# THE STRUCTURE OF IDEAS

# THE STRUCTURE OF IDEAS

## MAPPING A NEW THEORY OF FREE EXPRESSION IN THE AI ERA

JARED SCHROEDER

STANFORD UNIVERSITY PRESS
*Stanford, California*

Stanford University Press
Stanford, California

©2024 by Jared Schroeder. All rights reserved.

No part of this book may be reproduced or transmitted in any form or by any means, electronic or mechanical, including photocopying and recording, or in any information storage or retrieval system, without the prior written permission of Stanford University Press.

Printed and bound by CPI Group (UK) Ltd, Croydon, CR0 4YY

Library of Congress Cataloging-in-Publication Data

Names: Schroeder, Jared, author.
Title: The structure of ideas: mapping a new theory of free expression in the AI era / Jared Schroeder.
Description: Stanford, California: Stanford University Press, 2024. | Includes bibliographical references and index.
Identifiers: LCCN 2023040414 (print) | LCCN 2023040415 (ebook) | ISBN 9781503633230 (cloth) | ISBN 9781503639898 (paperback) | ISBN 9781503639904 (ebook)
Subjects: LCSH: Freedom of expression—United States. | Truthfulness and falsehood—United States. | Artificial intelligence—Social aspects—United States. | Information technology—Social aspects—United States.
Classification: LCC KF4770 .S37 2024 (print) | LCC KF4770 (ebook) | DDC 323.440973—dc23/eng/20231003
LC record available at https://lccn.loc.gov/2023040414
LC ebook record available at https://lccn.loc.gov/2023040415

Cover design: Aufuldish & Warinner
Cover art: Photo collage by Bob Aufuldish with *Arches National Park*, 2018, photograph by Jeff Finley/Unsplash
Typeset by Newgen in Sabon LT Pro in 10/14.5

# CONTENTS

*Acknowledgments* vii

**Introduction** 1

## PART I

### ONE
**An Endangered Space** 11

### TWO
**Fits and Starts** 30

### THREE
**Holmes and the Nothingness** 49

### FOUR
**Marketplace DNA** 71

### FIVE
**Maintaining the Space** 93

*Contents*

## PART II

### SIX
**Drawing a New Map**     115

### SEVEN
**The Balancer**     138

### EIGHT
**Baking Bread**     166

### NINE
**Monsters, Machines, and Truth**     190

### TEN
**Curators of Discourse**     213

**Conclusion**
**Revising the Space**     237

*Notes*     255

*Index*     307

# ACKNOWLEDGMENTS

A book about ideas and how we rationalize and protect their flow in a democratic society requires a lot of, well, ideas. This work required knowledge about the topics and, perhaps more importantly, the ability to deconstruct and reconstruct ideas. I am in debt to many who helped me in both realms. I want to thank friends who have shaped and challenged my thinking as I've explored and sought to get hold of the ideas that were, ultimately, constructed in this book. They include Chip Stewart, Wat Hopkins, Erika Pribanic-Smith, Tori Ekstrand, and Clay Calvert. I also want to thank Jeff Kosseff for his feedback and support throughout this project. Influential faculty in my graduate studies, more than a decade ago now, played a crucial role in helping me to structure ideas and engage with theories. They include Robert Kerr, Peter Gade, Charles Self, David Craig, Justin Wert, and Liz Watts.

I am thankful to the University of Missouri School of Journalism for its support of my work on this theoretical and historical project. I have wonderful colleagues, and graduate students, who challenge me to think and grow beyond the narrow scope of the law-and-policy field. In particular, I want to recognize my research assistant Xin Frida Qi for her help indexing the book. I also want to thank my former colleagues in the Meadows School of the Arts at Southern Methodist University, where I started this project. In particular, I want to thank my department chair,

*Acknowledgments*

Tony Pederson, for his early support of this work, as well as Melissa Chessher and her book-title-writing assistance. Also, my editor with Stanford University Press, Marcela Cristina Maxfield, was instrumental in helping me get these ideas organized and communicated clearly.

Finally, I must thank my family. I would be absolutely nowhere without my wife, Laura Schroeder. While my three teenaged sons, who are convinced it's not possible that I know anything at all, were no help in this process, I still wrote this with them and their futures in mind.

# THE STRUCTURE OF IDEAS

# Introduction

Mollie Steimer refused to stand. Everyone else rose from their seats as New York Court of Appeals Justice Bartow Weeks entered the courtroom. Steimer remained seated. Others in the courtroom urged the young woman to stand. Some might have thought Steimer didn't know the decorum, but the twenty-two-year-old Russian immigrant was well acquainted with courtrooms. She spent about ten days in federal court during a trial a year earlier in October 1918. Steimer and five others were convicted of violating the Espionage Act after they dropped thousands of leaflets that criticized the president and US foreign policy toward Russia from a New York City building.[1] The *New York Tribune*, during its coverage of the final day of her federal trial, described Steimer as "a tiny person, dressed in a red Russian blouse."[2] The newspaper noted she entered the courtroom that day smiling and carrying flowers. Clearly, Steimer knew her way around a courtroom. She was sentenced to fifteen years in federal prison but was out on bail while she appealed the conviction. She made the most of her time. That spring Steimer returned to court when she was charged with seeking to overthrow the government.[3] She was in federal court once again in September 1919, this time just a month before her refusal to stand as Weeks entered the courtroom, after

*Introduction*

dropping leaflets calling for "general strikes everywhere" and the "overthrowing of present society" from another New York building.[4]

Steimer was not on trial when she refused to stand for Weeks. She was in court that day to support friends. Still, she couldn't help making a point using silent protest. Weeks did not appreciate her point. The jurist had the four-foot nine-inch Steimer brought to the front of the courtroom, where she refused to respond to his questions. After learning her name from others in the room, he told her, "I am informed that you are one of the most pronounced abhorrers of this Government."[5] Steimer's reputation preceded her. Weeks let Steimer remain in the courtroom, reasoning a contempt charge would only make her a martyr. Her actions still grabbed headlines. The *New York Times* focused its trial coverage the next day on her behavior, headlining its story: "Girl Creates Stir at Anarchist Trial," and dismissively noting "the young Russian girl" enlivened the proceedings.[6] The story also listed past arrests for disorderly conduct and for having "thrown circulars from a roof of a building in Canal Street denouncing the National Security League's Constitution Day."[7] Steimer wasn't finished irking Weeks, however. Steimer booked another courtroom visit when she mailed Weeks an anarchist pamphlet titled "Arm Yourself" just days after she left his courtroom. Her helpful mailing to the jurist led to another arrest and more federal charges.[8]

Steimer seemed intent on testing as many of the boundaries of freedom of expression as possible in 1918 and 1919, particularly regarding the ideas the government would tolerate and the types of protections the First Amendment provided communicators. She wasn't alone. While her case was unique in that it changed the face of how we understand free expression, Steimer's protests came at a time of substantial change in US society. The headlines surrounding her various court visits tell the story of a quickly changing nation. World War I was transforming the industrial and diplomatic identities of the nation, as well as ushering in the Espionage Act, which represented a powerful, nationwide crackdown on unpopular expression. The temperance movement was fighting for prohibition. Massive waves of immigration in the 1880s and into the 1900s led overcrowded cities to swell with inequality and poverty.[9] Workers, including immigrants, began to protest and

*Introduction*

organize for labor. Thousands rallied in Haymarket Square in Chicago in 1887, for example. One person was killed and many injured when police scuffled with protestors. Ultimately, four protestors were convicted and sentenced to death after a bomb was thrown near the police. The Haymarket Riot inspired more workers' protests in major US cities.[10]

As workers started to fight for better wages and working conditions, women continued to fight for the right to vote. Alice Paul and the National Woman's Party began picketing in front of the White House in 1917, making front-page news in November after police arrested forty-one protestors.[11] While in government custody, Paul started her hunger strike, refusing to eat until being force-fed by guards. Women's suffrage efforts failed in Congress multiple times in fall 1918, just as Steimer was facing charges for violating the Espionage Act. The Nineteenth Amendment was passed by Congress in June 1919. The nation was shifting. How we understood freedom of expression, something that had received little attention from the Supreme Court until this time, required explanation.[12] Something had to change.

Steimer helped catalyze that change. Her protests and challenges to the ideas the government would tolerate led to a shift in how we understand free expression. These changes were of little help to her. The Supreme Court upheld her fifteen-year prison sentence for violating the Espionage Act, along with the sentences of three of her friends, in November 1919, about a month after her standoff with Weeks.[13] New York media documented Steimer's departure for a federal prison in Jefferson City, Missouri, noting she smiled and laughed, telling her mother and sister to cheer up.[14] After brief stays in prison, Steimer and three of her coconspirators were deported to Russia. In the absence of a clear set of free-expression safeguards, particularly in a quickly changing nation, the United States simply shipped its free-expression problems elsewhere.[15] While Steimer's time in the United States was over—she continued to fight for her beliefs in Europe before living her final years in Mexico City—her influence on free expression, if not her name, has endured.

Steimer is seldom mentioned in First Amendment textbooks, though newspapers often referred to her as a socialist or anarchist leader.[16] Her

*Introduction*

absence is largely because her case, *Abrams v. United States,* is named after her co-conspirator Jacob Abrams, whose story has become synonymous with one of the Supreme Court's earliest efforts to define the First Amendment's meaning.[17] The case represents a landmark moment in free-expression history, marking the first time a justice wrote in support of the First Amendment. *How* the justice wrote about free expression, as well as *who* the justice was, changed the path of how the First Amendment is understood. While Steimer and Abrams were eventually reunited in Mexico City, decades after being expelled from the United States for expressing unpopular ideas, their case introduced the crucial but complex idea that freedom of expression requires space. This is a book about that space.

We often think of freedom of expression in terms of personal rights. People speak of "my rights" or "their rights," but all expression must take place somewhere, whether it's in Weeks' courtroom, on Steimer's and Abrams's anti-government leaflets, on social media, or in the metaverse. The discussion about that somewhere started during a time of profound change in US society. Steimer's and Abrams's case marked a turning point in the discussion. In dissenting in their case, Justice Oliver Wendell Holmes introduced the concept of a space devoted to freedom of expression into the Court's discussions. He did not suggest a specific physical location. Instead, he suggested a conceptual space. He made it sound simple, beginning with facetious reasoning. He explained:

> Persecution for the expression of opinions seems to me perfectly logical. If you have no doubt of your premises or your power and want a certain result with all your heart you naturally express your wishes in law and sweep away all opposition.[18]

Holmes, in other words, reasoned limiting the flow of unpopular ideas only works if the government is certain of the truth.

Fundamentally, Holmes, a Civil War hero and a well-known legal mind, didn't believe anyone could really *know* the truth.[19] He blamed rigid, unmoving beliefs between North and South for causing a war that lead to the deaths of many of his friends.[20] The war might have been over for more than fifty years before Steimer and Abrams distributed their fliers, but he never forgot, keeping bullets that were pulled

*Introduction*

from his body and his bloodied uniforms for the rest of his life.[21] He reasoned, if no one can know absolute truth, society should be tolerant of a variety of ideas. He referred to the space in which ideas can be freely exchanged as a marketplace of ideas, explaining, "The best test of truth is the power of the thought to get itself accepted in the competition of the market."[22] He concluded, "That at any rate is the theory of our Constitution."[23]

His dissent didn't come at any ordinary time. The nation was struggling with all manner of protest and the Espionage Act, the first federal law to limit freedom of expression since the Alien and Sedition Acts of 1798. This wasn't just any stuffy political appointee to the Supreme Court lamenting free expression either. This was the same Holmes the nation had read about in "My Hunt After the Captain," his famous father's riveting tale of his desperate search for his injured son after the bloody battle of Antietam that was published in *The Atlantic* in 1862.[24] Importantly, the author who communicated these first ideas about the meaning of the First Amendment and a space for discourse was a well-respected legal mind. Holmes's words about a space for free expression led to supportive and celebratory letters.[25] His concern for a space for the exchange of ideas, in other words, made an impact, even if his ideas were part of a dissent.

Let's be clear, however, Holmes didn't invent the marketplace of ideas, and he absolutely did not complete it. His ideas were on the losing side of the case. A majority of the Court found limiting Steimer's unpopular ideas did not violate the First Amendment. This moment, in other words, did not resolve much regarding freedom of expression, but the nationally known legal thinker's concern for a space for discourse and his use of the marketplace concept ignited an important discussion about the exchange of ideas that has continued through more than a century of technological and social change. Alongside the marketplace concept, Holmes added truth and human rationality as foundational building blocks for why we should have freedom for expression. These difficult concepts remain central to how the space for the exchange of ideas is understood.

The marketplace ultimately, through decades of debate regarding its meaning, became the Supreme Court's dominant rationale for *why* we have freedom of expression. It also became justices' name for the

5

*Introduction*

space for the exchange of ideas in democratic society. Justices essentially attached freedom of expression to a particular map—the marketplace of ideas—which became the guide for what the space for the exchange of ideas looked like. While problems in the marketplace's assumptions about truth and human rationality, which are discussed later in the book, make it a flawed tool for mapping a crucial place, its role in creating a protected conceptual space for discussion is crucial.

What is a conceptual space? This book often refers to the conceptual place as a *space for discourse*, rather than the marketplace of ideas. These words are chosen carefully. The space for discourse is a conceptual place because it doesn't exist in a particular physical location. It is an imagined space that is meant to encapsulate and rationalize protecting freedom of expression. The space is, in other words, made up. It was created in jurists' and scholars' minds, ultimately entering the First Amendment's precedential history in Steimer's and Abrams's case in 1919 when Holmes introduced it as the marketplace of ideas. This book assumes democracy requires a space for discourse but does not assume the space must be called the marketplace of ideas or retain the traditional assumptions that characterize the metaphor. One of the crucial points of this book is that the shape and boundaries of the conceptual space have always remained up for debate. Technological and social changes, particularly the emergence of networked technologies and artificial intelligence (AI), have created new urgency to concerns that the marketplace of ideas, as it has been built, is not up to the task of acting as the primary tool for how we understand the space for discourse. We need a new way of thinking about the space for discourse.

The space requires clear understandings regarding its makeup and a new foundation in the twenty-first century. Much as was the case during Steimer's busy 1918 and 1919, the nature of the space has again changed, and the map no longer reflects the place it was created to describe. The space must be reimagined in light of these massive changes in how people make sense of the world around them, the AI entities that play persistent roles in molding our realities, and because its assumptions were never static or steady to begin with.

This book is divided into two parts in its examination of the future of the space for discourse. Part I encompasses the first five chapters and

6

*Introduction*

explores the nature of the space and the theoretical history and development of the marketplace concept. These chapters do not retell the same story about a static marketplace that was influenced by Enlightenment thinker John Milton and brought into the law by Holmes. Instead, these chapters tell the story of a living, dynamic idea that *came* to be a problematic and flawed Enlightenment-funded rationale for a space for human discourse. Chapters 1 and 2 do important work in providing a historically and theoretically grounded reframing of the traditional free-expression and marketplace-of-ideas narratives.

The chapters emphasize the space for discourse is an imagined place characterized by change, rather than stability. The marketplace of ideas, though justices generally present it as something that has always meant one thing, has been conceptualized in countless ways by many justices and scholars. These perspectives contribute a much more diverse set of understandings about how we should conceptualize the space for discourse in the networked, AI era. Chapter 3 continues to reframe and retrace the space's history, digging deeply into Holmes's philosophies regarding truth and human rationality. Both concepts, like Holmes himself, are fundamental to the US free-expression story. Chapters 4 and 5 trace the marketplace of idea's eventual ascendancy as the Supreme Court's primary tool for rationalizing and explaining freedom of expression. The chapters emphasize the uneven and highly contested development of the theory from a passing mention in Holmes's dissent in *Abrams* to its use as a seemingly static, absolute rationale for nearly unrestricted freedom of expression in more recent First Amendment precedents.

Part II shifts the focus from looking back to looking ahead. Chapter 6 examines the impact networked technologies and AI are having on the flow of ideas and the shapes and contours of the space for discourse. The four chapters that follow draw together a collection of diverse theoretical lenses through which to reconsider the conceptual space in the networked era. These chapters draw from jurists, philosophers, and the European Union's (EU's) fundamentally different approach to constructing a conceptual space for human discourse. Using building blocks from these interdisciplinary perspectives, as well as the frameworks of the space that were identified in Part I, the book concludes by identifying fundamental, theory-level changes involving the nature of

*Introduction*

the space and how we conceptualize it, changing the truth assumptions that are inherent in the way we understand and rationalize expression in the space, and describing and envisioning the space based on principles and ideas rather than comparisons to physical places. Ultimately, these revisions help preserve a space for democratic discourse by restructuring the foundations in ways that support free expression in the networked, AI eras.

# PART I

# ONE

## An Endangered Space

Arches National Park, outside Moab, Utah, is a one-of-a-kind place. Nature has formed more than 2,000 sandstone arches, creating incredible vistas of free-standing rock formations. More than 1.5 million people visit this shared space each year, crowding around and inside Double Arch, Turret Arch, and Skyline Arch to take pictures and stare in awe at these rare natural structures.[1] The iconic Delicate Arch, which stands alone in the rocky desert landscape, seems like a portal into a world of fiction. Perhaps Arches National Park is so popular and awe-inspiring because it is a real place that seems unreal. The marketplace of ideas, a metaphor that has been used for more than a century to conjure a shared, conceptual space for citizens to gather and communicate ideas, has the opposite problem. It is a work of fiction that we have treated as if it were real. Like a national park, the marketplace is a revered, shared space for the public. In fact, Justice Oliver W. Holmes, in a way, made the marketplace a conceptual national park in fall 1919 when he used the metaphor in his dissent in Mollie Steimer's and Jacob Abrams's case, making it the first Supreme Court opinion to argue for freedom of expression.[2]

The marketplace's designation as a shared space fits the times. The 1919 decision came nine months after Grand Canyon National Park was

*Chapter One*

created and just over a week before Zion National Park joined the growing list of shared, public parks.[3] Certainly, like the Grand Canyon, the concept of a shared space for human discourse is far older than its discovery and official designation, but Holmes's decision triggered a change in how we treated the space, much as is the case when any place becomes a national park. The person who named it, Holmes, and the manner in which it was done, via the first opinion to argue for free expression rights, triggered the beginnings of a transformation of the space in our national imaginations.

The greatest challenge for Marketplace National Park, despite sharing common characteristics with in-person physical spaces, is it exists in our imaginations and not on a map. If a nation, as political scientist and historian Benedict Anderson defined it, is an "imagined political community," then the conceptual space for democratic discourse is an *imagined* space where that community speaks with itself.[4] We cannot stand in the marketplace, like we can stand beside Delicate Arch, or gape into its depths like the Grand Canyon, and share an experience about the phenomena as we see it. As a result, the most dominant tool for creating a space for citizens to participate in democratic discourse has shifted and morphed in its meaning for more than a century as jurists and scholars have disagreed about what they see when they picture the marketplace of ideas.

The conceptual space did not start with foundational meanings. It might even be a stretch to credit Holmes with more than naming the space and using his power and authority to bring it attention. His dissent in the *Abrams* sedition case represents a catalyzing moment, but not the creation of the space itself. History tells us the marketplace's creation was a shared effort, which, like the Grand Canyon, took many years to form. The history of the marketplace as a shared space for discourse is defined by change and not by consistency. Holmes, a grizzled Civil War veteran and longtime jurist, set the process in motion in the final paragraph of a dissent in a case about anti-war protestors:[5]

> When men have realized that time has upset many fighting faiths, they may come to believe even more than they believe the very foundations of their own conduct that the ultimate good desired is better reached by free trade in ideas—that the best test of truth is

12

## An Endangered Space

the power of the thought to get itself accepted in the competition of the market, and that truth is the only ground upon which their wishes safely can be carried out. That at any rate is the theory of our Constitution.[6]

There is no doubt the passage marked a turning point for free expression.[7] The opinion, however, did not come with any footnotes or citations indicating what Holmes had in mind.[8] Despite taking part in multiple similar cases in the years that followed, Holmes never returned to the marketplace concept and made few statements in his opinions about freedom of expression after his dissent in *Abrams* in 1919.[9] Thus, the conceptual space was created, but lacked form, like an empty canvas left for others to fill. Contemporaries immediately associated Holmes's ideas with *Areopagitica*, in which Enlightenment thinker John Milton contended truth will win and falsity will fail in a free exchange of ideas.[10] In other words, without Holmes's input, others immediately began to paint what they thought the marketplace should look like and what the conceptual space should be. Holmes's personal correspondence from the time does not provide any indication he agreed with the Enlightenment foundations others placed on the empty canvas he created. In fact, his personal and legal writings contradict Enlightenment assumptions.[11] Despite this, over the decades that followed, justices slowly constructed a conceptual space based on Enlightenment ideas that truth is generally universal and the same for all and that people are rational and capable of making sense of the world around them.[12]

These assumptions became rationales for increasingly expansive protections for freedom of expression. Justices essentially concluded freedom of expression must be protected so truth can succeed and falsity can fail in an open exchange of ideas. The Court was perhaps most explicit about this in the *Red Lion v. Federal Communications Commission* fairness doctrine decision in 1969. The Court reasoned "It is the purpose of the First Amendment to preserve an uninhibited marketplace of ideas in which truth will ultimately prevail."[13] Importantly, this understanding *became* the majority vision of what the conjured space looked like. This vision of the marketplace's vistas was not present in 1919, nor has it remained static since. Using these assumptions, however, the Court

13

*Chapter One*

slowly staked out more and more acreage for Marketplace National Park, expanding free-expression protections to areas such as commercial, corporate, and online speech.[14]

Each of these expansions included unintended consequences for the conceptual space. The greater the space's reach, the more unwieldy its creaky Enlightenment foundations became. Then, in the late 1990s, like a volcanic eruption or an earthquake, networked technologies started to fundamentally transform the marketplace's landscape. Most of the conceptual park's vistas and landmarks changed. Information became increasingly plentiful, rather than scarce.[15] Access to publishing tools, once held by a limited group of gatekeepers, suddenly became available to anyone with an internet connection. The marketplace's terrain changed quickly and suddenly, but as a conceptual space, we could only guess about its new form. We could not observe and describe the changes, like we would the aftermath of a wildfire in Yellowstone or a hurricane in Everglades National Park.

In the networked, AI era, it is no longer clear what the conceptual space looks like. The traditional picture of the shared space does not seem to fit the information universe we live in. We do not *share* a marketplace anymore. Instead, we occupy mini-spaces within a broader multiverse of marketplaces.[16] People *choose* the information sources and individuals that come to dictate their realities about the world.[17] Beyond these matters of human choice, non-human actors substantially shape the conceptual space. Algorithms, using countless data points collected by private companies, make decisions for us regarding the ideas we do and do not see.[18] Bots engage with, and often manipulate, the space, overwhelming it with certain ideas and pushing human speakers out of the conversation.[19] Deepfakes and other manipulated content create believable lies that make it difficult to believe our own senses.[20] Our traditional vision of what our shared, conceptual space looks like no longer matches reality. The park maps that were drawn and printed as guides for visitors in the twentieth century are no longer accurate. Before examining the roles AI and other emerging technologies are having in undermining the marketplace approach and changing the way people make sense of the world around them, we must first look at the nature of the traditional space and its frail foundations.

14

*An Endangered Space*

## THE NATURE OF THE SPACE

While most scholars and jurists have, in *The Emperor's New Clothes* fashion, agreed the marketplace exists as justices painted it, a few have explicitly noted its imaginary status.[21] Legal scholar Jerome Barron, for example, concluded, "If ever there were a self-operating marketplace of ideas, it has long ceased to exist."[22] Barron, quite accurately, called the marketplace a "romantic conception."[23] Chief Justice William Rehnquist questioned the faith other justices placed in the marketplace concept in his dissent in *Central Hudson v. Public Service Commission* in 1980.[24] He concluded, "There is no reason for believing that the marketplace of ideas is free from market imperfections."[25] He was right. The metaphor that has been used to create a conceptual space for members of democratic society to share ideas and come to conclusions has significant flaws. We'll get to the flaws in the next section. First, we must address the nature of the marketplace as generally conceptualized by the Supreme Court, whose members have acted as the primary architects of the space for more than a century. Essentially, because of their power to interpret the Constitution and overturn laws, they have molded the conceptual space for human discourse.

If the space has changed in fundamental ways, how did it look when justices constructed an entire system of rights based upon its functionality? Justices' conclusions about the marketplace generally conjure an eighteenth-century, cobblestoned town square, much like the streets that were lined with the Enlightenment-era coffee houses and salons that represented the first spaces for the burgeoning professional middle class to receive news and engage with others about pressing matters in the community.[26] In *Reno v. American Civil Liberties Union (ACLU)* in 1997, for example, the Court celebrated the democratizing power of the internet, emphasizing it allows anyone with access to "become a town crier with a voice that resonates farther than it could from any soap box."[27] Using such reasoning, the Court struck down the government's first effort to limit online expression. Similarly, in *McCullen v. Coakley*, where justices struck down a law that created small buffer zones that limited abortion protest in front of clinics, the Court framed the issue as "Petitioners wish to converse with their fellow citizens about an

15

*Chapter One*

important subject on the public streets and sidewalks—sites that have hosted discussions about the issues of the day throughout history."[28] In both instances, justices conjured an idealistic, pastoral vision of human discourse, where citizens speak as equals in an open-to-all space. Such a vision of the space aligns with Enlightenment assumptions that tend to treat people as being generally the same, ignoring human diversity at nearly every level.[29]

Crucially, in justices' minds, the marketplace can be accessed by all, communication is orderly, and, above all, truth vanquishes falsity. These understandings construct a very particular type of conceptual space, one that aligns with Milton's contention that, when the government generally stays out of the flow of ideas that occurs in such spaces, truth succeeds and falsity fails.[30] In the *Thornhill v. Alabama* picketing case, for example, justices overturned limitations on public protest because such limitations afford "no opportunity to test the merits of ideas by competition for acceptance in the market of public opinion."[31] In the First Amendment-defining *New York Times v. Sullivan* decision in 1964, the Court reasoned the need for free expression for the "unfettered interchange of ideas" has "long been settled by our decisions."[32] Thus, the nature of the space, as mapped by the Court, is a generally wide open, egalitarian arena for the generally unfettered competition among ideas.

How wide open? Very. The final step in the modern, pre-networked-era development of the marketplace concept was justices' debate regarding a protected versus an expansive marketplace of ideas. In other words, should speech that harms rather than contributes to human discourse, such as intentional falsehoods or hate speech, be protected by the First Amendment? What about laws that protect the integrity of the marketplace, such as limits on contributions to political campaigns or advertising? Should limitations on speech be allowed to stand, in the name of safeguarding the space, or struck down as government limitations on expression? Crucially, majorities on the Court sided with an expansive marketplace, shunning concerns that the marketplace will be harmed and distorted when it is not protected. The Court struck down a law that criminalized lying about having earned military honors in 2012.[33] Citing Holmes's use of the marketplace metaphor in *Abrams*, justices reasoned, in true Miltonian fashion, "Suppression of speech by the government

*An Endangered Space*

can make exposure of falsity more difficult, not less so. Society has the right and civic duty to engage in open, dynamic, rational discourse."[34] Similarly, in *Virginia v. Black* in 2003, the Court struck down a law that criminalized cross-burning, reasoning that "The hallmark of the protection of free speech is to allow 'free trade in ideas'—even ideas that the overwhelming majority of people might find distasteful or discomforting."[35] In instances such as these, justices favored an expansive marketplace over one that is at least in some ways free of ideas that are intentionally false or created purely out of hate, rather than rational discourse.

Similarly, justices rejected arguments that limitations on campaign contributions and commercial speech should be used to protect the marketplace. In *First National Bank v. Bellotti* in 1978, Massachusetts contended its law prohibiting corporations from spending money to influence referendums was necessary to protect election integrity.[36] The Court rejected this reasoning, finding a speaker cannot be blocked from communicating ideas simply because it is a corporation, rather than a person.[37] In his dissent, Justice White agreed with the value of *protecting* the marketplace, explaining that corporate "expenditures may be viewed as seriously threatening the role of the First Amendment as a guarantor of a free marketplace of ideas."[38] Similarly, in *Citizens United v. Federal Election Commission (FEC)* in 2010, the Court struck down aspects of a federal law that limited large donors' power, including corporations, to influence political campaigns. The government contended the law was created to *protect* the marketplace from distortion.[39] A deeply divided Court disagreed, concluding the law threatened, rather than protected the marketplace of ideas because it could limit the exchange of ideas. Justices reasoned, "If the antidistortion rationale were to be accepted, however, it would permit Government to ban political speech simply because the speaker is an association that has taken on the corporate form."[40] Thus, the Court favored more expression, regardless of the artificial form of the speaker, over the well-being of the conceptual space.

The Court's reasoning in *Citizens United* had particularly powerful and unintended consequences for the nature of the conceptual space. The Court emphasized, as it did in *Bellotti* decades earlier, lawmakers cannot halt expression because it originates from an artificial entity.[41] Of

*Chapter One*

course, in 1978, and even in 2010, the artificial entities justices referred to were corporations, which are created by people. During the fourth wave of the internet, artificial speakers have come to include all manner of AI, particularly algorithms, bots, and generative, large-language tools, such as ChatGPT.[42] By explicitly protecting speech by artificial entities, the Court unintentionally expanded free-expression safeguards to entities that are having a substantial, often distorting, impact on the shape of the conceptual space, as well as the flow of information within it. Before examining AI-related concerns more closely, we must first consider long-standing structural flaws within the foundations of the marketplace's assumptions. Certainly, the growing presence of artificial entities within the conceptual space is causing the Enlightenment-founded assumptions to crack and strain under the pressure. These fissures and fault lines, however, have far deeper, older roots that run into the very foundations of the marketplace. In other words, AI and other growing concerns are merely exacerbating problems that have long been a part of the conceptual space.

## FUNDAMENTAL FLAWS

The marketplace concept was broken from the beginning. The conceptual, shared space for democratic discourse's failure in the twenty-first century has been in the works for more than a century—long before Steve Berners-Lee invented the World Wide Web in 1989 and Mark Zuckerberg started writing code for Facebook in his Harvard University dorm room in 2003. The sudden convergence and widespread availability of publishing tools to all who had access to the internet, the generally gatekeeper-less publishing process, and the explosion in sources of information all exploited the truth, rationality, and sameness flaws that had festered, but not stopped, the Enlightenment-based marketplace from persisting.

Remember, Holmes provided a relatively empty canvas by introducing the conceptual space in *Abrams*. He did not provide a clear framework for what he meant. Over the course of decades, justices, with support from prominent legal scholars, installed Enlightenment assumptions into the foundations of the space. Cracks began to show

18

*An Endangered Space*

immediately, all signs the Enlightenment-composed foundations were not up to the challenge of supporting a conceptual space for democratic discourse. Foremost among the weak spots in the foundations were the assumptions that truth is generally static and the same for all, and the related contention that people are rational and capable of discerning truth when confronted with ideas.[43] Alongside both of these concerns was the problematic overall assumption within Enlightenment thought that people are generally the same. Together, these problems, even without the emergence of networked technologies and fundamental changes in how people communicate, have undermined the functionality of the conceptual space.

Enlightenment assumptions about truth have almost universally been rejected by thinkers in a variety of fields. Legal scholar C. Edwin Baker, for example, concluded "truth is not objective," and, therefore, the marketplace approach is unworkable.[44] Philosopher William James, the founder of American pragmatism, contended "truth happens to an idea," rejecting assumptions that truth is a static, objective construct.[45] German thinker and hermeneuticist Hans-Georg Gadamer emphasized that people project themselves into what they come to believe is true. He explained, "A person who is trying to understand a text is always projecting. He projects a meaning for the text as a whole as soon as some initial meaning emerges in the text."[46] Even Holmes rejected absolute truth, which is discussed in greater detail in chapter 3. In a letter to a friend, he called truth a "mirage," and framed truth as the result of personal experiences.[47] In a law review article, Holmes concluded, "Men to a great extent believe what they want to."[48] In a letter to British jurist Frederick Pollock, Holmes contended people cannot know with certainty what the truth is, the best anyone can do is "bet."[49] Holmes invoked similar imagery in his dissent in *Abrams*, contending "Every year if not every day we have to *wager* our salvation upon some prophecy based upon imperfect knowledge."[50]

Thus, while Holmes did not paint a full picture of what the conceptual space should look like, his legal and personal writings rejected Enlightenment-funded truth. His conclusions have been supported by thinkers from a variety of fields and time periods. Ultimately, however, none of these warnings about the structural integrity of Enlightenment

*Chapter One*

ideas stopped justices from making the conceptual, shared place for discourse an Enlightenment-oriented space. Milton's *Areopagitica* was an early catalyst as scholars immediately associated Holmes's reasoning in *Abrams* with the Enlightenment thinker's impassioned seventeenth-century argument against licensing requirements for publication.[51] Felix Frankfurter, who was mentored by Holmes and taught at Harvard Law School before joining the Court in 1939, celebrated Holmes's *Abrams* dissent in a letter just after the decision was announced. He wrote, "I still read and rejoice over your dissents – and (Professor Roscoe) Pound has stolen from me when he says your paragraphs will live as long as the *Areopagitica*."[52]

A year later, in 1920, judicial philosopher and fellow Harvard Law professor Zechariah Chafee discussed *Areopagitica* and Holmes's *Abrams* dissent together in his seminal book *Freedom of Speech*.[53] Chafee opened the book with a quote from *Areopagitica*: "Truth be in the field, we do injuriously by licensing and prohibiting to misdoubt her strength. Let her and Falsehood grapple; who ever knew Truth put to the worse in a free and open encounter."[54] Importantly, the almost immediate association between Holmes's marketplace reference in his *Abrams* dissent and Milton's *Areopagitica* by leading legal scholars substantially influenced the otherwise blank canvas Holmes created regarding the conceptual space.[55] Frankfurter, from his powerful perch at Harvard Law School and his deep connections with Theodore and Franklin Roosevelt, writer Walter Lippmann, and political theorist Harold Laski, made for a particularly impactful messenger regarding an Enlightenment-based marketplace of ideas.

The positivistic assumptions and "capital T" truth that pervaded Milton's ideas and those of other thinkers from the period are indispensable to Enlightenment thought. The Enlightenment was started by thinkers such as Galileo, Francis Bacon, and Isaac Newton, who sought empirically based, dispassionate methods for explaining the natural world.[56] Importantly, their creation of a scientific method was a reaction to the doubt in the human senses that was created when Galileo invented the telescope and discovered humanity had been wrong about the way the world and universe worked for centuries.[57] In other words, the Enlightenment's revolution in knowledge, through which we garnered

20

*An Endangered Space*

the scientific method, was catalyzed by technological change. German thinker Hannah Arendt explained, "Galileo's discovery proved in demonstrable fact that both the worst fear and the most presumptuous hope of human speculation, the ancient fear that our senses, our very organs for reception of reality, might betray us."[58] The result was a method that sought to make all phenomena measurable. These thinkers concluded, if human senses cannot be trusted, then the problem could be solved by a dispassionate method that relied on measurements using agreed-upon standards. Political theorist H. B. Acton boiled the truth assumptions of Enlightenment-based, positivist thinkers to their most basic elements: "Positivism is the view that the only way to obtain knowledge of the world is by means of sense perception and introspection and the methods of the empirical sciences."[59]

These ideas about an a priori, waiting-to-be-discovered world crept from mathematics into social and political theory as thinkers such as Milton, John Locke, and Voltaire celebrated human rationality and individuals' abilities to reason and identify truth.[60] These assumptions led to Locke's argument for the rights of "life, liberty, and estate," as well as human equality and independence, in 1689.[61] Early US framers, such as Thomas Jefferson, who wrote the *Declaration of Independence*; John Dickinson, who wrote the "Olive Branch Petition" and "A Letter to the Inhabitants of Quebec;" and Benjamin Franklin, read and subscribed to this reasoning.[62] Franklin closely mirrored Milton's ideas in a piece he wrote in the *Pennsylvania Gazette* in 1731. He contended, "When Men differ in Opinion, both Sides ought equally to have the Advantage of being heard by the Publick; and that when Truth and Error have fair Play, the former is always an overmatch for the latter."[63] Jefferson nearly copied Locke's "life, liberty, and estate" with "life, liberty, and the pursuit of happiness" in the *Declaration of Independence*.[64] In short, the nation's founders were children of the Enlightenment, which, alongside the early associations legal scholars made regarding Holmes's dissent in *Abrams* and *Areopagitica*, helps explain how the conceptual space for democratic discourse came to be defined by Enlightenment thought. While the marketplace did not begin with these assumptions, they, along with their considerable philosophical baggage, were cemented into its foundations.

21

*Chapter One*

The problem is that truth is not universal and the same for all. And if we are going to reconceptualize the marketplace, it must address this fundamental flaw. There is no guarantee truth will overcome falsity in the free exchange of ideas.[65] The Enlightenment's problematic truth assumptions are also tied to the rationality expectation, which means both pillars must be rethought. The Court has reasoned an expansive marketplace of ideas is viable and needed *because* people are generally rational. Justices have gone all in on assuming truth is discovered as a result of human rationality and the ability to discern. What happens if people are not rational, if by rational we mean that they dispassionately evaluate ideas in order to discern truth from falsity? The assumption that people apply similar rationales and will share similar conclusions raises substantial, and important, questions.

Baker explained, "People individually and collectively choose or create rather than 'discover' their perspectives, understandings, and truths."[66] Similarly, legal scholar Frederick Schauer explained, "Our increasing knowledge about the process of idea transmission, reception, and acceptance makes it more and more difficult to accept the notion that truth has some inherent power to prevail in the marketplace of ideas."[67] Importantly, *who* people are, the characteristics that make them individuals, influence how they understand the world. Enlightenment thinking has ignored this, something legal scholar Derek Bambauer emphasized. He reasoned, "Cognitive psychology and behavioral economics shows that humans operate with significant, persistent perceptual biases that skew our interactions with information. These biases undercut the assumption that people reliably sift data to find truth."[68]

These more recent critiques of the marketplace's foundational flaws again find support in Holmes's writings from when the conceptual space was first introduced. In 1918, a year before the *Abrams* dissent, Holmes averred truth is created by each person's experiences.[69] He explained, "Property, friendship, and truth have a common root in time. One cannot be wrenched from the rocky crevices into which one has grown for many years without feeling attacked."[70] In the same passages, he emphasized that "While one's experience thus makes certain preferences dogmatic for oneself, recognition of how they came to be so leaves one able to see that others, poor souls, may be equally dogmatic about something else."[71]

*An Endangered Space*

Holmes's conclusions connect with the third fundamental flaw in the Enlightenment foundations of the marketplace approach, which is the problem of sameness. Enlightenment thinkers, in their quest to create an objectively measurable world, ignored a lot of variables. They had to oversimplify the world around them to make it measurable. Similarly, these thinkers, generally all white, land-owning men, tended to look around and conclude, since the people they surrounded themselves with were *like* them, that everyone was *like* them. In both boiling down human existence and the homogeneity of their worlds, these thinkers assumed people would come to the same conclusions about truth. Thus, the idea that truth will win and falsity will fail when all ideas are freely exchanged makes more sense when those involved in the space are generally the same. Historian David Hollinger recognized these problems, concluding, "The Enlightenment, it seems, has led us to suppose that all people are pretty much alike."[72] He explained that it "blinded us to uncertainties of knowledge by promoting an ideal of absolute scientific certainty."[73] These assumptions about sameness fall apart in a diverse society. The conceptual space cannot ignore individuality.

The Enlightenment-based marketplace not only assumes everyone is essentially the same personally, but also in regard to their access to ideas and their ability to participate in the exchanges that take place in the space. We know everyone does not have equal footing in the marketplace. Some have more power to get their ideas out than others. Messages reach individuals with different force and frequency, which is often dependent on the communities to which they belong. The force of a message is also influenced by personal biases. A person's race, religion, political affiliation, gender identification, and a host of other factors will affect how they evaluate a message.[74] Relatively recent events have highlighted the truth, rationality, and sameness problems that have been particularly evident in the marketplace's failing Enlightenment assumptions.

According to a Pew Research Center Poll, 75 percent of Trump voters believe he won the 2020 election, while 99 percent of Biden voters believe he won.[75] Similarly, the "birther" movement has argued former president Obama was not born in the United States. Even when Obama released his full, long-form birth certificate, the polls remained similar.[76] Of those polled before the long-form birth certificate was released, 55

23

*Chapter One*

percent believed he was born in the United States. Six months after its release, 59 percent believed he was born in the United States.[77] Either Biden won the election or he didn't. Similarly, either Obama was born in the United States or he was not. Despite the fact that a "truth" does exist in both instances, truth has failed to vanquish falsity. Instead, the two "truths" exist side by side. While the next section addresses the difficulties truth faces in the AI era, these examples reinforce the flawed truth, rationality, and sameness assumptions that were mixed into the conceptual space's foundations.[78]

## THE ARTIFICIAL MARKETPLACE

The "Plandemic" conspiracy video was posted on Facebook, YouTube, Vimeo, and one other website in May 2020. For a few days, it circulated in anti-vaccine and conspiracy-theory communities on Facebook, with links to YouTube.[79] Within seven days, it had worked its way out of the shadowy corners of online communities, reaching eight million views across social media sites. The video's claims were universally rejected by experts and fact-checkers.[80] Despite efforts to dispel the video's claims, and social media firms' decisions to remove it from their spaces, many of its falsehoods, including that COVID-19 was created in a lab and that National Institute of Allergy and Infectious Diseases Director Anthony Fauci and Microsoft founder Bill Gates helped create the virus for political or monetary gain, still resonated with many online communities.[81] In a poll from the same month the Plandemic video came out, 44 percent of Republicans believed Gates was trying to use vaccines to microchip citizens.[82] More than a year later, a majority of Americans believed the virus escaped from a lab in China, a conclusion most scientists have said is unlikely.[83]

The Plandemic was not an aberration. Certainly, the video's success reinforces the fundamental truth, rationality, and sameness flaws found in how the conceptual space for democratic discourse has been constructed. More than that, however, the video represents a growing realization by those who seek to manipulate the information environment that the conceptual space for human discourse has changed in fundamental ways. Propagandists and manipulators have developed a

*An Endangered Space*

playbook that remains several steps ahead of fact-checkers and people's information-literacy levels. The geography, nature, and the norms that govern the conceptual space have created new advantages for falsity and technologies that distort human discourse. Our map and understandings of the conceptual space are woefully inaccurate. When we no longer share a similar version of the changing conceptual space, the marketplace becomes more and more ripe for manipulation.

Crucially, virtual spaces are fundamentally different from physical spaces, making the imagined space for discourse even more complex to map. If the traditional marketplace is like an Olympic event, with distinctive rules and competitions, the artificial marketplace is like an entire Olympics, filled with all manner of sports—everything from badminton to fencing to trampoline gymnastics. The conceptual space becomes increasingly difficult to grasp and map in such an environment. Virtual spaces allow substantially more choice when it comes to the information, ideas, and people individuals engage with.[84] Virtual spaces also allow AI to function seamlessly around and within human discourse. Finally, virtual spaces make deception and falsity more impactful and widespread. Together, these changes take us even farther from the pastoral, egalitarian, cobblestoned streets the Supreme Court has conjured when speaking about the shared space for discourse.

Researchers have long found like-minded individuals are drawn to each other.[85] Social media have supercharged this phenomenon, allowing each person, in a choice-rich environment, to construct generally homogeneous people and information universes. We have deserted the imagined public square for countless side rooms. This does not bode well for a conceptual space for human discourse. As legal scholar Cass Sunstein explained, "When society is fragmented, diverse groups will tend to polarize in a way that can breed extremism, and even hatred or violence."[86] Sociologist Manuel Castells came to a similar conclusion, explaining "Social groups and individuals become alienated from each other, and see the other as a stranger, eventually as a threat."[87] He continued, "In this process, social fragmentation spreads, as identities become more specific and increasingly difficult to share."[88]

Thus, the conceptual space in the networked era suffers from fragmentation on a massive and complex scale. Individuals no longer share

25

## Chapter One

a space or common baselines of information, such as those that were provided by traditional news gatekeepers in previous eras. In this era, the conceptual space shatters into countless fragments, as groups form miniature conceptual spaces that limit the range of acceptable ideas to those that are generally part of the group's preexisting conclusions. They create sub-marketplaces that sell only certain ideas—those that are acceptable to the group. The ideological sameness within the intentional communities makes them more receptive to conspiracy theories and manipulation, since ideas that fit preexisting assumptions within the group are more likely to be accepted, and the ongoing effect of only hearing ideas that reinforce these accepted ideas makes people more extreme and never more open-minded. This realization helps explain the success of conspiracies and hoaxes, such as the Plandemic video. These "false" ideas find homes in like-minded communities that are primed for the type of information the conspiracy content provides. Thus, mapping out the imagined space in the networked era requires accounting for this shattered, but still somewhat interconnected, form to the conceptual space.

Of course, even sketching out the human aspects of the fragmented nature and choice-rich environment found in networked spaces leaves important actors out of consideration for how the marketplace should be reimagined. Before people make a single decision about the ideas and people they wish to encounter, algorithms have made thousands of choices for them. Algorithms, used by everything from social media firms such as YouTube and Facebook to product-oriented sites such as Amazon and the personal style firm Stich Fix, use information collected about individuals to select and present what the program believes they want to see.[89] The shift to predominantly online discourse has meant these decision-making programs have outsized influence on the people and ideas individuals encounter. In other words, the conceptual space has become an *artificial marketplace*, one that is substantially determined by non-human actors.

Importantly, algorithms are not independent robots. They are human-made tools. They could be programmed to make the conceptual space more functional for human discourse, such as by making a service more informative or to present people with more fact-based information. They are, however, intentionally programmed not to foster a functional space for human discourse. We often make the mistake of

## An Endangered Space

projecting journalism's public-service mission or the nature of physical public spaces on to social media firms, but these firms have created algorithms that maximize profit via interaction, rather than information value.[90] This means they are hesitant to remove high-interaction content. False and misleading content generally receives more interactions than truthful reports.[91] The Plandemic video, for example, exponentially outperformed other events from the same period in which it appeared.[92] Falsehoods also travel six times faster than truths on the internet, creating engagement and then an additional bump of interactions when people seek to set the record straight.[93] Facebook makes about US$40 a year from each user, so removing content or suspending accounts hurts revenue. Certainly, the firms have created policies that lead to banning and blocking certain content, but Facebook's algorithm has been found, by the company itself, to be a recipe for super-charging extremism.[94] Facebook found in an internal report that its algorithm-based recommendation tool accounted for a 64 percent increase in extremism on the platform.[95] Facebook was aware its "algorithms exploit the human brain's attraction to divisiveness" in 2018 and chose to do nothing about it.[96]

Similarly, YouTube's algorithm, which researchers have found often leads people to increasingly extreme content, accounts for more than 70 percent of its traffic.[97] In both instances, the algorithms represent a powerful, influential force on the conceptual space. By predetermining much of what we encounter and seeking to show us what we are thought to want to see, the algorithms increase fragmentation and polarization. They make it more difficult for people to hear ideas and for truth to be discovered, effectively nullifying Enlightenment assumptions about the marketplace.

Bots introduce another challenge to the conceptual space. Like algorithms, bots are programmed by humans and vary in their capabilities. Most importantly, however, they have the power to distort the marketplace by creating so many messages about a topic that it appears that truth has vanquished falsity because one idea has become dominant.[98] They can also make it difficult for human communicators to participate in the conceptual space for discourse, as bots can produce thousands of messages, making human discourse a needle in the haystack rather

*Chapter One*

than central to the exchange of ideas. In both instances, the fundamentally non-human nature of the actors powerfully transforms the space. In 2018, a Saudi Arabian company paid a firm about US$200 to artificially boost its grilled lamb sales using social media. Using an army of bots, the firm pushed "Grilled Lamb Delivery" into Twitter's trending topics.[99] The bots produced more than 17,000 tweets in a short period of time. While grilled lamb-related algorithm manipulation is not high on the list of problems facing the conceptual space, the idea that a firm could cheaply create an army of speakers that tricks an algorithm into emphasizing an idea illustrates the growing power of artificial communicators and that any re-mapping of the conceptual space in the networked era must account for the growing role these entities play.

Finally, emerging AI tools are making it easier for people to create deepfakes, which are audio or video clips of someone saying or doing something they never said or did.[100] These increasingly high-quality, believable fictions create new challenges to the marketplace's already shaky Enlightenment assumptions that rational individuals can discern truth from falsity. Social media firms have created policies against certain types of manipulated content, but this has not stopped deceptive content from persisting and circulating in fragmented online communities. A deepfake of Mark Zuckerberg appearing on CBS News to boast about his power over billions of people's personal data circulated in summer 2019.[101] Facebook refused to take the video down, despite CBS News's requests. The firm also refused to take a manipulated clip that made Speaker of the House Nancy Pelosi seem confused or intoxicated months earlier.[102] The marketplace, as it has been constructed within Supreme Court precedents and by scholars, is ill equipped to function in an environment in which believable reports about events that never happened and words that were never said are consistently published and shared, commented upon, "favorited," and liked throughout the fragmented artificial marketplace.

## A NEW MAP

The marketplace of ideas is full of contradictions. It is both a crucial space for democratic discourse and a work of fiction. It has existed for more than a century and, at the same time, never existed at all. What

*An Endangered Space*

we know, however, is democracy requires a conceptual space and the imagined marketplace of ideas that was created to fulfill that need is endangered. It is not only endangered by the obvious threats, such as algorithmic predetermination, the growing power of bots, and the increasing quality and believability of deepfakes and other manipulated content. The dangers it faces also include long-standing problems with how it has been imagined. Certainly, the contours of the space have been fundamentally altered by the seismic eruption of networked technologies and AI, but beneath the surface, the underlying assumptions that were built into the space are increasingly and unsettlingly precarious. Enlightenment ideas have never been up to the task of rationalizing widespread free-expression protections for a functional conceptual space for human discourse. These ideas regarding truth, human rationality, and assumptions regarding human sameness have long failed to accurately represent the conceptual space—emerging technologies have only exposed their inherent weaknesses. To rethink and repair the space for discourse, and to shore up its struggling foundations, we must first understand its nature and how it developed.

# TWO

## Fits and Starts

The marketplace of ideas is not a monolith. It is not a rigid, unmoving object that was created all at once and cannot be changed. Quite the opposite, the marketplace, as both a justification for expansive free-expression rights and a description of a particular type of space for citizens to gather and communicate ideas, has been defined by change. It is a dynamic space. If we are to get to the hard work of reconstructing the space for human discourse in the networked, AI era, we must come to grips with the reality we are not dealing with a static concept. The marketplace of ideas is not a real place, nor is it a historical artifact. It is an idea. In their reverence for the space and the expansive free expression rights it helps justify, jurists, historians, legal scholars, and others have often created a superhero's origin story for the marketplace of ideas that centers around Justice Holmes.[1] The narrative comes to treat the marketplace as something that *is* rather than something that is *becoming*. Framing the marketplace as a monolith is inaccurate. More importantly, it distorts the marketplace concept's nature and obstructs the important and continuous work that must be done to maintain a space for citizens to gather and communicate ideas in the face of massive, widespread changes in the flow of information.

*Fits and Starts*

Our initial work requires some clarifying. Holmes did not *invent* the marketplace of ideas. His role was crucial, but was closer to that of a stage-setter than an inventor. He catalyzed its development by using an economics-based metaphor to contend a space for free expression *should* exist, absent substantial government control, in the first opinion by a Supreme Court justice that argued for free expression.[2] This is a significant development, but it is not an invention of a space for human discourse. Similarly, the Bill of Rights' framers did not create the space, but the First Amendment laid the groundwork for such an idea. Going back even farther, classical and Enlightenment thinkers cannot be credited with creating the space, but their ideas about public discourse, truth, and human rationality eventually came to characterize its features.[3] In other words, the marketplace of ideas does not have an inventor. It has an evolution. The space is most accurately framed as an ongoing narrative that is defined by shifts and changes. Those changes have a powerful influence on how democracy functions.

The space's dynamic nature plays out in two primary dimensions. First, the marketplace's history tells the story of an imagined space that has shifted, in shape and dimensions, over more than a century. Justices and legal scholars have, for example, debated the relationship truth has to the marketplace, whether the space should include certain types of speech, and whether it should be protected from distortion.[4] Second, the dynamic nature of the space has been influenced by the philosophical assumptions that undergird it. The Enlightenment assumptions that came to structure the space and its free-expression rationales were installed over the course of fifty years, beginning many years after Holmes's first use of the market-based reasoning, and have continued to evolve during the Roberts Court era.[5] As emphasized in chapter 1, the marketplace is an *imagined space* we have treated as a real one. The space lives in our minds and, therefore, varies from person to person. It is virtually impossible for an imagined space's properties to become universally agreed upon. That is our challenge.

This chapter adds to the foundation of this book by framing the marketplace of ideas as more than a historical artifact. The space is not a historical relic or even a pastoral cobblestoned street. It's an idea. This

*Chapter Two*

chapter frames the space as a liquid rather than a solid. Sociologist Zygmunt Bauman explained in his book about modernity and change that "fluids do not keep any shape for long and are constantly ready (and prone) to change."[6] A solid, however, is the opposite. Solids resist change. Bauman contended history has been characterized by periods of social solidity, when society is stable, and periods of liquidity, when uncertainty and change occur.[7] Society has moved from these solids to liquids and then back to solids. Such a structure for understanding change can help us conceptualize how the space for human discourse, the space in a democratic society reserved for people to come together and communicate, has shifted over time. Importantly, the solid-to-liquid-to-solid process does not mean complete reinvention. Concepts retain aspects of their original forms during the process, though they are changed. The emergence of AI, algorithms, and networked communication tools more generally, have liquefied the structure of the space for human discourse, requiring a revision. Such a revision demands a history and context that accurately situates the space.

To do so, this chapter identifies three periods of liquidity within the marketplace concept's history. The periods do not represent a complete list, but together illustrate the dynamic, ongoing narrative of the space for human discourse. By exploring these, we learn about the concept as it has been and about the nature of its development. In other words, the goal is not to provide a rote history of the marketplace concept, but to frame its changing nature and the ways it has been altered in the past with an ongoing narrative defined by liquids and solids.

## 1919 PROBLEMS

Learned Hand idolized Holmes.[8] Hand was a judge for the Southern District of New York from 1909 until 1924. He served on the United States Court of Appeals for the Second Circuit until 1961, making him a constant supporting character in the story of the First Amendment's development for more than half a century. Like Holmes, Hand graduated from Harvard Law School, where he studied under professors who had been influential in Holmes's thinking. The two were in regular correspondence, sharing lively discussions about cases, current events, and

*Fits and Starts*

plans to meet.[9] In June 1918, for example, the pair discussed freedom of expression in a series of letters. Holmes wrote about truth, explaining:

> When I say a thing is true I mean that I can't help believing it—and nothing more. But as I observe that the cosmos is not always limited by my Cant Helps I don't bother about absolute truths or even inquire whether there is such a thing, but define the Truth as the system of my limitations.[10]

The tone of their correspondence was generally filled with kindness. The tone changed, at least briefly, in 1919. Hand confronted Holmes, a towering figure in American law and a revered Civil War hero, about a trio of First Amendment opinions he had written for a unanimous Court that spring.[11] The three cases dealt with the Espionage Act of 1917, which was passed just after the United States became involved in World War I.[12] The law sought to quash publications and speech that criticized the war effort, including the military draft, contending such expression was a danger to national security. The cases were the first in which the Supreme Court squarely addressed the meaning of the First Amendment. In all three, the Court found the Espionage Act, despite its clear limitations on political expression, did not conflict with the First Amendment. Holmes wrote all three opinions for a unanimous Court. In *Schenck v. United States*, the most articulated of the three decisions, Holmes reasoned:

> The question in every case is whether the words used are used in such circumstances and are of such a nature as to create a clear and present danger. . . . It is a question of proximity and degree.[13]

Suddenly, the direct, absolute wording of the First Amendment, which begins with "Congress shall make *no* law," wasn't as direct and absolute.[14]

Charles Schenck and fellow members of the Socialist Party had circulated pamphlets arguing compelled military service was a violation of the Thirteenth Amendment, which abolished slavery, and the act of despotic leaders.[15] They were convicted using the Espionage Act. Holmes's opinion for the Court in Schenck's case was not just any opinion. The decision was one of two crucial developments during a short but crucial period of liquidity regarding the meaning of the First Amendment's promises. *Schenck* represented the first First Amendment opinion: it

## Chapter Two

dealt with peaceful anti-war protest, and it was written by Holmes, a war hero from a blue-blood New England family who was already a well-known legal mind. The case, whatever the outcome, was destined to leave an indelible mark on free expression and the space for human discourse. Holmes's opinion, and the reaction it triggered, helped melt and reshape the otherwise solid assumptions about the First Amendment and a space for human discourse that had persisted generally uncontested on a national level since 1798.[16]

### Critical Responses

The *Schenck* opinion was unpopular. It seemed out of step with the Holmes who, at the outset of the Civil War, joined the Union cause because he believed slavery was wrong and who dissented, siding with workers' rights, in the Court's disastrous *Locher v. New York* case in 1905.[17] Holmes was not a sympathetic, civil liberties champion, but he'd been made into one.[18] Historian Louis Menand explained, "He had then become, to his pleasure (for he enjoyed being lionized) but also to his bemusement, a hero to progressives."[19] Perhaps he was an antihero. Either way, his Espionage Act opinions disappointed many and received criticism from friends and legal scholars. Magazines purloined his words.[20] In a letter in April 1919, he critiqued a letter a labor union sent him, finding their argument "at once cocksure and hopelessly ignorant of all about it."[21] In other words, the Espionage Act and Holmes's opinions in the three cases that initially dealt with it triggered an intense period of conversation about free expression and the exchange of ideas. Hand was a crucial part of that conversation. He thought Holmes used the wrong standard in *Schenck*.

Hand dealt with a similar case a year and a half earlier when, under the Espionage Act, the postmaster general refused to circulate *The Masses*, an anarchist magazine.[22] Hand had overturned the postmaster's decision not to circulate the anarchist magazine, concluding free expression could only be limited if it threatened an immediate incitement of violence.[23] Hand used the same argument when he conveyed his concern about *Schenck* to Holmes in a letter soon after the decision was announced.[24] Tentatively, he contended to his mentor, "I do

34

*Fits and Starts*

not understand that the rule of responsibility for speech has ever been that the result is known as likely to follow. . . . The responsibility only began when the words were directly an incitement."[25] In other words, he thought Holmes had erred by limiting too much expression in the name of national security and the Espionage Act. Holmes was dismissive in his response two days later, quoting his opinion from *Schenck* and finishing the matter with "I don't know what the matter is, or how we differ so far as your letter goes."[26]

Crucially, the matter was that two leading thinkers, with the power to influence how we understand free expression, were having a debate about the flow of information in the—at the time—amorphous, undefined, space for human discourse. Hand was not satisfied with Holmes's response. He approached Holmes on a train and made a similar argument in June, but again the justice was not convinced.[27] That same month, Zechariah Chafee, a professor at Harvard Law School and someone who was deeply connected with the justice's close friends, such as political scientist Harold Laski and influential Harvard Law professors Roscoe Pound and Felix Frankfurter, published "Free Speech in War Time" in *Harvard Law Review*. The article criticized Holmes, concluding "Justice Holmes in his Espionage Act decisions had a magnificent opportunity to make articulate for us that major premise under which judges ought to classify words inside and outside the scope of the First Amendment."[28] Chafee continued, "Instead, like other judges, he has told us that certainly plainly unlawful utterances are, to be sure, unlawful."[29] Perhaps Chafee knew just how to get Holmes's attention—by contending he had failed to be exceptional.[30]

Records of Holmes's correspondence from the period do not include any references to Chafee's article, though his letters from June and July 1919 include multiple defenses of the First Amendment opinions he wrote that spring. To Frederick Pollock, a British jurist, he wrote, "It was my misfortune to have to write opinions condemning [them, but] I suppose it was those opinions that led them to want to blow me up."[31] He shared similar sentiments with John Wigmore, dean of Northwestern's law school, contending it "seems to have let loose every damned fool in the country. On this question that comes before us I do not think there was room to doubt."[32] Regardless of Holmes's dismals and defenses, his

*Chapter Two*

correspondence, along with influential thinkers' responses, indicate free expression was being thought of and discussed in ways it had not been for more than a century. This was a national conversation and it centered around what Holmes had written.

During the same period, Laski, a political theorist who lectured briefly at Harvard before his socialist views led to his exit in 1920, also pushed back, however gently, against his dear friend Holmes's reasoning. Holmes mailed the three opinions to Laski, and mentioned them, rather apologetically, in a letter on March 16, 1919, about two weeks after they were handed down.[33] Holmes lamented, "I greatly regretted having to write them – and (between ourselves) that the government pressed them to a hearing."[34] Laski suggested a narrower limitation on expression, communicating particular concern regarding suppressing unpopular political views—a matter he was well acquainted with. He wrote:

> In the Schenck case I am not sure that I should not have liked the line to be drawn a little tighter about executive discretion. The Espionage Act tends to mean the prosecution of all one's opponents who are unimportant enough not to arise public opinion.[35]

In May, the *New Republic* ran a scathing critique of Holmes's First Amendment reasoning in the spring 1919 cases.[36] It was written by University of Chicago Law Professor Ernst Freund, who concluded:

> As in the case of all political persecution, the cause of the government has gained nothing, while the forces of discontent have been strengthened, and have been given an example of loose and arbitrary law which at some time may react against those who have set it.[37]

He continued, "Toleration of adverse opinion is not a matter of generosity, but of political prudence."

### *A Fleeting Glimpse at the Marketplace*

When the Court returned for the fall term in 1919, Mollie Steimer's and Jacob Abrams's case, *Abrams v. United States*, was on the docket. The case was, in many ways, *Schenck* all over again. A chance for a redo for the Court and, particularly, Holmes, who was not well acquainted with being criticized. Just as with *Schenck*, protestors were convicted for

36

*Fits and Starts*

speaking against US policy and military operations. The Court, using the clear and present danger test Holmes devised in *Schenck*, again upheld the convictions, finding the limitations on speech were not a First Amendment problem.[38] In a reversal from a few months before, and despite his numerous defenses of the earlier decisions over the summer, Holmes dissented. He penned a turning-point opinion that argued limitations on expression should only occur "if they so imminently threaten interference with the lawful and pressing purposes of the law that an immediate check is required to save the country."[39] Though he never admitted so, his reasoning sounded like Hand's.

Holmes didn't stop there, however—he added a justification for *why* we should protect expression that was not present in the precedential record before. He explained, "The best test of truth is the power of the thought to get itself accepted in the competition of the market, and that truth is the only ground upon which their wishes safely can be carried out."[40] What made him change his mind? Did the criticism get to him? We'll never know for certain.[41] He never admitted error. Friends wrote him celebratory letters, and his responses thanked them, but never explained any hint of a change of heart.[42] Hand celebrated the dissent, predicting it would become the dominant view in the future.[43] Holmes responded the next day, "Your letter gives me the greatest pleasure and I am very much obliged to you for writing to me."[44] Similarly, future Supreme Court justice Felix Frankfurter contended the dissent would "live as long as the *Areopagitica*."[45] Frankfurter's reference to John Milton's influential seventeenth-century argument for free expression, which is explored in chapter 4, was more correct than he could have guessed, but we are left to wonder what Holmes really intended in his use of the market-based argument for free expression.

What we can be certain of is this is our first instance where, now in a liquid form, the space for human discourse changed shape. Holmes's dissent changed the course of free expression in the United States. Importantly, it did so in very particular ways. He introduced the marketplace metaphor, contending "it is the theory of our Constitution" and reasoning, "We should be eternally vigilant against attempts to check the expression of opinions that we loathe and believe to be fraught with death."[46] Holmes's "competition of the market" reference, however,

37

*Chapter Two*

lacks any support or context. Nearly the entire opinion is off the cuff. It includes four case references, three of which are the much-criticized opinions he wrote in spring 1919. The opinion does not include any in-text references or footnotes that indicate how he understood such a space for human discourse. Despite taking part in several similar cases in the years that followed his *Abrams* dissent, Holmes never returned to the marketplace or any discussion of a space for human discourse. In fact, he generally avoided writing opinions in First Amendment cases after 1919, as Justice Brandeis took the lead in that area.[47] The structure of the space, however unclear and incomplete, started to solidify after *Abrams*. Justices had ample opportunity to continue to define the space in cases similar to *Abrams* in 1920 and 1921, but the reasoning did not return to the marketplace concept. We received a glimpse at a particular type of space for human discourse, then it was largely forgotten for nearly half a century. The actual phrase "marketplace of ideas" did not appear in a Supreme Court opinion until 1953.[48]

Market-based reasoning's disappearance was not helped by Holmes's personal and legal writings, which generally contradicted any assumption his "competition of the market" reference was intended to conjure a space in which truth would vanquish falsity in a free exchange of ideas.[49] In his dissent in *Abrams*, Holmes left us with the idea that there *should be* a space for human discourse, one that is generally protected from government intervention. What it looked like and how it should function—its shape—was not provided. The idea was enough to alter the shape of the space for human discourse, but not enough to define it.

## UNPOPULAR IDEAS (AND PEOPLE)

A socialist's blistering manifesto. Advocates for communism. The editor of a salacious, antisemitic newspaper in Minnesota. While this group sounds like the start of a very bad "three people walk into a bar" joke, the Supreme Court cases that surrounded this motley cast of characters helped liquefy and again reshape the space for human discourse between in 1925 and 1931. Importantly, the reshaping during this period took place without specifically referring to the space as a "marketplace." The marketplace concept, incomplete and unmoored in any type of legal

*Fits and Starts*

thought, was collecting dust. The legal conflict, acting as the melting agent for this period, was not a single federal law, like the Espionage Act and the world war that triggered it in 1917, but a series of relatively new state laws and one federal law intended to safeguard public order and national security.[50]

The challenges to these laws required justices take up the work the Court started during the brief liquid period between the Espionage Act's passage in 1917 and the *Abrams* dissent in 1919. All four decisions, three of which upheld limitations on expression, cited Holmes's free-expression-limiting reasoning from *Schenck*. His dissent from *Abrams* found little traction. While this period of liquidity was not characterized by a series of turning-point precedents for free expression, the dimensions and features of the space for human discourse gained substantial definition. Specifically, the reservoirs of rationales for *why* free expression is needed, and that government should generally stay out of the discourse, grew exponentially.

### *"Every Idea is an Incitement"*

The period begins with the Court's decision in *Gitlow v. New York* in 1925. The case is significant for a number of reasons, but for our purposes the tension between the majority and the dissenters, Holmes and Brandeis, regarding the government's role when it comes to unpopular and dangerous ideas is crucial. Benjamin Gitlow was convicted under New York's criminal anarchy law for publishing "The Leftwing Manifesto." The law was put in place in 1902, after President William McKinley was assassinated by an anarchist a year earlier. Though five new justices had joined the Court since *Abrams*, the outcome was nearly the same. Seven justices voted to uphold Gitlow's conviction, building part of their reasoning on Holmes's opinion from *Schenck*. The Court found the manifesto's "natural tendency and probable effect was to bring about the substantive evil which the legislative body might prevent."[51] Such a line of reasoning represents the solidified version of the outcome from the 1917–1919 liquid period, which generally reasoned expression could be limited to protect public order and national security. In other words, free expression was at best a luxury for popular ideas and at worst a

*Chapter Two*

menace to stability. Holmes helped liquefy the concept, in his final opinion about free expression, by reframing the approach to free expression the Court had again taken, arguing:

> It is said that this manifesto was more than a theory, that it was an incitement. Every idea is an incitement. It offers itself for belief and if believed it is acted on unless some other belief outweighs it or some failure of energy stifles the movement at its birth.[52]

While he did not return to the market concept, he built upon the idea he introduced in *Abrams* that a free exchange of ideas is more beneficial to democratic society than stringent government regulation of unpopular ideas. He continued:

> If in the long run the beliefs expressed in proletarian dictatorship are destined to be accepted by the dominant forces of the community, the only meaning of free speech is that they should be given their chance and have their way.[53]

Between *Schenck, Abrams*, and *Gitlow*, Holmes hardly created a clear picture of how a space for human discourse should function but, as Judge Richard Posner wrote in the preface to his collection of Holmes's writings, "If it is a crooked path, still it is one that most judges and mainstream legal scholars have been content to walk with him."[54]

The idea that unpopular ideas could somehow benefit society, which was perhaps an undercurrent in *Abrams*, received far more explicit treatment from Holmes in *Gitlow*. This was reinforced in a letter he wrote to Lewis Einstein, a US diplomat, about a month after the ruling was handed down. In far less formal language, Holmes explained, "I had my whack on free speech some years ago in the case of one Abrams and therefore did no more than recur to that and add that an idea is always an incitement."[55] He continued, "I regarded my view as simply upholding the right of a donkey to drool." Thus, Holmes saw his dissent as an extension of his efforts from *Abrams* and he designated his 1919 dissent as his statement about free speech. It should give us pause that he identified the *Abrams* dissent, which he and the rest of the Court had generally ignored for the past six years, as his position regarding free expression, rather than his often-used opinion for the Court in *Schenck* earlier that year. He never admitted error in *Schenck*, but clearly disowned it in

40

*Fits and Starts*

favor of *Abrams*. In the letter to Einstein, he continued that people tend to want to halt speech that shocks them, but the First Amendment was created for "when you do shock people."[56]

### Brandeis Reframes the Value of Speech

The *Gitlow* dissent, joined by Brandeis, added substantial dimension to *why* unpopular ideas should be protected in human discourse, but it did so in Holmes's much more off-the-cuff style. Few citations. Little connection with ideas or philosophies. The *Abrams* and *Gitlow* dissents are eloquent arguments that stand in relative isolation. Brandeis's concurring opinion in *Whitney v. California* in 1927, two years after *Gitlow*, directly addressed the value of a free exchange of ideas in human discourse and did so by interweaving historical and philosophical connections with free-expression rationales. The opinion was the first to do so, making it an influential tool for justices to draw from in future opinions. Anita Whitney was arrested in November 1919, a matter of weeks after the Court handed down its decision in *Abrams*, after addressing the Women's Civic Center in Oakland. Her case languished for years before the Court heard her appeal and affirmed her conviction under the California Criminal Syndicalism Act of 1919. The law's creation was not a coincidence as, in the wake of the Red Scare and the Espionage Act convictions during and after World War I, states passed laws to limit unpopular expression, often in the name of national security.[57] Whitney, however, is not the star of this case. In fact, Brandeis's turning-point concurring opinion wasn't meant for her case, which helps explain why it reads like a dissent.

Brandeis wrote the opinion as a dissent for *Ruthenberg v. Michigan*.[58] The Court heard arguments for a second time in *Whitney* in March 1926, but didn't hand down its opinion until May 1927. In the meantime, the Court heard arguments in *Ruthenberg*. Communist leader Charles Ruthenberg was convicted for violating Michigan's criminal syndicalism law, which, like California's, was passed in 1919. Brandeis constructed what is likely his most passionate and complete argument for free expression for his dissent in the case, but Ruthenberg died and there was no need for a ruling. Brandies and Holmes had agreed to

## Chapter Two

concur in *Whitney*, which was still languishing on justices' desks, so the opinion was repurposed for the *Whitney* decision. Brandeis's words, whichever case they were part of, have been labeled "Arguably the most important essay ever written, on or off the bench, on the meaning of the First Amendment."[59] Of course, its overall significance is not our focus here. We're after its role in *shaping* the space for human discourse.

Brandeis's opinion takes two important steps in this regard. First, it rejects the majority's view government limitations on unpopular and extremist speech are permissible for public safety and national security concerns. Brandeis contended limiting unpopular and extremist speech is a *danger* to civil society.[60] Second, Brandeis grounded his reasoning in history and political philosophy, providing a well-supported line of reasoning for justices and legal scholars to draw from in the future. Before examining these components, it is noteworthy Justice Holmes joined Justice Brandeis's opinion in *Whitney*. The concurring opinion critiques and carefully rejects Justice Holmes's reasoning from *Schenck* that the government had a right to limit speech "if the words used are used in such circumstances and are of such a nature as to create a clear and present danger."[61] Holmes's decision to join the concurring opinion reinforces his move away from his reasoning from *Schenck* toward his thinking in *Abrams*. We can think of the *Whitney* concurring opinion as a far more developed, nuanced version of Holmes's dissent in *Abrams*— absent, of course, any mention of the marketplace concept.

Brandeis reasoned, now eight years and many cases after *Schenck*, the Court had failed to clarify when free expression could be stopped because the speech was too dangerous.[62] He explained, "Fear of serious injury cannot alone justify suppression of free speech and assembly. Men feared witches and burnt women. It is the function of speech to free men from the bondage of irrational fears."[63] In another passage, he contended, "If there be time to expose through discussion the falsehood and fallacies, to avert the evil by the processes of education, the remedy to be applied is more speech, not enforced silence."[64] In other words, speech has value, even offensive or disagreeable speech. His reframing of speech as a public good, not a threat to security and order, is crucial in the development of a space for discourse. He reasoned, "Order cannot be secured merely through fear of punishment for its infraction; that

*Fits and Starts*

it is hazardous to discourage thought, hope and imagination; that fear breeds repression; that repression breeds hate; that hate menaces stable government."[65] Importantly, Brandeis did not present these ideas as his own or leave them unattributed. He tied them to history and the intent of the Framers. He argued these ideas were the outgrowth of the Framers' efforts to create a particular type of government.[66]

Thus, Brandeis provided a set of rationales for *why* free expression, even unpopular ideas, should be protected that was grounded in the history and political theory that was prevalent at the time of the First Amendment's creation. Together, Holmes's *Gitlow* dissent and Brandeis's concurring opinion in *Whitney* recast *why* expansive free-expression rights are valuable to society and the individual. In doing so, they provided building blocks for future justices when they constructed the marketplace as a justification for expansive free-expression safeguards and a particular type of space for human discourse. Brandeis's opinion from *Whitney* in particular is part of the DNA of nearly every future building block for a space for human discourse.[67] It provides a justification for free expression, an exchange of ideas, and a space for discourse that simply did not exist in the Court's record beforehand. Among the cases it influenced was *Near v. Minnesota*, the final case from this period of liquidity.

### An Unprecedented Decision

Jay Near's and Howard Guilford's *Saturday Press* might be the only paper in US history to be banned before it published a single issue.[68] The two Minneapolis publishers' reputations were so infamous, their reports so scandalous, the chief of police sent officers to take the *Press* off the stands before it could circulate its inaugural edition. Of course, Near and Guilford's reporting wasn't entirely false, though it was antisemitic, anti-Catholic, and filled with hate. The *Press* attacked grift. Near and Guilford named names when it came to public officials and business leaders who they suspected were supporting gangs, gambling rings, and crime. After Guilford was hospitalized having been shot in September 1927, Near escalated attacks on public officials and business leaders. Minneapolis police officially banned the paper in October. After

## Chapter Two

the paper's attacks on public officials continued, county attorney Floyd Olson filed a complaint, contending the state had a right under a 1925 "public nuisance" law to halt the *Press*'s publication.

When Near and Guilford challenged the law, a court upheld the ban. Four years later, the Supreme Court did something it had never done— it struck down a law because it conflicted with the First Amendment. The five to four ruling overturning Minnesota's law was unprecedented. There was *no* precedent from similar cases justices could ground their decision upon. Chief Justice John Hughes, who wrote the opinion, referenced Brandeis's opinion from *Whitney* and Holmes's opinion in *Schenck*, but mostly looked elsewhere, primarily in the British common law and the Framers' writings. His selections of these building blocks for the decision influenced the first Supreme Court opinion to rationalize striking down a law in support of free-expression safeguards in very particular ways. Importantly, Holmes—who was in his final full term on the Court—and Brandeis were silent in the decision. The pair had been, to this point, the only justices who had written opinions that rationalized free-expression safeguards.

Hughes joined the Court as chief justice in February 1930, a month *after* justices heard arguments in *Near*. He was not a judicial novice, however. After a term as governor of New York, he spent seven years on the Court before leaving in 1916 to mount a Republican challenge to Woodrow Wilson's re-election campaign. He narrowly lost, became secretary of state from 1921 to 1925, and then rejoined the Court. Now in his seventies, the Chief Justice left his mark on the space for human discourse by selecting three primarily historical building blocks to rationalize the Court's decision to strike down the Minnesota law: British jurist William Blackstone's commentaries, James Madison's writings, and John Dickinson's "A Letter to the Inhabitants of the Province of Quebec" from 1774. These eighteenth-century sources shared Enlightenment-era assumptions that truth is generally the same for all, people are rational, and government is intended to serve the individual. Essentially, in the first opinion that rationalized striking down a law because it conflicted with the First Amendment, Hughes opened a portal to the seventeenth century, connecting thinkers such as John Locke, John Milton, and David Hume to twentieth-century questions about the exchange of

44

*Fits and Starts*

ideas. The portal was not completely of his making, but its presence as a framing mechanism for the opinion's reasoning, and those that followed, cannot be underestimated. These thinkers put the reasons *why* we have free expression and the dimensions of what would become a space for human discourse on a particular trajectory that came to define the marketplace of ideas—though not yet, not in 1931.

Dickinson, who also wrote "The Olive Branch Petition" in 1775, was a former president of Pennsylvania and Delaware, a member of the Constitutional Congress, and among those who drafted early versions of the First Amendment.[69] He explicitly quoted Locke's thinking in his writing and in the Continental Congress's "Letter to the Inhabitants of the Province of Quebec," less than two years before the Declaration of Independence. He reasoned freedom of the press was needed to advance science, morality, and the arts, as well as the "diffusion of liberal sentiments on the administration of Government" and the "ready communication of thoughts between subjects."[70] The use of a seventy-word passage from Dickinson's letter in *Near* does more than argue for a free press. It laces assumptions about the value of a free exchange of information with Enlightenment ideas about truth and human rationality. Hughes also included a 250-word passage from James Madison, who was substantially influenced by Scottish Enlightenment thinkers, such as Adam Smith and David Hume.[71]

Madison, in one of the passages Hughes included in *Near*, reasoned "it is better to leave a few of its noxious branches to their luxuriant growth, than, by pruning them away, to injure the vigour of those yielding the proper fruits."[72] As with Brandeis's concurring opinion in *Whitney,* but more explicitly, the Court's opinion in *Near* continued to frame free expression as a public good, rather than a liability. Similarly, in choosing to draw from Blackstone's influential commentaries, Hughes associated *why* a free press is required in a democracy with Enlightenment reasoning about truth and rationality. He quoted Blackstone, who reasoned "Every freeman has an undoubted right to lay what sentiments he pleases before the public, to forbid this is to destroy the freedom of the press."[73] While *Near* remains a crucial precedent when it comes to government censorship, the building blocks Hughes selected to rationalize the Court's decision have immediate connections with the creation of

45

*Chapter Two*

a space for human discourse. The rationales include individuals having access to ideas and that government limitations can stifle the exchange of ideas. *Near* essentially adds new tools to justices' tool boxes of potential rationales for *why* a space for human discourse is needed and what is should look like. These tools have become well worn, but after *Near* they were, for a time, generally neglected as justices during World War II and much of the Second Red Scare era generally upheld government limitations on ideas that were considered subversive or dangerous. That changed with the final melt in this chapter, *New York Times v. Sullivan*.

## THE MARKETPLACE AWAKENS

*Sullivan*, decided in 1964, wasn't the first free-expression-related precedent after *Near*. It is the most important, however. This chapter's focus is on identifying crucial moments in which the shape and dimensions of human discourse liquefied, shifted, and resolidified. Chapter 4 provides a more comprehensive look at the marketplace's development as a rationale for free expression. Here, we focus on how *Sullivan*, and the conditions that surrounded it, melted a generally solidified way of thinking regarding *why* we have free expression, opening the door to a wave of cases that ultimately created the modern marketplace of ideas. It is no coincidence such an important case for the space for human discourse is also credited with creating the modern First Amendment.[74] The "Heed Their Rising Voices" advertisement that triggered the case ran in the *Times* as school integration battles and sit-ins raged throughout the South. In 1963, the March on Washington and 16th Street Baptist Church bombing, along with President Kennedy's assassination, prefaced the Court's hearings about the case in January 1964. At the same time, the conflict in Vietnam was escalating. In short, the space for human discourse was being liquefied as part of a national conversation that transformed US society.

The Court's decision to overturn a US$500,000 defamation verdict against the *Times* for falsehoods in the advertisement recast defamation law, particularly regarding public officials. Justices were not, however, satisfied to write a rationale for why the defamation verdict should be overturned. They aimed much higher. They wrote an argument for a

46

*Fits and Starts*

particular type of First Amendment, one that had massive repercussions for how a space for human discourse should operate. Essentially, *Sullivan* was the moment of synergy. All the pieces from the previous major melts came together in the same place for the first time. Justice Brennan, writing for the Court, reasoned the United States has "a profound national commitment to the principle that debate on public issues should be uninhibited, robust, and wide-open."[75] He continued, "The erroneous statement is inevitable in free debate, and that it must be protected if the freedoms of expression are to have the 'breathing space' they 'need to survive.'"[76]

We've come a long way from *Schenck* and the dominant assumption expression should be regulated as a threat to public order and national security. The priority shifted. The space for discourse became sacrosanct and indispensable to democracy. *Sullivan*'s "uninhibited, robust, and wide-open" thesis passage, even as a stand-alone rationale for expansive free-expression safeguards and a space for human discourse, is powerful. Its impact on the dimensions and shape of the space is multiplied by its context within the opinion. The passage is preceded by a quote from *Roth v. United States*, the landmark obscenity decision authored by Brennan seven years earlier. Brennan drew it into *Sullivan*, concluding the First Amendment requires an "unfettered interchange of ideas for the bringing about of political and social changes desired by the people."[77] He came awfully close to naming the space the marketplace of ideas. A year later, in *Lamont v. Postmaster General*, Brennan took the next step, using "marketplace of ideas" for only the second time in the Supreme Court's history.[78]

Soon after *Sullivan*'s "unfettered interchange" passage, Brennan incorporated a 150-word block quote from Brandeis's impassioned opinion from *Whitney*.[79] The passage emphasizes the importance of tolerating unpopular ideas and the dangers of limiting expression. A few pages later, Brennan included a footnote that reasons "even a false statement may be deemed to make a valuable contribution to public debate."[80] The footnote cites John Stuart Mill's *On Liberty* and Milton's *Areopagitica*, works justices in coming years used as templates to shape the modern First Amendment. Essentially, in *Sullivan*, the scattered seeds of ideas from the preceding eras of change came together and started bearing

*Chapter Two*

fruit in the form of a clearer, more discernible shape for an expansive space for human discourse. The case marks the beginning of the crucial period of liquidity, from roughly 1964 to 1980, as the space for human discourse justices gradually eked out became synonymous with the marketplace of ideas and the extensive and weighty theoretical baggage by which it is defined. Importantly, as justices recognized the space for human discourse as crucial, the space did not have to take the shape of the marketplace of ideas. That was only one path.

By constructing the marketplace, the shape and dimensions of the space took a very particular form—one dominated by Enlightenment assumptions about truth and human rationality. The space, particularly in an era dominated by algorithmic predetermination, AI communicators, and networked communication, does not have to be defined by the marketplace's guidelines. The marketplace, as this chapter has sought to contextualize, is only one of the possible forms the space for human discourse can take. In chapter 4, we map out the strange history of how the space became the marketplace of ideas. Many attribute the theory to Holmes. That is a mistake. In chapter 3, we'll separate Holmes's crucial contributions to the space for human discourse from marketplace theory.

# THREE

## Holmes and the Nothingness

Oliver W. Holmes went into the Civil War an idealist. He was six-feet three-inches tall and weighed 136 pounds when he joined the army, essentially resembling a telegraph pole. The twenty-one-year-old Holmes's mind, at the top of that pole, however, was full of ideas. He wrote poetry, inspired by his acquaintance with Ralph Waldo Emerson and other transcendentalist authors who had been part of his life growing up in Boston.[1] He penned the Class of 1861 poem for Harvard's graduation while training with his regiment. In the poem, he opined of the "Bloody birthright of heroic days" and letting "others celebrate our heroic endeavor."[2] He also supported abolition, in his writing and by attending rallies. When war broke out, he signed up to fight. He was motivated by ideas. He had an exuberance for what he believed was right. A young idealist, full of belief in a cause might seem like the perfect protagonist for Act I of the story of how a space for human discourse took shape. That's not how this story goes, however. Holmes altered the course of free expression protections and a space for human discourse because he *didn't* believe in truth or ideas. He believed in nothing. His idealism and any belief in causes were lost during the Civil War.

By the war's end, Holmes's faith in ideas was gone. He no longer believed in the Union cause—or any cause.[3] Truth and doing "what's

FIGURE 1 Holmes sat for this undated portrait at Silsbee, Case & Company in Boston. He turned twenty in 1861 a few weeks before Confederate troops attacked Fort Sumter.
Source: Library of Congress

## Holmes and the Nothingness

right" were vanquished. Such great losses did not mean his spirt was broken. By no means. What remained was a brilliant mind in a body with scars from three serious wounds, a host of nightmarish memories, many lost friends, and questions about truth, ideas, and human nature that had almost no mooring in any thought tradition. Lewis Einstein, an American diplomat who shared a decades-long friendship with Holmes, recounted the jurist telling him "After the Civil War the world never seemed quite right again."[4] The war shattered Holmes's privileged, homogeneous, Boston-centered understanding of the world.[5] Nothing replaced what was lost. This observation is crucial. He did not substitute his wounded ideology or seemingly failed set of beliefs about the world with new ones. He gave up on all of them. In a 1924 letter to his dear friend Harold Laski, a political theorist whose socialist ideas led him to leave the United States during World War I, Holmes concluded, "I had my belly fully of isms when I was young."[6] In a letter to Laski four years earlier, he explained he made it a practice to challenge the other justices on the Supreme Court to select any general legal philosophy and he would use it to decide the case.[7] What point was he trying to make? There is no one truth and it is a mistake to think otherwise. There is no one *correct* ideology and it is dangerous to believe so. In yet another letter to Laski, he explained, "If my fellow citizens want to go to Hell I will help them. It's my job."[8]

Holmes simply did not believe in causes or anyone who claimed to hold insight into what was true. In fact, the more strident a person's belief, the more dismissive he became. In a dissenting opinion, Holmes defended Benjamin Gitlow's right to publish the "Left Wing Manifesto" but privately rejected the socialist leader's impassioned stance. He wrote to Felix Frankfurter, "I gave an expiring kick on the last day . . . in favor of the right to drool on the part of believers in the proletarian dictatorship."[9] In other words, Gitlow was a fool, at least to some extent, because he believed too strongly in a cause. The same went for political activist Eugene Debs and the others who were convicted under the Espionage Act. After writing the Court's opinions to uphold their convictions in 1919, Holmes told a friend they "seemed to me poor fools."[10] He continued, "The greatest bores in the world are the come outers who are cocksure of a dozen nostrums. The dogmatism of a little education

51

*Chapter Three*

is hopeless."[11] They were not fools to Holmes because the truths or ideas they chose were incorrect. They were fools because they passionately believed in truths and ideas. To Holmes, the war had been a failure of ideas. It was the result of unyielding truths. And the costs of the war for him were incalculable. In the decades that followed, he made sure to undercut the argument of any person who passionately believed in a certain truth, cause, or set of ideas.

Much that has been written about Holmes's contributions to free expression and the marketplace of ideas is not accurate. Here, the task is simple. We do not need a biography or a hero's tale. We must clearly identify Holmes's role in setting the space for human discourse on a very particular course. This project requires a fresh, clear-headed construction of the conceptual building blocks Holmes's legal, scholarly, and personal writings contributed to the space for human discourse. These raw materials are crucial to how we should understand the space for human discourse in an era dominated by algorithms, AI, and highly homogenized networked spaces. Holmes was a primary contributor to two concepts that have become inseparable from the First Amendment—ideas and truth—the exact things he lost faith in during the war. Neither ideas nor truth are mentioned in the forty-five-word First Amendment, but how we have come to view ideas and the philosophical baggage we have assigned to truth all but define free expression in the United States.[12] The truth and ideas foci were part of the fits and starts regarding free expression highlighted in the preceding chapter. They find further prominence in the next chapter's examination of the transformation of the space for human discourse into the modern marketplace of ideas. In this sense, Holmes is indispensable to the story of *how* the space for human discourse developed, just not in the way he is often thought of. Holmes did not *create* the marketplace of ideas. He did not *believe* truth would vanquish falsity in an open exchange. He was not a progressive or champion of progressive movements. He was *not* a lot of things he is often credited as being.[13]

Perhaps Alexander Meiklejohn, a free-speech advocate and professor who knew a thing or two about First Amendment theory, captured Holmes's contributions best when he described him as "the leading hero, or villain, of the plot."[14] Meiklejohn, whom Justice Holmes wrote fondly of after they met in 1924, credited Justice Holmes with greatness, but

52

## Holmes and the Nothingness

concluded his work regarding the First Amendment "has no such excellence."[15] Such a distinction is helpful. Holmes's initial free-expression opinions in *Schenck v. United States* and *Abrams v. United States* are crucial waypoints in the story of the First Amendment's development, but his true impact on the shape and dimension of the space for human discourse makes far more sense when understood in the broader context of his extra-judicial writings. His greatness, or contribution, was not so much the primordial free-expression opinions he authored in *Schenck*, *Abrams*, and *Gitlow*, but his influence on how we approach ideas and truth.[16] Importantly, he only mentioned the "market" once. He spent a lifetime, however, reading, thinking, and developing an understanding about truth and how people interact with ideas.

It is from those lessons, rather than the relatively shallow waters of his passing reference to a "market" in his dissenting opinion in *Abrams*, that we gain the most from his contributions. Justice Holmes changed the shape of the space for human discourse and influenced a generation of legal scholars, but as a catalyst and contributor and not as an inventor. His expansive network of correspondence alone was influential. He exchanged, challenged, and celebrated ideas for decades with thinkers such as William James, the architect of American pragmatism; Felix Frankfurter, who eventually took Justice Holmes's seat on the Court; Learned Hand, who spent nearly half a century as a judge; Laski, a political theorist; and Morris Cohen, a philosopher and legal positivist. His network of connections, his birth into a family that was at the center of Boston's intellectual culture, his young adulthood that coincided with a life-altering experience fighting in the Civil War, and a host of other crucial elements formed Holmes into a unique thinker and gave him the power, heft, and influence to forever change the path of free expression in the United States. Importantly, the particular changes came because he believed in nothing, rather than something.

### "TOUCHED WITH FIRE"

Holmes's Ball's Bluff diary recounts his first experiences on the battlefield, including the sensation of having a bullet removed from his chest during battle. He described a sergeant grabbing him and pulling his

## Chapter Three

winded, wounded body to the back of the fighting after a bullet hit him "as if a horse had kicked me" in the chest.[17] He remembered the sergeant "squeezed it from the right opening—well—I remember the sickening feeling of water in my face—I was quite faint—and seeing poor Serg' Merchant lying near—shot through the head and covered with blood."[18] After pushing the bullet from Holmes's chest, the sergeant stuffed lint into the wound and handed the bullet to him. Holmes kept the bullet, like a medal, for the rest of his life. He stashed the bullets—the one from Ball's Bluff was the first of three—removed from his body during the Civil War in a safety deposit box. He also stored the blood-stained uniforms he was wearing when he was wounded in a closet, where they were found after his death in 1935, seventy years after the war's end.[19] Holmes left notes, telling those who found the bullets "These were taken from my body during the Civil War" and, regarding the uniforms, he wrote the blood was his.[20]

Holmes experienced the worst the war had to offer, from the nation's bloodiest day at Antietam, where he was shot in the neck, to his nearly deadly case of dysentery, to the weeklong nightmare of the Battle of the Wilderness. Clearly, part of him wanted to remember the horrific experience. Every year in September he drank a glass of wine on the anniversary of Antietam, a battle he narrowly survived.[21] In his Memorial Day speech in 1884, he wrote:

> I see another young lieutenant as I saw him in the Seven Days. . . . The officers were at the head of their companies. The advance was beginning. We caught each other's eyes and saluted. When next I looked, he was gone.[22]

Historians contend he was talking about his friend Henry Abbott, who was killed in the Battle of the Wilderness. After that battle in 1864, he wrote to his parents, "In the corner of the woods . . . the dead of both sides lay piled in the trenches 5 to 6 deep—wounded often writhing under superincumbent dead."[23] Despite the horrors, he was proud of his service, telling those gathered on Memorial Day, 1884, "We have shared the incommunicable experience of war; we have felt, we still feel, the passion of life to its top."[24] He contended his generation was "touched with fire" because of its experience in the gruesome, catastrophic war.[25]

54

*Holmes and the Nothingness*

Part of him, however, did not survive the war and its absence is crucial when we look ahead to when he was Justice Holmes, rather than a bleary-eyed, twenty-one-year-old officer fighting for his life near a muddy river bank in Northern Virginia.

A space for human discourse requires certain understandings about the nature of ideas and truth. Holmes spent his post-war life exploring ideas, truth, and human rationality not as a philosopher, though he considered the option, but as a lawyer, jurist, and, much like his father, a hub for a broad network of exceptional thinkers. Oliver Wendell Holmes Sr. was central to Boston society. He helped found *The Atlantic* magazine and wrote the poem "Old Iron Sides" as a tribute to the USS *Constitution*. This meant Oliver W. Holmes Jr. grew up in a house full of ideas. He grew up with elite thinkers and authors such as Emerson, Nathanial Hawthorne, James Russell Lowell, and Henry Wadsworth Longfellow in his home. Holmes's father, however, was a unionist, but not an abolitionist.[26] His views were tepid, comfortable, and safe. As dean of Harvard Medical School, he initially supported the admission of the first Black students, as well as the school's first woman, to the program. When a majority of the students rebelled, he returned the school to its all-white, all-male status.[27] Holmes, in his letters during the war, spoke respectfully to his father, but it was Emerson with whom he bonded. In 1930, he recounted meeting Emerson as the "moment when a spark started a flame" in him.[28] After the war, in 1876, Holmes sent Emerson a law paper and credited him with a "respect I feel for you who more than anyone else first started the philosophical ferment in my mind."[29] Before the war, Emerson spoke publicly against slavery and Holmes listened. Holmes's first publication was a tribute to Emerson in *Harvard Magazine* in 1858.[30]

By 1861, Holmes helped edit the magazine, and it continued to support abolition. He became close to abolition leader William Lloyd Garrison's son Wendell, who was a classmate at Harvard. Another classmate, Norwood Penrose Hallowell, who was shot alongside Holmes about a year later at Antietam, recruited him to help the abolitionist cause in Boston. When the war started, Holmes left Harvard early, just before graduation, to fight.[31] These experiences and actions tell the story of a young person who was driven by ideas, duty, and belief. All of these were extracted until only a unique type of nothingness remained by the war's end.

## Chapter Three

### *Waiting for Death After Ball's Bluff*

Of the 1,700 Union troops who sought to cross the Potomac River during the Battle of Ball's Bluff, only 800 came back.[32] Holmes was part of the Twentieth Massachusetts Regiment, which included many of his friends from Boston. The regiment saw some of the most intense fighting during the war. More than 60 percent of the regiment was killed or wounded, one of the highest numbers of any unit.[33] Many of those lost were his friends. After being shot early in the fighting, Holmes was taken to a house that was converted into a hospital. His diary indicates the bullet pierced his lung and he was struggling to breath and bleeding "very freely" from his mouth.[34] The diary describes a ghastly scene in the makeshift hospital.[35] Bloody body parts and amputations. Moaning and desperate cries for help. The doctor told Holmes his chances of survival were not good and he was left in the hospital to wait to see if he would live. We know how the story ends—Holmes died just shy of his ninety-fourth birthday in 1935—but there among the gore and fear of death, the twenty-one-year-old did not know if his story ended there.

He documented first considering dying "like a solider."[36] In other words, his idealism continued to play a crucial role. He wrote, "I was shot in the breast doing my duty up to the hub—afraid? No, I am proud."[37] He next considered his faith, and reaffirmed he had none. Late in the diary, well after he knew he would survive, he reflected:

> It is curious how rapidly the mind adjusts itself under some circumstances to entirely new relations—I thought for a while I might be dying, and it seemed the most natural thing in the world—The moment the hope of life returned it seemed abhorrent to nature as ever that I should die.[38]

Holmes convalesced in his home in Boston, where he received countless visitors.[39] His faith in truth and ideas appears to have survived, but his ordeal included the reflection that truth can change suddenly and is reliant upon circumstances.

He referred often to his near-death experience at Ball's Bluff.[40] In a 1918 letter to Laski, for whom he seemed to save his most vulnerable thoughts, he reaffirmed he associated the ordeal with truth and experience. He explained, "Our early impressions shape our later emotional reactions

*Holmes and the Nothingness*

and when one adds the experience of having been cocksure of things that weren't so, I can't help an occasional semi-shudder."[41] He continued:

> I am glad to remember that when I was dying after Ball's Bluff I remembered my father's saying that death bed repentances generally meant only that the man was scared and reflected that if I wanted to I couldn't, because I still thought the same.[42]

Holmes's wound at Ball's Bluff stayed with him, but the heart of the war, including two more wounds, a nearly fatal bout of dysentery, and the constant presence of death did even more to alter his belief in truth and ideas.

### Neck, Bowels, and Heel

A bullet grazed Holmes neck on September 17, 1862, at Antietam. The injury, by his own description, does not appear to have been life-threatening, though he was concerned enough about death that he wrote on a slip of paper "I am Capt. O. W. Holmes 20th Mass. Son of Oliver Wendell Holmes, M.D., Boston," to ensure his body would be identified and returned to Boston.[43] He kept the piece of paper for the rest of his life. Oddly, being shot in the neck was not the most transformative part of 1862 for Holmes. By the time he and his friend Norwood Hallowell, both wounded, were hiding in a house from Confederate troops during the bloodiest day of fighting in American history, Holmes had been unable to consistently digest food for more than a month. Dysentery was weakening him one day at a time. Before Antietam, his letters home indicate his idealism remained intact in spring 1862, as he learned he was to be promoted to captain, but stated he would reject the promotion because it would be disrespectful to a friend.[44]

Just the same, he was promoted to captain on May 1, 1862, and the war trod on. He recalled generally constant, intense fighting through much of the summer, writing to his parents in June that his unit spent a day burying the decaying bodies of Confederate soldiers.[45] He recounted:

> As you go through the woods you stumble constantly, and, if after dark, as last night on picket, perhaps tread on the swollen bodies already fly blown and decaying, of men shot in the head back or bowels—Many of the wounds are terrible to look at.[46]

## Chapter Three

After the neck wound, and surviving a day in which 6,000 were killed and 17,000 wounded, Holmes's letters home seemed increasingly positive. He reported to his concerned parents he was "really disgracefully well."[47] He explained, "I walk about all day & am in no respect in the condition of one who has been hit again within an inch of his life."[48] It is difficult to tell if his tone was authentic or a ruse to reassure his parents. Either way, the positive tone disappeared that winter.

He was hospitalized with dysentery in December. Being shot in the neck healed, but dysentery dogged him starting at least in September, based on his letters, and slowly weakened him for months. He later wrote dysentery nearly killed him, and if it had not, he might have died with his regiment in Fredericksburg, where his unit suffered massive losses in one of the Union's most ill-conceived battles.[49] He told his mother "I couldn't restrain my tears—I went to the Hosp.—the only tent left here—listless and miserable. They were just moving out a dead man."[50] Still in the hospital more than a week later, and after learning of the Union's terrible loss at Fredericksburg, he admitted in a letter to his father he was having doubts. He explained, "I see no further progress—I don't think either of you realize the unity or the determination of the South. I think you are hopeful because (excuse me) you are ignorant."[51] He continued by recounting the cause of the war and questioning whether those matters could be worked out in peace. He emphasized he would continue to serve, but "I am, to be sure, heartily tired and half worn out body and mind by this life."[52] The letter was similar to what he wrote his sister a month before. In the letter to her, he concluded, "I've pretty much made up my mind that the South have achieved their independence & I am almost ready to hope spring will see an end."[53] He continued, "The Army is tired with its hard, & terrible experience & still more with its mismanagement."[54]

The letters foreshadow a shift in Holmes. Beyond the expected fatigue from the war's gruesome experience were acknowledgments that the South's perspectives, its truths and ideas, were as real to its people as the North's conclusions about slavery and preserving the Union. He reflected on this in his Memorial Day 1884 address, where he reasoned, "We equally believed that those who stood against us held just as sacred convictions that were the opposite of ours, and we respected them as

*Holmes and the Nothingness*

every man with a heart must respect those who give all for their belief."[55] He came to see both sides had developed rigid, unmoving truths. Neither side could claim exclusive ownership of "the truth" of the matter. The result of such a divergence in who was *right* or whose ideas were true or good was massive carnage and death, which Holmes experienced first-hand. These observations found a home in Holmes's later writings about truth, ideas, and the law, but first the war was waiting for him when he recovered from dysentery.

He was hit again in May 1863 in the Battle of Chancellorsville. Metal from an exploding cannon shell cut into his heel bone. Medics dug the metal out, but the painful wound stole his ability to walk for several months. He wished the foot would have been amputated, so he did not have to fight in the war anymore.[56] Holmes was done. He no longer believed in the ideas behind the war. Still, he returned to duty in January 1864. The heel injury was his last, but the worst was still ahead of him. The Battle of the Wilderness, in early May 1864, was Holmes's final major conflict and it took much from him. Abbott died on the second day. Holmes admired Abbott's bravery and reflected on his friend's willingness to execute orders he knew were terribly wrong and would lead to many deaths. It could have been Abbott whom he remembered in "The Soldier's Faith," an address to the Harvard class of 1895. He reflected:

> I do not know what is true. I do not know the meaning of the universe. But in the midst of doubt, in the collapse of creeds, there is one thing I do not doubt, that no man who lives in the same world with most of us can doubt, and that is that the faith is true and adorable which leads a soldier to throw away his life in obedience to a blindly accepted duty, in a cause which he little understands, in a plan of campaign of which he has little notion, under tactics of which he does not see the use.[57]

His reflections wove truth, ideas, and human rationality into a solemn question about why people do what they do. What motivates a person to act? Of course, a part of that answer comes back to truth and ideas.

The Battle of the Wilderness was the most violent of the war.[58] Antietam represented the bloodiest day, but the Wilderness was more than a week of carnage. Holmes no longer led a unit. He was aide to a general and spent much of the battle, based on his letters, on horseback conveying orders, shoring up units, and bringing information back to

*Chapter Three*

headquarters. On May 11, he penned a terse, forty-two-word letter to his mother, "Fighting every day. . . . Just think of it—Today is the 7th day we have fought."[59] He guessed they were losing 3,000 soldiers a day. The next day, at the "Bloody Angle of Spotsylvania," men fought hand-to-hand, with bayonets, and with the backs of rifles for more than eighteen hours.[60] Holmes was there at least twice, as part of his duties during the battle. On May 12, he documented seeing "an angle in a space of 12 by 15 ft" where there were 150 bodies. The next morning, he described dead and wounded piled on top of each other. He noted, "Trees were in slivers from the constant peppering of bullets."[61] Experiences such as this are more difficult to associate with Holmes's transformation during the war. His body was, by all accounts, unharmed and his letters were generally more descriptive than dramatic.

In other words, it is not possible to identify when Holmes lost his faith in ideas. A letter to his mother in June 1864, after the Wilderness but before his final armed conflict in the Battle of Fort Stevens, he wrote to his mother that he felt he had completed his duty and wished to stop fighting. He explained to her he could not handle another battle. He wrote, "I started this thing as a boy. I am now a man and I have been coming to the conclusion for the last six months that my duty has changed."[62] He continued, "I have laboriously and with much suffering of mind and body *earned* the right."[63] Holmes was honorably discharged July 17, 1864. He entered the war believing the Union must be preserved and slavery must be abolished and he left believing in nothing. Both sides believed different truths. Those truths were the results of divergent ideas about what is right and the result was death on a historic scale. What good is truth if it leads to war? The most influential justice in determining *how* free expression and the space for human discourse would be shaped lost his faith in truth and ideas somewhere between Ball's Bluff and when he mustered out of the army in July 1864.

## THE MATTER OF TRUTH

Nothingness can be problematic. It leaves a void. The absence of a consistent Holmesian philosophy has vexed many who have searched for one. Like a Rorschach test or studying a Jackson Pollock painting, many

60

## Holmes and the Nothingness

have found what they're looking for in Holmes's writing. Holmes made this easy because he dabbled in ideas. He tried them on, but generally never committed to them. He looked into Social Darwinism, but let it go.[64] In his dissent in the Court's infamous *Lochner v. New York* ruling, which was decided using aspects of Social Darwinism, Holmes rebuked justices' use of the idea. He explained, "A Constitution is not intended to embody a particular economic theory, whether of paternalism and the organic relation of the citizen to the state or of laissez-faire. It is made for people of fundamentally differing views."[65] He provided a terser rejection in a letter in 1916. He explained, "I don't believe in H. Spencer."[66] In a letter the year before, he explained to a friend, "Herbert Spencer leaves some explosive qualities of man out of accounts."[67] Importantly, Holmes did not suggest an alternative theory. He explored the theory, critiqued it, and moved on.

Similarly, he debated pragmatism with James, but decided to reject the label.[68] He remained a fan of John Stewart Mill's work throughout his life but cannot be understood as a disciple of the late-Enlightenment thinker.[69] At times, slivers of these ideas appeared in his legal opinions or scholarship and it's easy to cherry-pick the overlaps and place him into one of these philosophical buckets. Taken as a whole, however, Holmes was an ideological free agent. This conclusion is reinforced by how few citations he placed in his opinions for the Court. When he wrote, he generally wrote his thoughts, not those of others. His crucial dissent in *Abrams* cites three opinions, all of which he authored.[70] He doesn't cite books or other thinkers. Similarly, in his short dissent in *Gitlow*, he cited three opinions, two of which he wrote.[71]

Holmes read voraciously and widely. He once joked to Laski "Books are the one element in which I am personally and nakedly acquisitive. If it weren't for the law I would steal them."[72] His personal library included works by Jane Austin, William Cullen Bryant, John Dewey, Johann Wolfgang Goethe, Nathanial Hawthorne, G. W. F. Hegel, Thomas Hobbes, Abraham Lincoln, Martin Luther, Edgar Allen Poe, and Plato.[73] His critiques of authors indicate the detached way he approached ideas. The more authoritative the author, the more he rejected the work. He found Hegel's philosophy "little better than an intentional mystification, though I daresay he thought he believed it."[74] He was

61

*Chapter Three*

more complimentary of Dewey's approach, but still held the ideas at arm's length, reasoning "It is badly written," but "Few indeed, I should think, are the books that hold so much of life with an even hand."[75] He hated Austin, concluding "it is for others—not for me."[76] Holmes's letters are filled with reflections about ideas. The ideas are most commonly considered, critiqued, and set aside in favor of the next book on his reading list or the next case awaiting the Court in conference.

As we frame Holmes as believing in *nothing*, this does not preclude him from searching—in his own detached, aristocratic approach—for a way to understand truth and ideas. What is crucial, however, is his search has been preserved in landmark court opinions and legal scholarship. His words, as a result of his position in society, carried immense weight. Before examining how Holmes constructed truth and interacted with ideas later in his life, this chapter looks at one more crucial formative moment that provides context for his contributions.

### *The Metaphysical Club*

The Metaphysical Club was a short-lived set of gatherings among a group of young Boston intellectuals that started in 1872. In many ways, the name is more memorable than the group's accomplishments. The context of the group's formation and some of the relationships it fostered, however, are noteworthy. Coming out of a war that undermined and damaged American thought, the group's interaction, however brief, can be seen as one of the first new blooms after the war scorched so many ideas. Holmes's involvement in the group was limited, but again, his future impact on free expression makes his membership noteworthy.[77] Holmes often treated people like he did ideas, entertaining them briefly before rejecting them and moving on. One of the group's principal organizers, Charles Sanders Peirce, certainly fell into that category. Peirce had a crucial role in the creation of American pragmatism, but Holmes found him "rather overrated."[78] The group, however, included two thinkers who made a lasting impact on Holmes. The first, William James, articulated pragmatic thought in his master work in 1907, thirty-five years after the Metaphysical Club's formation.[79] The second, Chauncey Wright, is far less known, likely because he died in 1875

## Holmes and the Nothingness

when he was forty-five. James and Wright could not have been more different.

Wright was a mathematician and a Darwinist. He had encyclopedic knowledge of countless topics.[80] Holmes cared greatly for Wright and took every opportunity to praise his ideas—even decades after his death. When an author asked Holmes about Peirce's contributions to the Metaphysical Club, he suggested he look into Wright, explaining, "I learned far more from Chauncey Wright."[81] To British jurist Frederick Pollock, Holmes wrote Wright was "a forgotten philosopher of real merit, [who] taught me when young that I must not say necessary about the universe, that we don't know whether anything is necessary or not."[82] Wright was an empiricist who was in the business of predicting phenomena. He worked for the *American Ephemeris and Nautical Almanac* creating tables that provided future movements of the sun, moon, planets, and major stars.[83] Could human behavior be predicted, based on a series of factors, like the sun or moon? Wright, in an 1865 letter to a Canadian astronomer, explained, "This problem is quite distinct from any anticipation we may have that we may become acquainted so intimately with the springs of human action as to be able to predict with certainty the course of an individual's conduct."[84] In other words, unlike natural phenomena, which he believed could be predicted, given enough information, human action included too many variables. It was impossible to *know* what was true. Perhaps Holmes was drawn to Wright because he offered an approach to thought that was generally agnostic regarding ideas. Wright didn't contend one truth was better than others, but emphasized the truth could not be known. Wright focused on what a person can and cannot know. He didn't have a cause or ideology. Wright provided a lens through which Holmes could understand the nothingness, his rejection of ideas and truth. In a letter to Laski in 1923, Holmes explained, "Chauncy Wright taught me that you couldn't affirm necessity of the universe."[85]

Wright helped Holmes on his journey regarding truth. If we can't know truth, we can guess at it. We can make reasoned conclusions. In this line of thought, late in his life, Holmes labeled himself a "bettabilitarian" and credited Wright's thinking as a contributor to this conclusion.[86] What is a bettabilitarian? In a 1929 letter to Pollock, Holmes

63

*Chapter Three*

reasoned, "We can *bet* on the behavior of the universe in its contact with us. We can bet we know what it will be. That leaves a loophole for free will."[87] Holmes's claim to "bettabilitarianism" draws a clear line from his experiences and disillusionment with truth in the war to his rejection of claims by any person or group that their ideas or truth is *the* final word on any matter. We can't know the truth, but we can make intelligent guesses based on what we think we know at that moment. Of course, a decade earlier, a similar version of this idea found its way into Holmes's crucial dissent in *Abrams.* Just after his reference to the "competition of the market," Holmes provided some fleeting context regarding his use of the economics-based theme. He explained, "Every year if not every day we have to *wager* our salvation upon some prophecy based upon imperfect knowledge."[88] He continued, "We should be eternally vigilant against attempts" to halt ideas we believe are false or dangerous.[89] The use of a "wager" or "bet" to describe how people interact with truth pulls the market-based metaphor away from a more Enlightenment-based assumption about truth vanquishing falsity in a free exchange of ideas and directs it toward reasoning free expression exists because we cannot *know* the truth. If everyone is guessing, we cannot limit expression because we dislike some guesses more than others.

William James was a different story. James is the central figure in American pragmatism, a philosophical approach that emphasizes that truth is internally constructed, largely based on a person's experiences.[90] In this sense, he identified understandings regarding the nature of truth and ideas—though they were incredibly flexible. In this sense his ideas skewed relatively closely with Holmes's agnostic approach because both thinkers acknowledge truth is dynamic and self-formed. The overlap, and Holmes's friendship with James, is one of the reasons Holmes has, at times, been labeled a pragmatist. James didn't believe truth *cannot* be known, like Holmes. He concluded truth is the result of experience, making it variable, depending on changing factors in a person's life. Truth, to James, was slippery and difficult to obtain. The two conclusions are not miles apart. A similar, dauntingly close line can be drawn between Holmes's and James's lives, which intersected and then traveled parallel for many years.

## Holmes and the Nothingness

Both became thought leaders for their generation, just in different ways. James was less than a year younger than Holmes and arrived at Harvard just as Holmes left for war. Their fathers were acquainted with Emerson and they grew up with his presence in their lives. Henry James, William's more famous, novelist brother, who was just more than a year younger, remembered "The winter firelight in our back-parlour at dusk and the great Emerson—I knew he was great, greater than any of our friends—sitting between my parents."[91] James's father later joined Oliver Wendell Holmes Sr.'s Saturday Club, which also included Emerson; Benjamin Peirce (Charles Sanders Peirce's father); Longfellow, and other thinkers. James's father, and, according to Holmes's letters, James himself, was argumentative. They would contest a point they disagreed with, while Emerson was eloquent and nonconfrontational.[92] He did not have to be right. Perhaps aspects of Holmes's detached approach can also be attributed to Emerson's willingness to let opposing ideas exist without his attachment to them.

The Metaphysical Club arose toward the end of Holmes's and James's friendship—at least their closest period. After the war, they spoke weekly, mostly about philosophy. In a letter in which Holmes discussed Immanuel Kant's *Critique of Pure Reason*, he started by emphasizing his thankfulness for their friendship. He wrote, "I believe I shall always respect and love you whether we see much or little of each other."[93] The friendship did not stick. By 1872, Holmes was recently married to Fanny Dixwell, who James had also pursued.[94] Holmes was deeply immersed in his legal studies. By 1876, James concluded Holmes was "a powerful battery, formed like a planing machine to gouge a deep groove through life."[95] Holmes's letters were not much kinder. Whatever souring occurred, the two exchanged one final discussion about truth and ideas in a series of letters in 1907, just as James's crucial work, *Pragmatism*, was being published.[96] *Pragmatism* constructed truth as a process, rather than an unmoving thing that awaits discovery.[97] He concluded, "New truths thus are resultants of new experiences and of old truths combined and mutually modifying one another."[98] In another passage, he explained, "The truth of an idea is not a stagnant property inherent in it. Truth happens to an idea. It becomes true, is made true by events."[99] *Pragmatism* came from a series of lectures James gave and the first of

65

*Chapter Three*

the lectures, titled "A Defense of Pragmatism," was published in *Popular Science Monthly* in March in advance of the book's release.[100]

James sent the article to Holmes, which resulted in one of Holmes's clearest explications of how he understood truth. Holmes started, of course, by rejecting the "pragmatism" label. He explained, "I have been in the habit of saying that all I mean by truth is what I can't help thinking."[101] He continued, "I have learned to surmise that my *can't helps* are not necessarily cosmic can't helps—that the universe may not be subject to my limitations."[102] Thus, while James contended truth was created by human experience, Holmes would not go that far. He staked his understandings even more broadly, contending truth amounts to what a person thinks they know—nothing more. Truth, in this sense, could even be understood as a system of biases or simply a person's reality. Holmes contended, "Truth then, as one, I agree with you, is only an ideal—an assumption that if everyone was as educated and clear as I he would feel the same compulsions that I do."[103] Holmes closed the uncharacteristically long letter with his usual, at-arms-length, assessment of James's work, explaining the work was "admirable."

That fall, James sent Holmes a copy of the full book, *Pragmatism*, for which Holmes thanked him. Holmes's assessment, again, was "I heartily agree with much—but I am more skeptical than you are."[104] Holmes's interaction with James's seminal work on pragmatism indicates how close the two came to coming to the same conclusions about truth. Holmes contended truth cannot be known, but each person makes guesses or *wagers* based on their understandings of the world. James contended truth can be known, but it is internally constructed and the outcome of personal experience. Both conclusions provide a particular lens through which to understand how a space for human discourse should be constructed. Essentially, truths and ideas should be protected from limitations because, according to James, ideas help individuals construct the world around them, which leads to the formation of truth. According to Holmes, truth and ideas should be safeguarded because it is not possible for anyone to *know* what is true, and information helps individuals *wager* on what is true. Importantly, as examined in chapter 4, neither approach is represented in the truth and ideas assumptions at the foundations of the modern marketplace-of-ideas rationales for expansive free-expression safeguards.

## Holmes and the Nothingness

James died in 1910. Holmes attended his funeral, but approached it as a spectator, rather than a participant. Holmes wrote to a friend, "Our relations had ceased, practically, except that he occasionally sent me a book . . . but it cuts a root deep in the past."[105] He emphasized he did not support James's pragmatism, critiqued the funeral's atmosphere, and then changed the subject in the letter to something else, as if the death of a person he'd known since his childhood was just another "can't help."

### An Apostle of Nothingness

Holmes's exchange with James about truth and pragmatism was, like much of his communication, formed as part of a series of letters. The discussion was not intended for a public audience. The same can be said regarding his extensive correspondences with people such as Einstein, Laski, Cohen, and Frankfurter—even Baroness Charlotte Moncheur, with whom he exchanged letters for nearly a quarter century. He was interacting with an audience of one in each letter, rather than trying to reach a discernible group. Certainly, the letters were influential to the thinkers they reached, as were his legal opinions, which receive more attention in the preceding and ensuing chapters, but our exploration of Holmes's thinking regarding truth and ideas would not be complete without considering his legal scholarship. What did Holmes want people in his field and in public-lecture audiences to know? The answer is quite predictable at this point—he wanted jurists, lawyers, and others to stop believing in absolute truth and ideologies. He complained about "a priori men," using the Latin phrase that denotes applying predetermined conclusions to understand the world.[106] He communicated that staying above associations with an absolute truth or a deep-seated personal ideology was crucial "for us to grow more civilized."[107] The only gospel Holmes preached was to not have a gospel at all.

Holmes did not wait until he was an esteemed Supreme Court justice to begin this work. He published *The Common Law* in 1881, when he was in his early forties. The work stemmed from a series of lectures Holmes gave the year before at the Lowell Institute. By this time, he had lectured on constitutional law at Harvard Law School for several years, joined and then broken away from the Metaphysical Club, and edited

67

*Chapter Three*

*The American Law Review* and a volume of *Kent's Commentaries*. He essentially used the period after the Civil War to explore ideas. We could dramatize this period as a wounded man's search for answers or a pilgrimage, but the evidence does not support, or deny, such a characterization. What we know is Holmes went to Europe to meet John Stewart Mill in 1866, immediately after he completed his law degree.[108]

He also rekindled his relationship with Emerson, who died in 1882, a year after the *Common Law* was published.[109] He engaged with James, Wright and, to a lesser extent, Peirce about truth and ideas. He poured himself into his legal studies. The editing experiences with *The American Law Review* and the commentaries gave him a chance to engage with the nation's leading legal minds, working through their writing while doing research of his own. The Lowell lectures, by his admission, accelerated the timeline for his plan to author an influential work in his field.[110] His book had exactly the impact he sought.[111] When one of his former law clerks republished the *Common Law* in 1968, a *New York Times* review emphasized the book's lasting impact on the field, as well as the fact that it did not favor any one theory.[112] Indeed, Holmes dispatched attachments to ideas, truths, and theories from the beginning of the book, explaining, "The life of the law has not been logic: it has been experience. The felt necessities of the time, the prevalent moral and political theories, institutions of public policy, avowed or unconscious even the prejudices which judges share with their fellow-men."[113] He continued:

> There are two errors equally to be avoided both by writer and reader. One is that of supposing, because an idea seems very familiar and natural to us, that it has always been so. Many things which we take for granted have had to be laboriously fought out or thought out in past times.[114]

His conclusion about truth and the assumptions people make reads like a toned-down version of what he argued in "Natural Law," which was published in *Harvard Law Review* in 1918, less than a year before he wrote the groundbreaking opinions in *Schenck* and *Abrams*. He reasoned, "Certitude is not the test for certainty. We have been cocksure of many things that were not so."[115] In both instances, Holmes started influential works by admonishing his audience to reject certainty and

68

*Holmes and the Nothingness*

ideology. In "Natural Law," he cautioned that each person's experiences draw them toward a certain world view. Such views, simply because they are familiar or seem natural and right, he reasoned, are not necessarily true. He explained, "But while one's experience thus makes certain preferences dogmatic for oneself, recognition of how they came to be so leaves one able to see that others, poor souls, may be equally dogmatic about something else."[116]

The passages bear substantial overlap with the letters he wrote his father and sister late in the war, as he recognized those from the South were fighting for a set of ideas or truths equally as real to them as the opposing ideas and truths held by the North.[117] The connections between the war and Holmes's legal scholarship are most stark in "Natural Law," where he explained "We all, whether we know it or not, are fighting to make the kind of world that we should like—but that we have learned to recognize that others will fight and die to make a different world."[118] He ultimately concluded "men to a great extent believe what they want to—although I see in that no basis for a philosophy that tells us what we should want."[119] In a speech to the Harvard Law School Association in 1913, Holmes made a similar argument, explaining, "I have no belief in panaceas and almost none in sudden ruin. I am not interested in one way or the other in the nostrums now strenuously argued."[120] He continued, in thinking that could be associated with his dissent in *Abrams*, penned six years later, that the "more civilized" approach would be for jurists to remain above the squabbling between ideologies.

Two years after his "Law and the Court" speech, he published "Ideals and Doubts," where he again rejected any person's ability to know what is true.[121] Many of the ideas, even exact phrases, overlap between "Natural Law" and "Ideals and Doubts." Crucially, "Ideals and Doubts" emphasizes holding to a certain truth or idea is a danger for an individual or an institution, such as a court. Holmes wrote, "To rest upon a formula is a slumber that, prolonged, means death."[122] This particular line is a good example of the impact of Holmes's thinking on his network of relationships. His quote about formulas has appeared in nine court decisions. Two of the references were by Frankfurter, who saw Holmes as a mentor. Frankfurter used the passage to attack the

69

*Chapter Three*

"preferred position" approach to free expression, reasoning against dogmatic, systematic thinking by the Court.[123]

Much as Holmes contended people tend to believe what they want in "Natural Law," his legal opinions, particularly his dissent in *Abrams*, have taken on a life of their own, one that is substantially separate and contradictory to his admonishment that the truth cannot be known, and deeply held ideologies are dangerous.[124] Holmes's dissent in *Abrams* does not include citations or references to a particular ideology. His legal scholarship, extensive record of correspondence, and experiences, from Ball's Bluff to the Wilderness, tell us the absence of an ideology in the primordial justification for free expression was intentional. He did not construct his understandings on a static set of truths or ideologies. Quite the opposite. Despite such an extensive body of texts, highlighted throughout this chapter, something he might have predicted but would have been abhorred by has occurred. His ideas, particularly from *Abrams*, have been transformed into an Enlightenment-based argument for the power of truth to vanquish falsity in a free exchange of ideas.[125] In other words, the modern name and characteristics of the space for human discourse do not match Holmes's strident contention that no one can know the truth and dogmatic ideas are dangerous. The space, which came to be known as the marketplace of ideas, largely because of Holmes's word choice in *Abrams*, fills in the nothingness he intended with a discernible ideology about the nature of truth. Understanding that the modern marketplace—which is struggling to function in the era of AI, algorithms, and networked communication—bears almost no resemblance to Holmes's understandings is crucial. Holmes's nothingness has something to contribute to how we define the space for human discourse, just not in the way it's been used to this point. If Holmes did not invent the Enlightenment-based marketplace of ideas, how did these assumptions come to dominate free-expression rationales and the space for discourse? Chapter 4 examines the marketplace's DNA.

70

# FOUR

## Marketplace DNA

Oliver W. Holmes made a passing, unsupported reference to truth and "the competition of the market" in 1919 in the first Supreme Court opinion in which a justice argued in favor of free expression.[1] He never returned to the idea. No one did—for decades. The market reference was forgotten. Yet somehow, somewhere between Holmes's "market" reference in the very last paragraph of the *Abrams v. United States* sedition case and today, the marketplace became the dominant tool for how the Supreme Court rationalizes expansive free-expression safeguards. More than that, it became part of the very DNA of the First Amendment. In the landmark *Red Lion Broadcasting v. Federal Communications Commission (FCC)* decision in 1969, for example, the Court reasoned, "It is the purpose of the First Amendment to preserve an uninhibited marketplace of ideas in which truth will ultimately prevail."[2] In other words, the concept has become interwoven with the First Amendment. The marketplace approach and First Amendment have been sewn together and treated as if they have common DNA. The merger of two separate concepts, free expression and market-based thinking, into a seemingly seamless strand of DNA raises two crucial points when it comes to conceptualizing the space for human discourse in the era of algorithms, AI, and networked communication. First, the marketplace is not original to

*Chapter Four*

the First Amendment. Their relationship is not inherent. The integration of the two resulted from a series of decisions over time, an evolution this chapter examines. Second, if the relationship is not inherent, there is no reason the space for human discourse *must* take the shape of a marketplace of ideas or, if it does, that it be founded upon the same assumptions.

Holmes, as we explored in the previous chapter, did not *invent* the marketplace and he would have bristled at and dismissed the adoption of a universal tool for conceptualizing free-expression safeguards. In other words, he would have rejected the marketplace concept many credit him with creating. Chapter 2 emphasized the dynamic, *becoming* nature of the marketplace. Here we continue the story by examining how the marketplace concept and free expression came to be treated as a single idea. In their origin story, we find many of the cracks and fissures that have come to plague the space for human discourse. The merger between the First Amendment and the marketplace was not as seamless as is often assumed, a matter that has been highlighted in the networked era as non-human entities overwhelm the space for human discourse and push human voices out of the marketplace. While AI entities and other networked-era concerns are relatively new to the party, the problems they highlight and exacerbate have been present since the First Amendment's and marketplace's genetic makeups were combined into what is in many ways a single rationale for expansive free-expression safeguards. The marketplace's DNA was flawed from the beginning. *How* it is flawed and *how* it was pressed into the service of holding up the increasing weight of expansive free-expression rationales helps identify places where the space for human discourse can be revised in the AI era.

## CERTAINTY AND DOUBT

The First Amendment and marketplace concepts were sewn together using Enlightenment thought as the thread. This point is crucial. Not just any thread binds the two. The Enlightenment thread introduced biases and assumptions that have shaped modern free expression and left the marketplace concept incapable of defining a functional space for

*Marketplace DNA*

human discourse in the AI era. The thread's craftmanship is poor. Enlightenment thought carries flawed assumptions about truth and human agency. Its use as a binding agent between the First Amendment and marketplace approach set the rationale for free expression on a problematic course.

Enlightenment thought was born from doubt. The Copernican Revolution followed Nicolaus Copernicus's conclusion in the sixteenth century that Earth and other planets revolved around the sun, rather than Earth marking the center of the universe. This revelation about celestial bodies might seem wholly unrelated to free-expression rationales, but it sent a shockwave of doubt throughout Europe. We were wrong about our place in the universe. Centuries of knowledge, derived from human senses, was called into question. The doubt that resulted from these revelations was incredible. We could no longer trust our senses to interpret phenomena. The doubt undermined centuries of certainty about nature and the universe.[3] During the period, English poet and thinker John Donne belied this doubt in his 1611 poem "Anatomy of the World":

> And new philosophy calls all in doubt,
> The element of fire is quite put out,
> The sun is lost, and th' earth, and no man's wit
> Can well direct him where to look for it.[4]

We suddenly needed a new way to understand the world around us. A new philosophy. As German thinker Hannah Arendt concluded, "Man had been deceived so long as he trusted that reality and truth would reveal themselves to his senses and to his reason if only he remained true to what he saw with the eyes of body and mind."[5] She continued, "If Being and Appearance part company forever, and this . . . is indeed the basic assumption of all modern science, then there is nothing left to be taken upon faith; everything must be doubted."[6] If we cannot believe our senses, what can we believe? How can we be certain of anything?

Out of this doubt came a revolution, which in many ways was catalyzed by thinkers such as Francis Bacon and Isaac Newton, who sought to overcome doubt and the human senses' fallibility by creating a systematic approach to science based on measurement and certainty. Bacon

## Chapter Four

created the scientific method, essentially establishing systems for identifying truth.[7] In his 1620 book *Novum Organum*, which translates to "true directions for interpretation of nature" or "the new instrument," he emphasized "impressions of the senses are erroneous, for they fail and deceive us."[8] He concluded, "Our only remaining hope and salvation is to begin the whole labor of the mind again; not leaving it to itself, but directing it perpetually from the very first and attaining our end as it were by mechanical aid."[9] The new approach, which Newton helped carry forward, emphasized empirical processes.[10] In this sense, truth is *discovered* via a disinterested, empirical approach.

### Truth Vanquishes Falsity

Enlightenment thought took root in the seventeenth and eighteenth centuries, when thinkers such as John Locke, John Milton, David Hume, Voltaire, and Adam Smith applied concepts about empirically obtained certainty to political and social concerns.[11] Milton, whose publications about divorce in the 1640s riled church and government leaders, published *Areopagitica* in 1644. Still, decades before publishing his most famous work, *Paradise Lost*, Milton struggled after his first wife, Mary Powell, went to visit her family soon after their marriage and did not return for three years.[12] Partially in response to his "Doctrine and Discipline of Divorce," published in 1643, Parliament passed the Printing Ordinance, which required all written works be licensed by the government before publication.[13] Milton responded with *Areopagitica*, which was not licensed and published as an act of civil disobedience against government censorship and control of published ideas.[14]

His argument against censorship in *Areopagitica* was constructed upon themes similar to Bacon's and Newton's scientific method. Milton reasoned truth is discovered through free inquiry and people are rational and capable of discerning truth from falsity.[15] He reasoned truth would vanquish falsity "in a free and open encounter."[16] He averred, "Where there is much desire to learn, there of necessity will be much arguing, much writing, many opinions; for opinion in good men is but knowledge in the making."[17] In other words, the search for truth will include unpopular ideas, but people, if given the chance, will discern truth from

*Marketplace DNA*

falsity. In this sense, Milton contended truth has a certain innate quality that leads to its discovery. *Areopagitica* has not been forgotten. When Holmes's dissent in *Abrams* was announced in fall 1919, future Supreme Court justice Felix Frankfurter, from his office in Harvard Law School, wrote to Holmes that his opinion would "live as long as *Areopagitica*."[18] Forty-five years later, Justice Brennan cited *Areopagitica* in the landmark *New York Times v. Sullivan* decision.[19]

Locke and Hume followed Milton in adapting empiricism into philosophy and political thought. Locke constructed arguments for natural rights founded upon assumptions of human rationality and inherent freedom. Historian D.W. Hamlyn described Locke's philosophy as "decidedly rationalist" because he "put weight on reason or the understanding, as distinct from sense or sense-perception."[20] If people are rational, Locke reasoned, they can employ disinterested processes and discern truth from falsity, ultimately governing themselves. Locke framed government as a tool for serving the individual, which was decidedly different from previous eras, when the individual served the government.[21] Such an approach was born from his belief in empiricism and human reason. He contended, "We must consider what state all men are naturally in, and that is a state of perfect freedom to order their actions and dispose of their possessions and persons as they think fit."[22] He emphasized a person's right to life, health, liberty, or possessions, words that, nearly to the letter, found their way into the *Declaration of Independence* and the Fifth Amendment.[23]

Hume, a Scottish thinker who was born in 1711, seven years after Locke's death, also built his ideas around natural rights. Hume did not put forth a certain idea but, using an empirical lens, dissembled and explored ideas, adding a certain amount of skepticism.[24] In his *A Treatise of Human Nature*, Hume credited Locke as "a great philosopher" and in conclusions similar to his, found

> Tis certain, that rights, and obligations, and property, admit of no such insensible gradation, but that a man either has a full and perfect property, or none at all; and is either entirely oblig'd to perform any action, or lies under no manner of obligation.[25]

Together, in the aftermath of the Copernican Revolution and Bacon's and Newton's scientific method, thinkers such as these constructed

75

*Chapter Four*

a lens through which to understand the world that was substantially based on three fundamental principles. First, truth is generally universal and discoverable. Second, people are rational and capable of discerning truth from falsity. Third, the purpose of government is to serve the individual. These three strands, interwoven with each other, made up the thread which, centuries later, sewed free expression and the marketplace of ideas together. They begin the story of the modern marketplace of ideas because they are the genetic ancestors of what has become the dominant rationale for *why* we have free expression. The Enlightenment thread carries very particular assumptions that have shaped the space for human discourse in ways other approaches to truth and human rationality would not have. The space for human discourse did not *have* to take the shape of a marketplace of ideas. The Enlightenment thread that sewed the two together was not happenstance, however.

## *Children of the Enlightenment*

John Adams was in awe of Milton's writing. As a twenty-one-year-old in 1756, Adams wrote in his diary, "His Genius was great beyond Conception, and his Learning without Bounds. I can only gaze at him with astonishment, without comprehending the vast Compass of his Capacity."[26] Adams, who helped Thomas Jefferson draft the *Declaration of Independence* and became the United States' first vice president, was not the only member of the founding generation who supported Enlightenment thought. Benjamin Franklin was also influenced by Milton. He constructed arguments similar to those found in Milton's *Areopagitica* in the *Pennsylvania Gazette* when he argued, "When men differ in Opinion, both Sides ought equally to have the Advantage of being heard by the Publick; and that when Truth and Err have fair Play, the former is always an overmatch for the latter."[27] The passage tracks very closely to Milton's contention that "Truth be in the field. . . . Let her and Falsehood grapple; who ever knew Truth put to the worse in a free and open encounter?"[28]

Jefferson read Milton with similar zeal.[29] As for Locke, he has been credited as the "philosopher of the American revolution," an incredible feat, considering he died more than seventy years before the *Declaration*

*Marketplace DNA*

*of Independence* was written. Crucially, his ideas were passed down by the Framers and etched into the nation's founding documents. Locke's ideas were woven into pre-revolution works, such as "The Olive Branch Petition" and "Letter to the Inhabitants of Quebec," both authored by John Dickinson, the "Penman of the Revolution," who professed admiration for the thinker.[30] Jefferson, who wrote the first draft of the "Olive Branch Petition," only to have it toned down by Dickinson, was the primary author of the *Declaration of Independence*. Jefferson lifted almost word-for-word from Locke's *Second Treatise of Government*, referring to "laws of nature" and the right of each person to "Life, Liberty and the pursuit of Happiness."[31] The similarities between Locke's words and Jefferson's were so close *Declaration of Independence* signers Richard Henry Lee and Adams accused Jefferson of plagiarism.[32]

The document is in many ways a love letter to Locke's work and a conduit through which Locke's Enlightenment ideas were officially cataloged into American thought. In the tempest of revolutionary fervor, a discernible philosophy regarding truth, human rationality, and the roles of individuals and the government was written into the nation's birth certificate. Locke's ideas' prominence in the document act as both a powerful framing tool regarding how human rights and truth would be understood by future generations and are an indication of just how influential Enlightenment thought was on the founding generation. Their influence was not at its end in 1776, however. James Madison's thinking, like his mentor Jefferson's, was substantially structured by Enlightenment thought. Such a realization is crucial, since Madison penned twenty-nine of the eighty-five Federalist Papers and drafted the Constitution and Bill of Rights. In drawing the blueprints for democratic government, Madison injected Enlightenment thought into the very foundations of the fledgling US structure. The Enlightenment assumptions were written into the wet cement of democracy, where they dried and remained, only to be found by justices seeking rationales for free expression.

Madison's work in enshrining Enlightenment ideas into the foundations of democratic thought went beyond his writing. In 1783, he compiled the initial list of books for the Library of Congress. His list was laden with Enlightenment thinkers, including two works by Hume, two by Locke, eight by Voltaire, and Adam Smith's *Wealth of Nations*.[33] In

*Chapter Four*

selecting these works, he not only cataloged the authors and ideas he favored, but also placed Enlightenment thought at the fingertips of the first congresses. Five years later, he published Federalist No. 10, one of the most crucial of the essays he, Alexander Hamilton, and John Jay wrote in support of the Constitution's ratification. Historians contend Madison penned Federalist No. 10, which lays out the argument for a republican form of government, with Hume's work "open on the table beside him."[34] No record exists regarding such a direct influence regarding the Bill of Rights, but the document is structured using Enlightenment assumptions, not simply in the explicit sense, as is seen in the Fifth Amendment's inclusion of Locke's ideas, but in a broader context that the rights Madison proposed were constructed upon very specific ideas about truth and human rationality. These assumptions were not a given. The government the Framers brought forth was the result of a series of choices. Their choices were substantially informed by Enlightenment thought.

### *Enlightened Baggage*

Howard Chandler Christy's famous painting "Scene at the Signing of the Constitution of the United States" is one of the most ubiquitous representations of the Constitutional Convention. The oil painting, which hangs in the US Capitol, depicts the thirty-nine delegates, including Madison, who signed the Constitution.[35] While it was not Christy's intention, the painting highlights some of the fundamental problems of Enlightenment thought, particularly as a thread that sews the First Amendment and the marketplace of ideas together. All thirty-nine delegates represented in the painting are white men. All are property owners. Fourteen are slaveowners. The painting depicts, quite accurately, a very homogeneous group. Enlightenment assumptions about truth and human rationality, that truth will generally "win" and falsity will fail in a free exchange of ideas among rational people, only have a chance of operating if those involved are similar. When everyone is generally the same race, religion, socioeconomic status, and gender, it is easy to assume they will come to similar conclusions about truth and the world around them. This is one of the great failures of Enlightenment thought. It assumes and requires sameness. It fails to account for human diversity, which is a crucial aspect

## Marketplace DNA

of twenty-first-century pluralistic society, as well as borderless and time-less online communication. In his critique of the dominant approach to thought and truth during the founding period, historian David Hollinger emphasized that "It is another mark of lingering Enlightenment assumptions, moreover, to focus on ostensibly autonomous individuals rather than the groups that provide individuals with their culture."[36] The Enlightenment foundations of the marketplace approach, in other words, fail because they do not account for a diverse society.

The sameness problem is one of three crucial flaws in Enlightenment thought that, when taken together, cast doubts regarding whether the marketplace concept, as it has been constructed, can adequately function as a dominant rationale for free expression in the AI era. The remaining problems, which question the truth-and-rationality assumptions, represent equally as devastating concerns as the sameness problem. Legal scholar C. Edwin Baker concluded, "The marketplace of ideas theory is unworkable, dangerous, and inconsistent with a reasonable interpretation of the purpose of the First Amendment."[37] Chief Justice William Rehnquist cited Baker's conclusions, as well as Milton's *Areopagitica*, in a dissent in a case regarding the extent to which advertising can be regulated by the government.[38] He concluded, "There is no reason for believing that the marketplace of ideas is free from market imperfections any more than there is to believe that the invisible hand will always lead to optimum economic decisions in the commercial market."[39] Similarly, legal scholar Jerome Barron reasoned, "Our constitutional theory is in the grip of a romantic conception of free expression, a belief that the 'marketplace of ideas' is freely accessible."[40] Together, these authors communicated a common skepticism that the marketplace approach, as a rationale for *why* we have free expression, can deliver what it promises. In particular, they were concerned the truth and human rationality assumptions simply do not hold water.

The two assumptions are intertwined, along with the failure to account for human diversity, because they, together, get at the question of how people come to understand the world around them. Legal scholar Stanley Ingber captured this tension when he admonished readers to "pierce the myth of the neutral marketplace of ideas and expose the flawed market model assumptions of objective truth and the power of

*Chapter Four*

rationality."[41] Scholars have concluded truth is not the same for all. Baker reasoned the marketplace approach must be revised to replace objective truth with "the view that people individually and collectively choose or create rather than 'discover' their perspectives, understandings, and truths."[42] Similarly, legal scholar Frederick Schauer concluded, "Our increasing knowledge about the process of idea transmission, reception, and acceptance makes it more and more difficult to accept the notion that truth has some inherent power to prevail in the marketplace of ideas."[43] In other words, how people come to understand what is true is not the outcome of a battle in which truth vanquishes falsity because truth has a certain inherent value that makes it recognizable to all. Instead, a variety of variables influence what is true to a person, including life experience and personal identity, access, and exposure to ideas, and the frequency and intensity of the ideas they encounter.[44]

These rips and snags in the Enlightenment assumptions that have come to sew the First Amendment and the marketplace together are particularly relevant in the era of AI, algorithms, and networked communication because the choice-rich environment has exacerbated the problems with assuming truth is generally the same for all, and people are rational in the sense that they view and understand the world in the same way. It's not that truth does not exist or people are not rational, it is simply that people come to different truths and are differently rational based on experience. Nevertheless, before the space for human discourse can be revised, it must be understood. The Enlightenment thread, with its rips and snags, was set in place by the founding generation. The next step was for justices to use the thread to sew the First Amendment and marketplace of ideas together.

### "TO TEST THE MERITS OF IDEAS"

Byron Thornhill was picketing with fellow workers as part of a union strike at Brown Wood Preserving Company in Tuscaloosa, Alabama, when he was arrested for violating a state law against loitering and picketing. Thornhill, the union president, was convicted and an Alabama appeals court upheld the decision in spring 1939. His conviction seemed simple to the appeals court. He was on company property. He led a union

*Marketplace DNA*

that had been picketing the company twenty-four-hours-a-day for weeks. He dissuaded a non-union employee from showing up for work. Despite these arguments, the Supreme Court overturned his conviction about a year later. The Court, to this point, had been willing to uphold nearly any limitation on free expression. How did justices rationalize overturning Thornhill's conviction because it conflicted with the First Amendment? In searching for rationales during a time when only one other precedent supported striking down a law because it conflicted with the First Amendment, they shook the dust off Holmes's "market" reference, which had languished in obscurity for more than two decades, *and*, in the same opinion, referenced Enlightenment ideas within the context of the meaning of the First Amendment. Crucially, the merger between the First Amendment's and marketplace approach's DNA strands took a crucial step forward in *Thornhill v. Alabama*. While the case remains a landmark decision in labor law and for the right to assemble, it is far more important as a starting point for the knitting together of these two crucial ideas.

On a Court that included Justices Hugo Black and William O. Douglas, whose opinions did more to expand the meaning of free expression than almost any other justices, and their nemesis, Justice Felix Frankfurter, who was known to write long, nuanced opinions about free expression, the turning-point opinion went to an unexpected author—Justice Frank Murphy. Murphy was the newest justice on the Court, having joined three weeks before justices heard arguments in *Thornhill*. Murphy is not known as a great Supreme Court justice. His most famous opinion might be his dissent in *Korematsu v. U.S.,* in which he disagreed with the Court's decision to uphold the government's efforts to force Japanese Americans to live in internment camps during World War II.[45] Before joining the Court, Murphy was a leader in the Democratic party. Franklin Roosevelt, as he considered whether to run for a third term, told Black he thought about handing the party's and the presidency's reins to Murphy. Roosevelt, however, wasn't certain Murphy could garner the Democratic Party's nomination and win the 1940 election.[46] Ultimately, Roosevelt concluded Murphy couldn't win and decided to run again, but thought highly enough of him, to make him the fifth of an astonishing eight appointments he made to the Court between 1937 and 1943. Murphy was a former governor of Michigan and an old friend of Black's.

*Chapter Four*

The two worked together to help re-elect Roosevelt in 1936, when Black was still a senator from Alabama. Once on the Court, Murphy tended to vote with Black, which riled Frankfurter, a longtime adviser to Roosevelt who expected to dominate the Court when he was confirmed in 1939.[47]

Murphy had little First Amendment precedent to work with when he sat down to write the Court's opinion in *Thornhill*. By 1940, the Supreme Court had struck down a couple of state laws in cases that dealt with free expression, but had otherwise generally upheld limitations.[48] Choosing from limited options, Murphy built the Court's opinion upon Chief Justice Charles Evans Hughes's reasoning from the *Near v. Minnesota* decision from 1931. In the first decision in which justices struck down a law because it conflicted with the First Amendment, the Court ruled Minnesota's "public nuisance" law was unconstitutional.[49] Hughes, in writing the Court's opinion in *Near*, drew heavily from Madison's writing, as well as his contemporary "Olive Branch Petition" author John Dickinson. Both men penned crucial works in the formation of the US government. Both were also substantially guided by Enlightenment ideas.[50] In *Thornhill*, Murphy cited Hughes's conclusions in *Near* that government censorship goes against the essence of the First Amendment.[51] Crucially, he did so in the same passage he referenced Milton's *Areopagitica*, drawing Enlightenment assumptions and the meaning of the First Amendment together in what is essentially the second major victory for free expression in the Court's history.[52] He wasn't finished. Near the end of the opinion, Murphy mixed Holmes's clear and present danger test from *Schenck v. U.S.* and the market reference from his dissent in *Abrams v. U.S.*[53] Murphy explained, limiting expression affords "no opportunity to test the merits of ideas by competition for acceptance in the market of public opinion."[54] He came close to using the phrase "marketplace of ideas," and certainly used the concept as a tool to help rationalize First Amendment protections. The opinion represents the initial stitches in a progression of cases that sewed the First Amendment and marketplace together.

### Frankfurter v. "The Axis"

The ideological conflict between Black and Frankfurter took over the discourse about the meaning of the First Amendment and how its

*Marketplace DNA*

safeguards should be rationalized the next year, pushing Murphy, and nearly every other justice—except Douglas—aside. The push and pull between the shrewd former senator from the east Alabama foothills and the former Harvard Law School professor who was mentored by two of the greatest justices in the Court's history, Holmes and Louis Brandeis, and was a founding member of the ACLU, left clear battle lines in the precedential record regarding how free expression is rationalized.[55] Black joined the Court in 1937. A leading liberal in the Senate, he was hesitant to leave his influential role for a spot on the Supreme Court, but agreed to accept the nomination when Roosevelt assured him that he needed him on the Court more than in the Senate.[56] Frankfurter, who was a close adviser to Roosevelt dating back to when he ran for governor of New York in 1928, joined the Court about a year and a half later. The pair voted together in *Thornhill*, but *Bridges v. California*, decided a year later, helped catalyze their split.

*Bridges* was first argued in 1940, not long after *Thornhill* was decided. The case centered around Harry Bridges, who led the longshoreman's union. Bridges messaged the secretary of labor regarding an ongoing case. He threatened to organize a strike and to shut down the Port of Los Angeles, and potentially other West Coast ports, if the Superior Court of Los Angeles County did not make the decision he wanted to see.[57] His message was leaked to several newspapers, including the *Los Angeles Times*. Newspapers ran editorials about the case, leading the judge to hold Bridges and the newspapers in contempt and fining them for interfering with an ongoing case. Bridges and the newspapers challenged the judge's fines, bringing another First Amendment argument before a Court that now included Black, Frankfurter and four other Roosevelt appointees. In conference, Chief Justice Hughes argued the judge had a right to fine Bridges and the newspapers and five justices joined him. Hughes assigned the opinion to Frankfurter, and Black went to work on a dissent. Frankfurter circulated a draft of the Court's opinion and Black sent around his dissent in June 1941.

This is where their styles conflicted. Frankfurter's opinion was complex and nuanced. It left room for limitations on expression, balancing the First Amendment with other concerns. Black's opinion spoke in absolutes. Black was an experienced negotiator, having worked in the

83

*Chapter Four*

Senate to gather votes for years. By summer 1941, Hughes and Murphy shifted their votes to Black's opinion. McReynolds, the lone dissenter from *Thornhill,* retired. Black's opinion now had five votes, making it the Court's decision, and Frankfurter's draft opinion, with only four votes, became the dissent. Frankfurter didn't forget the sting of losing the majority in the case. He came to call Black the leader of "the Axis," which included Douglas and Murphy. Frankfurter wrote in his diary in 1943, "In the Senate Black controlled one vote . . . on the Court he controls three votes out of nine in all important matters."[58]

Whatever Frankfurter's feelings were, the case represented a crucial choice between two approaches to what the First Amendment would come to mean. By gaining the majority, Black had his first opportunity to write his more absolute approach to the First Amendment into the Court's precedential record. He reasoned:

> The First Amendment does not speak equivocally. It prohibits any law 'abridging the freedom of speech, or of the press.' It must be taken as a command of the broadest scope that explicit language, read in the context of a liberty-loving society, will follow.[59]

Frankfurter separated Bridges's and the newspapers' behaviors from First Amendment safeguards, reasoning it simply did not apply to their behavior. Calling on his mentor Holmes's dissent in *Abrams,* he reasoned, "A trial is not a 'free trade in ideas', nor is the best test of truth in a courtroom 'the power of the thought to get itself accepted in the competition of the market'."[60] *Bridges* does not directly address the Enlightenment thread, but Black's more absolute approach, which debuted in the case, was based on a rationale that the founders intended "no law" to mean "no law" because they believed Enlightenment assumptions that rational individuals could discern truth from falsity in a free exchange of ideas. The fact that Black ended up with five votes, pulling the Court's opinion out of Frankfurter's hands, meant the development of *why* we have expansive free-expression safeguards was directed toward Enlightenment assumptions. Black and Frankfurter, with Douglas joining the fray, squared off again in *Dennis v. United States* in 1951 and *United States v. Rumely* in 1953. Justices in both cases drew Holmes's "market" reference into rationales for *why* free-expression should be protected.

84

*Marketplace DNA*

The *Dennis* case put the Court in a difficult position. Communist leader Eugene Dennis was convicted of violating the Smith Act, which criminalized advocating for the overthrow of the government or organizing or taking part in a group devoted to such a cause.[61] As the Court heard arguments in the case in December 1950, and circulated draft opinions into early June of the next year, Senator Joseph McCarthy and others led a high-profile, zealous crusade against communism in the United States. Justice Black, in his terse dissent in the case, admitted the national fervor was on justices' minds and hoped "in calmer times, when present pressures, passions and fears subside" the Court would rectify its decision.[62] The Court upheld, in a six-to-two ruling, Dennis's conviction. The problem was, Dennis never advocated for violence or the overthrow of the government. He and others planned to meet and exchange ideas. Dennis's plight led to Black's 725-word dissent, a longer dissent from Douglas, and a nearly 14,000-word concurring opinion by the long-winded Frankfurter. The Court's decision was the top story in the *New York Times* the morning after it was announced.[63]

Black knew he would dissent in the case, even if it turned the white-hot spotlight of McCarthyism squarely on him. His succinct dissent repeated the absolutist approach to the First Amendment he outlined in *Bridges*, adding inferred Enlightenment assumptions, primarily via Jefferson and other members of the founding generations' ideas, about truth and human rationality.[64] He reasoned:

> To the Founders of this Nation, however, the benefits derived from free expression were worth the risk. They embodied this philosophy in the First Amendment's command that 'Congress shall make no law abridging the freedom of speech, or of the press.' I have always believed that the First Amendment is the keystone of our Government, that the freedoms it guarantees provide the best insurance against destruction of all freedom.[65]

Black could not vote to uphold Dennis's conviction under the Smith Act because he understood the First Amendment as being written to protect individuals from government control over their lives. Black reasoned it was the founders' intent that the First Amendment protect an exchange of ideas among free individuals.

85

# Chapter Four

Douglas was far less definitive than Black but, crucially, devoted a substantial portion of his dissent to an argument for the "full and free discussion of ideas."[66] The dissent does crucial work in weaving the marketplace and the First Amendment together. First, Douglas came closer than any justice so far to a full application of what has become the modern marketplace approach when he reasoned, "When ideas compete in the market for acceptance, full and free discussion exposes the false and they gain few adherents."[67] He contended the free exchange of ideas is a *public good*. Society benefits when all ideas are freely exchanged. Douglas also elevated expression, much like Black, but used different reasoning. He contended, "Full and free discussion has indeed been the *first article of our faith*."[68] Douglas continued, emphasizing a trust in human reason to "choose the doctrine true to our genius and to reject the rest."[69] Together, Black's and Douglas's dissents continued to weave the Enlightenment thread, which was crafted before they arrived on the Court, between the First Amendment and marketplace. The dissents begin to merge the marketplace, though they are not quite explicit about it, with the First Amendment.

Frankfurter, playing his role as Black's and Douglas's nemesis, used his concurring option to attack the idea the conflict between national security and the First Amendment present in *Dennis* could be resolved through an expansive, absolute interpretation of the First Amendment. He reasoned, "If adjudication is to be a rational process, we cannot escape a candid examination of the conflicting claims with full recognition that both are supported by lengthy title deeds."[70] Essentially, Frankfurter championed a balanced, case-by-case approach, which would not have placed the marketplace or any other concept in the place of being a single concept that explains *why* we have free expression. He did not succeed.

Less than two years later, Frankfurter wrote the Court's opinion in the far-less-heralded *U.S. v. Rumely* decision. Edward Rumely, alongside newspaper publisher Frank Gannett and others, spent decades fighting Roosevelt's policies. Rumely gathered popular support against the New Deal and, according to some historians, coined the term "court-packing."[71] One of Rumely's main tactics was mailing persuasive literature to galvanize his followers. Rumely was subpoenaed by the House

86

*Marketplace DNA*

Select Committee on Lobbying Activities in 1950. The committee demanded his mailing lists and Rumely refused to provide them. Though Black and Douglas agreed with the Court's decision that Rumely's First Amendment rights protected him from having to provide the mailing list, the justices declined to join Frankfurter's opinion, which employed his usual balanced, case-by-case approach that treated free expression as one concern among many. Frankfurter was again upstaged by "the Axis." Douglas, in an opinion Black joined, introduced the first instance in which a justice specifically used the phrase "marketplace of ideas." Douglas explained, "This publisher bids for the minds of men in the marketplace of ideas."[72] He continued, "The aim of the historic struggle for a free press was 'to establish and preserve the right of the English people to full information.'"[73]

Of course, Douglas did not explicitly refer to Enlightenment thought, but he again included an assumption that people are rational and can discern truth when provided a free exchange of information. Douglas emphasized, "The safety of society depends on tolerance of government for hostile as well as friendly criticism."[74] Taken together, *Thornhill*, *Bridges, Dennis*, and *Rumely* mark a crucial shift in the very DNA that defines the First Amendment and marketplace concept that has come to be inseparably connected with it. The Court had opportunities, primarily through Frankfurter's approach, to move in a different direction, but Black and Douglas, with help from Murphy in *Thornhill*, took the Enlightenment thread that was crafted by the founding generation and started to weave the First Amendment and marketplace concept together.

## BRENNAN THE GENETICIST

As Frankfurter's health started to fade, and Black began to wonder how many terms on the Court they had left, he told a friend he trusted William Brennan to lead the Court. Black explained, "Bill is as smart as anyone on the Court. Everything is fresh to him. But when Felix and I decide a case now, it's just the last chapter of the book we've been writing."[75] Brennan lived up to Black's praise in *New York Times v. Sullivan,* the case that defined the modern First Amendment. The Court's decision

*Chapter Four*

in *Sullivan* did more to weave the meanings of free expression and the marketplace together than any other case, and Justice Brennan authored the Court's opinion. Justices heard arguments in the case in early January 1964—without Frankfurter. He left the Court in 1962 after suffering a stroke. Black visited Frankfurter at his home often as the two rekindled their friendship. Frankfurter's departure meant the chemistry and makeup of the Court lacked a powerful, divisive force that challenged justices to clearly explain their reasoning. His departure also meant, however, that the Court's chemistry changed. There were more chances to speak during conferences and more opportunities to write crucial opinions. Getting a word in had been difficult at times during Frankfurter's feud with Black and Douglas. Justices regularly complained Frankfurter's in-conference lectures were dull and long-winded.

In the void left by Frankfurter, Brennan emerged as the most artful tailor of them all when it came to using the Enlightenment thread to sew the marketplace and First Amendment together. Brennan took the initial stitching Black and Douglas completed in the 1940s and '50s and generally completed their work. By the time he left the Court in 1990, the marketplace was synonymous with the First Amendment. Brennan was not new to the Court when justices heard what became the landmark *Sullivan* First Amendment case in 1964. A World War II veteran and New Jersey appellate judge, Brennan was appointed to the Supreme Court in 1956 by President Dwight Eisenhower. Brennan weathered an entire day of questioning regarding alleged communist activities from McCarthy during his confirmation hearings.[76] His responses didn't satisfy the senator, who was the only one to vote against Brennan's confirmation.

### First Amendment–Marketplace Synergy

By the time *Sullivan* reached the Court, nearly four years had passed since the *New York Times* published the full-page "Heed Their Rising Voices" advertisement that triggered the case. The advertisement sought financial support for the Civil Rights Movement, particularly in regard to offsetting Martin Luther King's growing legal fees. In describing what was happening in the South, the advertisement's sponsors listed numerous instances when African Americans were attacked or mistreated by

88

## Marketplace DNA

police while taking part in peaceful demonstrations for their rights. L.B. Sullivan, the Montgomery, Alabama, public safety commissioner, contended the advertisement defamed him because it included false information that harmed his reputation. He was at least partially correct. The advertisement included numerous factual errors, none of which were crucial to the overall argument. The errors were, however, false, a crucial part of any defamation claim.

Despite the clear errors in the advertisement, justices were unanimous in their decision to overturn the Alabama Supreme Court's decision in favor of Sullivan when they met to discuss the case. The problem was, justices did not agree on the reasons why the US$500,000 defamation award against the *Times* should be overturned. Chief Justice Earl Warren tasked Brennan with writing an opinion that would satisfy everyone. During the next few weeks, Brennan wrote eight drafts of the Court's opinion, making revisions all the way up to the night before the Court's decision was announced on March 9, in an effort to get all the justices to sign on.[77] He succeeded and the rationales within the opinion regarding *why* we have free expression cemented the marketplace's and First Amendment's genetic code.

In rationalizing *why* the First Amendment protected a public official from succeeding in a defamation case simply because some of what was published was false, Brennan explained free expression requires "breathing space."[78] Such a space, Brennan reasoned, protects the exchange of ideas. The "breathing space" concept followed the decision's most famous line: "Debate on public issues should be uninhibited, robust, and wide-open, and that it may well include vehement, caustic, and sometimes unpleasantly sharp attacks on government and public officials."[79] The rationales that surround the passage are crucial to the First Amendment's DNA because they brought together, for the first time, the building blocks discussed in this chapter and assembled them into a cohesive, complete rationale for free expression. First, Brennan drew the marketplace concept into the Court's rationales when he highlighted the importance of an "unfettered interchange of ideas for the bringing about of political and social changes desired by the people" on the page that preceded the "uninhibited, robust, and wide-open" passage.[80] Thus, the marketplace concept, the need for an exchange of ideas among rational

*Chapter Four*

people so they can self-govern, helps set up his argument for the importance of generally unfettered expression. Second, Brennan drew Enlightenment thought into the opinion in two forms. He explicitly referred to Milton's *Areopagitica* in a note that also included John Stuart Mill's *On Liberty*.[81] The note references Milton's conclusion, "Truth be in a field, we do injuriously by licensing and prohibiting to misdoubt her strength. Let her and Falsehood grapple; who ever knew Truth put to the worse in a free and open encounter?"[82] Brennan also drew Enlightenment thought into the opinion in his references to Madison's ideas, which were shaped by thinkers from the Enlightenment period.[83] Using these ingredients, he presented a modern version of the First Amendment that was woven to the marketplace concept using Enlightenment threads. Quoting a lower-court decision from 1943, he reasoned:

> The First Amendment . . . "presupposes that right conclusions are more likely to be gathered out of a multitude of tongues, than through any kind of authoritative selection. To many this is, and always will be, folly; but we have staked upon it our all."[84]

In another passage, he emphasized, "The general proposition that freedom of expression upon public questions is secured by the First Amendment has long been settled by our decisions."[85] Ultimately, in *Sullivan*, Brennan completed weaving the First Amendment and marketplace concept together with the tattered Enlightenment thread.

### *Finishing Touches*

The weaving was complete. The First Amendment and marketplace approach were developed and joined, but two details remained. First, the Court, even by 1964, had used the exact phrase "marketplace of ideas" only once. Second, the Court had not explicitly drawn the marketplace concept and First Amendment together in a single statement. These finishing touches were not far away from Brennan's opinion in *Sullivan*. The next year, the Court heard *Lamont v. Postmaster General*, which dealt with whether a law requiring the Postal Service to review and hold "communist political propaganda" from foreign countries was constitutional. Mail addressed to Corliss Lamont was held under the law, and he contended it violated the First Amendment. A unanimous Supreme

*Marketplace DNA*

Court agreed. Douglas wrote for the Court, reasoning the law was "a limitation on the unfettered exercise of the addressees' First Amendment rights."[86] Quoting *Sullivan*, he concluded, "The regime of this Act is at war with the 'uninhibited, robust, and wide-open' debate and discussion."[87]

Brennan, though Douglas quoted his words from *Sullivan*, was not satisfied with the Court's opinion. He wanted to establish a right of each person to *receive* ideas, something the Court had not done before.[88] In arguing the right to receive was crucial, he contended that without such a right, "It would be a barren marketplace of ideas that had only sellers and no buyers."[89] His argument marked the second time a justice explicitly used the phrase "marketplace of ideas." Perhaps more important, since justices had referenced market terminology in other cases, was what he meant when using the phrase. When Brennan used the full phrase in *Lamont*, a year after *Sullivan*, he was employing a version of the marketplace that, for the first time, carried the full weight, meaning, and intent of the Enlightenment-founded construction of the space for human discourse. In other words, he tested out fully built marketplace rationales for free expression that are today, in many ways, synonymous with the First Amendment.

The final piece of the puzzle comes from an unexpected place. Four years after *Lamont*, the Court decided *Red Lion Broadcasting v. FCC*. The case in many ways foreshadows chapter 5, because it represents one of the justices' first disagreements about how the modern marketplace should be cared for and maintained. Here, however, the broadcast regulation case, in which justices concluded the FCC had the power to force a broadcaster to air content it did not want to air, provided the first explicit use of the marketplace and First Amendment as a single, fully woven together entity. The Court reasoned, "It is the purpose of the First Amendment to preserve an uninhibited marketplace of ideas in which truth will ultimately prevail."[90]

Such an evolution in how the First Amendment and marketplace concepts interact, from a passing undefined reference in *Abrams* to the idea the First Amendment *serves* the marketplace concept, communicates a massive shift in how free expression is understood and rationalized. In this scenario, the First Amendment, which was constructed in the late

91

*Chapter Four*

eighteenth century, essentially is understood as doing work for the marketplace concept, which at the same time has come to rationalize why we have expansive First Amendment rights. This represents some incredibly circular thinking, but it makes the point about the relationship between the two. The First Amendment and marketplace concept have been merged into a concept that shares common, intertwined DNA. The marketplace approach rationalizes expansive First Amendment safeguards. The First Amendment protects the space for human discourse. What ties them together? A tattered line of string constructed from fundamentally flawed Enlightenment assumptions about truth, human rationality, and the role of the individual in society.

# FIVE

## Maintaining the Space

Fred Cook demanded airtime on WGCB, a little radio station in rural southeast Pennsylvania. Right-wing broadcaster and white supremacist Billy James Hargis had attacked Cook during the "Christian Crusade" series on the station in November 1964. Hargis told listeners Cook was fired from *The New York World Telegram* for fabricating stories, supported alleged Russian spy Alger Hiss, and had written a book to smear Republican presidential nominee Barry Goldwater.[1] His criticism was not unprovoked. Cook's book, *Barry Goldwater: Extremist of the Right*, was by all accounts a political hatchet job orchestrated by the Democratic Party ahead of the 1964 presidential election.[2] The same year, Cook had published an article in *The Nation* headlined "Hate Clubs of the Air," which characterized Hargis and right-wing radio stations as "a potent and insidious barrage" of right-wing propaganda.[3] Cook responded to Hargis's attacks on his work and character with a letter demanding a transcript of the broadcast and equal air time on WGCB to respond. WGCB, owned by Red Lion Broadcasting, sent Cook a rate card. He was welcome to speak as long as he wanted on air—as long as he purchased the time.

Cook was not satisfied. He contended he had a right to *free* access to WGCB's audience. Cook filed a complaint with the FCC, citing the

## Chapter Five

"fairness doctrine," a policy that required broadcast license-holders to provide multiple perspectives regarding major public issues.[4] The FCC agreed with Cook and directed WGCB to provide him free airtime. Red Lion disagreed with the FCC's interpretation of the fairness doctrine and demanded it reconsider forcing the station to air Cook's response. In a letter to the FCC, Red Lion demurred: "Under the circumstances, we are at a loss to see the 'fairness' in the Commission's letter."[5] The letter continued, "We sincerely request . . . we be advised whether in good conscience and in 'fairness,' we should now be forced to give Mr. Cook free time to reply to an attack by one whom he has previously attacked."[6] The FCC didn't budge and Red Lion took its argument to the courts.

This seemingly petty political squabble between a liberal activist and a small, faith-based radio station in southeast Pennsylvania led to *Red Lion v. FCC*, a Supreme Court case that marked the completion of the Supreme Court's arduous, decades-long effort to construct and define a very particular version of the conceptual space for human discourse. While the decision marked the culminating moment in creating the marketplace approach's DNA, as discussed at the end of the preceding chapter, the case also introduced the next great question—how should this newly defined space be maintained? The transition from creating to maintaining is apparent in *Red Lion*'s central passage, which concludes "It is the purpose of the First Amendment to *preserve* an uninhibited marketplace of ideas in which truth will ultimately prevail."[7] In passages such as this, the Court put the finishing touches on its efforts to create a space for human discourse, having, over time, given it a catchy name, "the marketplace of ideas," and a shiny new (and fundamentally flawed) foundation constructed from Enlightenment assumptions about truth, human rationality, and the role of government in individuals' lives. At the same time, justices turned their attention to maintaining the space. The flashy new car was in the driveway. Now how would it be cared for? Should the government protect this freshly named and created space? Could lawmakers take actions to safeguard the marketplace from distortion and misuse, or do the Enlightenment-based marketplace's roots require an expansive, unfettered space where, absent government influence, ideas can succeed and fail based on the inherent value of truth? The Court struggled with these questions, beginning in *Red Lion*, and

*Maintaining the Space*

its answers, after several cases, have done as much to shape the imagined space for human discourse as the half century justices took to name and define the marketplace of ideas.

This chapter explores how the Supreme Court has conceptualized the marketplace's maintenance. This question of how the space should be cared for has only grown more important in the networked era, which has fundamentally shifted *how* information flows. New technologies, and how we use them, have transformed the marketplace's shape. Despite this transformation, policy, judicial, and other assumptions and reasoning about the space—essentially our map of the terrain—have remained relatively unchanged. We're navigating the contours of free expression using an outdated map. Within the changing communication terrain, algorithmic and AI actors have become part of the information formula, adding to the Enlightenment's long-standing shortcomings regarding human diversity, the nature of truth, and how people share and encounter information. Algorithmic predetermination changes the very terrain of the space for human discourse as search engines, social media products, and other services we use online apply the information they have gathered about users to make decisions for them.[8]

Algorithms predetermine the ideas, people, and communities users encounter. Their work is not entirely self-serving, since the vast, even endless, amount of information available online requires some preferences be made regarding what users encounter. A consequence of this shift, however, is that the behind-the-scenes sorting process effectively empties the shared marketplace of ideas as it sends people directly to specialty shops, where they are more likely to encounter ideas and people they agree with.[9] In the algorithm-based space, the conflict between truth and falsity among rational individuals never occurs. Truth is largely predetermined by decisions algorithms make on people's behalf. In this scenario, people do not evaluate truth like they would the merits of a product in a capitalistic society. Instead, truth is customized, packaged, and handed to them based on what the algorithms conclude they want. In this twenty-first-century space, concerns about access to the marketplace and the frequency and intensity with which people encounter ideas, which have long been attached to the marketplace concept, mutate into questions about a system in which individuals *never*

95

*Chapter Five*

encounter facts, information, and ideas about matters of public concern. Suddenly, a person's searches for conservative or liberal political information lead companies to suggest ideas and people that reaffirm those inquiries. We become more extreme.[10] Less informed. Less empathetic.[11] We become increasingly sensitive to ideas that do not align with ours, because we are not used to encountering them.[12] In this network-based scenario, the marketplace fails all together to describe the space for human discourse.

Algorithms are only part of the problem when it comes to maintaining the marketplace of ideas in the networked era. We share networked spaces with artificial entities such as bots that distort the marketplace of ideas in crucial ways. Their presence within our discourse is fundamentally new to human communication. Human existence was required in all previous generations of communication technology. Now AI communicators, whether they are simple programs or machine-learning entities that adapt and create speech, engage with humans in ways that are often indiscernible to us.[13] Bots, the most common form AI communicators take, are fundamentally not human. They do not grow tired. They do not sleep. They do not have empathy or a stake in any election. They are programmed to communicate ideas. A person can create an army of bots in an afternoon and that army can in turn dominate the discourse about an issue, such as gun control, a political candidate, or international affairs. Some bots key on hash tags or certain accounts, amplifying particular ideas or voices and seizing on the power of hash tags to concentrate discourse about a certain topic.

The bots can produce messages that make it appear a truth has "won" and been accepted in the free exchange of ideas, when in reality a series of non-human actors has merely overwhelmed and distorted the space with an idea. No exchange of ideas or battle between truth and falsity occurs in this scenario. Such entities dominate and distort the marketplace of ideas. The bots, in their countless artificially created messages, can also push human communicators from the marketplace. Human contributions to an issue can be lost in the sea of bot-based babble as fundamentally inhuman entities produce countless messages, never growing tired or questioning the ethics of their behavior. In this sense, the space for human discourse experiences market failure, and

*Maintaining the Space*

once again the landmarks and terrain that have come to make up the imagined space for democratic discourse cannot be reconciled with the rationales that drive its use as a justification for free expression. The conceptual space becomes something else—a concern explored more fully in chapter 6.

It is easy to read these concerns and think "something should be done about this." Exactly. Revising the conceptual space, however, requires understanding how we arrived at an expansive marketplace of ideas that is defined by features and contours that stem from a particular set of rationales for free expression. The very nature of human discourse, and the conceptual space for it, has been remade in the networked era. How will it be protected from distortion or manipulation? Examining how the Court has concluded the marketplace of ideas should be maintained might seem dull and unimportant, but the push and pull between a marketplace of ideas that can be protected from distortion by limited government regulation and an expansive, unregulated marketplace provides building blocks for how the space for human discourse can be reshaped in the networked era. The story regarding the conflict over how the marketplace of ideas should be maintained begins with Cook and his battle with Red Lion.

## OVERLAPPING CONCERNS

The Court's decision in *Red Lion* did not come about after a series of accidents. Cook was not a First Amendment hero, valiantly standing up for free speech. His motivations were political. Whatever his motives, Cook's article "Hate Clubs of the Air," which named and shamed Hargis, stumbled upon one of the fundamental, inherent weaknesses of the marketplace of ideas' Enlightenment-based assumptions. The article emphasized that one powerful group was using its massive financial resources and hold on broadcast licenses to dominate the ideas communicated on the public airwaves.[14] Much as with algorithms and bots in the networked era, truth was not vanquishing falsity in a Miltonian exchange of ideas on the public airwaves. Instead, one group, Cook argued, was distorting the space by artificially boosting its ideas and blocking others. Cook's solution, late in the article, was

*Chapter Five*

to leverage the FCC's contention that the public airwaves should serve public discourse by demanding "free air time to counter some of the radical Right's wild-swinging charges."[15] Hargis took the bait when he singled out Cook, triggering one of the earliest discussions among justices about how the marketplace should be maintained. The Court's explicit intermingling of the marketplace concept and the First Amendment in *Red Lion* was not accidental either. The Court's conclusion that the marketplace of ideas *benefited* when audiences encounter diverse ideas represents the first phase of the protected-versus-expansive marketplace discussion.

At the start, justices communicated they understood a protected marketplace as an expansive space. They did not see a conflict between the two. They saw synergy. In *Red Lion*, the Court reasoned, "It is the right of the public to receive suitable access to social, political, esthetic, moral, and other ideas and experiences which is crucial here. That right may not constitutionally be abridged by Congress or the FCC."[16] Thus, justices reasoned compelling a broadcaster to provide airtime to a speaker to whom it would not otherwise have opened its forum would enrich the space. The decision "preserved an uninhibited marketplace of ideas." Crucially, it did so using government regulation.[17]

The protective language gained more traction in the landmark *New York Times v. United States* censorship case two years after *Red Lion* in 1971. Justices, in a terse, unsigned opinion, rejected the Nixon administration's efforts to halt the *Times* from publishing classified documents about the conflict in Vietnam. In rationalizing a decision that stymied the executive branch's powers, justices turned to protective rationales. Justice Potter Stewart, in his concurring opinion, emphasized, democracy requires "an informed and critical public opinion which alone can here protect the values of democratic government. . . . For without an informed and free press there cannot be an enlightened people."[18] Justices Hugo Black and William Brennan wrote separate concurring opinions to emphasize the government should never be able to censor publications. Unlike *Red Lion*, justices in *Times* reasoned preserving the space required halting government efforts to control which ideas entered the marketplace of ideas. In other words, the integrity of the space was maintained by protecting it from government intervention.

98

*Maintaining the Space*

Similarly, a year later, justices in *Healy v. James* struck down a state university's decision to disallow a political group from forming a chapter on campus. Referencing the marketplace, justices emphasized, "The college classroom with its surrounding environs is peculiarly the 'marketplace of ideas,' and we break no new constitutional ground in reaffirming this Nation's dedication to safeguarding academic freedom."[19] Both cases called upon justices to maintain the marketplace by protecting it from government interventions into the space, making them different from *Red Lion*, where justices concluded government intervention in the space *enriched* the marketplace. *Red Lion*, *Times*, and *Healy* share a common concern for preserving the flow of information into the marketplace. Justices showed a willingness to do what was necessary, whether that meant halting government powers or upholding them, to protect the flow of ideas into the expansive marketplace.

Justices faced a more vexing challenge to their expansive *and* protected marketplace approach two years after *Healy* in 1973. In *Columbia Broadcasting v. Democratic National Committee*, CBS refused an anti-war group's request to purchase airtime for its messages. The group, with support from the Democratic National Committee, contended the network's refusal violated its First Amendment rights. The Court, which had welcomed four new justices since *Red Lion* was decided four years earlier, voted seven to two for CBS. Justices determined the marketplace was best served if those with the financial means to purchase advertising did not have the power to overwhelm the airwaves with their messages. The Court reasoned, "The marketplace of ideas and experiences would scarcely be served by a system so heavily weighted in favor of the financially affluent."[20] Justices rationalized their decision as *preserving* the marketplace of ideas from distortion, but in doing so they limited the expansive nature of the space. Some ideas might not be communicated as a result of their decision. Ultimately, justices communicated a concern for access and the flow of information into the marketplace, reasoning "There is substantial danger . . . the time allotted for editorial advertising could be monopolized by those of one political persuasion."[21] As with *Red Lion*, justices prioritized protecting the marketplace from distortion because they concluded doing so enriched the space. The decision came with a cost, however. The range of ideas would be limited.

*Chapter Five*

Brennan made the cost the Court's decision exacted on the range of ideas central to his dissent. Brennan, whose understandings of the First Amendment shaped the foundations of the marketplace as the space for human discourse in earlier cases, reasoned allowing the network to limit access to advertising on the public airwaves diminished the *amount* or *range* of ideas citizens could encounter. He contended, "The public have strong First Amendment interests in the reception of a full spectrum of views – presented in a vigorous and uninhibited manner – on controversial issues of public importance."[22] He continued, quoting from his opinion for the Court in the landmark *New York Times v. Sullivan* case nine years earlier, "The most effect way to ensure this 'uninhibited, robust, and wide-open debate' is by fostering a 'free trade in ideas'."[23] Thus, he found the Court erred in *protecting* the marketplace from distortion because in doing so it *limited* the range of ideas in the space. He prioritized an expansive exchange of ideas over a space for discourse that was more protected from distortion. His dissent planted the seeds for what would become the expansive, unregulated marketplace-of-ideas rationale in the cases that followed.

## BATTLE LINES

The *protected* and *expansive* marketplace-of-ideas rationales continued to drift apart after *CBS*. Justices in many ways came to see the two approaches as exclusive to each other, rather than coexistent. Justices stopped understanding government intervention in the space, for the purpose of protecting an expansive marketplace, as a viable rationale. This shift was particularly stark in *Miami Herald v. Tornillo,* decided in 1974, the term after *CBS*. The case was, essentially, *Red Lion* for newspapers. A Florida law required newspapers provide "a right of reply" to political candidates whom they criticized. Pat Tornillo, a candidate for the Florida House of Representatives, was criticized by the *Miami Herald*. Tornillo demanded the newspaper publish his responses. The *Herald* refused. The Florida Supreme Court, citing the Supreme Court's decision in *Red Lion*, concluded the law aligned with the First Amendment's concern for an informed public.[24] The state court found the right of replay requirement would *enhance* the space by providing

100

*Maintaining the Space*

more information for the public, essentially walking the protected *and* expansive marketplace-of-ideas line the Supreme Court followed in *Red Lion*.[25] The Supreme Court disagreed, rejecting the lower court's efforts to balance protected and expansive priorities. Justices unanimously overturned the Florida court's decision, finding the law gave the government the power to compel a private publisher to "publish that which 'reason tells them should not be published.'"[26]

The *Tornillo* decision is a crucial building block for publishers' rights, particularly in an era when state governments, such as those of Texas and Florida, have sought to compel social media firms to leave speakers and ideas in their spaces that they would otherwise remove, but it also represents a sudden, noteworthy shift by justices regarding the power of government to maintain the marketplace of ideas.[27] Justices rejected the idea government could intervene to protect the marketplace by compelling a more expansive space. The rationales the Florida Supreme Court provided for upholding the law aligned with the justices' reasoning from cases such as *Red Lion, CBS,* and *New York Times v. U.S.*, but the Court's opinion in *Tornillo* never even mentions *Red Lion*, despite the similarities between the cases. What changed? The Court shifted ideologically, becoming more conservative between 1969 and 1974, as four Nixon appointees, including Chief Justice Warren Burger, joined the Court.[28] Such a shift does not entirely explain the split between a protected and an expansive marketplace. The facts of the cases might also have played a part, since broadcasters' use of the public airwaves, which the government manages on the public's behalf, has generally meant justices have been more willing to allow government interventions on broadcasters' rights. Ultimately, *Tornillo* represented the first decision in which justices rejected the idea the government could help maintain the space. The discussion was not complete, however.

Justices further embraced the expansive, unregulated, approach, and ignored protected-marketplace-of-ideas rationales in a pair of landmark advertising cases, *Bigelow v. Virginia* and *Virginia State Pharmacy Board v. Virginia Citizens Consumer Council*, in 1975 and 1976 respectively. The cases challenged justices to address whether the government has the power to regulate speech that might distort the space for discourse or confuse citizens regarding commercial transactions. For a

## Chapter Five

majority of the Court in both cases, the answer was a firm "no." Justices instead, building upon the reasoning from *Tornillo* in 1974, favored an expansive marketplace. The Court rationalized in *Bigelow* "The relationship of speech to the marketplace of products or of services does not make it valueless in the marketplace of ideas."[29]

Similarly, in *Virginia State Board*, the Court reasoned, in a "predominantly free enterprise economy, the allocation of our resources in large measure will be made through numerous private economic decisions. It is a matter of public interest that those decisions, in the aggregate, be intelligent and well informed."[30] Thus, justices reasoned more information rather than less—even if information is by its nature persuasive and commercial—is preferred. When considered alongside *Tornillo*, the cases communicated that justices understood the expansive marketplace as being generally independent from any government efforts to enhance or protect it from distortion. By moving in this direction, justices increased their reliance upon the human rationality assumptions of the Enlightenment-based marketplace. The mantra became "more information" rather than a balance between an expansive information marketplace that is also protected from distortion.

An expansive, generally unmaintained marketplace only functions if we believe individuals can discern truth from falsity in an open exchange of ideas. In decisions such as these, the marketplace of ideas increasingly became an experiment in how the Enlightenment's assumptions would operate in the twentieth-century information environment. Justice William Rehnquist dissented in both commercial speech cases, reasoning the marketplace of ideas was better off without generally unregulated commercial speech. In other words, he found the marketplace would function more efficiently when the government had greater power to regulate the role commercial speech played in human discourse. In *Bigelow*, which dealt with a law that criminalized publishing information about procuring an abortion, Rehnquist dissented: "I am unable to see why Virginia does not have a legitimate public interest in its regulation."[31] In the next passage, he reasoned laws like the one involved in the case "protect the public from unscrupulous practices."[32] In *Virginia State Board*, which dealt with a Virginia law that proscribed advertising the prices of prescription drugs, he explained the Court's decision "elevates

102

*Maintaining the Space*

commercial intercourse between a seller hawking his wares and a buyer seeking to strike a bargain to the same plane as has been previously reserved for the free marketplace of ideas."[33] He continued, the case's implications "are far reaching indeed."[34] Rehnquist envisioned a different map and maintenance plan for the marketplace of ideas. His understandings allowed for some government regulation, in this instance commercial-speech-based limitations, in order to protect the space from speech that was more likely to mislead and was, in his analysis, of less value to democracy.

## MONEY TALKS AND CORPORATIONS ARE PEOPLE

Justices essentially canceled the marketplace of ideas' maintenance plan in the late 1970s. Forget a protected space. Forget concerns about distortion or market failure. They inspected the Enlightenment-based foundations, which were still relatively new, and concluded they could bear the massive weight of an expansive, increasingly unfettered set of free-expression protections. So, they tossed the maintenance plan. Claims the marketplace of ideas must be protected from distortion and misuse were dismissed. This process started in *Tornillo, Bigelow* and *Virginia State Board*, and was further nurtured in the murky *Buckley v. Valeo* campaign finance decision in 1976. A few years later, however, in *First National Bank v. Bellotti*, justices moved radically forward with the expansive approach.[35] The case did not initially seem like a turning-point matter. The disagreement between Massachusetts and a group of corporations about when businesses could take part in political discourse didn't have the fanfare of the civil-rights-movement infused *Sullivan,* or the showdown between the nation's leading news outlet—the *New York Times*—and the president in the Pentagon Papers case. What *Bellotti* lacked in fanfare it made up for in impact. By the time the Court ruled Massachusetts's limitations on corporations' participation in political discourse violated the First Amendment, it had eviscerated almost any idea a space for human discourse might require maintenance in order to remain effective.

Justices' conclusions in *Bellotti* can be summed up in two statements: Money equals speech and corporations are people. Both conclusions had

## Chapter Five

massive implications for how the marketplace of ideas would be maintained and, decades later in the networked era, which tools lawmakers and jurists would have available to address AI and algorithmic induced distortions and failures in the space for human discourse. Massachusetts had barred corporations from participating in most political expression because it sought to *protect* human discourse. Lawmakers' reasoning included "preserving the integrity of the electoral process" and "preventing corruption."[36] The commonwealth concluded corporations are different in nature than people and their presence in the marketplace of ideas would distort discourse. The Supreme Court's five-to-four decision to strike down the law supercharged the expansive marketplace approach. The decision did more than reject state lawmakers' efforts to set aside the marketplace of ideas for *human* communicators.

Justices went out of their way to indicate the nature of the speaker cannot determine its ability to contribute ideas to the marketplace of ideas. Justice Louis Powell, writing for the Court, explained, "If the speakers here were not corporations, no one would suggest that the State could silence their proposed speech."[37] He continued, "The inherent worth of the speech in terms of its capacity for informing the public does not depend upon the identity of its source, whether corporation, association, union, or individual."[38] The Court contended an entity, such as a corporation, despite its fundamentally non-human nature, has rights equivalent to human speakers because limiting the entity's rights would limit the flow of ideas into the space for human discourse. The focus, justices emphasized, was on the flow of information, not the nature of the speaker. The question was not *who* was speaking, but *what* could be contributed. Justices found the corporations could contribute to the flow of ideas.

The *Bellotti* dissents contended the nature of the speaker was crucial. The primary dissent was written by Justice Byron White, who wrote the *Red Lion* opinion, and was joined by Brennan and Justice Thurgood Marshall. Brennan is likely the justice most instrumental in constructing the Enlightenment-based marketplace, but in *Bellotti* he joined a dissent that would have upheld a law that allowed the government to limit the role non-human entities played in the space for human discourse. White's thesis is a crucial counterpoint to the expansive marketplace approach.

104

*Maintaining the Space*

He reasoned protecting the space from distortion *supports* the First Amendment, rather than detracts from it. He explained, "The Court's fundamental error is its failure to realize that the state regulatory interests in terms of which the alleged curtailment of First Amendment rights accomplished by the statute must be evaluated are themselves derived from the First Amendment."[39] The dissenters essentially reasoned free expression is for humans, not entities. The dissent found some protection of the space for human discourse preferrable to the distortive effects these communicators posed to the marketplace of ideas. By protecting corporate speech rights, the dissent contended, the Court had erred in prioritizing information over the original conception of free expression, which was based on individual rights. White averred: "What some have considered to be the principal function of the First Amendment, the use of communication as a means of self-expression, self-realization, and self-fulfillment, is not at all furthered by corporate speech."[40]

Rehnquist's shorter dissent focused on corporate personhood. He reasoned the Court had gone too far in expanding corporate rights to include freedom of expression. Rehnquist quoted Justice John Marshall's reasoning from an 1819 case, which emphasized "A corporation is an artificial being, invisible, intangible, and existing only in contemplation of law."[41] Rehnquist emphasized, when a corporation is created, it does not immediately gain "all the liberties enjoyed by natural persons."[42] Instead, he found the rights of such entities should have boundaries. *Bellotti* refreshed the battle lines regarding how the space should be maintained. A majority of the Court radically expanded the Enlightenment-based trust in human discernment and the ability of truth to emerge from a relatively unmitigated exchange of ideas. The dissenters, including Brennan, contended the First Amendment is safeguarded when the focus is on protecting individual rights.

The battle lines were revisited two years later when justices struck down a New York state policy that limited electric utilities from promoting energy use.[43] Powell wrote for the Court, with Brennan joining in part and Rehnquist again dissenting. The Court reiterated information, in whatever form, was paramount. Powell explained, "Even when advertising communicates only an incomplete version of the relevant facts, the First Amendment presumes that some accurate information is

105

## Chapter Five

better than no information at all."[44] The Court reasoned, in ways consistent with *Bigelow* and *Virginia State Board*, commercial speech loses its First Amendment protections when it ceases to provide information to the public. Powell found "There can be no constitutional objection to the suppression of commercial messages that do not accurately inform the public about lawful activity. The government may ban forms of communication more likely to deceive the public than to inform it."[45]

The decision reinforced the expansive marketplace, striking down government attempts to limit a certain type of speech because the expression might not benefit the public. Justices, however, created an exemption for false or illegal commercial speech. Such speech, they reasoned, could be limited because justices found it was valueless in the marketplace of ideas. Brennan concurred with the judgment, but disagreed with the reasoning. He found the Court's decision to allow the government to regulate commercial speech that does not inform the public limited free expression. Thus, Brennan moved back to the expansive marketplace side in the case. He saw no distinction between commercial speech and other areas of expression.[46] To Brennan, a central author of the marketplace of ideas' foundational thinking, no distinction should be made between commercial and other types of expression. In such an approach, all ideas compete, however uneven their footing and unfair the opportunities they encounter, in the marketplace of ideas.

Rehnquist did not budge. He continued his consistent dissents arguing against the expansive marketplace. The dissents do not tell us Rehnquist, the most conservative justice on the Court at the time, supported government interventions into the space to protect the marketplace of ideas. That would be a leap. Instead, Rehnquist was consistently suspicious that commercial speech was worth First Amendment protection and that of the marketplace of ideas functioned at all. His dissent in *Central Hudson* represented his most complete critique of the marketplace approach. He contended:

> While it is true that an important objective of the First Amendment is to foster the free flow of information, identification of speech that falls within its protection is not aided by the metaphorical reference to a "marketplace of ideas." There is no reason for believing that

*Maintaining the Space*

the marketplace of ideas is free from market imperfections any more than there is to believe that the invisible hand will always lead to optimum economic decisions in the commercial market.[47]

Rehnquist found the marketplace approach problematic. This and other dissents in similar cases tell us he, at the same time, generally concluded the government had more power to regulate certain areas of speech, including commercial and corporate speech, than most of his fellow justices believed. Thus, the greatest antagonist of the expansive marketplace of ideas approach cannot be neatly placed into the protected space side of the argument. Rehnquist's critique did not generally include concern for the flow of information or the success of the space. He didn't believe the space functioned. His conclusions simply conveyed that he found some expression simply wasn't worth protecting.

## THE PROTECTED MARKETPLACE MEETS ITS END

The Reuters Pitchbot is a satirical Twitter account that creates fake news headlines about real events.[48] The bot has more than thirty thousand followers. When Elon Musk moved to purchase Twitter in spring 2022, the bot tweeted "World's biggest clown purchases world's largest circus."[49] In other words, the bot contributed a take on a news event that was on par or better than most people's postings regarding the much-discussed purchase. Of course, not all bots are as harmless. The Reuters Pitchbot is labeled and clearly states it is not a real news organization. Many AI entities are not as forthcoming. Bots have been associated with spreading false and misleading information, particularly regarding election-related information.[50] Bots are just one non-human entity that communicates ideas in the twenty-first century, as discussed more fully in chapter 6. A Google search result, produced by an algorithm, is a form of communication. Similarly, machine learning is used to produce deepfake audio and video clips, which can be interpreted as a form of speech that emanates from computer programs. All of these are non-human entities that *speak* in ways that can influence the flow of ideas and the space for human discourse, whatever shape it takes in the twenty-first century. Should the Court remain agnostic, as it did in cases such as *Bellotti* and *Central Hudson*, regarding the nature of the speaker or speech?

## Chapter Five

Well before vast, heavily populated computer networks provided spaces for AI and algorithmic communicators, justices tempered *Bellotti*'s enthusiastic support of non-human entities. The Court, in a six-to-three decision in *Austin v. Michigan Chamber of Commerce* in 1990, upheld a Michigan law that halted corporations from using treasury funds to pay for political messages. The law at the heart of the case was similar to Massachusetts's regulation in *Bellotti*, but it allowed corporations to take part in political discourse through independent funds, such as political action committees. The Court's decision to uphold the law breathed new life into a protected approach to the marketplace of ideas that had not found a majority of justices' support since the early 1970s. Crucially, justices accepted the rationale that the law was constitutional *because* it protected the space from distortion. Marshall wrote for the Court, concluding "We find the Act is precisely targeted to eliminate distortion caused by corporate spending while also allowing corporations to express their political views."[51]

Crucially, Brennan *and* Rehnquist, who was now chief justice, joined justices' decision to uphold the law. Brennan was in many ways the bellwether justice for marketplace-of-ideas thinking because he did so much to write Enlightenment assumptions into the theory's foundations, particularly in *Sullivan*.[52] In the term before *Austin*, Brennan had authored the Court's opinion in the *Texas v. Johnson* flag-burning case. Building and expanding upon free-expression rationales he wove into *Sullivan* twenty years before, Brennan created "the bedrock principle" of the First Amendment. He concluded, "The government may not prohibit the expression of an idea simply because society finds the idea itself offensive or disagreeable."[53] His reasoning in the landmark *Johnson* case only added more weight onto the Enlightenment assumptions that people are rational and truth will defeat falsity in a generally unregulated marketplace. Such an opinion, written just nine months before *Austin*, makes his support for the Michigan law particularly noteworthy. The justice who did more than anyone to invest in a very particular type of space for discourse found in *Austin*, as he did when he joined the dissent in *Bellotti*, that a marketplace of ideas that receives at least some protection against distortion from the government was preferrable to a fully expansive and unregulated space.

*Maintaining the Space*

Brennan wrote a concurring opinion in *Austin* to emphasize that the use of funds assigned to an independently funded entity, such as a political action group, was different from a corporation potentially using investors' money to advocate for issues or candidates without their support or knowledge.[54] He explained, "Just as speech interests are at their zenith in this area, so too are the interests of unwilling Chamber members and corporate shareholders forced to subsidize that speech."[55] Importantly, Brennan emphasized government should not determine *who* speaks or *what* they say, but it can limit the power of a non-human entity from speaking for people, using their funds, without their knowledge or permission. Justice Antonin Scalia took up the expansive marketplace argument in his dissent, contending "The Court today endorses the principle that too much speech is an evil that the democratic majority can proscribe."[56] He continued, "that principle is contrary to our case law and compatible with the absolutely central truth of the First Amendment: that government cannot be trusted to assure, through censorship, the 'fairness' of political debate."[57] Scalia's conclusions, along with fellow dissenter Anthony Kennedy's, moved to the forefront twenty years later in *Citizens United v. FEC*, where a conservative majority, led by two of the three dissenters from *Austin*, dismantled any idea the marketplace of ideas required maintenance or protections from distortion or misuse.

Much like *Bellotti*, *Citizens United* fractured the Court. Citizens United, a non-profit political organization, contended a section of the Bipartisan Campaign Reform Act, which limited the amount of money corporations and other groups could spend on campaign contributions, violated its First Amendment rights. As in *Bellotti*, justices were asked to determine the constitutionality of a law created to *protect* the flow of ideas from the type of distortion non-human entities can create. Justices, in another five-to-four ruling, doubled down on *Bellotti*. The Court rejected any argument the marketplace of ideas could be helped by a law that allowed the government to limit expression. The protected marketplace rationale, the Court communicated, has no place in how the First Amendment should be understood. Kennedy, who wrote for the Court, attacked the reasoning from *Austin*. He reasoned, "If the antidistortion rationale were to be accepted, however, it would permit Government to ban political speech simply because the speaker is an association that

109

*Chapter Five*

has taken on the corporate form."[58] He continued, later in the opinion, "*Austin* interferes with the 'open marketplace' of ideas protected by the First Amendment."[59]

Chief Justice John Roberts's separate opinion, which is labeled a concurrence but is more of a letter of support for Kennedy's opinion for the Court, contends the Court was obligated to fix its wrong thinking in *Austin*. Roberts explained, "Congress may not prohibit political speech, even if the speaker is a corporation or union."[60] Thus, justices in *Citizens United* didn't simply conclude the law in question overstepped. They went after the entire line of reasoning that would support limiting expression for the purposes of maintaining a functional space for human discourse. Crucially, non-human entities, which have become crucial actors in democratic discourse, were at the heart of the question.

## THE EXPANSIVE MARKETPLACE—ON STEROIDS

The protected marketplace approach was vanquished in *Citizens United*. Game over. The back-and-forth among justices that began in *Red Lion* in 1969 came to an end as a consistent majority of justices galvanized around the expansive marketplace of ideas and churned out increasingly bold decisions in that regard. By *Citizens United* in 2010, early in the Roberts Court era, any argument that government could create limitations on expression, even if the limits had nothing to do with the content of the ideas, was dispatched. The argument that the space for discourse must be maintained was pushed to the fringes. At the same time, most of the cases within the expansive-versus-protected-marketplace debate centered upon the non-human nature of the speaker, particularly in *Bellotti*, *Austin*, and *Citizens United*. Justices in *Bellotti* and *Citizens United* were emphatic the non-human nature of a speaker was not a valid rationale for limitations. The expansive, unmaintained marketplace took control. Justices reaffirmed and pushed the boundaries of the space even further in the terms that followed *Citizens United*.

The next year, justices reaffirmed protestors who communicate hateful and heartbreaking messages during military funerals and other sacred events are not liable for damages for the emotional harm they cause in *Snyder v. Phelps*.[61] Roberts, writing for the Court, concluded,

110

*Maintaining the Space*

the nation has chosen "to protect even hurtful speech on public issues to ensure that we do not stifle public debate."[62] While the speakers in the case were human, the decision reaffirmed and pushed the boundaries of the marketplace, rejecting the idea that certain speech should be removed. Months later, the Court struck down a California law that prohibited the sale of violent video games to those younger than 18. Justices reasoned, "Video games communicate ideas—and even social messages."[63] The Court continued, "And whatever the challenges of applying the Constitution to ever-advancing technology, 'the basic principles of freedom of speech and the press, like the First Amendment's command, do not vary' when a new and different medium for communication appears."[64] The Court emphasized video games create virtual worlds, which are a form of expression. Justices contended these virtual spaces, and the ideas, characters, and stories within them, can contribute to the flow of ideas, ultimately expanding the marketplace of ideas to types of spaces and expression that previously had not been included. Finally, a year later, in *United States v. Alvarez*, the Court pushed even deeper into the expansive marketplace approach. Justices struck down a federal law that criminalized lying about having earned military honors.

The case arose after Xavier Alvarez, who was elected to a California water board, claimed he earned the Congressional Medal of Honor, served in the Marines for twenty-five years, and had been awarded the Purple Heart. None of it was true. Alvarez was indicted for violating the Stolen Valor Act, but he contended the law violated his First Amendment rights. In other words, he argued the law violated his right to intentionally mislead people about having earned the nation's highest military honors. The Court agreed with Alvarez and used the case as an opportunity to stretch the already vastly expanding marketplace of ideas. Kennedy, who also authored the *Citizens United* opinion, reasoned the law was unconstitutional because the lies Congress sought to protect the public from would be exposed and corrected in the marketplace of ideas. He explained, "The Government has not shown, and cannot show, why counterspeech would not suffice to achieve its interest. The facts of this case indicate that the dynamics of free speech, of counterspeech, of refutation, can overcome the lie."[65] In other words, let Alvarez lie, the marketplace's Enlightenment-based foundations can handle the weight of

111

*Chapter Five*

his and other falsehoods—truth will prevail. Thus, a government effort to protect the discourse from intentional lies about military honors violated free expression.

The concern in these instances is not whether each of these post-*Citizens United* decisions was rightly decided. Crucially, each represents a different type of push toward an increasingly wide open, unregulated vision of what the imagined space for discourse looks like. The vision for such a space for discourse places the maximum amount of trust possible in Enlightenment ideas about truth, human rationality, and the place of the individual in society. The expansive marketplace does not account for there being multiple truths, the influence of each person's experiences on their realities, or massive discrepancies regarding the frequency and intensity of messages that reach different groups. The expansive marketplace is not concerned about access. All of these nuanced concerns were rejected. This is the version of the marketplace that welcomed AI communicators into human discourse and algorithmically predetermined information bubbles for online communities. This is the marketplace that fails to match the new terrain created by the AI era. The imagined space for human discourse—the expansive, Enlightenment-founded marketplace of ideas—does not line up with the pastoral, cobblestone streets justices appear to conjure when they explain how they understand the space. The Enlightenment-based, expansive marketplace has created market failure in the space for human discourse.

# PART II

# PART II

# SIX

## Drawing a New Map

Akihiko Kondo and Hatsune Miku were married during a small ceremony in Tokyo in 2018. Kondo's family and coworkers refused to attend. They did not support the marriage. Strangely, the bride was not present either, at least not in a traditional sense.[1] Kondo placed a wedding band on a plush-toy replica of the bride. Miku did not attend the wedding because she has never existed in human form. Kondo married an idea. He married a fictional anime character associated with software that replicates a young woman's singing voice. Miku has opened for Lady Gaga and performed on the "Late Show," but she's never taken a breath, had a heartbeat, or fallen in love. Kondo's relationship with Miku was primarily conveyed through a Gatebox, which is an artificially intelligent home companion marketed primarily to Japanese men.

The companion is programmed to make the user feel cared for and not lonely. In one advertisement, the user tells his companion how good it felt to know someone was at his apartment, waiting for him to get home from work.[2] Kondo married an AI representation of a fictional character based on feelings he developed for it. His experience, while more extreme than most, represents a small, novel glimpse into a fundamentally changed, dynamic space for human discourse that simply cannot be squared with the traditional contours judges and thinkers

115

*Chapter Six*

have identified and used to describe its terrain. Kondo's love for Miku might be the least of our concerns as many AI communicators and other non-human entities have far greater impacts on human discourse. They influence political and social debates, along with the ideas and communities people engage with.

The space is being changed by four primarily AI-based innovations. First, by AI communicators, such as Miku, and countless similar and simpler entities that interact with each other and humans in shared virtual spaces, such as social media platforms and apps. The Replika app, for example, offers users a customized AI companion for their mobile devices.[3] Bot-based Twitter accounts, such as @RedDebate and @TexasSammiD poured political content, disinformation, and conspiracy theories into followers' feeds before they were suspended.[4] AI entities are doing far more than providing companionship. They are influencing the ideas and *truths* human participants in the space for discourse come to understand, which leads to the second group. The space is also being *organized* differently, with algorithms, another type of computer program, constructing customized marketplaces of ideas for each person, based upon personal information corporations have collected about them. Algorithms transform the space for discourse from a shared place, one that envisages a pastoral, cobblestoned, eighteenth-century European town square, to one that is personalized for a single shopper.

In the AI era, we each have our own store, rather than a shared space for the exchange of a broad spectrum of ideas. This is a problem for democracy. The shift encourages extremism and handicaps compromise as people become increasingly incapable of considering ideas different to their own.[5] In this sense, ideas become beliefs, and beliefs do not require accuracy or evidence. Truth becomes irrelevant. Third, deepfakes are produced by machine-learning entities that work together to create believable video and audio clips of people saying and doing things they never said or did.[6] These fictional creations undermine audiences' abilities to conclude what is true and false regarding what they see and hear. Finally, the metaverse promises to provide an even more immersive experience with AI communicators, algorithms, and deepfakes as we go from visiting virtual spaces to living in them.[7]

*Drawing a New Map*

These four transformative, AI-infused influences on the space for human discourse continue to fundamentally reshape how people understand the world around them. This is no small thing and cannot be written off as purely a matter of technological change. These are not simply modern-day conveniences. These four creations amount to a revolution in how people know and understand the world around them. They shift how reality—the truths people come to accept—is formed. We do not have AI overlords. Not yet. How people use these technologies, and networked communication tools in general, however, plays a substantial role in how the marketplace of ideas is being transformed. People believe in and share bot-based content, deepfakes, and false information because they reinforce existing beliefs.[8] People flock to virtual spaces, including the metaverse, to find like-minded others and to perform behaviors and share ideas that might be unacceptable in their local, physical communities. Kondo's story tells one small part of that tale. He married a fictional character for a reason. He explained he was lonely and struggled to build meaningful connections with people. Engaging with AI helped him meet unmet human needs.

Kondo isn't alone in his loneliness. Studies show people are lonelier than ever.[9] They are struggling to engage in meaningful, rewarding human relationships. Sociologist and human-technology expert Sherry Turkle, in her aptly named book *Alone Together,* emphasized people are more connected than they have ever been, but those virtual human connections often only simulate actual relationships. Texts, social media posts, and emails do not replace in-person communication. Turkle explained, "In the half-light of virtual community, we may feel utterly alone. As we distribute ourselves, we may abandon ourselves."[10] In other words, virtual spaces often simulate human discourse, but end up acting like a placebo for the real thing. Loneliness and isolation represent one way the space for human discourse is changing. Most importantly, it shows the space is being transformed because *we* are changing.

The differences, as Turkle indicated, go beyond loneliness. People express themselves differently online than they do in person. Online communication lacks the social cues embedded in body language, people have less control over which constituencies will encounter their messages, and the forums themselves often limit the length of messages.

*Chapter Six*

Subconsciously or not, people, to certain extents, take these changes into account when communicating online. The outcome is oversimplified messages. Ideas become more blunt, less nuanced, and, often, more extreme. Communication scholar Zizi Papacharissi explained, "The individual must then engage in multiple mini performances that combine a variety of semiological references so as to produce a presentation of the self that makes sense to multiple audiences."[11] Add that people create less trust and empathy online and that social networks are constructed to encourage engagement rather than discourse, and we begin to get a glimpse of some of the new contours and terrain found in this transformed space for discourse.

The idea that the very architecture of online spaces transforms the nature of discourse as the places people communicate reward extreme, attention-getting, and performative behaviors, rather than incentivizing informed, meaningful discussion alone is crucial—yet these are part of the shift.[12] Without realizing it, people act out identities to garner virtual attention, in the form of likes, favorites, shares, new followers, or other interactions that reward them and increase their stature within the algorithms' programs.[13] Hour after hour and post after post, we begin to forget we're performing. The virtual performative identities begin to take the place of people's actual identities, making people more likely to act out extreme behaviors, both online and in person. Finally, after algorithms sort people based on programmed criteria, individuals further divide themselves into generally like-minded groups in an information environment that has shifted from being characterized as limited in terms of information sources to choice-rich.[14]

When people are given nearly infinite options regarding the ideas and people with which they can engage, they tend to narrow the range to sources that reinforce their existing beliefs. This is a problem for democracy and the marketplace of ideas. Constitutional scholar Cass Sunstein explained, "If like-minded people stir one another to greater levels of anger, the consequences can be literally dangerous."[15] Similarly, sociologist Manual Castells concluded, "When communication breaks down when it does not exist any longer . . . social groups and individuals become alienated from each other."[16] He continued, they "see each other

*Drawing a New Map*

as a stranger, eventually as a threat, as identities become increasingly difficult to share."[17]

The result is an "othering" process, where people become less and less likely to entertain or have tolerance for ideas that do not align with their own or those found in their like-minded communities. In this scenario, the space for human discourse, historically conceptualized as a marketplace of ideas, transforms into a series of walled gardens that operate as dividers between echo chambers. The space for human discourse doesn't simply take a new shape. The very fabric of how truth is constructed in a democratic society takes on a new set of assumptions about the flow of information and how people come to understand what is true. Part I of this book mapped the shapes and contours of the traditional marketplace of ideas, which continues to dominate how we think of human discourse and rationalize expansive free-expression safeguards.

Now we begin to consider what a new map of the space for human discourse should look like. The space for discourse has always been an imaged place. As discussed in Part I, justices named the space the marketplace of ideas and installed Enlightenment assumptions about truth and human rationality into its foundations. Based on these assumptions, they constructed an expansive, generally unregulated space for the exchange of ideas. The ushering in of the networked era, followed by the AI era, has shifted the shapes and contours of the space. This chapter begins the second half of the book by examining *how* the space for human discourse has shifted, particularly in regard to how individuals in a networked world come to understand the world around them and use those realities to make decisions.

## NEW NEIGHBORS

Bots are not new—the environment where they thrive is. Mathematician Alan Turing, who created one of the very first computer programs, envisioned thinking machines that could replicate human communication as early as 1950.[18] Computer scientist Joseph Weizenbaum programmed what was likely the first bot, though he certainly didn't call it that, in 1966, when he created ELIZA. The program functions like a psychologist, providing conversational responses to information users provide.

*Chapter Six*

ELIZA's responses are simple, but effective. The program responds to human inputs with phrases such as "tell me more" or "what do you think?" Turkle who taught with Weizenbaum and worked with the program in the 1970s, was fascinated that Weizenbaum's students knew ELIZA was not human and could not empathize with their problems, but still enjoyed engaging with it.[19] She explained, students "wanted to chat with it. More than this, they wanted to be alone with it. They wanted to tell it their secrets."[20]

ELIZA, and programs like it, were under house arrest, however. They were trapped on individual computers, sequestered away in musty offices and labs in poorly lit university buildings, because no technology existed that would allow computer programs to seamlessly interact with people. Then, they were freed. The creation and widespread adoption of networked communication tools created an environment where AI could participate alongside human communicators—no physical form required. The networked era essentially opened a portal that invited a new type of participant to take part in discourse, forever altering the flow of information. Unlike almost any other form of communication, virtual spaces do not require human existence. As the famous *New Yorker* cartoon from the early 1990s quipped, "On the Internet, nobody knows you're a dog."[21]

We're a long way from ELIZA. While corporations increasingly use AI for two-way conversations in customer support, most bots are employed in one-way communication, triggering on key words, hash tags, or particular accounts to convey ideas. The ideas entities communicate can shape financial markets, elections, and the way people understand the world around them. AI makes decisions about and influences stock trades, causing the market to ebb and flow based on key words and the artificial spread of certain information through online networks.[22] The Syrian Electronic Army, for example, hacked the Associated Press's Twitter account in 2013 and tweeted a false message that a terror attack occurred at the White House.[23] The Dow Jones industrial average immediately dropped 140 points before recovering when the post was corrected. Similarly, the Dow unexpectedly dropped 1,000 points in what was labeled a "flash crash" in 2010. Investigators concluded bots, set to make trades based on key words, caused the sudden drop.[24] So-called

*Drawing a New Map*

robo advisers, which are AI-based financial traders who manage people's investments, have grown in popularity. They buy and sell stocks and mutual funds, while remaining immune from "behavioral aspects that are linked to financial advisors."[25] In other words, they do not suffer from being human.

AI communicators' influence on political discourse is even more concerning. Researchers found about half a million bots communicated nearly four million tweets about the 2016 presidential election.[26] Their messages accounted for about one-fifth of the entire conversation about who should be president on the platform. Bots were used to supercharge disinformation in the French elections the next year in 2017 and "conservative bots played a central role in the highly connected core of the retweet network" during the 2018 US midterm elections.[27] That same year, interest groups used bots to fan the flames of a political controversy regarding a four-page memo written by a Republican congressman about whether the FBI violated its policies while looking into Donald Trump's presidential campaign.[28] The hashtag #releasethememo was artificially boosted by armies of bots, using what one expert labeled "computational propaganda," which is "the use of information and communication technologies to manipulate perceptions, affect cognition, and influence behavior."[29]

That's exactly what we're talking about. A congressional aide checking their employers' Twitter account would immediately see hundreds of seemingly real arguments for one idea, as if a *truth* had emerged in the discourse taking place in the virtual marketplace. At the same time, a human user's messages would be lost within the bot-based babble. From both perspectives, AI entities distort the space for human discourse. Their fundamentally non-human nature, such as their ability to publish countless messages and their lack of any ethics or stakes in the ideas they convey, unnaturally influence the frequency and intensity of ideas that flow in the marketplace of ideas. Bots are one reason the twentieth-century marketplace, founded upon eighteenth-century ideas, is not in a position to describe the twenty-first-century space for discourse.

Bots evolved by 2020. A cybersecurity firm identified a network of nearly 14,000 Facebook accounts programmed to post about fifteen times per month.[30] The bots published about a variety of political issues

121

*Chapter Six*

and each account included a profile photo and a friends list, making it seem as if all the accounts, the equivalent of a town's population, were real people. Bot accounts, with extensive and active networks, and that have operated for longer periods of time, are among the most difficult to identify. During the COVID-19 outbreak in 2020, "bots were found to be pushing a number of conspiracy theories, such as QAnon, in addition to retweeting links from partisan news sites."[31] In all these instances, and many others, AI entities engaged in major political debates, distorting expression, pushing human speakers out of the space, and, in many instances, spreading false information. While not all bots have nefarious programming, their presences throughout human discourse represents a fundamental shift in the way individuals come to know and understand the world around them. These entities' engagement within human debates has greater impact when they are understood alongside the power of algorithms and the choice-rich networked environment to make people more extreme, less tolerant of ideas, and more likely to believe information that reaffirms existing beliefs.

## PERSONAL SHOPPERS—FOR IDEAS

Grocery stores surround checkout areas with items people are likely to purchase on a whim—candy bars, magazines, breath mints. They aren't on the shopping list, but for a dollar or two, what would it hurt to add them? Stores also place items at the ends of aisles or in special displays to get customers' attention. The system is organized using the assumption people, even when they have shopping lists, will encounter, consider, and, at times, purchase items they did not plan to buy. Personal shoppers, however, don't make spontaneous decisions. They don't consider whether to pick up an extra loaf of bread or gallon of milk. They aren't going to splurge and buy a box of cookies. They follow the list provided. The twenty-first-century, algorithm-based information system is essentially a personal-shopper system. Algorithms limit the likelihood people will encounter ideas or information they did not intend to consider, which enhances convenience.

The "grocery store," in the networked era, is essentially an endless universe of information. It would be impossible for a person to shop

*Drawing a New Map*

through the entire space. Algorithms, like personal shoppers, save time and energy. They help us by shrinking the spectrum of potential ideas to a manageable selection. Something, however, is lost along the way. The customer—us—never actually enters the public space and never encounters a full range of ideas. The algorithms, to the best of their ability, provide us the reality we seek. The chances citizens engage with people or ideas they did not seek to engage with disappear. At this point, the marketplace of ideas transforms into an office cubical—small, enclosed, and made for one person.

The algorithm-based information system redefines the space for human discourse, in many ways returning the concept of publicness and an exchange of ideas to the tail end of the High Middle Ages era, which ended in 1300. Something started to change in thirteenth-century Europe. A merchant class, separate from the nobility, church, and commoners, began to emerge.[32] They traveled from town to town, exchanging their wares. Their popularity gradually led to a shift from self-sufficient, generally household-based, private economies to the necessity of public gathering places where among the trade, people—particularly the burgeoning middle class—began to exchange news that traveled with the merchants from town to town, and to discuss the problems and questions that concerned them in public.[33] These marketplaces became a sort of *commons*. People left their private spaces and physically stepped into a shared, public space. The result, ideally, was informed, public discussions, which marked the first iterations of the concept of public opinion. The idea citizens would leave their private, household-based lives to engage with others and come to conclusions about important issues was novel in the High Middle Ages. We've come to assume its existence in the twenty-first century, as we *imagine* what the space for human discourse looks like.

The shared marketplaces of the High Middle Ages were defined by *public* presences, exchanges of information, and generally limited control by nobility or government officials, characteristics that historically bear the most resemblance to the type of space jurists and lawmakers have imagined and sought to create when rationalizing expansive safeguards for free expression. These spaces were, essentially, marketplaces *with* ideas. They were created for the exchanges of goods, but came to

123

*Chapter Six*

host exchanges of ideas. The ideas included those people did not intend to encounter, did not agree with, and those they found unsettling. It's no coincidence that these marketplace spaces evolved alongside the massive shifts that catalyzed the Enlightenment era. Remember these three foundational elements to the primordial space for human discourse: publicness, information, and, at least to some extent, freedom from government control. What happens to each of these elements when networked technologies exponentially multiply the *range* of potential information and ideas each person must consider, but algorithms work to group people based on information corporations have collected about them?

First, the publicness and information characteristics are immediately transformed. We go from shoppers in the market to solitary actors selecting items. Ideas become what we *want* to encounter using our networked devices. This is similar to searching for specific items while shopping online and placing them in a virtual cart for our personal-shopper order. Consider what this shift does to the imagined, Enlightenment-based marketplace of ideas examined in Part I. In the algorithm-infused, personal-shopper scenario, no battle between truth and falsity occurs. The algorithm generally serves up the "truths" users were looking for. If people seek one idea, the algorithm, like a personal shopper, is happy to deliver it. Presence in a public space also traditionally requires certain behaviors. People are, for the most part, expected to treat others with respect. They usually feel obligated to listen politely, even when they disagree with a person's thinking. People are also likely to encounter ideas they did not expect to engage with, just as a shopper spies something that's not on their list as they walk through an aisle at the grocery store. Contrast these expectations with algorithmically determined private spaces. Private spaces demand less decorum. People do not have to sit through ideas they do not wish to encounter, or listen politely. A private-based form of human discourse limits the range of ideas people encounter and supersedes the need to engage with and tolerate opposing views. We also get out of the practice of exercising basic courtesies to others.

Second, the reasoning behind *who* controls the space for human discourse and *how* it is regulated weakens in a private-based, personal-shopper-oriented marketplace. The Enlightenment-based marketplace of ideas rationalizes expansive free-expression safeguards so government

124

*Drawing a New Map*

has little power to control the exchange of ideas and the ultimate supremacy of truth over falsity in an open exchange of ideas. If no such exchange is occurring, should the rationales for free expression emphasize protecting the flow of information, rather than the competition between truth and falsity? Protecting the flow of information could strengthen the *protected* marketplace approach, discussed in chapter 5, and allow some regulations on AI entities that distort the flow of information in detrimental ways. Furthermore, corporations, which control virtual spaces, have become far more influential in both authoring the algorithms that in many ways preempt the exchange of ideas, and setting community guidelines that dictate the ideas and people who can engage in the space. In this regard, the space for human discourse is being transformed regarding *who* controls the space and *how* we rationalize expansive free-expression safeguards.

## FAKE AND FAKING IT

Deepfakes are not helping these problems. Human and bot-based false information travels six times faster than truth in virtual spaces. That's before we account for deepfakes.[34] Choice-rich, fragmented, idea-based online communities are primed to accept information that reinforces their beliefs, even if the content's sourcing and logic are obviously flawed. People *want* to believe their ideas are winning more than they want to know what is true. When we add increasingly believable fake audio and video clips, truth doesn't stand a chance. Audio and video tend to have an extra level of credibility because they have historically allowed people to hear and see what is happening with their own senses. Now, with the help of machine-learning tools, even seemingly authentic clips of what we hear and see can be false.

Machine learning helps computers build believable, deceptive clips using adversarial networks. This means one computer constructs a deepfake and a second computer evaluates it, indicates problems, and returns it to the creating computer for revision. This cycle works because the programs are capable of learning and improving the quality based on how they analyze audio or images they have been provided. The results are higher-quality, more realistic fake clips that reach audiences that

*Chapter Six*

*want* to believe in the messages. A "cheapfake" clip of US Speaker of the House Nancy Pelosi that made her sound as if her speech was slurred, which was titled "Drunk Pelosi," circulated on social media in spring 2019.[35] The clip was deemed a "cheapfake" because it was manipulated only slightly to make the audio sound slurred. The fake received more than a million views on Facebook and was shared on the forum by former New York mayor Rudy Giuliani. Then-president Donald Trump retweeted the clip, writing "Pelosi stammers through news conference" in all caps.[36]

A year later, a deepfake showed President Joe Biden sleeping, snoring loudly, on live television while an anchor tried to rouse him for an interview. The clip was made using video footage from singer Harry Belafonte, who did fall asleep during an interview, and audio and video from when Hillary Clinton endorsed Biden during the presidential election.[37] The clip was shared tens of thousands of times. We will never know how many people believed the Pelosi and Biden clips were real and developed conclusions based on the false information, but researchers have found people are incapable of identifying a deepfake from an authentic video.[38] One study found people had a lower than 50 percent chance of accurately identifying a video as authentic or fake. Even worse, respondents made their often-incorrect choices with a high degree of confidence. They were confidently wrong, overestimating their ability to discern between real and fake. Finally, deepfakes do more than create believable, false information that fragmented online audiences are ready to believe. They also undermine truth altogether by creating what legal scholars Bobby Chesney and Danielle Citron called the "liar's dividend."[39] In other words, people caught on audio or video doing something wrong can claim authentic clips are false. They can say the evidence is a deepfake. The authors explained, "Liars aiming to dodge responsibility for their real words and actions will become more credible as the public becomes more educated about the threats posed by deepfakes."[40]

The Enlightenment assumptions that truth will generally vanquish falsity in a free exchange of ideas and people are rational and capable of discerning truth crumble in the face of this substantially changed information environment. Keep in mind, these are the assumptions at the foundation of the marketplace of ideas. When confronted with the

126

*Drawing a New Map*

reality that algorithmically formed communities, which are further limited by human preferences toward information that reinforces preexisting beliefs, alongside the increasing power of bots and deepfakes to distort the flow of information, the assumptions justices constructed for expansive free expression and a space for human discourse fail. And they do so before we even get to the metaverse.

The metaverse is what happens when people stop visiting social media sites, online communities, and apps and start *living* in a virtual space.[41] Using virtual reality (VR) equipment, the metaverse would allow Kondo to forgo the Gatebox and plush toys and actually spend time with Miku in a virtual world of their choice. For others, the metaverse could include attending concerts without ever leaving their homes. Epic Games' *Fortnite* has already experimented with this, tying in a theme from the game: Ariana Grande headlined the Rift Tour, performing virtually for millions of players who attended, each person represented by their virtual avatar, which are called skins.[42] No VR equipment was required. Researchers are predicting schools could hold classes in the metaverse, with students never leaving their homes.[43] Employees could meet to do work in the space. The global pandemic moved the workplace closer to this reality, with virtual meetings becoming the norm for many.[44] What does the space for human discourse look like when people *live* in a virtual realm?

At first glance, the metaverse appears to recreate the publicness and exchange of ideas that characterized the developments in public opinion during the High Middle Ages. In the metaverse, people can engage in a type of public forum, albeit virtually, with others. The idea doesn't work, however. Instead, the metaverse represents the apex of each area discussed in this chapter. The interaction between human and AI entities becomes more seamless as non-human entities gain virtual physical features, enhancing the likelihood people project human emotions, such as love, trust, and empathy, on the AI entities. A bot programmed to communicate ideas in support of a political idea such as gun control on Twitter or Instagram has the power to reach communities with ideas. The metaverse, however, allows that same bot to take human form. The shift to the metaverse enhances the power AI entities have in the space for discourse, as they can play upon social and cultural norms to take

*Chapter Six*

the most convincing form possible when trying to inform or convince someone. Suddenly, saying "no" to the bot means rejecting a human-like form that looks like a friend or trustworthy person, is using a human-sounding voice, and is mimicking human emotions. The metaverse essentially gives AI entities even more power to distort discourse in the space for human discourse.

The power of algorithms to determine what people encounter also increases exponentially in the metaverse as corporations have even more data to use when making decisions for each user. Those who provide the spaces can track even more sensory data, alongside traditionally mined information, in the metaverse and use that data to create a world fundamentally different in appearance to that their neighbor experiences.[45] If two people are sitting on the same couch, using VR equipment to enter the metaverse, one could see messages supporting stricter gun laws and representations of politicians, as bots or recordings, that would advocate for limits, while the other sees arguments for why gun ownership should be protected and expanded. In other words, the metaverse, as a result of algorithmic and human choices, will likely exacerbate the abandonment of any semblance of a marketplace where people gather, encounter ideas and people they did not seek out, and make rational decisions about the world around them.

What about deepfakes? Manipulating reality becomes far easier when people are already in a virtual environment. The line between real and unreal is grayer. The line becomes even more indiscernible when the technology used to create believable deepfakes overlaps with the tools needed to create an immersive virtual-life experience. The disappearing line between truth, belief, and fiction fades even more in the metaverse as people live in spaces that are created to remove the inconvenient aspects of life and replace them with attractive, engaging, and profitable experiences. Essentially, we're not talking about *a* metaverse. We're talking about a multiverse of metaverses, countless versions of reality. The outcome is similar to the countless marketplaces of ideas, each customized for small groups or individuals. Truth and human rationality, the foundational landmarks in the Enlightenment-based marketplace-of-ideas version of the space for human discourse, transform into matters that are personal, rather than shared.

128

*Drawing a New Map*

## OTHERING

These changes have consequences. Increasingly, people do not share common experiences or information. The "general-interest intermediaries," as Sunstein labeled newspapers and other information sources oriented toward broad audiences, have diminished in their role as sources for shared facts that individuals can use to inform discourse in the marketplace of ideas.[46] In the place of general-interest intermediaries, with help from algorithms, bots, deepfakes, and the metaverse, people are bombarded by information that affirms their beliefs—and suspicions. Their ideas are not challenged. They get out of the practice of encountering ideas they do not plan to hear or do not agree with. The racist's online world tells them, every time they open social media, they were right all along about other races. The member of the baby-boomer generation finds in their information sources everything is as they suspected—all the generations that followed theirs are lazy and good for nothing. The Republican finds the liberals are lying, cheating, and ruining everything. The devout member of one faith finds the other faiths are blasphemous. Through the drumbeat of countless online interactions with like-minded people and ideas, people become, by degrees, a little more extreme each day. All the while, the imagined space, the marketplace of ideas, has become like many shopping malls. It sits relatively empty. Few go there anymore. Why go there when the ideas and truths are delivered to us?

The shift in the networked, AI era from shared spaces and ideas to algorithmically determined and choice-based communities has resulted in unexpected consequences. Networked communication is a fundamentally globalizing technological advance. No tool has ever facilitated instant, borderless, and global discourse more effectively than networked communication. Yet, at the same time, the *ability* to encounter and examine ideas from people and cultures around the world has not, for many, translated into an interest or culture of doing so. Quite the opposite. Faced with the massive, global power of the networked world, many have retreated to the identity-affirming safeties of more localized communities.[47] Castells explained, when faced with the overwhelming immensity of the networked world, people shrink "the size of human experience to a dimension that can be managed and defended . . . in the

*Chapter Six*

whirlwind of a destructured world."[48] In other words, people's response has generally been to seek control by limiting the range of ideas and returning to what is stable and known.

The effort to safeguard identities, however, has led to unhealthy side effects. Faced with fear and uncertainty brought on by the globalization of communication and the increasing power of AI-influenced technologies, people have constructed defensive identities. These identities are built using traditional materials, such as faith, nationality, and ethnic foundations, but are reimagined and repurposed as bulwarks against perceived threats. The Tea Party political movement that became popular among many conservatives beginning in 2009, for example, took its name from the 1773 Boston Tea Party, but ultimately distorted and stretched the meanings and events from the heart of the original. In instances such as this, identities and the building blocks used to construct them become distorted. National history narratives become more intense and more likely to leave out important details. Religious faiths become stricter and more unforgiving.[49]

These identities become shields and swords to fight off perceived threats. Add the non-human influences of bots and deceitful deepfakes which prey on these fears and stoke the fires of defensive identities, and the power of algorithms and self-selection to wall people off from fact-based reports and opposing ideas, and a wave of othering sweeps through society. People not only fail to encounter opposing ideas; they find these ideas, and those who believe in them, threatening. Those who we once encountered in the public marketplace of ideas are now seen as threats. They are *others*.

Defensive identities are externally focused, but they are the results of internal processes. Internally, in the networked, AI era, people act out their defensive identities via performances for virtual audiences. These are carefully curated identities oriented toward two goals. First, they influence how people interact with those within their algorithmically and intentionally chosen communities. Interactions generally include reaffirmation of the elements of the group's defensive identity.[50] People seek to perform a version of the identity that is acceptable to the community. As Turkle explained, when people write in a journal or diary, they write for themselves. When they publish on social media,

130

*Drawing a New Map*

they "go into performance mode."[51] Second, performative identities seek to garner affirmation and algorithmic success as each share, like, new friend, or other interaction increases the likelihood that their messages will reach larger audiences. Both considerations encourage extreme behavior, which is more likely to be rewarded by the community and the social media companies' algorithms, which will give heavy-engagement messages more exposure.[52]

Meta is well aware Facebook's algorithm encourages extremist groups. Company documents leaked in 2021 concluded extremism and false information succeed in Meta's online spaces because the algorithms encourage them.[53] The internal report found "We also have compelling evidence our core product mechanics, such as virality, recommendations, and optimizing for engagement, are a significant part of why these types of speech flourish on our platforms."[54] Facebook chose not to make substantive changes that would discourage extremism. Similarly, YouTube's algorithm, by degrees, encourages people toward progressively extreme content, leading viewers down rabbit holes one video suggestion at a time.[55] Thus, a spiral ensues as algorithms tug people toward more extreme content and communities as people seek to craft performances that reinforce the perceived beliefs, or truths, within the groups to which they belong. As people perform to fit into groups and to satisfy algorithms, their content becomes more extreme. One behavior feeds into the other, as performing for the group reinforces belongingness, which creates more engagement within the algorithm. Of course, publishing messages that go against the group's accepted defensive identity beliefs can also trigger massive engagement, but the author can damage their place in the community.

These performances need not be purely online. People increasingly use in-person experiences, such as photos, videos, and live streams, as ways to reaffirm online credentials with defensive-identity-based communities and to gain algorithmic success in virtual spaces. A selfie at a Trump rally or with Vice President Kamala Harris, for example, can be a powerful way to perform an identity for an online community. The January 6, 2021, riot in Washington, DC, might be the most potent example. Extremist groups, such as the Proud Boys, organized the riot on social media.[56] Many rioters documented every step as they fought

131

*Chapter Six*

their way into the US Capitol.[57] Rioters wore costumes and took selfies in front of statutes and in congressional offices, establishing their presence to such an extent that it seemed documenting *being there* on social media was the end goal for many who participated. Ultimately, the effort to gain acceptance by repeating the group's accepted ideas and receive social-media-platform-based affirmation encourages performance identities toward more extreme content. Nothing in the system draws people toward those in other ideological groups for discourse and a test of truth against falsity in the marketplace of ideas. Quite the opposite. The prevailing currents draw people away from a generalized meeting place for citizens to encounter and discuss ideas with others.

## MAPS AS LENSES

Justices, along with others, used the Enlightenment-based marketplace of ideas to map the space for human discourse. They ascribed contours and features, mile-markers and landmarks, based on an open, relatively expansive space where individuals could employ their rationality and independence in coming to conclusions regarding truth and falsity. More than anything, the map was written with a very particular version of truth as its compass. The cartography assumed truth was generally the same for all and that it would vanquish falsity in a free exchange of ideas. The map was also written with a very specific, imagined space in mind. Justices drew and rationalized a guide for the space that assumed a pastoral, European market center that is generally equal and open to all and where information and ideas could be freely exchanged. This space has never existed, though aspects of it have. At first glance, the networked, AI era has ushered in something quite close to the map justices constructed. After all, networked devices allow nearly anyone to take part in democratic discourse. Doesn't the internet essentially create the very first, truly open marketplace of ideas? A closer look, as this chapter has provided, indicates the internet did the opposite. AI communicators, algorithms, deepfakes, and the metaverse, have emptied the shared marketplace of ideas. In doing so, they have fundamentally remapped the space for human discourse.

132

*Drawing a New Map*

They have remade *how* people conclude what is true, undermining the map's compass. They have also introduced new features and contours, such as an entirely new form of communicator, AI entities, and a different type of organizing system, algorithms. The old maps no longer explain and guide us regarding the space. As we seek to construct a new rationale for protecting a space for human discourse, this chapter concludes by identifying three potential ways we can picture the space for human discourse in the networked, AI era. Each attempts to describe the complex, imagined, and crucial space *as it exists*, before the remainder of the book goes to work providing different lenses through which a new map could be understood, ultimately outlining a new map in the final chapter.

## *A Multiverse of Marketplaces*

We could understand these changes as creating a multiverse of marketplaces. Such a map would expand from the staid, two-dimensional, twentieth-century map, to a complex, multidimensional rendering that accounts for the disintegration of the shared marketplace. In other words, to understand the shape of the space for discourse, we can't use a two-dimensional map. The multiverse map replaces the conceptualization of a single marketplace with countless smaller, interconnected, interest-based spaces for discourse. This version accounts for the algorithmic predetermination and personal choices that lead to intentional communities that generally never meet to test their truths in a free exchange of ideas. The multiverse approach does not require public presence or general-interest intermediaries, though it is certainly hurt by the absence of both. The countless interest-based communities that make up the multiverse are characterized by concepts discussed in this chapter. They limit the spectrum of potential ideas to those accepted within the community. Participants generally perform defensive identities, which, with the help of algorithms, tend to pull people toward more extreme perspectives and away from general-interest information sources. Truth is, for the most part, predetermined by the accepted beliefs within the community. These remain limitations, as do the power of AI entities and false information to distort the discourse and reality formation within

*Chapter Six*

the smaller marketplaces. The goal here is to accurately model the space, however, not to rewrite it, which is the goal for the rest of the book.

How would human discourse function in this rendering? The communities within the multiverse of marketplaces, rather than individuals in a marketplace, identify what is true. When an issue is crucial enough that it pervades through a multitude of otherwise divided communities, one idea or conclusion regarding the issue can come to dominate enough mini-marketplaces that these communities can form coalitions. Thus, truth is the result of a critical mass of small multiverses coming to a shared conclusion that, with the weight that it brings, can exert influential pressure on democratic discourse that is similar to the power a shared discovery of truth would have in vanquishing falsity in the Enlightenment-based marketplace of ideas. Problematically, democracy, in this model, faces all the problems the traditional marketplace model faces. The multiverse approach, however, is a more accurate rendering of what the space for discourse looks like in the networked, AI era.

### *Nodes and Holes*

Network analysis research provides another multidimensional way to map the twenty-first-century space for discourse. The field understands a "node" as a social actor within a communication network.[58] A "structural hole" is a connection between two actors within a network.[59] Importantly, not all nodes are equal. Similarly, not all holes have the same strength. When we consider a space for discourse in the networked, AI era, we can imagine the marketplace of ideas as a communication network, rather than a shared space for human discourse. Once again, we discard the pastoral, cobblestoned streets justices have envisioned in favor of a conceptualization of the space that accounts for a vast, decentralized network that is both fragmented and interconnected. This approach's strength is its ability to account for the varying strengths of actors and connections within the network. Thus, within virtual spaces, a certain actor, such as a politician or athlete, represents a powerful node that, in essence, operates like a marketplace. When they communicate an idea, the discourse that ensues, which is based in their social

*Drawing a New Map*

media account or other forum, transforms the space into a forum for the exchange of ideas.

Truth and falsity *can* compete in such a space, though the forces discussed earlier in this chapter, such as algorithms, deepfakes, and bots can lead to idea-based, rather than general-interest forums. Elon Musk's Twitter account, which has about 100 million followers, is a good example. Within a vast, interconnected communication network, his account, with his many unpopular statements, transforms into a forum for discourse. A simple tweet about who should be mayor of Los Angeles or environmental policy can garner tens of thousands of replies. And those replies receive replies. Ultimately, people *meet* in the space, or node, for discourse. Ideas are exchanged.

Meeting in an individual or organization's virtual space, whether it's a social media account, message board, website, or other forum, requires a connection. That's where the structural holes come in. The network analysis-influenced map of the space accounts for how close actors are to each other. Generally, encountering a message that leads a node to engage in a forum that ensues in another node, such as Musk's, requires a connection. The nature of these connections varies, depending on how much social capital is shared between two nodes. A person with close ties to a forum-creating node will see all the ideas conveyed by the communicator and be more likely to respond candidly. A person who is distant and has weaker ties, might still see the ideas, if they are shared by a node they are connected with. A large, concentrated node, such as Musk's, like a massive planet, has the gravity to draw many toward it. Less powerful nodes, those with few connections, are less likely to become forums for discourse. Of course, AI entities don't have to follow these rules. They don't evaluate an idea from another node and consider whether to join the discourse. They can flow throughout the entire communication network, joining conversations based on key words, hash tags, certain accounts, or other triggers.

The network-analysis-influenced node-and-hole rendering provides another lens through which the twenty-first-century space for discourse can be imagined. Importantly, the space still suffers from the changed nature of communication in online spaces, which includes less empathy, more extreme statements, and the presence of AI entities. These spaces

135

## Chapter Six

are hardly equivalents to justices' imaginations of the marketplace of ideas, where all speakers meet in a public space, on relatively equal terms, to rationally consider ideas, and discern truth from falsity. Of course, that space has never existed to begin with. The virtual spaces in the nodes and structural holes map are managed by corporate interests, rather than being understood as public forums, which are generally protected from government control and are cared for as a public good. Algorithms sort and encourage nodes toward some and away from others, still causing fragmentation problems. Communication scholar Itai Himelboim described "polarized clusters" as large, dense groups formed around certain nodes. Polarized clusters generally remain disconnected from each other; thus, it remains common that like-minded individuals will not connect with dense, active clusters because algorithms, and people's ideological currents, draw them away from each other.[60]

Bots still distort discourse and falsity continues to be readily accepted in idea-based communities. These shifts in communication must be accounted for in any rendering of the twenty-first-century space for discourse, and they are certainly influential in the network analysis model.

### The Personal Marketplace

The final imagination of what the space for discourse looks like in the twenty-first century envisions the place shrinking from a shared, public space, as justices envisioned when they constructed the Enlightenment-based marketplace of ideas, to a personal space. A marketplace of one. This rendering concludes no space for human discourse exists. Certainly, individuals engage with others and spaces for communication still exist. Spaces for democratic discourse, however, which are characterized by general-interest information sources, unplanned encounters with others and ideas, and little government or corporate control regarding free expression, have, to whatever extent they once existed, disappeared. Emerging technologies, outlined in this chapter, certainly point in this direction. Algorithms, and personal choices, limit the likelihood people will engage with ideas that diverge from their own. People, AI entities, and deepfakes spread false and misleading information that is readily accepted by communities that are primed to believe their messages. The

136

*Drawing a New Map*

metaverse promises more seamless interactions with AI entities as well as the ability to customize a livable virtual world. Furthermore, online communication encourages weaker relationships with others, less empathy, and more extreme messages, all of which work against shared spaces. All of these concerns detract from a shared space.

Ultimately, the shared spaces came out of necessity, not because they were designated as community-building places for democratic discourse. Public squares were ideal for merchants to sell their wares. These spaces became marketplaces *with* ideas. The marketplace for goods and services came about because a common space was needed. The marketplace of ideas, at least as justices imagined it, came about because people congregated in those spaces. The need for a common space to buy and sell goods, alongside shared spaces for discourse, has in many ways been replaced with an individual-based system, where people never engage with others when making purchases. They go online, tell a website or app what they want, and it appears soon after. Something similar happens with ideas in the networked, AI era. People go online and find the ideas they expected to encounter. Ideas are delivered.

This is a chapter of problems. New technologies have remade the space for discourse. In doing so, they have also remapped how people come to understand the world around them. In a democracy constructed upon the assumptions that people are rational and capable of making sense of the world around them and that truth will vanquish falsity in an open exchange of ideas, remaking how citizens construct reality is no small matter. This chapter ended with three different ways based on technological and societal changes that we can map or imagine the space for discourse as it operates now. With these renderings in mind, the rest of the book considers possible theoretical approaches that could reconstruct the space in a way that acknowledges the changes, but maintains a rationale for expansive free expression and a space for human discourse, which is crucial for democracy.

# SEVEN

## The Balancer

We don't talk much about Justice Felix Frankfurter's free-expression legacy. Perhaps for good reason. His legal opinions were dense, long-winded, and heavily nuanced. His time on the Court, including the opinions he wrote that outlined how he imagined the space for human discourse, was overshadowed by the First Amendment-shaping ideas of his nemeses, Justices Hugo Black and William O. Douglas. Frankfurter referred to the two justices, and those who consistently voted with them, as "the Axis." It was not a compliment.

Much of history's forgetfulness of Frankfurter's years on the Court is well-earned. One historian called Frankfurter "perhaps the greatest disappointment in the high court."[1] He was to lead the Court. Instead, he bickered with Black and Douglas for decades, often writing legal opinions that attacked them and their ideas rather than interpreting the Constitution. His time on the Court wasn't entirely forgettable, however, especially when it comes to our questions about the future of the space for democratic discourse in the networked, AI eras. The lengthy legal opinions from the well-connected, influential thinker provide a needed alternative lens regarding how the space for human discourse could be constructed and maintained. Within Frankfurter's meticulous efforts to *balance* free expression safeguards with protecting the space

138

## The Balancer

and those who seek to operate in it, we get a glimpse of another way to understand the imaged space during a time of massive change in communication and society. Much of that glimpse was galvanized in a more than two-decade struggle between Frankfurter, Black, and Douglas, on the Court.

Frankfurter's story is characterized by missed opportunities. Joining the Court in 1939, he was in the perfect position to complete the work his mentors Justices Oliver W. Holmes and Louis Brandeis started in the early twentieth century regarding *how* we rationalize free expression and imagine a space for human discourse. Frankfurter was a respected thinker before joining the Court, having spent decades teaching at Harvard Law School and advocating for civil liberties. After his nomination to the Supreme Court, a profile in *New York Times Magazine* called him one of "the keenest legal minds in the country."[2] He helped found the ACLU in 1920 and worked as a legal adviser to the National Association for the Advancement of Colored People (NAACP). In 1927, he risked his name and reputation to stand up for Italian immigrants Nicola Sacco and Bartolomeo Vanzetti, who were convicted, under questionable circumstances, for murder.[3] He was a trusted adviser to Franklin Roosevelt, providing insights into New Deal policies and recommending nominees to the Supreme Court.

By 1939, when Roosevelt considered who should replace Justice Benjamin Cardozo on the Court, Frankfurter was at the top of his list. Some feared, given what was happening in Europe, appointing a Jew would stoke antisemitism in the United States.[4] Others wanted a justice from a Western state. Secretary of Commerce Harry Hopkins, Secretary of the Interior Harold Ickes, and Solicitor General Robert Jackson advised Roosevelt to select Frankfurter. Ickes told the president "If you appoint Felix, his ability and learning are such that he will dominate the Supreme Court for fifteen or twenty years to come."[5] Jackson, who would soon join the Court and be entangled in Frankfurter's feud with Black and Douglas, told Roosevelt Frankfurter could stand against Chief Justice Charles Evans Hughes's forceful personality.[6] Roosevelt took their advice, appointing Frankfurter to the seat once held by his mentor, Holmes. Frankfurter, along with many others, believed his time to lead the New Deal, Roosevelt Court had come.

139

*Chapter Seven*

They were wrong. A hardscrabble lawyer from Alabama and a former waiter, janitor, and cherry picker didn't get the memo. Black, a former Senate leader who Frankfurter advised Roosevelt against nominating for the Court in 1937, and Douglas, who joined the Court just months after him, outshined Frankfurter during their decades together as justices. Black and Douglas, as discussed in chapter 4, took the early sketches and drawings regarding a space for human discourse and bases for expansive free-expression rationales left by Holmes and Brandeis and developed them into a relatively complete set of rationales for free expression, ultimately creating an Enlightenment-founded marketplace of ideas. Frankfurter was relegated to an antagonist's role in a show in which he believed he was cast as the main character. Fittingly, in a book about great Supreme Court justices, legal scholar Jeffrey Rosen devoted a chapter to the differing styles of Black and Douglas. Frankfurter receives only passing attention. Rosen noted, "Black and Douglas . . . drove Felix Frankfurter to distraction."[7] Importantly, he continued, "A former Harvard Law School professor and celebrated civil libertarian, Frankfurter disappointed his liberal supporters on the Court by embracing a strenuous vision of judicial restraint."[8]

As a legal scholar and devoted follower of Holmes and Brandeis, Frankfurter saw the Court and its role, as well as the Constitution, differently than Black and Douglas. Frankfurter set out to lead the Court by holding its course. Black and Douglas, as outsiders, sought to use the Court to shape the nation. Frankfurter saw the Court as a static institution. Black and Douglas saw it as a tool. On a Court that included seven New Deal, Roosevelt appointees, their progressive understandings and efforts to build American civil liberties were celebrated and cemented into the foundations of free expression and the space for human discourse. Frankfurter's message of judicial restraint and the measured, careful role of the Court found little support. Frankfurter's ideas were largely forgotten.

Crucially, for us, the feud between Frankfurter, Black, and Douglas carried into the Court's decisions, as Frankfurter constructed numerous concurring and dissenting opinions that sought to counter Black and Douglas's conclusions. Historian Joseph Lash explained, "The emotional intensity with which Frankfurter invests these episodes gives . . . the

140

# The Balancer

sense that the great marble blocks of the Court must have shaken with the vigor of the battle."[9] Black biographer Roger Newman concluded, "If eventually in many, and among the most important, ways the Court was Black's lengthened shadow, his conflicts with Frankfurter played a significant part."[10] The justices pushed each other to stake clear arguments during a period in which the Court faced difficult free-expression questions. Frankfurter's ideas faded over time as Black's and Douglas's became building blocks for the marketplace-of-ideas approach. This chapter, as part of our search for how to rationalize free expression and reconstruct the space for human discourse in the networked, AI era, identifies potential building blocks within Frankfurter's understandings.

This chapter contends Frankfurter's ideas provide a valuable lens through which to understand the future of the space. Frankfurter imagined a dynamic space for human discourse that could not be constructed using an unwavering, one-size-fits-all approach, such as the Enlightenment-founded marketplace of ideas. He expected to see a public-good value and social order in free expression. He further understood the space as requiring protection from distortion. Frankfurter's alternative imagining of the space provides a different lens through which to view and conceptualize how democratic discourse *can* function and how we can revise our understandings of the space in the networked, AI era. Frankfurter's understandings might not provide *the* answer to our question, but they provide crucial materials—ideas—that can be considered for the task.

## HALF BROTHER, HALF SON

Holmes is not known for his warmth or empathy (see chapter 3). In describing his judicial philosophy, he once explained, "if my fellow citizens want to go to Hell I will help them. It's my job."[11] He chose not to have children. He told Judge Learned Hand "This is not the kind of world I want to bring anyone else into."[12] Frankfurter was an exception. Holmes explained, in a letter to a friend, that the Austrian-born lawyer "walked deep into my heart."[13] He told US diplomat Lewis Einstein "I am very fond of him."[14] Holmes had a soft spot in his war-hardened heart for Frankfurter, providing the young lawyer access to one of the great jurists in history's legal thinking and reasoning.

*Chapter Seven*

Holmes advised Frankfurter not to take a teaching position at Harvard Law School, while Brandeis, his other mentor, encouraged him to accept the job. Brandeis, who shared a Jewish faith with Frankfurter, referred to his mentee as "half brother, half son."[15] The pair exchanged nearly 700 letters over three decades. They met in 1905, when Brandeis, a reform-minded lawyer based in Boston, came to speak to the Harvard Ethical Society. Brandeis admonished the law students in attendance, to care for everyday people and avoid unethical corporations. Frankfurter took his advice, choosing to work for the US Attorney for the Southern District of New York when he graduated. The position paid less than a private firm but offered Frankfurter a chance to make a difference in people's lives. He and Brandeis started corresponding in 1910, when Brandeis was becoming a nationally known reformer. They saw each other often when Frankfurter worked for the War Department during World War I. Unlike with Holmes, Brandeis and Frankfurter shared similar interests and personalities. Historians Melvin Urofsky and David Levy emphasized they "possessed a set of progressive social, political, economic, and judicial articles of faith very nearly identical to his counterpart."[16]

Holmes's and Brandeis's mentorship of Frankfurter is worth a pause. Two of the greatest legal minds in the nation's history personally invested in him. Holmes, for example, watched over Frankfurter's career, particularly in 1919 when his mentee faced an effort to push him out of Harvard Law School. Despite Frankfurter writing to assure his mentor "There is absolutely no occasion for concern,"[17] Holmes was not satisfied. He wrote to British economist Harold Laski, who was a dear friend to both, that he had asked Brandeis for advice about Frankfurter's situation. Holmes wrote that he was considering writing a letter to the president of Harvard to support Frankfurter.[18] He explained Harvard Law School, which he attended, "would lose its soul" if it lost Frankfurter. When the danger passed, he wrote a short letter to Frankfurter, thanking him for his friendship. He explained, "You have brought a great deal of comfort and companionship to the natural loneliness of old age and I ask nothing better than that it may continue while I last."[19] Frankfurter made a special trip to the Holmes house to announce his engagement to Marion Denman in 1919. Holmes's wife, Fannie, gave Frankfurter a

142

# The Balancer

precious stone as a gift for his fiancé. Holmes wasn't the only influential person in Frankfurter's life. His wedding was officiated by future justice Benjamin Cardozo in influential federal judge Learned Hand's New York office.

Holmes's philosophy of general judicial restraint, which meant whenever possible the Court should uphold the laws and decisions of elected officials, and Brandeis's concerns for people and the power of elites—what he called "the curse of bigness"—influenced Frankfurter's imagination of the space for human discourse. As Black and Douglas cited Holmes's and Brandeis's reasoning to rationalize what became an Enlightenment-based marketplace of ideas, Frankfurter contended his mentors' ideas were being misused and offered alternative constructions of the space. One other influence, however, is crucial. Frankfurter was close friends with Roosevelt and at the center of the New Deal and the president's conflict with the Court that followed. Roosevelt and Frankfurter met in 1906, while both were young lawyers in New York. Roosevelt was assistant secretary of the Navy during World War I, which meant they worked together often on War Department affairs. Years later, Frankfurter helped Roosevelt in his bid to become governor of New York. By 1932, he was working on Roosevelt's presidential campaign—always remaining close to Roosevelt, but never joining his administration. While Frankfurter remained at Harvard, the so-called Hot Dogs, the nickname people in Washington gave to the young lawyers he placed in the Roosevelt administration, helped write the New Deal.[20]

Frankfurter publicly supported the New Deal and suggested the Supreme Court find it constitutional. The Court, including his mentor Brandeis, and Cardozo, who officiated his wedding, disagreed. As Supreme Court historian Robert McCloskey concluded, "The Court tore great holes in the New Deal program of recovery legislation."[21] The Court started by unanimously striking down the National Industrial Recovery Act in 1935. The decision, and similar rulings that struck down New Deal legislation, forced Frankfurter to consider two competing conceptualizations of the Court's power. As a Supreme Court historian, he found the decisions were in line with the Court's role in the checks-and-balances-system within the government. He understood New Deal laws ceded broad powers from the legislative branch to the executive.

143

FIGURE 2 Frankfurter joined the Harvard Law School faculty in 1906.
Source: Library of Congress

*The Balancer*

At the same time, he remembered his mentor Holmes's reasoning that the "felt necessities of time" often influence judicial decision-making.[22] He understood the New Deal as something that was needed to help the nation out of the Great Depression. Years later, conflicting understandings such as these plagued Frankfurter's time on the Court, contributing to his complex and unclear legacy. Should justices be strict or pragmatic in their interpretations? In the moment, still four years before he would join the Court and despite his close relationship with Brandeis, Frankfurter sided with Roosevelt. His decision during the clash between the judicial and executive branches drove a wedge between him and his mentor.[23] Their relationship was never the same. Frankfurter did not go so far as publicly supporting Roosevelt's court-packing plan, which emerged after the Court struck down large parts of the New Deal, but advised the president that an information campaign, along with continued pressure from the White House, would pressure the Court into changing its mind. He might have been right. Roosevelt followed Frankfurter's advice and also went forward with his court-packing plan in 1937. In 1938, in a case that is referred to as the "switch in time that saved nine," the Court changed the way it interpreted the constitutionality of New Deal provisions, finding them constitutional.[24]

The pragmatic Holmes. The reform-minded Brandeis. The charismatic Roosevelt, who demanded loyalty. The decades of teaching and studying law and the history of the Court. All of these influences bore upon Frankfurter's complex, dynamic construction of free expression and a space for human discourse. These influences formed a unique lens, one that departs greatly from the dominant rationales and imaginings for a space for human discourse in the twenty-first century. Of course, his foes, Black and Douglas contributed to his ideas as well.

## DEFENSIVE POSITIONS

Roosevelt waited more than four years before he had a chance to nominate a justice for the Supreme Court. After Roosevelt flirted with packing the Court with justices who would uphold New Deal legislation in early 1937, conservative Justice Willis Van Devanter announced his retirement, effective in June. Roosevelt finally had a chance to bring a

145

*Chapter Seven*

New Deal-supporting justice on to the Court. He struggled to pick the right person to nominate. He asked longtime adviser Frankfurter whom he should select. Frankfurter suggested Solicitor General Stanley Reed. Roosevelt asked Frankfurter about Democratic Senator Black. Frankfurter advised against nominating Black. He explained, Black would "have to muster an immense amount of rather technical jurisdictional learning."[25] In other words, Frankfurter did not believe Black was qualified or ready to join the Court. Roosevelt nominated Black anyway. The Alabama senator joined the Court in August 1937. Justice Harlan Stone, who had been on the Court since 1925 and later became chief justice, immediately saw Black was capable, but had concerns about Black's grasp of technical concepts and the Court's traditions. In this sense, Frankfurter was correct, Black was not ready to join the Court. Frankfurter and Stone were concerned Black wasn't staying within the traditional boundaries of the Court. Stone asked Frankfurter to tutor him.

The tutoring must have been amicable. Less than two years later, Roosevelt nominated Frankfurter to take Cardozo's seat on the Court. Black celebrated the nomination, telling Laski "I am looking forward to the pleasure of many years of service with him."[26] Roosevelt nominated Douglas to join the Court a few months later, after Brandeis retired. Like Black, Douglas shared a friendship with Frankfurter *before* they were on the Court together. In early 1933, Douglas wrote in a letter to Frankfurter "I have missed you more than I can say."[27] In April 1937, Douglas professed, "My affection for you is so abiding . . . I will nevertheless arrange to come up there this month."[28] These friendships soured quickly. Historian Melvin Urofsky dedicated an entire section in his collection of Douglas's letters, titled "Felix," to the justices' complex relationship. By 1954, Douglas wrote to Frankfurter, "We all know what a great burden your long discourses are. . . . I do register a protest at your degradation of the Conference and its deliberations."[29] Frankfurter's diaries include extensive passages about his distaste for Black's power over the Court and Douglas's political ambitions. Frankfurter wrote to Hand, "Hugo is self-righteous, self-deluded part fanatic, part demagogue, who really disbelieves in law."[30] In the same letter, he called Douglas, one of "the most completely evil men I have ever met." Hard-working, methodical Black and brilliant-but-distracted Douglas became unlikely friends, forming

146

*The Balancer*

the basis of what Frankfurter called "the Axis." The Axis, a set of three to five justices, voted as a bloc, thwarting Frankfurter's efforts to lead the Court. While the bloc changed from term to term, Black and Douglas were always at its heart.

The ideological and personal differences between Frankfurter and fellow Roosevelt appointees Black and Douglas shaped the nature of how the space for human discourse is imagined and protected, via expansive free-expression rationales. The struggle between these personalities led to heated exchanges during justices' conferences and concurring and dissenting opinions that expressed alternative approaches to free expression during a time when the Court considered crucial First Amendment cases.

## FLAGGING SUPPORT

The disagreements among new Roosevelt appointees in First Amendment cases began almost immediately. Just after the Nazis occupied Denmark and Norway, and as they invaded Holland and Belgium, the Court heard and considered a case in which a group of Jehovah's Witness's children refused to recite the Pledge of Allegiance in a Pennsylvania public school. The district expelled the students, claiming it had a right to compel students to recite the pledge. The Court had to decide in *Minersville School District v. Gobitis* whether the district's policy violated the First Amendment. When justices met to vote and decide who would write the Court's opinion, Frankfurter argued the value of patriotism and the role public schools play in society demanded the Court uphold the district's power to compel student speech.[31] In what he likely envisioned as his role as the leading mind on the Court, his argument persuaded a majority of justices to side with him. Chief Justice Hughes assigned the opinion to Frankfurter, reasoning "an immigrant could really speak of the flag as a patriotic symbol."[32] Frankfurter constructed a rousing opinion that conveyed early hints of his balancing approach regarding the space for human discourse.

He opened the opinion by contending "A grave responsibility confronts this Court whenever in course of litigation it must reconcile the conflicting claims of liberty and authority."[33] He emphasized the

147

*Chapter Seven*

importance of religious freedom, but cautioned "the manifold character of man's relations may bring his conception of religious duty into conflict with secular interests of his fellow-men."[34] Frankfurter, weighing religious liberty and free expression against the state's interest in patriotism and love of country, concluded the school district's decision must stand. In other words, he sided with state authority. The government could, in his reasoning, compel speech if that speech was a *public good* for society. As we will see in cases that follow, Frankfurter imagined a space for human discourse that was, among other features, protected and orderly. In the opinion's final paragraph, he added it is not for the judicial branch to tell a school district how to educate children. His reasoning overlaps with Holmes's efforts to limit judicial interference but departs from Frankfurter's history of fighting for civil liberties. Many were surprised by his opinion. Where was the champion of civil liberties who helped found the ACLU and argued for fellow-immigrants Sacco and Vanzetti? Eleanor Roosevelt, while Franklin Roosevelt was mixing drinks for Frankfurter and his wife, told the justice it seemed wrong to force children, against their conscience, to salute the flag.[35] Frankfurter wrote in his personal journal that he received many letters that argued he "as a Jew, ought particularly to protect minorities."[36] He rejected these concerns, emphasizing that as long as he was on the Court, "all considerations of race, religion, or antecedence of citizenship, are wholly irrelevant."[37]

His opinion, however unpopular, led seven justices, including Black and Douglas, to go along with his reasoning. The mantle of leadership Frankfurter expected to carry onto the Court appeared to be taking shape. Only Justice Stone, who wrote an equally passionate dissenting opinion, declined to join the majority. Black and Douglas did not see Stone's dissent until it was too late to change their votes. They came to regret siding with Frankfurter. Decades later, Black wrote, "we knew we were wrong, but we didn't have time to change our opinions."[38] He continued, "We met around the swimming pool at [Justice Frank] Murphy's hotel and decided to do so as soon as we could."[39] Douglas remembered, "We thought we'd been taken in and we mentioned this several times. . . . It was a matter of, that we wished we hadn't . . . gone along."[40]

*The Balancer*

They had their chance in 1943, when a nearly identical Pledge of Allegiance case reached the Court. True to their word, the Axis justices, Black, Douglas, and Murphy, joined Jackson, Wiley Rutledge, and Stone to overturn the precedent set in the Pennsylvania case in *West Virginia State Board v. Barnette*. Justice Jackson, who as solicitor general had lobbied Roosevelt to nominate Frankfurter to the Court four years previously, spoke for the new majority that sought to overturn Frankfurter's vision. The Court reasoned First Amendment rights could not be limited by elected officials. Black wrote a concurring opinion, joined by Douglas, in which they admitted they were wrong in 1940. Black explained, "Neither our domestic tranquility in peace nor our martial effort in war depend on compelling little children to participate in a ceremony which ends in nothing for them but a fear of spiritual condemnation."[41] Frankfurter dissented. His nearly 8,400-word dissent, more than double the Court's opinion's length, can be seen as the first instance when the division between himself, Black, and Douglas, influenced a Court opinion.

In his personal journal, he blamed Black for the shift in the Court's opinion.[42] His dissent in the case, in many ways, reads as if he was writing to one person—Black. Its opening lines belie how personally he took the negative feedback from the 1940 *Gobitis* opinion and the Court's organizing against him. He opened his dissent with: "One who belongs to the most vilified and persecuted minority in history is not likely to be insensible to the freedoms guaranteed by our Constitution."[43] Murphy and Jackson, as well as Chief Justice Charles Evans Hughes, advised him to remove the line.[44] He ignored their advice. His dissent continued, emphasizing judicial restraint requires justices be detached from personal beliefs and willing to uphold laws they disagree with. Citing his mentor Holmes, he contended elected officials, not judges, "are ultimate guardians of the liberties and welfare of the people."[45]

Ultimately, the flag-salute cases convey Frankfurter's tendency to *balance* free-expression concerns with other matters, such as judicial restraint, public order, and the importance of social values. Biographer Joseph Lash framed the shift in 1943 as a product of Frankfurter losing the leadership mantle he carried to the Court.[46] Justices Murphy and Jackson, both appointed by Roosevelt after Frankfurter's nomination,

*Chapter Seven*

initially followed Frankfurter, but were drawn by Black's personality and his experience as a senator. Black, unlike Frankfurter, had experience working to gather coalitions and collect votes to get legislation through Congress. He used those skills to connect with other members of the Court and gather consensus. After *Barnette*, Douglas documented that the initial veneer of leadership and good will Frankfurter had come to the Court with was fading. Douglas explained:

> We began to realize that here was a man who instead of being a friend and a champion of civil liberties was using his position on the court to line up allies for a constitutional doctrine that we didn't, we couldn't go with.[47]

With seven seats on the Court occupied by Roosevelt appointees, many of whom had been in the president's orbit alongside Frankfurter before joining the Court, Frankfurter was losing the ideological and personal mantle of leadership to Black. And he knew it.

## ORDERLY SPEECH

The Black-led shift in the Court's thinking in flag-salute cases in 1943 wasn't the first slight Frankfurter attributed to the former senator from Alabama. Justices decided two cases regarding disorderly expression in 1941, not long after *Gobitis*. In both instances Frankfurter and Black were at odds regarding how free expression should be conceptualized. The outcome in *Bridges v. California* was particularly galling to Frankfurter. In *Bridges*, union leader Harry Bridges, along with a group of newspapers, including the *Los Angeles Times*, were held in contempt after publishing intimidating comments regarding pending court cases.[48] Bridges, for his part, sent a telegram to the secretary of labor contending if a decision in a pending court case was not satisfactory, he would lead union workers to paralyze work at the Port of Los Angeles and beyond. Similarly, a group of newspapers had published editorials that commented about pending cases. In conference, Hughes contended the contempt decisions should be upheld, and he was joined by Clark McReynolds, Stone, Roberts, Frankfurter, and Murphy. Hughes, as he did in *Gobitis*, assigned Frankfurter to write the opinion. Black began work on a dissent.

150

*The Balancer*

Frankfurter's draft opinion for the Court focused on history, tradition, and, crucially, limitations to free expression. Once again, using balancing to approach the issue, Frankfurter reasoned, "Deeming it more important than ever before to enforce civil liberties with a generous outlook, but deeming it no less essential for the assurance of civil liberties that the federal system founded upon the Constitution be maintained."[49] In other words, he noted the value of free expression, but contended the work of the judicial branch is more important to social order and the public good. Citing his mentor Holmes's market reference from his dissent *Abrams v. United States*, Frankfurter reasoned, "A trial is not a 'free trade in ideas,' nor is the best test of truth in a courtroom 'the power of the thought to get itself accepted in the competition of the market.'"[50] He emphasized a court has defined limits on speech that are created to protect the dispatch of justice. Ultimately, Frankfurter communicated order, on the balance, is more crucial than free expression. The speech in this case, he reasoned, threatened the orderly flow of justice, thus it could be limited.

Black, predictably, paid attention to one primary concern—the wording of the First Amendment. Building his reasoning upon Frankfurter's mentors Holmes's and Brandeis's conclusions in *Schenck, Abrams*, and *Whitney*,[51] Black reasoned that the justices' ideas "do no more than recognize a minimum compulsion of the Bill of Rights."[52] Then, for the first time, Black outlined his absolute interpretation of the First Amendment. He explained:

> The First Amendment does not speak equivocally. It prohibits any law 'abridging the freedom of speech, or of the press.' It must be taken as a command of the broadest scope that explicit language, read in the context of a liberty-loving society, will allow.[53]

Thus, where Frankfurter was nuanced, careful, and balanced in his examination of the issue and his conclusions, to his great frustration, Black was direct and simple. Where Frankfurter reasoned free expression *can* be limited when it conflicts with other values, such as threatening public order, Black simply stated that "Congress shall make no law" means "Congress shall make no law."[54]

Both opinions were circulated to the justices in June 1941. By that time, McReynolds and Hughes retired. Murphy changed his vote. The Court reheard the case, this time with Stone in the chief justice's seat

151

*Chapter Seven*

and James Byrnes and Jackson on the Court. Jackson sided with Black's opinion, giving him five votes. Frankfurter's draft opinion for the Court was relegated to a dissent as he watched Black's ideas receive a majority of the Court's support.

Less than a week after the Court announced the *Bridges* decision, justices heard arguments in *Milk Wagon Drivers Union v. Meadow-moor Dairies*. With the differing visions of free expression still fresh in justices' minds, the case again challenged the Court to rule and rationalize regarding a difficult First Amendment question that would influence the space for human discourse. In the case, a delivery drivers' union in Illinois sought to rein in non-union milk deliveries by picketing at dairies. Beyond picketing, some union members burned non-union trucks, broke windows, attacked drivers and storekeepers, threatened people at gun point, and drove one truck into a river.[55] Meadowmoor Dairies asked Cook County to stop the union from picketing on or around its facilities and its clients' stores. The county agreed, making it a crime for even peaceful picketing by union members to take place. The Supreme Court of Illinois upheld the limitations on free expression, but the union argued the limits on even peaceful picketing violated its First Amendment rights. The union emphasized the US Supreme Court had established picketing was protected by the First Amendment in *Thornhill v. Alabama* in 1940. Predictably, Frankfurter reasoned the county's limitation on expression was justifiable and did not violate the First Amendment. Five justices joined his opinion as the Court upheld the limitations on expression.

Frankfurter recognized, in the opinion, that peaceful picketing is protected by the First Amendment. He wrote picketing has become "the workingman's means of communication."[56] That's when the journey through Frankfurter's complex set of rationalizations begins. Frankfurter sought to thread a narrow, winding course of reason to explain why this specific instance of government limitations on ideas does not violate the First Amendment. In doing so, he provided a glimpse into how he imagined the space for human discourse. He explained:

> It must never be forgotten, however, that the Bill of Rights was the child of the Enlightenment. Back of the guarantee of free speech lay faith in the power of an appeal to reason by all the peaceful means for gaining access to the mind. It was in order to avert force and

## The Balancer

explosions due to restrictions upon rational modes of communication that the guarantee of free speech was given a generous scope. But utterance in a context of violence can lose its significance as an appeal to reason and become part of an instrument of force. Such utterance was not meant to be sheltered by the Constitution.[57]

Frankfurter imagined a space in which free expression safeguards vouchsafe reason-based, peaceful exchanges of ideas. In this case, he found the presence of *potential* intimidation or violence was a threat to the space for discourse. The space was made better, safer, and more functional when disruptions were removed. Thus, he weighed the importance of a safe, orderly space over one that included the broadest possible spectrum of ideas. To Frankfurter, the threat to rational discourse was enough to allow the government to be the monitoring agent. In this case, that means allowing the county to halt violent *and* peaceful expression. In the opinion, Frankfurter reasoned, "The momentum of fear generated by past violence would survive even though future picketing might be wholly peaceful. . . . We cannot say that such a finding so contradicted experience as to warrant our rejection."[58]

While *Milk Wagon Drivers Union* is not a landmark case, it provides glimpses of all the building blocks of Frankfurter's alternative imagining of the space for human discourse. The space is safe for all to participate. It is made to protect reasonable discourse. The public good, rather than individual good, is paramount. Finally, the Court's role is to defer to those who are closer to the question. In this case, Frankfurter emphasized the lower courts and county officials are in a better position to make this call than the US Supreme Court. Certainly, hints of these themes were present in *Bridges* and the flag-salute cases. Here, however, Frankfurter is most clear about the space. Of course, this imaging of free-expression rationales and the space for discourse is forming in a parallel line alongside what Black and Douglas are constructing. Frankfurter's nemeses, predictably, dissented. Black, Douglas, and Reed would have overturned the law. Black penned a dissent, which Douglas joined, that, compared to Frankfurter's delicately woven path, is as simple as a long, never-ending stretch of West Texas highway. Black reasoned the case dealt with one simple question: Did the injunction against peaceful expression violate the participants' First Amendment

153

*Chapter Seven*

rights? He concluded it did. He explained, "Freedom to speak and write about public questions is as important to the life of our government as is the heart to the human body."[59] He continued, "In fact, this privilege is the heart of our government. If that heart be weakened, the result is debilitation; if it be stilled, the result is death."[60]

Where Frankfurter saw a crucial First Amendment right, one of several viable concerns, Black saw a foundational right that stood above all others. Frankfurter interpreted free expression and the space for discourse as a public, societal concern. Black imagined the space as crucial as well, but its value came down to individual liberties to "speak" and to "write."[61] These differing imaginings of the space and how free expression is rationalized continued, along with the simmering feud between Black, Douglas, and Frankfurter.

## *Disturbances*

Morris Cohen and Frankfurter were from Jewish families that immigrated to the United States via Ellis Island in the 1890s. Both attended City College of New York as undergraduates before studying at Harvard. Both were brilliant. The pair roomed together during Frankfurter's final year at Harvard Law School and remained in the same circle of friends and mentors, including Holmes, Brandeis, and Laski, the British economist. Cohen was a philosopher whose interests included legal matters. He studied with Josiah Royce and William James, Holmes's old friend. Frankfurter and Cohen remained close after graduating. How close? Cohen named his first-born Felix. As Frankfurter prepared to teach his first semester at the law school, it was Cohen he asked for help.[62] As Frankfurter struggled to advise Roosevelt as the Supreme Court struck down New Deal legislation, Frankfurter confided in Cohen, who responded with what he called "affectionate castigations."[63] Cohen kept Frankfurter's feet on the ground.

Frankfurter's decades-long friendship with Cohen failed when he joined the Court. The reason is crucial. Cohen no longer recognized Frankfurter as a fellow progressive champion. Frankfurter had exchanged his civil libertarian fight, which he showed in work for the ACLU, his unsuccessful fight for minimum wages for women and

154

## The Balancer

children in Washington, DC, and for Sacco and Vanzetti, for a tepid, conservative approach.[64] By the end of the 1943 term, Frankfurter had the second-most conservative record on the Court.[65] That year, after suffering from a stroke, Morris Cohen asked one of Rutledge's clerks to arrange a visit for him to the Court's building. He wanted to meet Hugo Black. He specifically did not want to see Frankfurter.[66] After four years on the Court, even Frankfurter's oldest friend saw Black as the Court's leader when it came to civil liberties. Despite the loss of his longest friendship, Frankfurter didn't budge. In a pair of difficult First Amendment cases in 1949, he continued to construct a parallel space for human discourse. All the while, Black and Douglas kept chipping away as they installed the foundations of the space and free-expression rationales that have come to dominate and define the marketplace of ideas.

The differences in approaches were placed in stark contrast in *Kovac v. Cooper* in 1949. Charles Kovac was convicted of violating a Trenton, New Jersey, ordinance that limited vehicle-mounted loudspeakers from making "disturbing noises." Kovac had used a speaker mounted on a vehicle to play music and communicate ideas about a local labor dispute. He challenged his conviction, contending the Trenton ordinance limited free expression. The case provided a new opportunity for Frankfurter and Black and Douglas to develop their differing conceptualizations of free expression and the space for discourse. The city ordinance, after all, directly influenced the space for discourse. It was created to limit unwanted and intrusive noise, challenging justices to choose between a protected, orderly space and a wide open one, where some speakers have more power to distort the space—a concern with direct parallels to the power of algorithms and AI communicators in the networked, AI era.

The Court, in a five-to-four-decision, upheld the Trenton ordinance. Frankfurter, supporting the Court's decision, framed the case as a matter of public order. He contended, "Wise accommodation between liberty and order always has been, and ever will be, indispensable for a democratic society."[67] In other words, he again *balanced* free expression with competing concerns, finding public order more important than individual rights and First Amendment safeguards. He went a step further this time, however. Frankfurter devoted more than 2,000 words of his opinion to attacking the idea that free expression should receive a "preferred

155

## Chapter Seven

position." Justice Reed, writing for the Court in *Kovac*, referred to the idea exactly one time, in passing, at the close of his opinion for the Court. Reed contended, "The preferred position of freedom of speech in a society that cherishes liberty for all does not require legislators to be insensible to claims by citizens to comfort and convenience."[68] The reference, which generally aligned with Frankfurter's more balanced, public-good approach, still triggered a lengthy concurring opinion.

Frankfurter called the "preferred position" approach "mischievous." In the type of lecture-like opinion that riled Black and Douglas, he traced the history of the phrase, rightly finding its origins in Stone's famous Footnote 4 of the *U.S. v. Carolene Products* decision from 1938. In a decision that led to the "switch in time that saved nine," because it recast how justices interpreted New Deal legislation and, potentially, staved off Roosevelt's court-packing plan, Stone reasoned challenges to fundamental rights, such as free expression, should face higher bars to success than other concerns.[69] Frankfurter's lecture was almost certainly aimed at one person—Black. The preferred position approach is only slightly less supportive of individual free expression than Black's absolutist approach, which generally contended any limitation on the flow of ideas is a violation of the unequivocal language of the First Amendment.[70]

Preferred position is defined by its presumption "that government action that limits free speech and free press to protect other interests is *usually* unconstitutional."[71] Frankfurter, using his mentor Holmes's reasoning, contended any dogmatic approach to deciding cases, whether it is absolutism or preferred position, can lead to "mechanical jurisprudence" and "oversimplified formulas."[72] In *Kovac*, he reasoned, a dogmatic, absolute approach ignored the power of new technologies to distort human discourse. Frankfurter reasoned, "Only a disregard of vital differences between natural speech, even of the loudest spellbinders, and the noise of sound trucks would give sound trucks the constitutional rights accorded to the unaided human voice."[73] Nuanced. Argumentative. A little vindictive. Frankfurter's opinion included all his signature elements. If we can look past Frankfurter's condescending tone, which helps explain why his leadership on the Court never materialized, the legal scholar's opinion essentially constructs an alternative component to the space for human discourse. He communicated a concern that

156

*The Balancer*

new technologies can endanger and distort the exchange of ideas. His solution—be flexible. Frankfurter's balancing approach does little to secure crucial First Amendment protections, a crucial weakness, but it contributes important considerations regarding a dynamic, rather than static space.

Beyond the war of personalities within the Court, his opinion in *Kovac* added a concern that new technology can create problems for existing axioms. Frankfurter envisioned a dynamic space for discourse, while Black continued to develop a clear, simple, and static approach to free expression. Frankfurter contended conditions *might* change and a rigid system will be ill-prepared to address them. In *Kovac*, Black, joined by Douglas and Rutledge, contended the ordinance privileged those who can afford to own mass-media outlets because it outlawed vehicle-mounted loudspeakers "upon any vehicle in any of the public streets."[74] Black was concerned the law limited the scope of ideas to those that might be acceptable to broadcast-license-holders or newspaper and magazine publishers. Ultimately, the differences in perspectives illustrate diverging understandings about free expression and the space for discourse. Those differences continued the very next day. The Court announced its decision in *Kovac* on January 31, 1949. On February 1, the Court heard arguments in *Terminiello v. Chicago*, another case concerning the government's power to control speech that threatened social order and rational discourse.

Just after dark, on a cold February day in Chicago, Christian nationalist Arthur Terminiello delivered a hate-filled speech to about one thousand people in the West End Woman's Club. Invitations for the event encouraged "Patriotic Friends" to come to the event to hear "one of the boldest and bravest public statements to which you have ever listened."[75] As the event neared, protestors gathered outside the building. Police watched as more and more, eventually about one thousand, formed picket lines to block the entrances and protest the speaker and his ideas. When Terminiello stepped to the stage, he insulted and assailed the crowd outside. Protestors responded by throwing rocks and stink bombs. Windows were broken and doors were bashed in. Chicago police decided to put a stop to the event. They arrested Terminiello and he was charged and convicted of disorderly conduct. He challenged

*Chapter Seven*

his arrest and conviction, contending the government violated his First Amendment rights when it halted his speech and fined him.

Terminiello's case presented a variation on an ongoing disagreement between Frankfurter and Black and Douglas, opening the door to the next installment of their differing rationales for free expression. The Court, in another five-to-four vote, agreed with Terminiello, overturning his conviction for disorderly conduct. Douglas wrote the Court's opinion, emphasizing the exchange of ideas "is often provocative and challenging."[76] He continued, "It may strike at prejudices and preconceptions and have profound unsettling effects as it presses for acceptance of an idea."[77] With these acknowledgments in mind, Douglas contended free expression must be protected from government limitations on ideas. In reasoning that inched closer to the marketplace of ideas we know today, he explained,

> It is only through free debate and free exchange of ideas that government remains responsive to the will of the people and peaceful change is effected. The right to speak freely and to promote diversity of ideas and programs is therefore one of the chief distinctions that sets us apart from totalitarian regimes.[78]

Thus, even in the face of violence and danger to physical well-being, the Court reasoned the government could not halt the speaker without violating his rights. Such an understanding emphasized the individual rights of each citizen, conceptualizing personal rights as, taken together, creating public and social goods. The understanding also recognizes and accepts expression might not be orderly, but the risk of placing the government in a position to decide what is orderly and what is not is greater than that of concerns for security and safety within the space. Frankfurter, as expected, was having none of any of this.

Frankfurter, in his dissent, wanted the five-justice majority to know they were doing their jobs incorrectly. He contended Douglas and the rest of the majority reached beyond the primary question raised in the appeal, a departure from the Court's traditions. He was also aghast the Court would set a precedent about free expression in a case that dealt with this particular speaker and such a small US$100 fine. He contended:

> Freedom of speech undoubtedly means freedom to express views that challenge deep-seated, sacred beliefs and to utter sentiments that

*The Balancer*

may provoke resentment. But those indulging in such stuff as that to which this proceeding gave rise are hardly so deserving.[79]

His concern regarding the limited value of the speakers' ideas and minor nature of the fine, not the principle within the case, reinforces his balancing-based standard. It also communicates his concern for the Court's traditions and how he valued them beyond the Court's power to shape civil liberties. Taken together, Frankfurter's opinions in *Kovac* and *Terminiello* belie a limited appreciation for expansive free-expression safeguards. His rationales, however, continue to construct an alternative lens through which to understand the space for discourse. The lens includes concern for the public and social goods over individual rights, emphasis on order and the ability to participate, and the expectation that technologies will change and rigid approaches to free expression will limit the Court's ability to adapt.

## PROCESS AND DIGNITY

Somewhere in Arkansas, during a road trip to New Mexico, William O. Douglas and his first wife, Mildred, heard on the radio Roosevelt had selected a new chief justice to replace Hughes, who retired at the end of the 1941 term. Douglas hoped Roosevelt would select Black. The president chose to elevate Stone. Douglas took a moment from his vacation to pen a letter to Black. Douglas told his friend his first thought when he heard the news of Stone's appointment was "Felix has done it again."[80] He continued, "You will recall that I expressed fear that Felix would make that move. I am sorry that it did not go to you."[81] Douglas was correct. Frankfurter, who was close to Roosevelt, advocated for Stone. Douglas's sympathetic letter to Black included one other crucial sentiment. About Stone, Douglas wrote "Unless the old boy changes, it will not be a particularly happy or congenial atmosphere in which to work . . . I wired Stone, however, extending my congratulations."[82] Douglas knew Stone's strengths and limitations well. Beyond serving on the Court with him, Douglas was one of Stone's students at Columbia Law School in the 1920s. Douglas was correct again. Stone, a well-respected justice and author of perhaps the most famous footnote in Supreme Court history,

159

*Chapter Seven*

is generally considered one of its least effective chief justices.[83] One of Stone's chief difficulties—navigating the feud between Frankfurter, Black, and Douglas.

Stone retired in 1946 and Harry Truman nominated Fred Vinson, his Secretary of the Treasury, to be chief justice. He couldn't rein in Frankfurter, Black, and Douglas either. Frankfurter wrote of Vinson in his personal journal, "He is confident and easy-going and sure and shallow."[84] Not a ringing endorsement. When Vinson died of a heart attack in 1953, Frankfurter said it was an act of providence, because the Court was in such great a need for leadership. Stone's and Vinson's struggle to put out the fires of division among justices contributed to Frankfurters' and Black's and Douglas's diverging visions of free expression and the space for human discourse. By the time the Court considered crucial First Amendment cases in the early 1950s, the Court was in shambles. The landmark *Dennis v. United States* decision in 1951 included five separate opinions, each constructing differing rationales regarding the fate of Communist Party leader Eugene Dennis and others who were convicted of teaching and advocating for the overthrow of the US government. A year later, it happened again. Justices produced five opinions in the less-heralded *Beauharnais v. Illinois* group-defamation case. Frankfurter, Black, and Douglas were right in the center of the fractured Court's inability to agree and present at least somewhat united fronts regarding fundamental First Amendment questions.

The Court voted six to two to uphold Dennis's and others' convictions under the Smith Act. The post-World War II law criminalized advocating for the demise of the US government. Of course, any such law that vests the government with the power to halt unpopular ideas immediately collides with First Amendment questions. Vinson wrote a tepid opinion for the Court. Only three justices, one of which was a Roosevelt nominee, joined his opinion. Frankfurter and Jackson wrote separate concurring opinions, creating a plurality of justices who found, for diverging reasons, the law did not conflict with the First Amendment. Frankfurter's opinion is likely his most complete statement about the meaning and purpose of the First Amendment and the space for human discourse. It's also his most extreme. His 12,500-word missive, which includes an appendix, examined the history and purpose of the First

## The Balancer

Amendment. It reads like a seminar. Again, the seminar appeared to have only one enrollee, Black, who wrote his own dissenting opinion. In both the apex of his First Amendment writings on the Court and a complete departure from his civil libertarian roots, Frankfurter reasoned:

> Civil liberties draw at best only limited strength from legal guaranties. Preoccupation by our people with the constitutionality, instead of with the wisdom, of legislation or of executive action is preoccupation with a false value. . . . When legislation touches freedom of thought and freedom of speech, such a tendency is a formidable enemy of the free spirit. Much that should be rejected as illiberal, because repressive and envenoming, may well be not unconstitutional. The ultimate reliance for the deepest needs of civilization must be found outside their vindication in courts of law.[85]

In short, free expression rights should be sussed out in public. The kicker, however, is that to Frankfurter, free expression was what the public, *via* democratically elected representatives, thought it was. Thus, he reasoned it is generally not the judicial branch's role to step in to halt laws and policies being executed by elected officials. Such a conclusion aligns with ideas he conveyed in other opinions and with Holmes's influence, but is placed in far more stark terms in this opinion. In a twenty-first-century sense, Frankfurter's thinking would likely allow the government to force social media firms to take down or leave up content, because those decisions would represent the will of the people, via elected officials' actions. The First Amendment, in this view, is maintained by the executive and legislative branches. Free expression is *balanced* with other concerns. Frankfurter, in his opinion, assumes public officials always seek to serve the public good. While Frankfurter's reasoning is anathema to our constructions of free expression and the space for discourse, it is noteworthy there is precedent in the Court's history for a different approach.

Frankfurter's opinion also affirmed the US government has a right to protect itself, again placing perceived public good and generalized concerns above those of individual liberties. In this sense, the First Amendment allows the government to act as a guardian in the space for human discourse. Frankfurter acknowledged this path might mean protected expression will at times be limited in the government's efforts to halt dangerous speech. He explained, "It is a sobering fact that in sustaining

## Chapter Seven

the convictions before us we can hardly escape restriction on the interchange of ideas."[86] Frankfurter's understanding of the First Amendment in *Dennis* is truly in an alternative realm when compared to Black's and Douglas's constructions and the Enlightenment-based marketplace of ideas and expansive marketplace understanding that have come to define how the space for human discourse is imagined.

Black's 725-word dissent speaks volumes. It constructs a space for free expression that is generally free of government intervention in the exchange of ideas. Perhaps as a direct response to Frankfurter, he reasoned if judicial review does not apply in cases such as this, "the First Amendment amounts to little more than an admonition to Congress."[87] Douglas's separate dissent contended individual rights to share and receive ideas amount to social and public goods. In constructing his reasoning, he went directly to the foundations of what would become the Enlightenment-based marketplace of ideas. He contended, "Free speech has occupied an exalted position because of the high service it has given our society. Its protection is essential to the very existence of a democracy."[88] He continued, "When ideas compete in the market for acceptance, full and free discussion exposes the false and they gain few adherents."[89] There they are. In Black's and Douglas's dissents, we see the continuous efforts both made to construct an expansive space for free expression. Frankfurter's balancing approach weighs free expression with other concerns. As we have seen, free expression generally does not receive much weight in his thinking.

Frankfurter wrote the Court's opinion for a deeply divided Court in *Beauharnais*, less than a year later. His opinion, which may well be his best articulation of his vision for free expression and the space for discourse—certainly not the longest—introduces concern for the well-being of others and systemic social problems that the Enlightenment-based space fails to account for. Joseph Beauharnais led a hate group called The White Circle League. The group was based in Chicago and generally organized against the rights of Black Americans, particularly in their efforts to integrate traditionally white neighborhoods and schools.[90] One of his group's pamphlets, which degraded Black people and threatened violence against them, led to his conviction under an Illinois law that criminalized distributing information that degraded people

162

*The Balancer*

based on their "race, color, creed or religion."[91] Beauharnais challenged the law's constitutionality, contending it violated his speech and press rights. The Court found the Illinois law did not conflict with the First Amendment. Frankfurter's opinion included his usual argument—local elected officials, in this case Illinois lawmakers, are in a better position to address problems than the Court. Crucially, he went further, turning his attention to the purpose of the law and its place in the space for human discourse.

Frankfurter contended Beauharnais's expression has no place in the exchange of ideas. He reasoned, it is not a public or social good. Quite the opposite. He explains:

> A man's job and his educational opportunities and the dignity accorded him may depend as much on the reputation of the racial and religious group to which he willy-nilly belongs, as on his own merits.[92]

In other words, this expression can encourage systemic oppression, which when balanced with expansive free expression, is more important. Thus, Frankfurter extended his reasoning that expression must be balanced with other concerns to weighing the power of words and ideas to harm and limit opportunities for others. Frankfurter also remained consistent in his construction of a space that is accessible to all who seek to contribute to the public and social good, but limited to those that would disrupt or distort it.

Black and Douglas dissented. Black reasoned the First Amendment protected Beauharnais's ideas. Though distasteful, Black reasoned Beauharnais's expression had value because it communicated ideas regarding a matter of public concern. He contended the First Amendment precludes the government from deciding which ideas are good or bad. Black wrote, "The Court does not act on this view of the Founders."[93] He continued, "It calculates what it deems to be the danger of public discussion, holds the scales are tipped on the side of state suppression, and upholds state censorship. This method of decision offers little protection to First Amendment liberties."[94] Douglas's separate dissent reinforced Black's, though he used "preferred position" reasoning, rather than absolutist. He warned against content-based restrictions, again reinforcing the solidifying foundations of the Enlightenment-based marketplace

## Chapter Seven

approach. He warned of "a new orthodoxy—an orthodoxy that changes with the whims of the age or the day, an orthodoxy which the majority by solemn judgment proclaims to be essential to the safety, welfare, security, morality, or health of society."[95] In this scenario, he warned, "Free speech in the constitutional sense disappears."[96]

What Douglas lamented Frankfurter celebrated. His balancing approach emphasized free expression rationales and the space for discourse should be sensitive to change. That sensitivity, he contended came in the form of flexible approaches to free expression and a willingness to let elected officials construct solutions to problems in their constituencies. Unlike Black and Douglas, Frankfurter also saw the space for discourse as being safeguarded from distortion and disruption by the government, therefore allowing speech that failed to establish its public-good credentials to be limited. In *Beauharnais*, the safeguarding included protecting people from speech that encouraged systemic oppression. All of these ideas were generally antithetical to Black's and Douglas's constructions of the space. We know how the story ends (see chapters 4 and 5). Black and Douglas were joined by William Brennan in 1956.

Together, they cemented their understandings of the space for human discourse. Frankfurter's ideas collect dust, along with the countless complaints he made about his nemeses.

To be fair, the feud ended with kindness. Frankfurter left the Court in 1962, after a stroke and failing health. Black visited Frankfurter often as his health declined. They became friends again. When Frankfurter died, in 1965, Black cried.[97] He wrote a tribute to Frankfurter in *Harvard Law Review*. In it, he explained:

> I am happy to have had the opportunity to have served with him . . . to argue with him; to agree with him; to disagree with him; and to live a large part of my life in the light of his brilliant intellect, his buoyant spirit and his unashamed patriotism.[98]

Frankfurter left an alternative lens for understanding the space for discourse. While it may not be suitable as a replacement or revision for the marketplace system, it can be understood as providing building blocks toward that goal.[99]

FIGURE 3 Decades into their ideological battle about free expression, Douglas, Black, and Frankfurter join their colleagues for a photo of the Court in 1957. Brennan, who joined the Court a year before, helped solidify Black's and Douglas's expansive approach to the space for discourse. Sitting left to right: Douglas, Black, Warren, Frankfurter, Burton; standing left to right: Brennan, Jr., Clark, Harlan, Whittaker.
Source: Library of Congress

# EIGHT

## Baking Bread

William James met Fanny Bowditch Dixwell in spring 1866 while living in Cambridge, Massachusetts. He was immediately enthralled. The twenty-four-year-old James, recently home from a long, mosquito-infested year assisting famed scientist Louis Agassiz in his studies along the Amazon River in Brazil, wrote glowingly of Dixwell. He exclaimed to a friend "I made the acquaintance the other day of Miss Fanny Dixwell of Cambridge (the eldest), do you know her?"[1] He continued, "She is decidedly A1, and (so far) the best girl I have known. I should like if possible to confine my whole life to her."[2] There was one catch. Fanny was his friend Oliver Wendell Holmes's girlfriend. Dixwell's father had been Holmes's private tutor. Dixwell and Holmes met and began a friendship when they were ten. She remained part of his life throughout the Civil War.[3] James knew all of this. He was close friends with Holmes during this period and the men's fathers were part of the Saturday Club, which included Ralph Waldo Emerson, Henry Wordsworth Longfellow, Nathaniel Hawthorn, Benjamin Peirce, James Russell Lowell, and Agassiz.[4] James, who would later become the father of American pragmatism, should have known better.

He called on Dixwell often when Holmes was in London for the summer, meeting John Stewart Mill and other leading British thinkers,

## Baking Bread

after finishing his law degree.[5] James visited the Dixwell family home so often that Holmes's mother, Amelia, took notice. In a letter that begins by chastising her son for failing to write her more often while he was abroad and worrying about his well-being, Amelia noted, "Fanny is living quietly in Cambridge with the exception of visits from Bill James, who appears to go there at any time from 9 o'clock in the morning."[6] Amelia did not see James as a threat to her son's long-standing relationship with Fanny. She continued, "I told her to let me know how the flirtation got on . . . I had a little fun with her, about him, & told her I should write to you about it."[7] Amelia was right, James's efforts were unsuccessful. Dixwell married her son, Oliver, in 1872.

James's attempt to woo his friend's longtime love interest helps with two important aspects of this chapter. The story evidences the broader picture of James's struggle to discover himself and where he belonged, an effort that helped shape his massive contributions to American thought. As one biographer explained, "His own somatic problems led him to study psychology, and his personal concern with the relations of his mind and body underlay all his philosophical speculations."[8] Unlike Holmes, James wrestled with depression, chronic physical ailments, and an inability to settle on what he wanted to do with his life.[9] James tried painting, chemistry, and biology, before settling on medical school, which he started, left, and later finished. In true James fashion, he never practiced medicine. Another biographer captured James's Charlie Brown-like existence succinctly: "William James was fragile; he was socially insecure; and he could never make up his mind."[10] Together, these struggles defined James's lifelong search for a way to understand himself and the world around him.

The Fanny Dixwell story also identifies a crucial intersection in American thought. James's and Holmes's friendship was closest just after the Civil War. They shared common acquaintances with Charles Sanders Peirce, who created the term "pragmatism," and Chauncey Wright, who was a massive influence on both men's thinking before he died in 1875, at the age of 45.[11] One of James's biographers labeled Wright as the "intellectual-boxing master" to Peirce, Holmes, and James during the early 1870s.[12] James's and Holmes's ideas overlapped, to some extent, before they drifted in separate directions. Holmes's impact on the space for

167

*Chapter Eight*

human discourse and how we rationalize free expression is well documented (see chapter 3). He authored the first Supreme Court opinions to address the meaning and scope of the First Amendment in 1919.[13] Later that year, he wrote the first opinion that supported protecting free expression.[14] As a result, Holmes is often mistakenly credited for creating the Enlightenment-based marketplace of ideas.

James was not like Holmes. Often physically and mentally unwell, and deeply concerned with religion and belief, James *felt* the world. Holmes glided on top of it. As a result, James provided an alternative lens through which to conceptualize the crucial space for democratic discourse, particularly in the twenty-first century, during an era characterized by massive, widespread changes to the communication landscape. James knew nothing of algorithms, AI, the metaverse, or networked technology, but his struggle to understand the human mind, including his own, led to a discernible and alternative approach to the Enlightenment-based assumptions that have come to dominate free-expression rationales and the map for the space for human discourse (see chapter 4).

James was not successful in wooing Dixwell, or in anything early in life, but in his own roundabout way, he became the father of American pragmatism. He did not invent pragmatism—that honor goes to Peirce, who, along with James, Holmes, and Wright, took part in the Metaphysical Club in Cambridge beginning in 1871.[15] Peirce read a draft paper to the group that outlined a pragmatic approach to understanding. Six years later, a revised version of the paper appeared in *Popular Science Monthly*. Peirce explained, "Consider what effects, that might conceivably have practical bearings, we conceive the object of our conception to have. Then, our conception of these effects is the whole of our conception of the object."[16] Decades later, James went out of his way to credit the then down-on-his-luck Peirce with the initial kernel of an idea for pragmatism. He acknowledged Peirce's ideas from the Metaphysical Club during his first lectures about pragmatism at Berkley in 1898, a *Popular Science Monthly* article, and *Pragmatism: A New Name for Some Old Ways of Thinking*, published in 1907, which outlines American pragmatism.[17]

Peirce might have coined the term, but James built the theory. James's *Pragmatism* is the most complete explanation of pragmatic thought. In the work, as in earlier lectures, James complained that too much

168

FIGURE 4 William James
Source: Haughton Library, Harvard University

*Chapter Eight*

philosophy "bakes no bread."[18] He found the empiricist's reliance on science and the rationalist's emphasis on abstract principles and ideas failed to get at the crucial, practical, and necessary truths required for resolving important questions. He sought to construct a philosophy that bakes bread. His recipe—the "pragmatic method," which "turns away from abstraction and insufficiency, from verbal solutions, from bad a priori reasons, from fixed principles, closed systems, and pretended absolutes and origins."[19] He explained, the pragmatist "turns towards concreteness and adequacy, towards facts, towards action, and towards power."[20]

Crucially, James came to pragmatism as much for himself as for his work in philosophy. His ideas were part of a quest to understand his own being and place in the world. James's search led to an inwardly focused pragmatic method. He taught psychology, after all, and wrote the field-defining work, *Principles of Psychology*, which was published in 1890. John Dewey, who was in his early thirties and had recently completed his dissertation on Emmanuel Kant's psychology, read James's book soon after it was published. It changed his life.[21] James's thinking reorganized the way Dewey thought about pragmatism. In a 1930 essay, Dewey credited James's *Psychology* as "one specifiable philosophic factor which entered into my thinking so as to give it new direction and quality."[22] Dewey built on James's work, creating a second wave of American pragmatism. Dewey, particularly as a result of his partnership with Jane Addams and her settlement program at Hull House in Chicago, however, sought answers to social, rather than personal, problems. He focused pragmatic thought externally, seeking to apply the approach to improving civil society.

Dewey's pragmatism became a rationalization for a particular form of democracy. Essentially, Dewey created a pragmatism-based model for the space for human discourse. His model emphasized the need to protect the *process* of democracy, rather than the idea. In his essay "Creative Democracy—The Task Before Us," Dewey explained, "Democracy is a way of personal life controlled not merely by faith in human nature in general but by faith in the capacity of human beings for intelligent judgment and action if proper conditions are furnished."[23]

Dewey built on James's pragmatism, constructing a case for free expression and a space for human discourse based on individual fulfillment

170

*Baking Bread*

within community and active citizenship. His work was widely read. In fact, Holmes had three of Dewey's books in his personal library when he died in 1935.[24] Regarding one of Dewey's books, the jurist wrote, "I read sentences I didn't understand, for his style is horrid, but I thought that I never anywhere had read a philosophical work that felt our universe so deeply and so widely."[25] Dewey's work made an impression. Unlike the Enlightenment-based marketplace-based approach, which is founded upon protecting individuals' abilities to *discover* universal truth and eschew falsity in an open exchange of ideas, the alternative lens provided by Dewey's pragmatism emphasized discourse. The discourse-based space Dewey built, using James's initial ideas, rationalized free expression as a tool for individual fulfillment within community and the shared adoption of practical truths that emerge via free exchanges of ideas among citizens. In this sense, pragmatism is a process-based alternative to the outcome-based marketplace approach. This chapter establishes the foundational assumptions of James's pragmatic method and examines Dewey's construction of pragmatism as a rationale for a living, breathing version of democracy. Such a lens provides another way to understand how the space for discourse can be constructed in the networked, AI era.

## JAMES AND EXPERIENCE

James didn't fight in the Civil War. He wanted to join the army in 1861, according to a letter from his father.[26] He never joined. There's no documented reason he stayed on the sidelines. The 19-year-old could have changed his mind about enlisting. He was often indecisive. His health could also have prevented him from joining. James suffered from a variety of maladies. Alternatively, his father could have kept him, and his third brother, Henry, out of the war to protect his most gifted sons.[27] His younger brother, Henry James, who later became famous for novels such as *The Turn of the Screw* and *The Portrait of a Lady*, was injured putting out a fire in 1861, which for a period made him ineligible to fight. Henry never joined, however. Younger brothers Garth, who they called "Wilky," and Robert, both fought. Wilky helped lead the first Black regiment from Massachusetts. The unit was the focus of the 1989

*Chapter Eight*

film "Glory." When the 54th Massachusetts marched through Boston on its way to fight, with Frederick Douglass's sons Charles and Lewis, and Wilky in the procession, William James watched the fanfare from the sidelines. Essentially, unlike his friend Holmes, the philosopher who made experience central to the way of thinking he established did not take part in his generation's transformational experience.

James's experience, and pain, came from within as much as from without. Unlike his friend Holmes, who was careful to never adopt any faith and moved through life with confidence and direction, James spent his life searching for meaning. He marveled at his friend's vigor, writing to Henry that Holmes was "a powerful battery, formed like a planing machine to gouge a deep groove through life."[28] James's experience was far different. As friends and family, including Holmes, left for the war in 1861, James enrolled in science courses at Harvard. He completed only three semesters before deciding to leave. New faculty member Charles Eliot taught James's chemistry courses. Several years later, after Eliot became president of Harvard, he remembered James "was a very agreeable pupil, but was not wholly devoted to the study of chemistry. . . . He possessed unusual mental powers, remarkable spirituality, and great personal charm."[29]

Eliot, however, referred to James's struggles with depression, which might have led him to leave Harvard in spring 1863.[30] James studied on his own, reading widely in science and philosophy. He returned to Harvard to begin medical school in 1864 but left in 1865 to do field research with Agassiz, who had gone to the Amazon River to find evidence to disprove Darwin's theory of evolution. Darwin's *The Origin of the Species*, published in 1859, had overturned the science world. Agassiz found the opposite of what he sought in the Amazon. He found support for Darwin's theory while James discovered he never again wanted any part of field work.[31] From Rio de Janeiro, Brazil, James wrote Henry about "unlimited perspiration; unlimited itching of the skin caused by fleas & mosquitoes, and worst of all, on both cheeks and one side of neck by virulent ring-worms which appeared on board ship."[32]

James returned, ring-worm free, to Cambridge in 1866. He started his ill-fated pursuit of Fanny Dixwell, before leaving for Europe to deliver some of Agassiz's specimens to a colleague and to undergo medical

172

## Baking Bread

treatments on his back. When he returned, he finished his medical degree in 1869 only to fall into a deep depression. James admitted to Henry in a letter that he overdosed on chloral hydrate, a drug used to aid sleep and reduce anxiety.[33] His cousin, Mary Temple, died of tuberculosis in spring 1870. James's relationship with Mary—he called her "Minny"— has confused historians. Their letters, especially during her final six months, indicate a deep, loving bond.[34] None of the exchanges admit a romantic relationship. Whatever label history might provide their relationship, Minny's death was devastating to James.[35] In his biography, *Notes of a Son and a Brother*, Henry James explained:

> Much as this cherished companion's presence among us had represented for William and myself—and it is on his behalf I especially speak—her death made a mark that must stand here. . . . We felt it together as the end of our youth.[36]

Neither forgot her. Henry's leading female characters from *Portrait of a Lady* and *Wings of a Dove* were patterned after Minny Temple.[37] Commiserating with his brother, Henry wrote, soon after her death, "I feel as if a very fair portion of my sense of the reach and quality and capacity of human nature rested upon my experience of her character."[38] William James experienced her loss, both in a depression that lasted until 1872, and in a change in the way he understood the world. Temple's death influenced how James experienced reality, forcing him to reconsider the control he or any person had over what happens in their lives.

James climbed out of his depression. He began teaching at Harvard, with help from Eliot, in 1872. He also started an academic exploration of how people make meaning and come to truths. He published an unsigned tribute to Wright after his death in 1875. In 1879, he criticized Herbert Spencer's ideas about evolution in *The Nation* and asked "Are We Automata?" in an essay for *Mind*. He examined "The Association of Ideas" in *Popular Science Monthly* a year later. While these are considered minor works, taken together, they evidence James was converting the types of questions he faced in his losses, illnesses, and depression, into a line of inquiry. His thinking took a decisive step toward pragmatic thought in "The Will to Believe," an essay published in 1896 that arose from an address to the Philosophical Clubs of Yale and Brown

*Chapter Eight*

Universities. In the work, he questioned how people come to make decisions and follow through on them. The topic might seem mundane, but it gets at the heart of pragmatic thought. He reasoned, "We find our passional nature influencing us in our opinions, but that there are some options between opinions in which this influence must be regarded both as inevitable and as a lawful determinant of our choice."[39] He contended truth is the outcome of internal perceptions. Put another way, James concluded truth is the outcome of experience. In this sense, truth is conditional. Truth is dependent on what is known or perceived to be known at the moment of choice. He explained, given another moment of choice at another time, different truths might influence the outcome. Earlier in the essay, he reasoned, "I live, to be sure, by the practical faith that we must go on experiencing and thinking over our experience, for only thus can our opinions grow more true."[40]

Two years later, before a heart condition sidelined him for three years, James specifically discussed pragmatism in a lecture to the University of California Philosophical Union. The lecture was a turning-point moment in American thought. Pragmatism became a central part of philosophical debate for the next few decades.[41] By all accounts, James did not intend to create a discernible branch of philosophy. He used "pragmatism" because he remembered his friend Charles Peirce using it when they were in the Metaphysical Club.[42] James returned to pragmatism when he gave the Lowell lectures in Boston in December 1906. His work, *Pragmatism*, published a year later, was drawn from the transcripts of the lectures. All the while, his health was failing. He returned to Europe at least three times after 1898 to heal and seek cures.

### JAMES BAKES BREAD

The publisher's prints for *Pragmatism* arrived at James's home on a spring morning in 1907. In an upbeat letter to Swiss psychology professor Théodore Flournoy, James emphasized the book was going to be "exceedingly untechnical."[43] He continued, "I can't help suspecting it will make a real impression."[44] James's confidence, once something in short supply, was well-founded. By the end of 1910, the year he died,

# Baking Bread

*Pragmatism* was on its tenth printing. The work, compared with Georg Wilhelm Friedrich Hegel's or René Descartes's seminal works, is untechnical, even pragmatic, in outlining James's philosophy. *Pragmatism* is also constructed as a lecture, with little deviation from its initial form as a spoken work. Thus, it contains James's tentative, unassuming personality. The foundational work on American pragmatism is not delivered with the tone of a firebrand believer. Rather, James outlined the philosophy as if he was considering its problems and faults along the way. His tone fits his character. The same person who struggled with depression and physical illness all his life outlined a careful, thoughtful philosophy that, as it was constructed, acknowledged weak points and potential lines of criticism.

James started the work by contending every person has a philosophy. He reasoned most, because they seldom consider the matter, make decisions about the world around them based on a mishmash of empirical and rationalist perspectives. Thus, while philosophers continue to argue whether empirically based, sense-experience knowledge or principle-based rationalism best reflect how people understand truth, James emphasized the disagreement does little to aid people in the decisions they must make every day. He explained, "The whole function of philosophy ought to be to find out what definite difference it will make to you and me, at definite instants of our life, if this world-formula or that world-formula be the true one."[45]

James emphasized most people's philosophy, particularly those outside university philosophy programs, is a pragmatic endeavor. Each person must make difficult decisions in their daily lives and there is no time or need for lengthy, philosophical disagreements about being and truth, rationalism and empiricism, or idealism or materialism. The hallowed halls of philosophy, detached from the world of experience and choices, provided ideas and disagreements that "bake no bread" when it comes to determining truth, James contended.[46] He reasoned philosophy *should* bake bread and his pragmatic approach was intended to do so. He explained, "Now, what does *thinking about* the experience of the persons come to compared with directly, personally feeling it, as they feel it? The philosophers are dealing in shades, while those who live and feel know truth."[47] James's pragmatism does not pick a side in

175

*Chapter Eight*

the long-standing debates between empiricists, who understand truth as static and universal—essentially the outcome of careful processes and measurement—and rationalists, who construct truth via enduring principles, such as logic and ethics. He framed pragmatism as a middle path between the staked ground held by the two approaches.

James constructed truth as a *process*. Whether it is initially composed of facts or principles, truth is subject to change when new facts or a shift in principles takes place. He explained:

> The truth of an idea is not a stagnant property inherent in it. Truth happens to an idea. It becomes true, is made true by events. Its verity is in fact an event, a process: the process namely of its verifying itself, its verification. Its validity is the process of its validation.[48]

Thus, truth is dynamic, but not in a postmodern sense. James contended truth can be known. His conception of truth remains grounded in facts and beliefs, but it is treated as a liquid, rather than a solid. The truth process, to James, is fundamentally directed by experience and informed by prior truths. An individual might come to a conclusion about a matter, but they can, and should, be willing to adjust what had previously been perceived as truth when the factors used to make that conclusion shift. He reasoned, "New truths thus are resultants of new experiences and of old truths combined and mutually modifying one another."[49]

James, in his polite and unassuming way, did not transform how truth is constructed. He acknowledged pragmatism's foundational components were not new.[50] Instead, he worked to cut away any thinking or debating that failed to contribute to how people think and come to understand the world around them. James's pragmatic approach essentially recast experience and truth as partners in a cycle. Experience, he contended, creates perceptions. Those perceptions drive what people accept as true or false. Such conclusions, however, are subject to changes that come from new experiences. James emphasized people do not verify every fact, like a scientist might. They rely on shortcuts. The shortcuts are made from experiences, which have produced other generally unverified truths. In *The Meaning of Truth*, which James labeled "a sequel to *Pragmatism*," he explained, "To continue thinking unchallenged is, ninety-nine times out of a hundred, our practical substitute for knowing

*Baking Bread*

in the completed sense."[51] In the same passage, he continued, "The experiences of tendency are sufficient to act upon—what more could we have done at those moments even if the later verification comes complete?"[52] Thus, the truth process includes checking new ideas or necessary decisions against existing perception-based truths. Pragmatism, in this regard, identifies and explicates this ongoing process between experiences and truths. Such an approach bears particular value in the networked, AI era, as people encounter countless ideas from human and non-human speakers.

James's pragmatism makes three crucial contributions to this chapter's lens for understanding how the space for discourse can or should be constructed. First, his vision of pragmatism understood truth as being individually constructed based on personal experience. While the Enlightenment thought that shaped the marketplace approach's thinking also focused on individual rationality, it assumed people are generally the same and will come to similar conclusions. James's approach understood individuals, based on experience, weigh different facts and principles when discerning truth. Of course, James's emphasis on the individual, rather than society or democracy, aligns with his background in psychology, along with his lifelong, personal search to understand himself and others. Second, the definition of truth, which in the empiricist-dominated marketplace thinking is a static universal, becomes conditional and fluid. Truth becomes more akin to a perception, impression, or belief. James, in one instance, explained, "Truth . . . becomes a class-name for all sorts of definite working-values in experience."[53] In another passage, he reasoned, "Truth, as any dictionary will tell you, is a property of certain of our ideas. It means their 'agreement,' as falsity means their disagreement with reality."[54] Third, pragmatism builds a process-based model regarding how people interact with the world around them. The marketplace's Enlightenment foundations emphasizes static truths that are discovered. The outcome is predetermined, and in rationalizing expansive free expression, justices have sought to safeguard the discovery outcome. The pragmatic, discourse-based model emphasizes the fluid movement of truth, via individual experiences.

The approach essentially resituated truth, framing it as a type of provisional belief or idea. The model's inflection point, therefore,

*Chapter Eight*

emphasizes safeguarding the *process* that happens when people encounter new ideas, checking them against their existing truths, and making appropriate adjustments. James explained, "Since almost any object may someday become temporarily important, the advantage of having a general stock of extra truths, of ideas that shall be true of merely possible situations, is obvious."[55] Thus, pragmatism rationalizes protecting the exchange of ideas for the purpose of safeguarding a *process*.

## JANE ADDAMS RE-EDUCATES JOHN DEWEY

Dewey wasn't heir to James's pragmatism when he arrived as head of philosophy at the University of Chicago in 1894.

He wasn't even on James's list of philosophers in his field. Dewey was a lightly published, thirty-five-year-old academic from Vermont. He wasn't anyone's first choice for the University of Chicago job. University president William Rainey Harper wanted a big name to lead the philosophy department.[56] He asked James for a recommendation. Dewey didn't make James's list. James, always loyal to Peirce, suggested his old friend, who had been dismissed from Johns Hopkins and was destitute.[57] Peirce's reputation for being difficult to work with and for bringing substantial controversy led University of Chicago faculty members to reject the suggestion.[58] Harper had to continue the search. He offered the position to three other scholars, all of whom turned him down.[59] Another faculty member suggested Dewey, whom he had worked with at the University of Michigan. Dewey's candidacy didn't overwhelm Harper. A reference described him as "simple, modest, utterly devoid of any affection or self-consciousness."[60] Still, Harper needed to fill the position and Dewey met the requirements. He offered Dewey the job.

Dewey came to Chicago with a PhD from the Johns Hopkins University, where he'd crossed paths with Peirce, but was disappointed by the only course he took with him.[61] He'd published four modest works, including a text on psychology, but was far from the well-known progressive advocate who was an initial member of the NAACP (1909), co-founded the American Association of University Professors (1915), and helped establish the ACLU (1920). By all accounts, however, by 1894, Dewey's education was complete. Yet, something was missing. In 1930,

178

FIGURE 5 John Dewey.
Source: Library of Congress

*Chapter Eight*

in an essay titled "From Absolutism to Experimentalism," he framed himself as being "unacquainted with any system of thought that satisfied his head and heart" early in his academic career.[62] In other words, he had not been able to connect what he cared about with his scholarly pursuits. In the same essay, he emphasized "The forces that have influenced me have come from persons and from situations more than from books."[63] Addams was paramount among those influential persons.

She, in many ways, completed his education.[64] Addams, already a reformer and advocate for the poor, and Dewey, a quiet, scholarly thinker, met at Addams's Hull House in fall 1894, just after the Pullman Strike divided the nation. The partnership that grew from their initial meeting, and disagreements, transformed Dewey's thinking. Dewey wrote his wife, Alice, after hearing Addams speak for the first time in 1894. He described her speech, and their conversation afterward, as "the most magnificent exhibition of intellect and moral faith I ever saw."[65] A biographer characterized Dewey and Addams as "intellectual soul mates from the moment they met."[66]

They became close friends, educating and supporting each other. Dewey assigned Addams's books as class readings at the University of Chicago. He dedicated *Liberalism and Social Action* to Addams and named one of his daughters, Jane. For her part, Addams wrote a stirring eulogy for Dewey's son Gordon, who died of typhoid fever in 1904. He was ten years old. Dewey and his wife Alice had already lost Gordon's older brother, Morris, in 1895. Addams characterized Gordon as smart and sensitive. She explained:

> He was destined to feel the smart and pang of the degrading poverty in the world, as he would have shared a growing belief newly common among men, that it may be possible not only to alleviate but at last remove it, if the race but makes a concerted effort.[67]

Thus, even in eulogizing her dear friend's lost son, she associated his life with her work toward a more equitable society. Addams opened Hull House in 1889 after deciding to devote her life to helping the poor.[68] She bought an old mansion, once owned by real-estate magnate Charles Hull, and turned it into a home for impoverished working people. Addams lived in the home, working with her partner, Ellen Gates Starr,

*Baking Bread*

to create a community of support for those in the area. The Hull House ultimately expanded to thirteen buildings southwest of downtown Chicago. Addams's programs included schools for children and courses on civil rights and civil duty.[69]

Dewey joined the board of trustees and worked in the Hull House. He gave lectures and facilitated conversations with activists from a variety of viewpoints. These speakers were drawn to Hull House as a meeting place for ideas. It was a safe space for discourse. Essentially, the Hull House community became a physical manifestation of a particular version of the conceptual space, something Dewey observed carefully. Those who gathered in the space shared concerns and communicated ideas in ways that informed the community. They practiced active forms of citizenship, making democracy a way of life, rather than an abstract concept. As one biographer noted, "Dewey owed much to the influences he encountered at Hull House."[70] Of course, behind Hull House's space for discourse was Addams, who challenged Dewey's ideas and convinced him to consider new approaches. Two years before she met Dewey, Addams outlined three arguments for social settlements, such as Hull House. Her reasons sound much like Dewey's later work regarding pragmatism and its relationship with civic engagement. She summarized her reasons as:

> The first contains the desire to make the entire social organism democratic, to extend democracy beyond its political expression; the second is the impulse to share the race life, and to bring as much as possible of social energy and the accumulation of civilization to those portions of the race which have little; the third springs from a certain renaissance of Christianity, a movement toward its early humanitarian aspects.[71]

Addams's vision for Hull House was, essentially, what would today be labeled a Deweyan public. Dewey's prominence has not gone unnoticed by feminist scholars, who have emphasized Addams's role, alongside Dewey, in constructing these assumptions.[72] Crucially, Addams articulated many of these ideas decades before such a space appeared in works such as *The Public and Its Problems* (1927) and *Liberalism and Social Action* (1935). The pair's advocacy went beyond sharing ideas.

*Chapter Eight*

Addams, alongside Dewey and Felix Frankfurter (see chapter 7), helped found the ACLU. She and Dewey were also among the first members of the NAACP. Addams won the Nobel Peace Prize in 1919. Her influence on Dewey, however, is most crucial to the lens for understanding the pragmatic-based space for democratic discourse. Addams died in spring 1935, just months after Holmes.

Dewey wrote five more books, each overlapping with ideas the two shared regarding an active form of citizenship that takes place in a space for discourse.

## CIVIC PRAGMATISM

James might not have thought of Dewey when Harper sought candidates for the head of philosophy at the University of Chicago in the early 1890s, but he knew who he was when he wrote *Pragmatism* in 1906 and 1907. James referenced Dewey fifteen times in *Pragmatism* and *The Meaning of Truth*.[73] He clearly admired Dewey, who was seventeen years younger. Dewey, for his part, specifically mentioned James as shaping his thinking. Referring to James in his usual congested writing style, he emphasized, "As far as I can discover one specifiable philosophic factor which entered into my thinking so as to give it a new direction and quality, it is this one."[74] Though they admired each other, the thinkers were not close friends. They exchanged cordial letters, but there is no record of them working together or meeting. Their differences are crucial. James developed pragmatic thought as a tool for understanding largely internal processes. He wanted to know how personal experiences—including his own struggles—shape the way people understand the world around them. Dewey didn't have the same demons with which to wrestle. His "head and heart" were devoted to applying pragmatic thinking to better society.[75]

Perhaps Addams's and the Hull House's influences were, in a large part, responsible for the differences between James's internally focused and Dewey's socially concerned approaches to pragmatism. Ultimately, Dewey's pragmatic assumptions regarding experience and truth overlap with James's, but the scope of his thinking is fundamentally on a societal level. For our purposes, Dewey constructed pragmatism as a blueprint

FIGURE 6 Jane Addams, who won the Nobel Peace Prize in 1931, founded and ran the Hull House settlement program in Chicago.
Source: Library of Congress

## Chapter Eight

for a very particular design for the space for human discourse. In particular, he introduced concern for the nature of human-formed publics, the place of the individual in society, and the flow of information into James's existing pragmatic formula. The building blocks of each of these discourse-based approaches operate upon different assumptions from the Enlightenment-founded marketplace approach that has dominated the design of the space for democratic discussion for decades. Dewey's writing, it's worth noting, is far from eloquent. As Holmes commented about Dewey in a letter to a friend, "He can't write and therefore doesn't make pleasant reading, but to my fancy he gets closer to the cosmic wiggle than anyone else I know."[76] Let's examine that wiggle.

Through all of Dewey's writing—however convoluted and ungraceful it is—Addams's influence and her Hull House community echo in the background. Dewey understood a public as a group of individuals who freely associates for some purpose or end. He explained, "Those indirectly and seriously affected for good or for evil form a group distinctive enough to require recognition and a name. The name selected is The Public."[77] In other words, a public forms based on a shared interest or concern, and is defined by the active nature of its participants. Such a construction is fundamentally different to what we often colloquially refer to as *the* public, which is a sort of generalized term for a mass of ordinary people. Dewey did not see *the* public in that sense. He saw *publics*.

Within the masses of people, he saw discernible communities of individuals who associate based on shared concerns, beliefs, interests, or other bonding factors. Dewey rejected the idea *the* public can be constituted as an entrenched government institution. A public can organize to create a political entity, but that entity does not inherently remain a representative of the public. In fact, such an institution's power can keep a public from effecting important change on society.[78] Similarly, an institutionalized marketplace of ideas can be understood as failing to function in its role in creating a space for discourse. Dewey's construction of publics overlaps with the way virtual communities function in the networked, AI era, as people move seamlessly through interest-based associations that ebb and flow online.[79] In the early twentieth century, however, these associations looked like the lectures and discussions he

184

observed and participated in at the Hull House. People from diverse groups gathered to address problems and questions, such as poor working conditions, low wages, or the scourge of Standard Oil.[80] They formed associations with one another, sought common ground, and, in doing so, lived an active form of democratic citizenship.

The final aspect, active citizenship, related to another feature of Dewey's discourse model. He understood individuals' engagement in publics as the only path toward self-fulfillment. Put another way, a person could not reach their potential without being an active member of some association with others. He explained, "Liberty is that secure release and fulfillment of personal potentialities which take place only in rich and manifold association with others."[81] In another passage, he reasoned, "To learn to be human is to develop through the give-and-take of communication an effective sense of being an individually distinctive member of a community."[82] Dewey essentially reasoned association with others benefited democracy, because he understood democracy as a "way of life."[83] At the same time, the individual, who grows and finds meaning through engagement, benefits as well. Such a vision of the individual and community is in near complete opposition to Enlightenment-based understandings that the individual's freedom is the paramount concern.[84]

When Dewey considered these association-and-individual dynamics, he was talking about experience, a crucial pillar of pragmatic thought. The experience of the individual and the experiences of those who engage with them are influenced by how these associations form and operate. While James focused on an internal process in which personal experience helps influence how people evaluate ideas and come to truths, Dewey emphasized the process occurs in interactions with others. He contended, "No man and no mind was ever emancipated merely by being left alone."[85] The shared experiences that come from associations help people understand themselves and others, making them better citizens and influencing their constructions of truth. In one of his essays on democracy, he reasoned, "Democracy is belief in the ability of human experience to generate the aims and methods by which further experience will grow in ordered richness."[86] Dewey essentially contended democracy is a pragmatic endeavor. He reasoned democracy requires active citizenship that generally takes the form of subject or interest-based associations

## Chapter Eight

that become publics and, intermingling with other publics, exert pressure on institutions to create a better life for citizens. Certainly, within these assumptions, we also see the progressive nature of Dewey's thinking. His construction of pragmatism assumed social progress. Within the process he envisioned, Dewey understood the associations people form as helping them share experiences and create individual fulfillment.

We are still missing one crucial, space-for-human-discourse-related building block of Dewey's pragmatic vision. He was deeply concerned with the flow of information. The formation of associations and publics and the self-fulfillment that comes from active, way-of-life democracy cannot function without the free exchange of ideas. Dewey's understanding of the exchange, however, was markedly different from the Enlightenment assumptions that undergird the marketplace approach. He explained, for example, democracy requires "perfecting the means and ways of communication of meanings so that genuinely shared interest in the consequences of interdependent activities may inform desire and effort and thereby direct action."[87] He emphasized that such communication requires a flow of ideas, but also restraint and protection for that flow. Dewey contended:

> There can be no public without full publicity in respect to all consequences which concern it. Whatever obstructs and restricts publicity, limits and distorts public opinion and checks and distorts thinking on social affairs. Without freedom of expression, not even methods of social inquiry can be developed.[88]

Dewey communicated concern for distortion in the space for discourse. He raised questions about those who seek to mislead or artificially influence the experience-based formation of truth within the associations and publics he outlined. Dewey also emphasized legal protections are not sufficient to protect free expression and a space for discourse. He explained, "Intolerance, abuse, calling of names because of differences of opinions about religion or politics or business, as well as because of differences of race, color, wealth or degree of culture are treason to the democratic way of life."[89]

Thus, Dewey implied the discursive space he envisioned included protections for free expression. Put differently, he was not conjuring a

186

# Baking Bread

space for absolutely protected free expression. Dewey hinted expression that distorts the space or shames people from participating would harm democracy. He went no further, however. His version of the map of the space for human discourse does not detail *how* the space can be protected from distortion in a way that still safeguards free expression.

We do know, however, Dewey's discursive vision for the space emphasized engagement, via associations, that created mutual, shared solutions and conclusions regarding social concerns. He did not go into detail about how the discursive space he envisioned should be safeguarded. His general solution was inclusive communities and a willingness to work together. The associations he described required "the common man to respond with commonsense to the free play of facts which are secured by effective guarantees to free inquiry, free assembly, and free communication."[90] We are left to ask ourselves what such a hopeful space would look like in the networked, AI era. After all, Dewey was not a lawyer and he did not make a legal argument. He has never been cited by the Supreme Court in a free-expression case. Importantly, as we seek alternative lenses through which we can understand the space for discourse in the twenty-first century, Dewey comes to the matter of free expression and how it is rationalized from a pragmatic philosopher's perspective. His thinking had some overlap with Holmes's.

Dewey and Holmes were not friends. There is no documentation they ever met. They read each other's work carefully, however. Dewey quoted Holmes's ideas extensively in his 1924 essay "Logic Method and Law" and again in his 1925 book *Experience and Nature*. In explicating the difference between empirical logic and pragmatic experience, he quoted Holmes's conclusion, "The actual life of the law has not been logic: It has been experience," for example.[91] Dewey's use of Holmes's reasoning to support largely pragmatic thinking added fuel to the fire that Holmes was a pragmatic thinker, though he denied that designation, as well as any other label others tried to place on his thinking (See chapter 3). It's likely Holmes was introduced to Dewey's work because the younger thinker was complimentary of Holmes's ideas, which contributed to Holmes's positive feedback. In a 1927 letter to Elizabeth Shepley Sergeant, a journalist who was among the first contributors to the *New Republic*, he noted Dewey's work is "very badly written but unless I am

187

*Chapter Eight*

mistaken a really great book. If I am misled it is not because he gives me a compliment. He really seemed to me to have more of our Cosmos in his head than anyone."[92] In a letter to another friend about a year later, Holmes labeled Dewey as having "the leading place in American philosophy."[93] Thus, Holmes, who introduced the marketplace concept—although rather incompletely (see chapter 2)did not reject Dewey's ideas. While he did not hold them to the scrutiny he would the question before the Court in a case, Holmes was often critical of the authors he read. He never picked apart Dewey's ideas in the ways he did Hegel's or Kant's—or Peirce's or James's, for that matter.[94]

Whether or not Holmes's consistently supportive words about Dewey's ideas—if not his writing style—amount to an endorsement of the pragmatic, discourse-based model for the space he set forth, it is crucial that Dewey constructed a set of foundations for the space that are in near complete opposition to Enlightenment thought. While the Enlightenment-founded marketplace creates outcome-based rationales for free expression and the space for discourse, Dewey's pragmatic system emphasized a *process*. The space for discourse takes a different shape when it includes assumptions that individuals enrich communities and communities enrich individuals in interlocking ways. Dewey's map of the space emphasized human engagement for the purpose of association and shared problem-solving. Truth functions differently in such a space. Truth in a pragmatically constructed space, as James most clearly explicated and Dewey supported, is transformed from a static, universal matter that awaits discovery to a dynamic, personally constructed set of beliefs or conclusions based upon experience and a mishmash of personal philosophies. If the space and nature of truth are changed in these ways, we must ask whether the rationales for free expression also change. James, in his fervor to understand his being—and that of others—had almost nothing to say regarding this matter. Dewey indicated the space he envisioned is vulnerable to distortion.

While the marketplace-based map of the space faces similar vulnerabilities, such weaknesses have been ignored or cast aside in favor of the Enlightenment-based faith that truth will generally vanquish falsity. Dewey's approach recognized the problem, but he left us without a solution. He never explicitly addressed how the discursive space could be

*Baking Bread*

protected. We must also note Dewey's discourse-based model is idealistic. It is predicated on a democratic society that seeks to work together to solve problems. It assumes consensus that comes from citizens who *want* to find solutions and move forward to better others and their own lives. Perhaps Dewey's thinking's greatest weakness is its hope and optimism regarding citizens in a democratic society. Similarly, what we learn from James regarding a pragmatism-based space for discourse suffers from his largely internally focused explication of his theory. Neither of these concerns mean the pragmatic lens cannot contribute to how the space for human discourse *can* or *should* be constructed in the networked, AI era.

# NINE

## Monsters, Machines, and Truth

By all accounts, Adolf Eichmann was a monster. A high-ranking member of the Nazi's feared SS corps, Eichmann was the logistical mastermind behind the systematic murder of millions of Jews. He arranged for their removal from Nazi-occupied Austria in 1938 and performed the same duties in Prague in 1939.[1] Eichmann excelled at following orders and getting things done. He was rewarded with an invitation to Nazi headquarters and, in 1942, at a lakeside villa southwest of Berlin, was trusted by the Nazi's highest leaders to organize the "final solution to the Jewish question." He was essentially named chief executioner.[2] The five-foot-nine, thirty-six-year-old from western Germany began immediately, arranging for Jews from throughout Europe to be taken to places like Auschwitz and Treblinka, both in Poland, where they would be murdered.

Then the Third Reich began to falter. British, US, and Canadian troops landed in Normandy, France, on D-day, June 6, 1944, forcing Germany to fight on eastern and western fronts. Later that month, Soviet troops began pushing west, driving German forces back from Belarus into Poland. Adolf Hitler killed himself in his Berlin bunker in late April 1945. Little more than a week later, Germany's unconditional surrender was celebrated throughout Europe. Twelve Nazi leaders, including Ernst Kaltenbrunner, who recruited Eichmann into the SS in 1932,

190

*Monsters, Machines, and Truth*

were sentenced to death by the Nuremberg military tribunal in 1946. Eichmann, the monster, disappeared. He escaped US custody in 1946, lived under a false name in Germany for several years, and then slipped away on a ship to Argentina. The man a 1960 Associated Press report referenced as the "greatest living enemy of the Jewish people," got away.[3]

Almost. Israeli secret service operatives found Eichmann's wife, Veronika, in 1959, learning she had remarried and was living near Buenos Aires with Eichmann's children. Secret service agents began to observe Veronika Eichmann and her new husband, Ricardo Klement. They were almost certain he was not new at all. Agents became increasingly convinced they had found Adolph Eichmann, who was using a false identity and working at a Mercedes-Benz factory. One evening, operatives pretended to be working on their car on the road the man going by Klement usually walked on his way home. When he passed, they grabbed him. In a struggle, they fell into a nearby ditch.[4] They ultimately wrestled him into a vehicle and took him to a safe house. There, the captors asked their target one question, "Who are you?" He responded, "Ich bin Adolf Eichmann." They had their man.

Hannah Arendt was vacationing with her husband, Heinrich Blücher, in the Catskill Mountains in New York when she heard the news.[5] Arendt, a German and a Jew, had been captured and interrogated by the SS for eight days in 1933, fled her home in Berlin, lived as a refugee in Paris, and narrowly escaped on a steamer to the United States after the Nazis invaded France. By the time Eichmann, who was born the same year and fewer than two hundred miles from Arendt, was captured and whisked away to Jerusalem to stand trial, she was a world-renowned thinker. Her life, and thought, were defined by antisemitism, totalitarianism, and death. Now, the fifty-three-year-old thinker wanted to see the monster. She wanted to look the physical embodiment of the evil that had killed so many and overturned her life in the eye. After reading of Eichmann's capture, she started to arrange to be in Jerusalem for the trial of the man whose photo was below a headline that read "Killer of 6,000,000" in the *New York Times* a few weeks after his capture.[6] She immediately volunteered to cover Eichmann's trial in Jerusalem for the *New Yorker*. Editors agreed and she set about clearing away obligations. She requested new terms for a grant she had with the Rockefeller

## Chapter Nine

Foundation, reasoning "You will understand I think why I should cover this trial; I missed the Nuremberg Trials, I never saw these people in the flesh."[7] Weeks later, she canceled a lecture at Vassar College. She explained:

> This is for me the first . . . opportunity to watch one of the chief actors of totalitarianism in the flesh. As you probably know, Nazism has played a considerable part both in my personal life and my life as an author.[8]

Arendt concluded, "To attend this trial, I feel, is somehow an obligation I owe to my past."[9]

Eichmann's trial before a tribunal of the Jerusalem District Court started April 11, 1961. When he entered the courtroom, Arendt described Eichmann as "medium-sized, slender, middle-aged, with receding hair, ill-fitting teeth, and nearsighted eyes, who throughout the trial keeps craning his scraggy neck toward the bench."[10] Arendt did not find the monster she expected. The monster, to Arendt, was a pathetic, ordinary man with a "nervous tic to which his mouth must have become subject long before this trial started."[11] Eichmann was not a strident ideologue who espoused Nazi ideas. He did not stand up in his glass box at the trial and scream at those in attendance. He was a small man with small ideas, devoid of independent thought or meaningful reflection. She explained, "He did not enter the Party out of conviction, nor was he ever convinced by it."[12] Arendt framed Eichmann as a lazy, unsuccessful man who was insignificant in society's and his own eyes, but found success and purpose in the Nazi Party. While her conclusions regarding the type of monster she observed led to substantial criticism, she emphasized his behavior represented "the banality of evil."[13] The unthinking citizen, engulfed in a wave of Nazi-infused like-mindedness, orchestrated the deaths of millions without ever directly killing anyone by his own hand. To Arendt, this was the danger posed by modern society. The life-transforming tools and lack of an active, thoughtful life endangered the future. The space for discourse had failed to operate. Eichmann was a result.

Eichmann dropped out of high school—the same school in Linz, Austria, Hitler attended several years earlier. He enrolled in trade school but did not finish. Arendt quoted him as explaining, he "had not exactly

## Monsters, Machines, and Truth

been the most hard-working" student.[14] By his early twenties, he had few prospects. He worked odd jobs, selling radios and vacuum oil. By 1932, the vacuum-oil-sales job was gone too. Kaltenbrunner, a family friend, found a place for the twenty-six-year-old in the SS. In *Eichmann in Jerusalem*, Arendt's full account of the trial, she explained, "Kaltenbrunner had said to him: Why not join the S.S.? And he had replied, Why not? That was how it had happened, and that was about all there was to it."[15] In other words, Eichmann was not a true believer. He was not an idealist. He joined the Nazis in the same way a person might agree to see a movie. He shrugged and said "okay." Eichmann never read Hitler's book, *Mein Kompf*, and was not able to explain what the Nazis stood for. Eichmann portrayed himself as a mere cog in the Nazi machine, an argument Arendt's account, to some extent, supported. He contended he never killed anyone. Eichmann reasoned he was simply following orders.

Arendt wanted to know how an unexceptional person like Eichmann could casually stumble into a role that orchestrated mass genocide and never stop to consider whether it was evil, why the death was happening, or his contribution to the tragedy. To Arendt, Eichmann's greatest sin, and qualification for service in the Nazi war effort, was his inability to think. She wrote, "From a humdrum life without significance and consequence the wind had blown him into History."[16] In another passage, she descried him as "a leaf in the whirlwind of time."[17] The monster was an unthinking citizen. In scrutinizing his case, she found connections to her previous works on community, citizenship, and the flow of ideas. His final words only reinforced her conclusions. Eichmann was executed in 1962. His last words were a mixture of clichés and nonsensical, conflicting statements about his faith. Arendt reasoned, "It was as though in those last minutes he was summing up the lesson that this long course in human wickedness had taught us—the lesson of the fearsome, word-and-thought-defying banality of evil."[18]

Arendt in many ways made it her life's work to understand the evil Eichmann embodied. In works such as *Origins of Totalitarianism* and *The Human Condition*, both published in the 1950s, she sought to understand the factors that influence whether civil society fails or flourishes. In *Origins of Totalitarianism*, she explained "this book has been written against a background of both reckless optimism and reckless

193

*Chapter Nine*

despair."[19] Her interests were not a mere hobby. Arendt faced antisemitism as a girl in school, was forced to flee her home during World War I, experienced the hopeless feeling of being stateless as a refugee in Paris when the Nazis rose to power, survived near misses with the Nazis in Germany and France, and watched, shocked, as the world learned about the Nazi's crimes in the mid-1940s. Ultimately, Arendt provided a crucial, discernible lens through which to consider the space for human discourse in the networked, AI era. Her construction of a democratic space for discourse is particularly relevant because it emphasizes the requisite boundaries for public and private speech, the extent to which tools and machines humans create influence society and the self, and how truth is constructed. Because Arendt's life is inseparable from her thinking, this chapter begins by examining her experiences until just after her harrowing escape from Nazi-occupied France in 1941.

## PARVENU OR PARIAH

Arendt's mother, Martha, instructed her daughter to never tolerate antisemitic remarks from her teachers or classmates. If an anti-Jewish remark came from a teacher, Hannah was to get up and leave the school. Her mother would deal with the teacher and administrators. If the remark came from another student, however, Martha expected her daughter to fend for herself.[20] Arendt recalled in a television interview "All Jewish children encountered antisemitism. And the souls of many children were poisoned by it."[21] Arendt's family's faith and ethnicity, while her parents were not particularly devout, immediately led her to consider identity, community, and the role of government. She was born in Hanover, Germany, in 1906, but grew up in Königsberg, an ancient East Prussian city that was home to Immanuel Kant in the 1700s and, in the twentieth century, housed a substantial Jewish population. Long before her hometown was destroyed in World War II, Arendt felt the tension between Jewish culture and assimilation with middle-class life in Königsberg.

She framed the choice she and others faced as being between pariah, those excluded from society, and parvenu, those who left behind their culture to assimilate socially and economically into the culture.[22] She explained, Jews

194

*Monsters, Machines, and Truth*

always had to pay with political misery for social glory and with social insult for political success. Assimilation, in the sense of acceptance by non-Jewish society, was granted them only as long as they were clearly distinguished exceptions from the Jewish masses.[23]

Arendt was already considering the forces that exerted pressure on the space for discourse.

Alongside these experiences, Arendt lost her father in October 1913. He slipped away slowly, suffering from syphilis. He was moved to a psychiatric hospital in 1911, where she visited him until he no longer recognized her.[24] The next year, the Arendts spent ten weeks in Berlin as Russian forces threatened to overrun the German army near Königsberg during World War I. The family returned home after the threat had passed and Arendt's mother married a widower named Martin Beerwald. As she entered her teens, Arendt was becoming difficult for her mother and new stepfather to handle. She refused to attend family events. As one biography explained, "she claimed, as a matter of principle, that she did not regard family ties as sufficient reason for sociability."[25] Arendt was expelled from school when she was fifteen. A teacher offended her with a comment—it's not clear what was said—and Arendt organized a boycott of the teacher's classes.[26] Her mother argued on her behalf, but the principal would not change his mind. Arendt took advantage of her expulsion, entering a crucial, formative period in her early thinking.

Arendt lived with relatives while sitting in on courses in Greek, Latin, and theology at the University of Berlin, although she was not enrolled there. She also read existentialist philosopher Søren Kierkegaard's and Kant's principle works when she was sixteen. Looking for more reading, she encountered Karl Jaspers's *Psychology of the World*, newly published in 1919, as well as the work of a young thinker named Martin Heidegger.[27] These influences became the foundational building blocks for her thoughts regarding the space for discourse. She remained grounded in classical Greek philosophy and influenced by Jaspers's and Heidegger's thinking throughout her life.

Arendt chose to attend the University of Marburg, in the rolling, wooded hills of central Germany, at least partially because Heidegger was there. Heidegger, a thirty-five-year-old junior faculty member, who

195

*Chapter Nine*

was studying with respected thinker, and pioneer of phenomenological thought, Edmund Husserl, had just come to Marburg after lecturing at the University of Freiburg. He was drafting his master work, *Being and Time*, the same year Arendt came to the university. She sat in his lectures and absorbed and observed Heidegger's efforts to develop the very ideas that came to characterize his philosophy-altering conceptualization of being.[28] Heidegger's questions were inward, existence-focused, but included concern for the nature of being in the world. In marking his eightieth birthday, in 1969, Arendt reflected that she and her classmates came to Marburg to hear thinking "come to life again."[29] She continued, "People followed the rumor about Heidegger in order to learn thinking. What was experienced was thinking as pure activity."[30] Contextually, her reflection had particular meaning in depressed World War I Germany. Decades later, elements of Heidegger's ideas regarding thinking and being were among the foundational building blocks Arendt used to described Eichmann's particular form on monstrousness. He was thoughtless. Living required thought, she reasoned.

## STATELESS AND RIGHTLESS

As she hoped, Heidegger helped Arendt to think. Their relationship, however, extended beyond the student-teacher boundaries. They had a secret affair in 1925, as Heidegger continued to construct his philosophy. Arendt was nineteen years old. Heidegger was married with two children and seventeen years older than his student. The affair ended and Arendt left Marburg to study at the University of Heidelberg with Jaspers. While the affair ended, Heidegger and Arendt maintained a bond until her death in 1975. Welcomed by Heidegger's wife, Elfriede— the two were cordial to each other—she visited him in Freiburg before her unexpected death later that year. Arendt wrote a friend, "I came home very depressed. Heidegger is now suddenly very old, very changed from last year, very deaf and remote, unapproachable as I never saw him before."[31]

Their lifelong relationship faced more challenges than the feelings from the 1925 affair. Heidegger joined the Nazi Party in 1933 and became the party's approved rector of the University of Freiburg. This

196

FIGURE 7 Hannah Arendt was detained and questioned for eight days by the Nazi SS in 1933. She was 27. Arendt confused the officials with lies and sent them on errands to buy her cigarettes. She and her mother fled Germany after her release.
Source: Wikimedia Commons

*Chapter Nine*

ended communication between Arendt and Heidegger for many years. It also ended Heidegger's and Jaspers's friendship. Heidegger wrote Jaspers in 1950 to tell him he was ashamed of his behavior.[32] Arendt had little time to reflect on Heidegger's support for the Nazis. As he ascended as rector, Arendt was arrested and questioned by Nazi officials for eight days about her library searches in 1933. After convincing the police to buy her cigarettes and coffee, she told them a string of lies and they let her go.[33] She and her mother soon fled Germany, using an underground network of paths in the woods used by many Jews near the mountains that made the border with Czechoslovakia.

Arendt joined countless other refuges who gathered in Paris, where she lived from 1933 until 1941, when the Nazi invasion of France meant she was again uprooted and forced to run. As she worked odd jobs, her years as a refugee influenced the way she understood the structures of government and society. She found herself stateless and, therefore, without rights. She explained, "There was no place on earth where migrants could go without the severest restrictions, no country where they would be assimilated, no territory where they could found a new community."[34] Arendt also observed that being stateless and rightless meant people lacked government protection. She and others became a burden, lacking the rights of citizens. She reasoned, "Their plight is not that they are not equal before the law, but that no law exists for them; not that they are oppressed but that nobody wants even to oppress them."[35] In *Origins of Totalitarianism*, Arendt lamented the absence of a space for community. She emphasized the meaninglessness of opinions and actions for people who lack a shared space, physical or imagined. Arendt explained stateless people are "deprived, not of the right of freedom, but of the right to action; not of the right to think whatever they please, but of the right to opinion."[36]

Her time in Paris was not all tragedy. She crossed paths with French existentialist Jean-Paul Sarte, reconnected with a childhood friend, and married Blücher. As the Nazi threat loomed, the French government moved all German refugees into internment camps. Arendt and her new husband were separated and lost each other. In the chaos of France's sudden defeat, Arendt escaped her assigned camp with only a toothbrush and the clothes she was wearing. She found Blücher, who, after living in

198

*Monsters, Machines, and Truth*

a barn with thirty other men, had found his way out of a camp in southeast France. The couple narrowly escaped France's puppet government's increasingly restrictive policies. She was fortunate to leave. The Nazis later took over the camp the French relegated her to in 1940. Ultimately, Eichmann, the monster, transported nearly 6,000 Jews through its gates, where they lived in terrible conditions. A few years later, most who survived were sent to extermination centers.

## THE PUBLIC AND PRIVATE REALMS

Arendt had only twenty-five dollars when she walked off the ship in New York in May 1941. She, her husband, and her mother, struggled to establish new lives in the United States They were again stateless. Arendt started writing for a weekly newspaper that served the German refugee community in New York and teaching part-time at Brooklyn College. Blücher, a scholar in his own right, worked in a chemical factory. This was the beginning of Arendt's transformation into an international thinker. Her grounding in Greek philosophy and training with pioneering philosophers such as Heidegger and Jaspers, drawn together with her lifetime of harrowing experiences, led to four works that examine the requisite ingredients for a space for human discourse from a very particular lens. She started writing *Origins of Totalitarianism* in 1944, which was not published until 1951, the year she became a US citizen. *The Human Condition* was published in 1958, followed by *Eichmann in Jerusalem*—the tale of the monster—in 1963. Arendt died in 1975 and her final work, *The Life of the Mind*, which was incomplete, was published in 1978.

Her works include a complex, nuanced conceptualization of the private and public realms and how what occurs in such realms influences the space for discourse. She categorized the private realm as what, in antiquity, constituted the household or estate, a place that included family members and laborers. The private realm was internally focused and dominated by a head of the household. Such a space was where necessary functions occurred. In this sense, the private realm was characterized by authoritarianism, a solitary leader who managed affairs and everyone else in the household followed. Only the necessities, the labor

*Chapter Nine*

needed to maintain existence and manage personal affairs, existed in the private realm. In her vocabulary, these functions equated to "labor." Labor activities, to Arendt, were those that maintained life and were inseparable from the human condition.[37] She explained, "Natural community in the household therefore was born of necessity, and necessity ruled over all activities performed in it."[38] The opposite of labor, in Arendt's thinking, was "work." Work was the creative outcome of being. She explained, "Work provides an 'artificial' world of things, distinctly different from all natural surroundings."[39] In this regard, work was distinctive, individual, and enduring, whereas labor was necessary and generally a burden each person carried as a matter of the human condition. Finally, the third aspect of living was *vita activa*—the active life. *Vita activa* required community and public presence. To Arendt, the active life, the idea-filled state of being, could not happen in the private realm. She concluded:

> To live an entirely private life means above all to be deprived of things essential to a truly human life: to be deprived of the reality that comes from being seen and heard by others, to be deprived of an 'objective' relationship with them that comes from being related to and separated from them through the intermediary of a common world of things.[40]

Arendt set the public realm aside as the space for an active life and democratic discourse. In her understanding, the individual leaves the private, labor-based realm, stepping into the world of appearances to engage with others. She constructed the public realm as being fleeting and always in danger of failure. No matter how tenuous the public realm was in her understanding, however, its foundational ingredients contribute crucial building blocks to the question of how a space for discourse could be understood in the networked, AI era. Arendt emphasized the public realm required community and communication, creating an overlap with James's and Dewey's pragmatic thinking from chapter 8. Aside from these topical intersections, however, Arendt's thinking about the space was generally constructed using different assumptions. The public space, to Arendt, was where the individual could engage with others as equals in an effort to create meaningful acts and deeds. She emphasized, "The public realm, in other words, was reserved for individuality; it was

*Monsters, Machines, and Truth*

the only place where men could show who they really and inexchangeably were."[41] The performance of meaningful words and deeds in the public realm required a space. Such a space required political freedom in the sense that government was generally absent. Government could neither create the space nor safeguard it. Government's best contribution, according to Arendt, was preserving political freedom.[42] Nothing else.

Arendt was particularly critical of the human-rights assumptions that were at the heart of Enlightenment thought. To Arendt, the assumptions were just words and ideas, not realities. She explained, in the 1940s, these paper-thin promises regarding inherent, natural human rights "broke down the very moment when those who professed to believe in it were for the first time confronted with people who had indeed lost all other qualities and specific relationships—except that they were still human."[43] The assumptions not only failed in Germany, Arendt reasoned, they also fell apart in France, where she lived as a refugee, and throughout Europe. In other words, governments made commitments to certain ideas, promising to create and safeguard a space for equality and human discourse— all in the name of a belief in inherent human rights. When these ideas were tested, the space that had been created using Enlightenment assumptions turned out to be merely an abstract idea. Arendt experienced these failures while stateless in Paris and observed them in the Nazi's actions. Arendt concluded, "The world found nothing sacred in the abstract nakedness of being human."[44] Her rejection of high-minded Enlightenment ideas about inherent human rights provides one of the most explicit connections between her personal experiences and her thinking.

Her concerns, however experience-based, contribute to a valuable, nuanced construction of the space for discourse. The public realm was not, to Arendt, a government-created and maintained space. Such a space also could not be constructed using Enlightenment assumptions about inherent human rights. The realm, crucially, was about people and the functional value of an organic public space. With these factors in mind, she constructed a space that was not inherently a physical or government-maintained realm. The space required only political freedom from the government. She reasoned, "Wherever people gather together, it is potentially there, but only potentially, not necessarily and not forever."[45] Thus, her conceptualization of the public realm relied on

201

*Chapter Nine*

individuals who chose to live the active life and stepped forward into the space to think and exchange ideas.

Crucially, the public realm was undermined, and potentially destroyed, by one other threat—the private realm. To Arendt, when the private realm bled into the public space, its inherent authoritarianism and unthinking, labor-focused mindset, undermined the freedom and equality of the *vita activa*-dominated public realm. In other words, the private realm's movement into the public space replaced the life of ideas, innovation, and meaningful work with base, herdlike activity.[46] Such a space fostered the conditions for the monster, Eichmann. The herd, and the labor-based orientation of the private space, would quickly overwhelm freedom of thought. In the closing passages of *The Human Condition,* Arendt concluded, "No other human capacity is so vulnerable, and it is in fact far easier to act under conditions of tyranny than it is to think."[47] When private-realm matters seeped into the public space, thoughts and ideas became endangered.

To illustrate this concern, Arendt described two types of people, *animal laborans*, which were defined as unthinking laborers, and *homo faber*, who are thoughtful, active-life world-builders.[48] She explained, "Unlike the *animal laborans*, whose social life is worldless and herdlike and who therefore is incapable of building or inhabiting a public, worldly realm, *homo faber* is fully capable of having a public realm of his own."[49] In *The Human Condition*, Arendt did not explicitly connect these concerns about the space with her life experiences with antisemitism and, eventually, the Nazi regime, but between the lines, her classifications between *animal laborans* and *homo faber*, and private and public, get at how rational thought was lost in favor of nationalism and genocide in Nazi Germany. In *Eichmann in Jerusalem*, she explained, "Conscience as such had apparently got lost in Germany, and this to a point where people hardly remembered it and had ceased to realize that the surprising 'new set of German values' was not shared by the outside world."[50]

Arendt framed this concern about the deterioration of the public space in favor of a mass or social space based on the private realm's needs differently in *The Human Condition*, explaining:

> Where the main public realm is society, there is always the danger that, through a perverted form of 'acting together'—by pull and

*Monsters, Machines, and Truth*

pressure and the tricks of cliques—those are brought to the fore who know nothing and can do nothing.[51]

The public space, to Arendt, encompassed the very nature of *being* in the world. The heart of that *being* was thought. She explained:

> Even the greatest forces of intimate life—the passions of the heart, the thoughts of the mind, the delights of the senses—lead an uncertain, shadowy kind of existence unless and until they are transformed, deprivatized and deindividualized, as it were, into a shape to fit them for public appearance.[52]

Arendt concluded the public realm was the space of *vita activa*. Such a space was where being, what Heidegger described as *Dasein*, took place.[53] The private realm was crucial to existence, but the public space was for living. She emphasized, "We are not born equal; we become equal as members of a group on the strength of our decision to guarantee ourselves mutually equal rights."[54] Thus, Arendt's public space shared some assumptions and concerns with Dewey's. Both reasoned engagement with others and the realization of the self within engagements with others was crucial, though their paths to such conclusions were markedly different.[55] Both also constructed the space upon assumptions of equality, reasoning people must come together in the space as equals.

## APPEARANCES AND TRUTH

Arendt's decision to frame Eichmann as a different type of monster during her coverage of his trial for the *New Yorker* led to a wave of criticism from the Jewish community. She was traveling throughout Europe in the months surrounding when *Eichmann in Jerusalem*, the work that combined her reports from the trial into a book, was published in 1963. Friends at home in New York wrote to her that her conclusions about Eichmann were all anyone in their community was talking about.[56] The Anti-Defamation League distributed negative talking points and criticisms for reviewers to use before the book even appeared. The *New York Times* devoted pages to letters to the editor that streamed into its offices after the book and its review were published.[57] The review itself was particularly critical. Written by a judge who attended the trial, the *New*

*Chapter Nine*

*York Times*'s review contended her book "sympathized with Eichmann" and argued "it would be 'preposterous' to believe he personally slew five million people."[58] Writing from Rome, Arendt defended her thinking and questioned the reviewer's motives in a letter to the editor in the *New York Times* soon after.[59] Siegfried Moses, the first comptroller of Israel, with whom Arendt had cordial correspondence for many years, asked her to halt the publication of her book.[60] In a warm letter, Arendt sought to reassure him that she had added a supplement to the book that would assuage concerns.[61] Ultimately, Arendt lost friends and received piles of angry letters, all criticizing how she framed Eichmann and his trial. Her conclusions from the trial created an unexpected firestorm. Arendt found the controversy only reinforced her conclusions.

In the supplement she promised Moses, she contended the public outcry had in many ways altered the ideas in her book. The *truth* she sought to communicate about the trial was transformed by people into an opinion-based attack. She explained, "The clamor centered on the 'image' of a book which was never written, and touched upon subjects that often had not only not been mentioned by me but had never occurred to me before."[62] She revisited to the outcry and transformation of her ideas into unintended meanings in an essay titled "Truth and Politics," which was published in 1967 in *The New Yorker*. The essay includes a footnote, indicating "this essay was caused by the so-called controversy after the publication of *Eichmann in Jerusalem*."[63] Arendt did not apologize for her conclusions regarding Eichmann and his trial.

As she did with the trial, she turned the event, this time the wave of criticism she faced, into a study in the flow of ideas and the space for discourse. Early in the essay, Arendt emphasized, "What kind of reality does truth possess if it is powerless in the public realm, which more than any other sphere of human life guarantees reality of existence?"[64] She contended unpopular truths struggle in the public realm because they encounter individuals who are *conditioned* to accept certain ideas and reject others. Her nuanced construction of Eichmann as banally evil because of his thoughtlessness was, to Arendt, an unpopular truth. People wanted to see the monster they expected, not the monster she observed.

The construction of truth is vital to the space for discourse, as we have seen in preceding chapters. The marketplace approach is founded

## Monsters, Machines, and Truth

upon Enlightenment-based assumptions that truth is generally static and universal, something that exists outside of human control. Truth, in this regard, is to be discovered amid a free exchange of ideas. Arendt was critical of these assumptions, identifying their origins in the wave of doubt triggered by Galileo's invention and use of the telescope to identify what she labeled as the "Archimedean Point," "a point outside the earth from which to unhinge the world."[65] In Arendt's reasoning, people had believed their senses, which told them the Earth was the center of the universe, for ages. The revelation that human senses had been wrong about the way the universe functioned and the place of the earth in the solar system undermined all previous conclusions about what was *true* about human existence. Arendt explained, "Galileo's discovery proved in demonstrable fact that both the worst fear and the most presumptuous hope of human speculation, the ancient fear that our senses, our very organs for reception of reality, might betray us."[66] The betrayal led to a new quest for certainty, one that sought to separate human senses and truth.

The outcome was Enlightenment-based positivism, a development Arendt critiqued in unique ways. Positivism sought to remove thought, Arendt reasoned, from the truth-discovery process by using dispassionate approaches, such as the scientific method, to discern truth. In this process, philosophy and science were separated from each other for the first time. Removing thought from science, to Arendt, was a mistake. In *The Life of the Mind*, which Arendt was writing when she died in 1975, she contended, "The simple-minded positivism that believes it found a firm ground of certainty if it only excludes all mental phenomena from consideration and holds fast to observable facts, the everyday reality given to our senses" fails to grasp truth.[67] Again, this time in thinking about how truth is constructed, Arendt emphasized an unthinking system is problematic. Crucially, Arendt was inspired to write *The Life of the Mind* by the Eichmann trial.[68] Positivistic thought, to Arendt, failed because it separated thought from truth's development, which, in a microcosm, Eichmann's actions exemplified, as he failed to associate thought and his actions.

In removing thought from the truth process, Arendt emphasized positivism—a foundation of Enlightenment assumptions—failed to identify

205

*Chapter Nine*

the difference between truth and appearance. The scientific method often reveals appearances, but not truth, because identifying truth requires thought, rather than processes. Her use of the words "truth" and "appearance" represents another crucial, nuance-loaded use of terminology in Arendt's thinking. She sought to separate actual reality—truth—the very existence of a phenomena from how it appeared to an individual's senses. This separation between truth and appearance was crucial in Heidegger's work, which Arendt acknowledged.[69] Identifying the truth, or being, behind the appearance, to Arendt, required thought—an unwillingness to accept initial impressions of an idea or object as fully, accurate representations.

The concern for truth, rather than the appearance of a phenomenon, relates with Arendt's contention in "Truth and Politics" that people are conditioned to believe those ideas that align with their assumptions about the world. In this regard, it's not just easier to accept appearances rather than search for truth. Appearances often lend themselves to acceptance because they align or conflict with conditioned assumptions. Complaints about her coverage of Eichmann's trial, according to Arendt, were based on conditioned responses and appearances, rather than thoughtful examinations and truth. Similarly, the space for discourse, the public realm in Arendt's terms, will struggle when individuals forgo thought, accepting appearances as truth.

Importantly, Arendt emphasized the word "conditioned" rather than "experience," in her work. Her use of "conditioned" drew her thinking down a slightly different path than James's or Dewey's pragmatic thought, which emphasized experience as crucial to the truth-building process.[70] Those who focus on experience affix value to the events in a person's life that influence the lenses they employ to understand the world. Conditioning, as Arendt used the term, adds experience to a broader understanding of influences, particularly societal concerns that color a person's perceptions. Eichmann's experiences, for example, might have predisposed him to success in the Nazi Party, but his conditioning included the powerful influences the Nazi propaganda machine had on society, as well as the persistent antisemitism in much of Europe during his life. The conditioning influences, to Arendt, could not be ignored or removed from the reality-building process, no matter the accuracy or

*Monsters, Machines, and Truth*

complexity of the positivistic, scientific methods. Arendt quite succinctly reasoned "human existence is conditioned existence."[71] Thus, the controversy about how Eichmann's trial was framed, to Arendt, amounted to a failure to think and to look beyond appearances for truth.

Ultimately, Arendt contended each individual must step into the public realm with a willingness to evaluate ideas beyond their initial appearances, an effort that requires acknowledging the pre-conditioning factors that influence how truth is constructed for them. How a phenomenon presents itself and how a person, conditioned by their lives, receives the idea's appearance in the world, vary. Arendt reasoned in *The Life of the Mind*, "Although everything that appears is perceived in the mode of it-seems-to-me, hence open to error and illusion, appearance as such carries with it a prior indication of *realness*."[72] Such thoughts are similar to Heidegger's conclusion that "Looking at something, understanding and conceiving it, choosing, access to it—all these ways of behaving are constitutive for our inquiry, and therefore are modes of Being for those particular entities which we, the inquirers, are ourselves."[73]

Similarly, Hans-Georg Gadamer, who was briefly a student alongside Arendt when she was at Marburg studying with Heidegger, concluded in his master work, *Truth and Method*, "A person trying to understand something will not resign himself from the start to relying on his own accidental fore-meanings."[74] In their own words, the three interconnected thinkers contended appearances are not sufficient carriers of truth. Thought, particularly when acknowledging prejudices and conditioning, is the crucial, needed element. Combined with Arendt's earlier conclusions in *The Human Condition*, in which she reasoned "Men are conditioned beings because everything they come in contact with turns immediately into a condition of their existence," truth in the space for discourse evolves when thinking individuals delve beyond the appearances of ideas to identify what is true.[75] Arendt's *Eichmann in Jerusalem* concluded his failure to think made him a monster. In *The Human Condition*, she emphasized the public realm fails, and becomes dominated by the private, when people fail to think. In *Life of the Mind*, Arendt examined truth and appearance. Overlapping in all these works is a concern for thought, the very foundation of the *vita activa*.

*Chapter Nine*

## THE MACHINES

Arendt was particularly concerned with the power of human-constructed tools and machines to condition the lenses people use to understand the world and the public realm. In other words, she lamented the power of inventions, which society often celebrated and welcomed, to undermine the *vita activa*. Her concern did not, of course, specifically include algorithms or artificially intelligent communicators, such as those that have fundamentally remapped the space for human discourse in the twenty-first century and were discussed in chapter 6. Her words of warning, however, *seem* at times as though she had a glimpse in the 1950s into our networked, twenty-first-century present. She explained, for example:

> The world of machines has become a substitute for the real world, even though this pseudo world cannot fulfill the most important task of the human artifice, which is to offer mortals a dwelling place more permanent and more stable than themselves.[76]

In another instance, she referred to "mute robots" that are meant to improve human existence.[77] Regardless of her powers of prophecy and time-travel, Arendt's ideas make crucial contributions to how we can construct the space for human discourse in the networked, AI era.

She was principally focused on the power of the tools and machines people create to condition human experience and, in a related sense, on society's failure to weigh and consider the influence the creations will have on human existence. She emphasized, "If the human condition consists of man's being a conditioned being for whom everything, given or man-made, immediately becomes a condition of his further existence, then man 'adjusted' himself to an environment of machines the moment he designed them."[78] In other words, technological advances, and their adoptions by people, condition human existence. The change cannot be helped. It's inherent. Such inventions change the way people understand themselves and others. When we think about truth versus appearances and the conditioning influences that shape how each person perceives the world around them, Arendt emphasized tools and machines must be accounted for. She contended, "The machines

*Monsters, Machines, and Truth*

demand that the laborer serve them, that he adjust the natural rhythm of his body to their mechanical movement."[79] If technological inventions are conditioning forces, changing the way people encounter the world, then, Arendt reasoned, society must evaluate *how* they influence people's life worlds.

She emphasized tools were intended to help *homo faber,* whom she understood as the world-builder, go about creating and doing meaningful works. The tools were not meant to improve the human condition, particularly those needs that were to be met in the private, rather than public realm.[80] Problematically, to Arendt, tools and machines have mistakenly come to be thought of as making life easier, rather than facilitating world-building. To use her dichotomy, tools and machines have come to be understood as ways to alleviate the toil of *animal laborans*, the simple laborer, rather than to empower *homo faber* to do great, meaningful, and lasting works. She contended:

> The discussion of the whole problem of technology, that is, of the transformation of life and world through the introduction of the machine, has been strangely led astray through an all-too-exclusive concentration upon the service or disservice the machines render to men.[81]

Thus, the crucial concern, to Arendt, was not that society and human existence are changed by technology. Rather, the emphasis should be on *how* it is changed. Arendt emphasized the conditioning power of new tools and machines should be considered alongside their potential uses.

Arendt's primary concern was the *vita activa*, which was her original title for *The Human Condition.* Her publisher suggested the change.[82] Arendt contended new tools and machines often undermine the active, meaningful life that takes place in the public realm. The realm was already poisoned by "clichés, stock phrases, adherence to conventional, standardized codes of expression and conduct" that end up "protecting us from reality."[83] These new inventions, she reasoned, threatened to further fill the public realm with base, valueless expression and thought-stifling limitations. Her concerns became specific enough, even in the 1950s, to consider machines that could think like human beings. She explained, "The newly invented electronic machines, which, sometimes to the dismay and sometimes to the confusion of their inventors, are

*Chapter Nine*

so spectacularly more 'intelligent' than human beings, would indeed be *homunculi*."[84] Homunculi is Latin for small humans. Arendt contended there is no life in such "artificial improvers." They could replicate human work, but not life. Thus, in the public realm, they can only bring the distractive force of *animal laborans* and the human necessities of the private realm, into the space.

Arendt's conclusions about electronic machines were generally drawn from early computers and calculators, rather than the complex, AI-influenced networked environments that characterize the space for human discourse in the twenty-first century. Her list of deeply layered concerns about the active life and public realm, however, remains crucial and instructive regarding the space for discourse. First, her ideas emphasize the conditioning power of tools and machines to undermine already problematic distances between appearances and truth. Arendt explained, "it is no longer the body's movement that determines the implement's movement but the machine's movement which enforces the movements of the body."[85] In other words, these innovations often encourage people to employ less critical approaches, making it more likely individuals simply accept what appears to them, rather than seeking truth. Second, as a related matter, the tools and machines are conditioning forces. She reasoned, for example, "If one makes man a measure of all things for use, it is man the user and instrumentalizer, and not the speaker and doer or man the thinker, to whom the world is being related."[86] In this sense, the tools and machines do not inherently devalue human life and expression, but the way society comes to view them conditions existence. These creations have the power to alter the lenses people use to understand the world around them.

## ARENDT'S SPACE FOR DISCOURSE

Arendt found Eichmann's failure to think the most monstrous thing about him. His role in facilitating the deaths of millions of people was secondary, a symptom of the larger problem of an unthinking, heavily conditioned existence that was substantially based on appearances, rather than truth. How was this monster created? In seeking to resolve this question, and in her other works, Arendt drew a unique, but limited,

*Monsters, Machines, and Truth*

map for the space for human discourse. The map is characterized by a requirement for individuals to live meaningful, active lives in the public realm. This feature shares characteristics with the discourse model put forth by James and Dewey, discussed in chapter 8, but departs from their assumptions in crucial ways. Arendt had little concern for the type of community-building Dewey understood as a democracy-enriching exercise. A person's active role in the public realm, to Arendt, meant fulfillment first for them and their lives in creating "works and deeds and words."[87] The active life was a thoughtful life and a thoughtful life was a remedy for the monster, whether its name was Eichmann, the Nazis, or the totalitarianism that forced her from home multiple times in her life. Arendt's space for discourse emphasized the need to protect and foster the active, thoughtful life, from the forces that undermined individuality, such as the baseness of the private realm and its forays into the public space.

Thus, the active life, to Arendt, must be characterized by habits and practices that look beyond the appearances of phenomena, all the way to the truth that is somewhere behind them. Such a life must also acknowledge the conditioned nature of human existence. The conditioned nature makes seeing behind appearances more difficult, as each person is predisposed to accepting those ideas that align with their pre-understandings. Arendt's construction of the space, uniquely, incorporated a concern for how technology influences the space for discourse. She generally contended tools and machines condition human existence. In other words, their influence is built in. They inevitably color the lenses individuals use to construct truth. Her reasoning conveyed a generally negative picture of such tools, not because they were intended to harm the space for discourse, but because the way they are used tends to lead to a more conditioned, appearance-rather-than-truth-based space for discourse. Such a space encouraged thoughtlessness.

The difficulty in Arendt's thought, however, is she offered few mechanisms for safeguarding the public realm. Her list of concerns for the space is thorough. Her descriptions of thoughtlessness and the nature of truth and appearances are detailed. Yet, we find little beyond normative admonishments that society *should* encourage thought in the public realm and the innovations can contribute to an unthinking society. Her

211

*Chapter Nine*

map of the space for discourse does little more than mark the dangerous areas and suggests ways to safely navigate the space. Her lack of a complete, detailed map, however, does not mean her ideas cannot contribute conceptual building blocks to how we can construct a space for democratic discourse in the networked, AI era.

# TEN

## Curators of Discourse

Claude Vorilhon, a French racecar driver and journalist, felt an unexplainable urge one day to stop his car during an otherwise routine drive through the mountains around Clermont-Ferrand in central France. He got out of the car and walked along a volcanic crater, where he saw a bright light in the distance. Vorilhon walked toward the light and an unidentified flying object (UFO) landed nearby. As he neared the UFO, an alien walked out to meet him. The alien explained to him that extraterrestrials had created every living thing on Earth as part of an experiment and, after an atomic bomb was dropped on Hiroshima in 1945, it would be Vorilhon's job to be the Last Prophet of the Age of the Apocalypse.[1] The 1973 encounter changed his life. He changed his name to Raël and founded Raëlism a year later. The sect has grown to more than 60,000 members in fifty-two countries. In 1997, the group created Clonaid, which claims to have cloned human children as part of Raëlism's belief that cloning is part of the path to immortality.[2]

The Raëlian movement continues to spread its controversial message, which includes rejecting all other world religions and supporting "unusual sexual preferences," which include "pleasure from biological robots designed as sex slaves."[3] The group also contends the world should be led by the most intelligent, which should be determined using

213

## Chapter Ten

scientific measures. Such ideas have led to concerns about eugenics. The Raëlian movement expends substantial resources on outreach, hosting lectures and meetings around the world while keeping active social media presences. The group's outreach efforts collided with the EU's understandings of freedom of expression in a European Court of Human Rights (ECtHR) case in 2012.

The standoff started in 2001, when the group sought permission from Swiss authorities to display a thirty-eight- by twenty-seven-inch poster in a public space in Neuchâtel, a small town in eastern Switzerland. The poster, which read "A Message from Extraterrestrials," included a link to the organization's website, images of aliens' faces, a pyramid, and a flying saucer. City authorities rejected the organization's request to display the poster, finding the group's ideas were immoral and a danger to public order. The Raëlian movement challenged the decision, claiming it had a right to free expression. The city's leaders rejected the appeal, reasoning their duties included safeguarding the public from the organization's dangerous ideas, particularly those regarding human cloning and sensual meditation.[4] On appeal two years later, the city's decision was again upheld. This time those considering the case noted the poster itself was not offensive. They concluded the group's overall ideas, beyond the poster, were, however, sufficient reason to protect the public from potentially dangerous content. In each step of the legal process, the sect's claims to free-expression rights were countered by government officials' beliefs that they had a custodial duty to safeguard citizens from immoral, dangerous, or unhealthy ideas.

Eleven years and five decisions after the group's first request to display the poster for a two-week period in April 2001, the ECtHR upheld the Swiss authorities' ban.[5] The ECtHR, which was created to ensure EU member states respect the rights outlined in the European Convention on Human Rights, found the government officials' claims were valid exceptions to free-expression safeguards. Ultimately, the ECtHR found the city was justified in banning the poster. Jurists reasoned member states have broad powers "when regulating freedom of expression in relation to matters liable to offend intimate personal convictions within the sphere of morals, or, especially, religion."[6] In other words, expression can be limited when it fails to be a public good or threatens people's

214

*Curators of Discourse*

abilities to live in a pluralistic, tolerant society. The ECtHR supported the Swiss courts' reasoning that the poster itself was not problematic. Jurists reasoned the website listed on the poster, however, opened the gateway to ideas that *could* support eugenics and sexual abuse of children.[7] The ECtHR reasoned "It was indispensable to ban the campaign in question in order to protect health and morals, protect the rights of others and to prevent crime."[8]

Protecting health and morals. Safeguarding personal convictions and other religious beliefs. Concern for public order. These rationales for limiting expression provide a substantial contrast to the United States' generally wide-open, marketplace-of-ideas model. Crucially, the ECtHR's decision in *Mouvement Raëlien Suisse v. Switzerland* was not an isolated incident, others including having a conversation with alien visitors, for example. Using policies, legislation, and legal decisions, EU lawmakers and jurists have employed substantially different free-expression assumptions than their counterparts in the United States when constructing a space for human discourse. While the US Supreme Court's construction of the space—the marketplace of ideas—is built upon very particular understandings of Enlightenment assumptions about truth and human rationality and has come to justify rejecting nearly any limitation on the flow of ideas in democracy, the EU has taken a different approach, emphasizing expression is expected to be a public good and something that should be balanced with the needs of a pluralistic society.

Crucially, in constructing a space for discourse that is safeguarded from a variety of threats, EU lawmakers and jurists have placed government officials in a custodial role, an approach that has generally been treated as an anathema in the United States. The ECtHR decisions, as discussed later in this chapter, indicate EU thinkers have generally concluded government is best suited to ensure the space for discourse is safe and undistorted. For this, and other reasons, the EU's more curatorial approach to the space for discourse provides a final lens through which to understand ways in which the flow of ideas can be conceptualized in the networked, AI era. The approach is particularly relevant because the global, often-borderless nature of online discourse has meant massive EU-originated laws, such as 2018's General Data Protection Act and 2022's Digital Services Act, can have the effect of imposing

*Chapter Ten*

EU constructions of the space for discourse on the rest of the world as online firms change their entire products—worldwide—to comply with EU policies.[9]

Thus, the EU's construction of the space for discourse is already having an impact on the shape and contours of networked communication around the world. It is no mistake news organizations have noted the EU is "the world's top regulator" and "the world's super-regulator in AI."[10] The EU lens, in many ways, portends to become the dominant approach, isolating and undermining the United States' expansive marketplace model. This chapter begins by examining and contextualizing the origins of the EU's protected, pluralistic approach to free expression and the space for discourse before identifying foundational building blocks within crucial ECtHR decisions that, like *Mouvement Raëlien Suisse*, rationalize and explain the bloc's assumptions that government should curate the space and expression should be a public good. Finally, the chapter examines EU policies and recommendations that influence free expression in the networked, AI era, such as those that address bots, deepfakes, extremism, and disinformation.

## ORIGINS OF THE EU SPACE

Switzerland's case against the Raëlian movement's poster was largely based on paragraph 2 of Article 10 of the European Convention on Human Rights (ECHR) Article 10, which is divided into two paragraphs, is the EU's foundational statement regarding freedom of expression. Paragraph 1 is written in absolute terms, much like the First Amendment. Article 10 begins "Everyone has the right to freedom of expression."[11] Paragraph 2, however, provides an expansive list of limitations on expression, including concern for national security, public safety, public order, health and morals, and safeguarding the rights of others.[12] The ECtHR drew from paragraph 2 in its reasoning in *Mouvement Raëlien Suisse*, with the Court explaining Switzerland's "interference with the applicant association's right to freedom of expression must be 'prescribed by law,' have one or more legitimate aims in the light of paragraph 2 of Article 10, and be 'necessary in a democratic society.'"[13] Thus, Article 10's limitations on expression create the conditions for a

216

*Curators of Discourse*

substantially different shape for the space for discourse than that which US jurists and scholars have built into the marketplace of ideas. While the First Amendment is written in absolute terms, and does not include a second paragraph with limitations, the EU model lays the foundations for a space that is intended to be safe for all to participate—allowing limitations on hate and extremism, for example—and is protected from distortion. This crucial difference introduces substantially different rationales into the shapes and contours of the space.

While US jurists and scholars are loath to read exceptions into a guiding free-expression statement that does not explicitly include any, Article 10 supplies a wide range of limitations that leave ample room for interpretation. Crucially, the exemptions to free expression give EU lawmakers and jurists substantial flexibility in adjusting the space for discourse to fit social and technological changes, such as the creation and adoption of social media, the introduction of bots, and the proliferation of deepfakes. Ultimately, the United States' marketplace-of-ideas rationale has been conceptualized as creating a rigid, unmoving space, while the EU's Article 10 laid the groundwork for dynamic, changing space. The ECtHR, for example, reasoned in one case that the ECHR is "a living instrument which must be interpreted in the light of present-day conditions."[14] Such an approach runs in opposition to the thinking of many US jurists, who seek to interpret the Constitution based on the original intent of its eighteenth-century authors.[15] The contexts surrounding the creations of the US and EU statements regarding free expression help explain the different ways in which they influence the map for the space for discourse.

As examined in chapter 4, the *Declaration of Independence*, *Constitution*, and *Bill of Rights* were written in the late eighteenth century by thinkers who were children of the Enlightenment.[16] The authors, including Thomas Jefferson, Benjamin Franklin, John Dickinson, and James Madison, were heavily influenced by Enlightenment thought, particularly John Milton, John Locke, and David Hume's ideas.[17] As a result, the authors wrote Enlightenment assumptions into the founding documents, ultimately providing the tools jurists and scholars later used to construct the generally wide-open, unregulated marketplace-of-ideas version of the space for discourse. Crucially, the Enlightenment

## Chapter Ten

assumptions emphasized government was created to serve the individual, truth was universal and generally the same for all, and people are rational and capable of making sense of the world around them.[18] These assumptions, through a centuries-long watering-down process and substantial repurposing by justices and legal scholars, became the foundational building blocks for a space for discourse in which—harm and public good be damned—the government would generally not have a role in controlling the exchange of ideas. These justices and scholars reasoned only individuals, in their rationality, and the inherent value of truth, should control what is accepted and rejected in the marketplace of ideas.

The ECHR was written under much different circumstances. While the First Amendment was written within the wave of influence created by Enlightenment thought and in the shadow of a revolution that overthrew a monarchy, the ECHR emerged from the shock and sorrow that followed the end of World War II in Europe. Early American thinkers wrote the *Constitution*, and *Bill of Rights* that soon followed, in response to many of the British monarchy's and army's aggressions that were top-of-mind after the war.[19] Similarly, the ECHR was written with dangers such as extreme nationalism and disinformation in mind. Before the ECHR was drafted, the newly formed United Nations created the Universal Declaration of Human Rights (UDHR) in 1948. The UDHR was created after "the international community vowed to never again allow atrocities like those of that conflict to happen again."[20] The UN sought to safeguard human rights—and human dignity.[21] These concerns are central to the UDHR, creating a difficult tension between the promise of freedom and an expectation of responsibility to others. Article 1 reads "All human beings are born free and equal in dignity and rights. They are endowed with reason and conscience and should act towards one another in a spirit of brotherhood."[22] The article ultimately communicates people are free, but that freedom comes with a responsibility to use such rights for the public good.

A similar understanding is woven into promises of free expression. Article 19, which carries the primary promise of freedom of expression in the UDHR, reads "Everyone has the right to freedom of opinion and expression; this right includes freedom to hold opinions without

218

*Curators of Discourse*

interference and to seek, receive and impart information and ideas through any media and regardless of frontiers."[23] The article includes no exceptions. As a document, however, the UDHR includes expectations that people's actions don't harm others. Article 29, for example, outlines, "Everyone has duties to the community."[24] Other articles promise human dignity.[25] Such duties and promises of dignity provide room for exceptions to expression and ensure a constant tension between freedom and responsibility.

When members of the Council of Europe met at The Hague, two years after the UDHR was drafted and approved, they drew from the new international document to construct a set of rights for the European bloc. Ultimately, the council copied Article 19, making it, word-for-word, paragraph 1 of Article 10 of the ECHR. The European leaders, however, added paragraph 2, which writes limitations on expression into the very document jurists and lawmakers are to use when conceptualizing the space for democratic discourse. With the Nazi's effective wave of misinformation and disinformation—as well as their use of othering to dehumanize entire groups of people—fresh on their minds, free expression was *balanced* against concerns for national security, health and morals, and the rights of others. The EU's more balanced approach has allowed jurists and lawmakers to construct a space for discourse that is written more in pencil than pen. Crucially, unlike in the rigid US system, government officials, including lawmakers and jurists, hold the pencil. Paragraph 2 of Article 10, and the overall expectation that freedom comes with a responsibility to others, opens the door for officials to, as is needed, erase and rewrite the lines and features that make up the boundaries of the space for discourse in the bloc. The list of limitations on expression make the EU system flexible and, at the same time, place government actors in a custodial role. Those who seek to limit expression do not have free rein to do so, however. Limitations must be tied to exemptions listed in paragraph 2 of Article 10, especially the "necessary in a democratic society" and "prescribed by law" passages.[26] Ultimately, the EU rationales for expression allow for a more limited space for discourse in the name of the *public good*—a blanket term that encapsulates the limitations outlined in paragraph 2.

## Chapter Ten

The ECtHR upheld Swiss authorities' decision to block the Raëlian movement's poster because the ban met "a pressing social need" that aligned with the limitations to expression outlined in the ECHR's Article 10, paragraph 2.[27] Ultimately, the ideas the sect sought to convey were not shared in the space for discourse because government officials reasoned they were not a public good. Such a conclusion, which would be unthinkable within the marketplace-of-ideas rationale in the US system, begins to illustrate the crucial differences between the spaces for discourse. The EU's space is characterized by two crucial differences: The government acts as a curator and expression that seeks protection is expected to be a public good. Both differences require nuance. The EU's space for discourse, and its underlying rationales for expression, after all, should not be considered under a simple good or bad assessment. Crucially, for our work here, the EU's approach provides an alternative lens through which to understand the space for discourse in the networked, AI era.

The government's curatorial role and public-good expectations were on display in the landmark Article 10 case *Handyside v. United Kingdom* in 1976. Richard Handyside distributed the *Little Red Schoolbook*, which included a twenty-six-page section on sex, to an intended audience of twelve- to eighteen-year-old students. UK officials seized more than a thousand copies of the book and charged him with violating an obscenity law. Handyside argued he had a right, under Article 10, to publish and distribute the work. The ECtHR sided with the government. More important than the verdict, however, was the reasoning. The jurists celebrated the crucial role free expression plays and emphasized the Court's obligation to protect "the principles characterising a 'democratic society.'"[28] The Court continued that Article 10 protects a wide range of expression, explaining that it

> is applicable not only to "information" or "ideas" that are favourably received or regarded as inoffensive or as a matter of indifference, but also to those that offend, shock or disturb the State or any sector of the population. Such are the demands of that pluralism, tolerance and broadmindedness without which there is no "democratic society."[29]

The Court, in line with the freedom-and-responsibility tension found in both the UDHR and ECHR, followed its support of free expression

*Curators of Discourse*

with a substantial qualification. The jurists explained, "Whoever exercises his freedom of expression undertakes 'duties and responsibilities' the scope of which depends on his situation and the technical means he uses."[30] In the same passage, the jurists reasoned it was the Court's role to ensure the government's limitations on expression remained appropriately narrow. Thus, in one of the crucial, and most cited, Article 10 cases, the Court communicated it understood free expression as a crucial matter that is to be balanced with a public-good expectation. The Court also conveyed it expects limitations on ideas to be limited and proportional and the government has a role in curating the space.

## THE SPACE'S KEEPERS

While *Handyside* set a substantial precedent regarding the tension between the ECHR's promise of free expression and expectation of responsibility, decisions that followed solidified and clarified the related idea that government officials have a crucial curatorial role in the space for discourse. This understanding was certainly present in *Mouvement Raëlien Suisse*, where the Court reasoned the government could block the public display of a group's poster because people *might* encounter ideas that were deemed "dangerous for the public."[31] Crucially, in a dissenting opinion, Portuguese Judge Pinto De Albuquerque contended the United States' construction of the marketplace of ideas as a generally open, government-intervention-free space, was the better approach.[32] He reasoned, for example, the Raëlian movement's support of cloning was not, in-of-itself, dangerous. Had the poster included concrete plans to break Swiss laws, it could be halted, he contended. De Albuquerque's dissent aside, the Court's decision emphasized the government, for the good of the public, had a right to remove perceived threats to the space.

Four years earlier, in *Animal Defenders v. United Kingdom*, in 2008, the Court upheld the government's right to halt an animal rights group's twenty-second advertisements from airing on television.[33] The group had challenged the limitation, contending the passage of the Communication Act of 2003 that government officials cited in limiting their expression violated Article 10. The jurists once again deferred to

221

## Chapter Ten

the government, reasoning "The general measure was necessary to prevent the distortion of crucial public interest debates and, thereby, the undermining of the democratic process."[34] The Court continued, emphasizing the government's limitation was "relevant and sufficient."[35] Thus, the range of ideas was limited to *protect* the space. A similar space-protecting, distortion rationale appeared in *Hertel v. Switzerland*, a 1998 ECtHR decision that considered whether a ban on a researcher's conclusions about the dangers of eating microwaved food violated his rights under Article 10.[36] Hans Ulrich Hertel and other researchers conducted a study, primarily based on changes in blood samples, that found microwaved food is a danger to public health. The study was published in a quarterly journal, which led the Swiss Association of Manufacturers and Suppliers of Household Electrical Appliances to demand Hertel be halted from suggesting microwaves were dangerous to people's health.

The organization argued his false conclusions would distort the economic market for microwaves. Lower courts accepted the organization's reasoning, granting and upholding a ban on Hertel's research. The ECtHR, however, struck down the gag on Hertel's research, reasoning the order against him was outside the appropriate role of government in maintaining the space.[37] While the government officials' remedy for Hertel's unpopular research was rejected by the Court, jurists never questioned the power of officials to limit expression to preserve an undistorted space for discourse. The jurists merely concluded the Swiss officials' solution was not sufficiently limited and proportional.

Considered from a different angle, the ECtHR found Delfi, a news portal based in Estonia that also reaches Latvian and Lithuanian audiences, was liable for damages for hateful and false comments posted on its website. Delfi took the comments down when it became aware of them, but the Court still reasoned the company failed to fulfill its responsibilities as an organization that conveys information to the public. In analyzing the case, the Court reasoned,

> While the Court acknowledges that important benefits can be derived from the Internet in the exercise of freedom of expression, it is also mindful that the possibility of imposing liability for defamatory

*Curators of Discourse*

or other types of unlawful speech must, in principle, be retained, constituting an effective remedy for violations of personality rights.[38]

In this regard, jurists reasoned the government had a role in maintaining a balance between free expression and human dignity. The government did not halt ideas, as it did in *Mouvement Raëlien Suisse* and *Animal Defenders*. Instead, by creating liability for a news portal that allowed reader comments, it incentivized private firms to limit the range of ideas. In evaluating Estonia's initial decision to find Delfi liable for the posts, the ECtHR reasoned the harm to expression was moderate and the government's decision was limited and proportional. In each of these cases, the Court agreed with government claims that it had a role in curating the space for discourse. Jurists, however, expected that curatorial role to remain limited, proportional, and connected with concerns outlined in paragraph 2, Article 10 of the ECHR.

Ultimately, in *Mouvement Raëlien Suisse, Animal Defenders, Delfi,* and *Hertel,* the Court communicated it understood government as the space's keeper, a substantially different approach than the US model for the space, which generally requires the government remain on the sideline while individuals are free to evaluate ideas, whether, in many cases, they are potentially dangerous to the public or not.

## PUBLIC GOOD – ON THE BALANCE

The Hungarian Helsinki Committee (HHC), a Budapest-based legal-rights group, was zeroing in on what it perceived to be a corrupt, non-transparent system used by government officials to assign public defenders to those who were charged with crimes. As part of its campaign to improve the system, the group in 2009 filed open-records requests, seeking the names and numbers of assignments for public defenders in twenty-eight police departments in Hungary. Six departments refused to comply, contending the information was private, personal information. The HHC averred the government's refusal to provide the information it sought violated its free-expression rights under Article 10, because it limited the group's right to receive and impart information.[39] The government, however, reasoned Article 10 protected free expression, not a right of access to documents. Article 10, the government continued,

## Chapter Ten

had nothing to do with its standoff with the rights group. The ECtHR disagreed with the government's logic, ultimately siding with the HHC. The Court reasoned:

> by denying it access to the requested information . . . the domestic authorities impaired the applicant NGO's exercise of its freedom to receive and impart information, in a manner striking at the very substance of its Article 10 rights.[40]

Crucially, the Court did not indicate *all* Article 10 claims regarding access to information would be successful. The jurists emphasized the rights group's intent was to use the information for the betterment of society. It's intent, and the information it sought to share, were a public good. Chastising the government officials, the Court emphasized "The domestic authorities made no assessment whatsoever of the potential public-interest character of the information sought."[41]

The HHC's case, *Magyar Helsinki Bizottság*, represents another crucial aspect of the EU's approach to the space for discourse: Ideas often must be demonstrably associated with the public good. Such an expectation finds its foundations in the tension between freedom and responsibility found in the UDHR and the ECHR. The public-good emphasis is inferred in Article 10, where paragraph 1 explains "Everyone has a right to freedom of expression," yet paragraph 2 cautions "the exercise of these freedoms, since it carries with it duties and responsibilities, may be subject to such formalities, conditions, restrictions, or penalties as are prescribed by law and are necessary in a democratic society."[42] Within the push and pull of the opposing interests in freedom and responsibility, the EU space for discourse finds another point of contrast with the United States' marketplace approach. Misinformation and disinformation, for example, are generally protected in the wide-open, hands-off marketplace of ideas in the United States, while the EU's public-good expectation provides an avenue for government to remove such content.[43] While the law-and-policy influences on the space for discourse are discussed later in the chapter, EU jurists have consistently contended information that lacks value to the public, or threatens it, can lose Article 10 protection. Such an expectation was present in *Mouvement Raëlien Suisse*, where jurists rationalized the government could reject a group's request to display a poster because the sect's ideas were not beneficial to society.[44]

224

*Curators of Discourse*

Similarly, the cash value of the communicators' ideas was central in the *Delfi* and *Animal Defenders* decisions. In *Delfi*, the company took down threating and allegedly defamatory reader comments when the subject of the vitriol's lawyers demanded they be removed. The victim still sued the company, and Delfi was found liable and fined about €320. When Delfi challenged the Estonian courts' decisions, contending they violated the company's Article 10 rights, the ECtHR *weighed* the value the commentors' ideas had to the public against the victim's right to dignity. The Court emphasized, the "balance might, however, depend on the nature of the information in question and its sensitivity for the data subject's private life and on the interest of the public in having that information."[45] The jurists, having weighed the value the comments had to the public good against the victim's rights, upheld the fine, reasoning the penalty was only a slight amount of money and the corporation could have done more to manage the comments published in its spaces.

The ECtHR generalized the public-good criteria even further in *Animal Defenders*, reasoning televised political advertisements in general threatened "distortion of the political debate."[46] Thus, while the animal rights group's messages were about a matter of public concern, the Court upheld the government's decision to disallow them from airing because the form of media, combined with the subject matter, was found to be potentially distorting and, to that end, not a public good. The ECtHR generally accepted the government argument that the ban was needed "to protect effective pluralism and the democratic process."[47]

The public-good expectations do more than provide rationales for limiting expression in the EU's construction of the space for discourse. Public-good-related concerns helped rationalize pro-free-expression decisions in *Aguilina v. Malta* and *Steel and Morris v. U.K.* In *Aguilina*, a 2011 case, Sharon Spiteri, a reporter for the *Times of Malta*, covered a raucous bigamy trial where the accused's lawyer didn't show up. She was certain she heard the magistrate say he found the absent lawyer in contempt of court. Unable to verify the information with the magistrate or deputy registrar, she asked another reporter, who said he heard the same thing. She reported the lawyer was held in contempt, but the lawyer complained that had not happened. The reporter checked the court's records

*Chapter Ten*

the next day and no contempt decision could be found. The newspaper quickly apologized, but the no-show lawyer sued all involved, contending the report was false and was not a fair and accurate account of the proceedings. Spiteri lost her case, since there was no record of the contempt charge, though no witness from that day disagreed with what she reported.

The ECtHR overturned the Maltese courts' decision, reasoning her efforts to report on the proceedings were a public good. The Court reasoned journalism has a crucial role in informing the public exchange of ideas. That role includes "in a manner consistent with its obligations and responsibilities – information and ideas on all matters of public interest, including those relating to the administration of justice."[48] The jurists reasoned the reporter's conclusion that the contempt charge had been announced by the magistrate comported with traditional journalistic practices in that she reported what she saw and heard and corroborated it with others who were there. The journalist's efforts, while they might not have led to an accurate report, were of great enough public good, in principle, that the Court overturned the judgment against her. In a parting shot to the person who brought the case, the jurists noted the no-show lawyer was the last person who could give an accurate account of what happened in the courtroom that day.

The Court's decision in *Steel and Morris*, decided in 2005, represents similar understandings regarding the public-good expectations. Helen Steel and David Morris, members of Greenpeace London, helped create and distribute a leaflet that called McDonalds "McDollars, McGreedy, McCancer, McMurder, McDisease," and claimed the company exploited workers, led to starvation in impoverished countries, destroyed the rainforests, and was part of a colonial invasion into many nations around the world.[49] McDonalds sued them for defamation and British courts ruled in the corporation's favor, awarding tens of thousands of pounds in damages against Steel and Morris. The activists appealed the decisions to the ECtHR, contending their free expression rights, under Article 10, were violated. The Court weighed arguments from both sides, noting the UK courts' decisions interfered with Steel and Morris's free-expression rights and, conversely, emphasizing the decisions followed English law. The deciding question, to the Court, was whether

*Curators of Discourse*

the limitations were "necessary in a democratic society."[50] The Court reasoned it "must weigh a number of factors in the balance when reviewing the proportionality of the measure complained of."[51] The jurists emphasized small groups, such as Steel's and Morris's, can contribute to democratic discourse and the matters they addressed were of concern to the public.

Thus, the ECtHR ultimately framed the question before it as whether the ideas in question were beneficial or a hinderance to democratic discourse. The Court explained, "There exists a strong public interest in enabling such groups and individuals outside the mainstream to contribute to the public debate by disseminating information and ideas on matters of general public interest such as health and the environment."[52] Using such reasoning, the Court found Steel's and Morris's free-expression rights were violated. Crucially, the ECtHR did not set a precedent that similar expression cannot be limited in the future. The jurists lamented the size of the damages, reasoning they were unreasonably large, and the public-good value activists' messages had within democratic discourse. Absent one or both arguments in the applicants' favor, the Court could have upheld the decisions against them.

The Court's reasoning in *Steel and Morris* was influenced by public-good reasoning derived from *Zana v. Turkey*, a 1997 decision that cites *Handyside* and is cited in *Hertel*.[53] Mehdi Zana, a former mayor in a town in southeastern Turkey that was, at the time, contested by Kurdish fighters, voiced support, from jail, for the Kurdish liberation movement. He was convicted under a law that criminalized supporting those who commit crimes and endanger public safety. In assessing Zana's case, the ECtHR emphasized the crime in question was prescribed by law but questioned whether the decision was "necessary in a democratic society."[54] In approaching this question, the Court investigated both the government's actions and the speaker's rights, balancing each concern on a scale that pivoted upon the necessity of both parties' actions. In this regard, the public-good question was the fulcrum on which the matter was weighed. Did democracy require halting the expression? Did the expression constitute a public good? As with *Steel and Morris*, the "necessary" question required the speakers' ideas be identified as a positive or valued contribution to discourse. In *Zana*, the Court upheld the former

## Chapter Ten

mayor's conviction, reasoning, on the balance, his expression in support of the Kurdish group was more a danger than a public good.

Ultimately, as these cases indicate, the EU space for discourse is constructed more like a tension bridge than one of the stone arch bridges that dot rivers throughout the bloc. The US system, which places nearly all the weight of free-expression rationales on a series of Enlightenment assumptions, bears more resemblance to a stone arch bridge. The entire system, in other words, is supported up by a series of weight-bearing assumptions about truth and human rationality. Such a design requires little in the way of balancing between the push and pull of opposing promises. The built-in tension between freedom and responsibility in the EU, however, creates a balanced space that requires that the opposing foundational structures continue to pull in opposite directions, like a tension bridge. This continuous tension between freedom and responsibility holds up the bloc's assumptions regarding the space for discourse. The balancing the tension provides includes questions about the intent of the publisher, how information will be used to benefit the public, concern for free expression versus distortion in the space, the public's right to know, and human dignity. Coupled with the broader conceptualization of the government as the curator of the space, the balance between the public-good value of information and other social concerns is largely measured by officials who, based on Article 10 and the precedential record that surrounds it, are empowered as the space for discourse's caretakers.

### LAWMAKERS AS FELLOW CURATORS

Jurists are not the only government actors empowered by the ECHR's efforts to balance the space for discourse's shape and contours within the carefully balanced, built-in tensions between freedom and responsibility. The "duties and responsibilities" wording within paragraph 2 of Article 10, as well as the public-good and curatorial roles established within jurists' precedents, have opened the door for lawmakers to actively manage and safeguard the space for discourse within the bloc. As US lawmakers have generally approached pressing questions, new and old, about distortion, falsity, and harm as if free-expression

*Curators of Discourse*

rationales are static and immovable barriers, largely as a result of an Enlightenment-based interpretation of the marketplace of ideas, EU lawmakers have experimented with laws that both protect and limit the flow of ideas. While this chapter looks at individual laws as examples, it is crucial to note from the outset that, as a whole, the very existence of such regulations and protections get at a fundamentally different understanding of free expression and the space for discourse than that which exists in the United States. The existence of measures such as the Digital Services Act (DSA), Digital Markets Act (DMA), the proposed Artificial Intelligence Act (AIA), and the European Media Freedom Act—as a group—is a testament to the EU's far more dynamic construction of the space. Many, if not most, of the requirements of these laws would conflict with the United States' expansive marketplace approach and be found unconstitutional. The tension between freedom and responsibility in the EU, however, opens the door to such experimentation when it comes to addressing emerging problems for the space for discourse.

The DMA, which came into effect in fall 2022, exemplifies this thinking. The law defines large online platforms, including firms such as Meta, Twitter, and Google, as gatekeepers. Under such a designation, the EU requires such firms ensure competing third-party services and products are treated equally on gatekeepers' spaces, disallows companies from forcing pre-installed software that cannot be removed on consumers, and halts firms from limiting consumers' abilities to work with other businesses outside their platform.[55] Each of these requirements, and a host of others, represent government officials' efforts to prune and clip the growing branches of the virtual space for discourse, helping to keep them within certain boundaries. Inherent within these requirements is an EU assumption that government officials are the best landscapers for the space, a substantial contrast to the US model, where market forces—as well as the assumed innate natures of truth and human rationality—are tasked with organically caring for the space for discourse. EU lawmakers' landscaping work, particularly in the networked, AI era, provides a helpful contrast to the United States' hands-off approach.

The DMA's sibling, the DSA, was approved by EU lawmakers in autumn 2022, just as the DMA came into effect. While the DMA focuses

229

*Chapter Ten*

on business structures and market forces, such as competition and product design, the DSA takes aim at content regulation. The law, labeled by one news organization as "the potential gold standard for online content governance,"[56] requires firms remove hateful, extremist, and terroristic content. Misinformation, disinformation, and harassing content are also limited.[57] While many online firms have internal policies about some of these areas of content, and a very narrow slice of them are limited within the United States' generally wide-open approach to the space for discourse, the DSA enforces a common legal standard on all large technology firms and, in many instances, substantially broadens the definitions of each category.

While a US politician's social media post, for example, might include racism, attacks on the LGBTQ community, conspiracy theories, or implied threats, the First Amendment would generally protect it from the government forcing its removal from the space for discourse. The DSA, with support from decades of EU legal precedents that support the government-as-curator approach and a public-good expectation, would strongly incentivize companies to remove this type of content. If companies failed to do so, the DSA empowers the government to impose multimillion-dollar fines on the companies. In other words, the law itself, as well as related fears stemming from the threats of fines, effectively shrinks the range of ideas and cleanses the space for discourse. Which ideas are too extreme, dangerous, or hateful? The law leaves government officials to determine these matters, reinforcing the curatorial role jurists staked out in the precedential record. The EU reasoned in its information about the DSA, "The responsibilities of users, platforms, and public authorities are rebalanced according to European values, placing citizens at the centre."[58]

Such a sweeping, ambitious approach to content moderation belies EU officials' beliefs that government can be a force for good by caring for the space for discourse. The approach also reinforces the constant tension between freedom and responsibility within the EU's guiding principles. Crucially, such a caretaking role does not end at the edges of the bloc's geographic boundaries. Online technologies often do not heed the marks and squiggly lines on maps. As we saw with the General Data Protection Restriction (GDPR), a massive EU online privacy law

230

*Curators of Discourse*

that went into effect in spring 2018, massive laws like the DSA can catalyze global revisions to the services online firms provide.[59] In the case of the GDPR, aspects of the law reached across the Atlantic, influencing, as a side effect, US citizens' privacy. Sites such as those of Arkansas State Parks and Mount Rushmore, clearly not within the EU's borders, came to include GDPR compliance information within their spaces.[60] The DSA promised to do the same, encouraging companies, as they seek to comply with the bloc's law, to make EU-friendly content moderation policies on a global scale. Such a move would circumvent the United States' static, hands-off marketplace approach to the space for discourse in favor of Europe's more government-as-curator role as companies, pushed by the EU to change their practices, limit the spectrum of ideas in the space for discourse.

Finally, EU lawmakers proposed the AIA in spring 2021. The law would require publishers to label AI-influenced entities and works, such as bots and deepfakes, and create liability for their works' "through the whole AI systems' lifecycle."[61] The proposal emphasized that AI can harm human rights, particularly in regard to human dignity and privacy. The law avers some AI "should be prohibited because they contradict Union values of respect for human dignity, freedom, equality, democracy, and the rule of law."[62] While bots have already influenced US elections and deepfakes have been used to confuse voters and victimize and shame individuals, no substantial federal regulation has been seriously considered.[63] The White House released a "Blueprint for an AI Bill of Rights" in fall 2022, which included a passing mention of freedom of expression.[64] The non-binding document, however, portended to have little or no direct influence on the space for discourse in the United States. If enacted, however, the EU's AIA would again place government regulations and officials in a curatorial role, much as is the case in the DMA and DSA. Such regulations, in the name of protecting the space and those who engage in it, would limit the flow of ideas and speakers in the space for discourse. Ultimately, the differing conceptualizations of the space, particularly regarding the role of government, substantially explain the ways concerns regarding AI-based distortions and harms are being approached.

Taken as a group, the DMA, DSA, and proposed AIA reinforce the assumption—outlined earlier in the chapter within the context of

231

*Chapter Ten*

courts—that EU constructions of the space for discourse place government officials in a curatorial role. These laws assume government officials, for the good of the public and the space, should shepherd the exchange of ideas. Furthermore, government curators are expected to work to protect the space for discourse from distortion. Their curatorial powers are limited, however, as court decisions emphasized earlier in the chapter. While restrictions must be balanced within the freedom-and-responsibility tension the EU has constructed, laws such as the DMA, DSA, and AIA all reinforce understandings that EU officials see government as a crucial curator of the space for discourse.

### INFORMATION—GOOD AND BAD

The EU wants to protect information—at least some of it. The bloc proposed the European Media Freedom Act (MFA) in fall 2022. The law, among other safeguards, would protect news organizations from people and government entities that seek to use power and threats to influence editorial decisions. The law would also safeguard journalists from spyware and hacking attempts and require media organizations seeking to take over smaller rivals to prove such a deal would ensure media pluralism and editorial independence.[65] The group that put forth the law also advised the EU it should create a media services commission to monitor information regulation efforts among the bloc's member states. Months earlier, the EU announced clarified restrictions on disinformation, which include stripping the ability to profit from false information from publishers, transparency for political advertising, and giving users more power to flag disinformation.[66] In announcing the revised efforts to fight disinformation, the EU reasoned, "Users will be better protected from disinformation."[67]

The MFA and anti-disinformation efforts followed a spring 2022 directive aimed at helping to protect communicators from strategic lawsuits against public participation (SLAPPs), which are frivolous lawsuits increasingly used by those in power to cause financial, emotional, and reputational harm to publishers.[68] Similarly, in 2021, EU leaders recommended legal frameworks that would strengthen safety measures for journalists.[69] The recommendation emphasized freedom and

*Curators of Discourse*

responsibility, highlighting "The EU is founded on the values of respect for human dignity, freedom, democracy, equality, the rule of law and respect for human rights. This includes respect for media freedom and pluralism and the right to freedom of expression."[70]

These four efforts reinforce EU officials' understandings that government should act as a curator for the space for discourse. Importantly, however, they also emphasize a crucial, conceptual understanding of information. The EU efforts to *protect* some information, while limiting other content, illuminates the bloc's foundational expectation that information should be a public good. Put another way, information that fails to show itself as valuable to the betterment of society can be more easily regulated than public-good content. In announcing the MFA, for example, one EU leader explained, "Media are a pillar of democracy. . . . Journalists should be able to do their work, inform citizens and hold power to account without fear or favour."[71] Similarly, in rationalizing the EU directive against SLAPPs, the bloc reasoned, "In order to secure meaningful participation, citizens must be able to access reliable information, which enables them to form their own opinions and exercise their own judgement in a public space in which different views can be expressed freely."[72] In supporting improved restrictions against false information, the EU explained, "The spread of both disinformation and misinformation can have a range of harmful consequences."[73]

The statements, along with the regulations and directives being considered, communicate that EU officials understand information, at least some of it, as a crucial part of democratic society and, therefore, the space for discourse. Each of the government measures listed is founded upon assumptions, communicated by lawmakers, that the flow of information must be protected because it is *good* for society. Along with such an understanding, however, is the assumption that some information will fail to make the public-good argument for protecting the flow of ideas. Europe's Democracy Action Plan, a large, umbrella initiative under which the efforts to protect journalists, journalism, and the flow of information are listed, also emphasizes countering disinformation and election interference, as well as strengthening media literacy.[74] The presence of such concerns in the plan reinforces the conclusion that

*Chapter Ten*

information is expected to be a public good. Information that does not meet such criteria can be limited.

Such an approach represents another departure from the US system—though not a complete one. The static, Enlightenment-funded marketplace approach makes few judgments regarding the cash value of information seeking protection under the First Amendment. Thus, there generally is not a public-good expectation for information within the US system and the space for discourse it creates. Jurists, however, have not ignored information's value when evaluating entire classifications of ideas. Areas such as obscenity, defamation, and fighting words—those words that, at "their very utterance, inflict injury or tend to incite an immediate breach of the peace"[75]—are not protected by the First Amendment because, justices have rationalized, they are of little or no value to the space for discourse.[76] Importantly, however, almost nothing is obscene under the Supreme Court's definition of obscenity and justices have all but forgotten the fighting words exemption to free speech.[77]

The differences between the two approaches to information and the space for discourse, once again, come down to the foundational assumptions that undergird the systems. The US system places its hefty theoretical weight on foundations that were fashioned from Enlightenment assumptions regarding objective, universal truth, and a one-size-fits-all form of human rationality that is assumed to be inherent in each citizen. The EU does not place the entire girth of its space for discourse upon any single set of assumptions. Instead, it seeks to create a tension-based balance between freedom and responsibility. A free and responsible individual, according to founding documents such as the ECHR and UDHR, will use free-expression protections to benefit society. Content that fails to meet such an understanding can generally be limited. The tension between freedom and responsibility creates the public-good expectation for information. The measuring stick such an expectation gives government officials, who understand themselves as curators of the space for discourse, is a powerful rationale to limit expression and ideas that fail to establish meaningful cash-value benefits for society.

234

*Curators of Discourse*

## THE EU SPACE

Whether the question revolves around the Raëlian movement's request to display a small UFO-adorned poster for a few weeks in a little town that is overlooked by an iconic castle in Switzerland or the massive, online flow-of-ideas-shaping DSA, the EU has fashioned substantially different understandings than the United States regarding the shape and contours of the space for democratic discourse. The crucial differences, however, are not on the surface. The important ECtHR legal decisions and sweeping EU regulations are all undergirded by a set of foundational assumptions about the flow of ideas and the role and place of government. It is because of these foundational building blocks that the EU space for discourse diverges substantially from the US system. These differing building blocks also make crucial contributions to this book's overarching question regarding how we should conceptualize the space for discourse in the networked, AI era.

The US model is constructed upon Enlightenment-based assumptions that truth is generally objective and universal and people are rational and capable of identifying truth from falsity. Courts have used these building blocks to construct a static and expansive space for discourse, in which most expression, however distortive or concerning, is protected and government has little or no role in maintaining the space. While the Enlightenment ideas at the heart of such assumptions are *from* Europe, the EU's approach shuns them in favor of understandings that place government in a curatorial role and include expectations that expression have some identifiable value to the public. Any such government intervention into the flow of ideas in the space for discourse would be an abomination to free-expression champions in the United States—largely because of the Enlightenment-based assumptions at the heart of the marketplace of ideas approach—but they are woven into the very fabric of free expression in the EU.

Crucially, the government's curatorial role in the EU, which would send shudders though most First Amendment scholars, include built-in safeguards. Restrictions must be proportional. Jurists, as examined in the cases earlier in this chapter, expected government officials to be able

235

## Chapter Ten

to rationalize limitations on expression within the framework of paragraph 2 of Article 10's requirement that restrictions must be "prescribed by law and are necessary in a democratic society."[78] This thinking was seen in *Mouvement Raëlien Suisse*, for example, where the Court concluded "The national authorities did not overstep the broad margin of appreciation afforded to them in the present case, and the reasons given to justify their decisions were 'relevant and sufficient' and met a 'pressing social need'."[79] Conversely, in *Hertel*, the Court found the government overstepped its curatorial role, reasoning "the measure in issue cannot be considered as 'necessary' 'in a democratic society.' Consequently, there has been a violation of Article 10."[80] The expectations create gray areas, but the precedential record, in cases such as these, as well as *Handyside*, *Animal Defenders,* and *Delfi*, help clarify the government's boundaries.

Fundamentally, we are not looking here to determine whether the EU's system is good or bad. It is sufficient to conclude the EU's approach provides a unique lens through which the space for discourse can be understood as we seek to revise how free expression should be rationalized and protected in the networked, AI era. Among the crucial characteristics of the EU approach is the careful, difficult-to-achieve balance between freedom and responsibility. The balance creates flexibility. Jurists and lawmakers in the EU are free, based on the foundational guiding documents, to take action to limit problems and distortions that harm the space for democratic discourse. The dynamism, while far more complex and nuanced than the United States' static approach, makes it possible for EU leaders to respond to threats, such as those posed by AI, deepfakes, and the metaverse, to people, democracy, and the space.

# CONCLUSION

## Revising the Space

Flemish cartographer Gerardus Mercator revolutionized mapmaking in 1569 when he converted the globe's curved longitude and latitude lines into straight ones. In doing so, he published the first two-dimensional maps of the world. The Mercator projection, as it is called, has remained one of the dominant representations of what the world looks like for nearly five hundred years—even though we have known it is terribly inaccurate for centuries.[1] Mercator's map represents North American and European land masses as being much larger than they really are and shrinks South America and Africa to mere fractions of their actual sizes. His map shows Greenland as larger than Africa, though the continent's land mass is fourteen times the size of Greenland. Alaska appears to be larger than Mexico, though the nation is three times larger than the state. The map also centered on Europe. In short, if it is a map's purpose to accurately represent the shapes and contours of a space, Mercator's work fails. But we still use it.

Boston schools made news in 2017—centuries after the Mercator projection was created—when it became the first major US district to reject the old map in favor a more accurate version.[2] The move from the flawed, long-established map of the space, which many concluded represented sixteenth-century imperialist and colonial biases, to a different

## Conclusion

representation caused a stir. Some complained about the school district's intent, which was to decolonize the maps students use to learn about world geography.[3] Others complained the new maps were flawed, but in different ways than the old ones.[4] Another perspective, which appeared in an episode of the *West Wing* about the conflict regarding world maps, included a character simply concluding the alternative version of the map was "freaking me out."[5] Change can create discomfort.

Disagreements about intent, alternative versions of the space, and human preferences for stability and what is known do not make the Mercator projection more accurate. Cartographers have known of the map's shortcomings for centuries, but governments and schools have generally rejected accurate maps in favor of the traditional, inaccurate one. The stubbornness seems irrational. If we know we are using inaccurate representations of the world we live in, why not correct the maps? The world, after all, is tangible and visible. It can be measured and observed. How is this still a problem? The same question must be asked of the Enlightenment-based marketplace of ideas, which represents the dominant, most-accepted map of the space for discourse in the United States. Like the Mercator projection, the marketplace metaphor, as a tool that maps an expansive space for democratic discourse, is deeply flawed. These flaws, with their primary failings in the foundational assumptions of Enlightenment thought, were examined most directly in chapter 4. Despite the irreconcilable flaws in the approach's assumptions regarding truth and human rationality, the marketplace map has stubbornly persisted in the minds of jurists and legal scholars.

The flawed natures of Mercator's and the marketplace's representations of the spaces they were created to describe can, perhaps, be defended because they were intended to be used in different ways than they are now. Mercator sought to provide accurate navigation information, not a reference map of the world's nations and features. The result was a focus on the places where people like him lived and sought to go, which at the time were largely colonial trading lanes.[6] Similarly, Enlightenment thought was constructed as a means for individuals to gain certainty in a world in which human senses can fail to grasp phenomena.[7] These ideas were applied to a space for discourse as it was imagined by eighteenth-century thinkers and interpreted by jurists in the twentieth century. The

238

*Revising the Space*

way we use the space for discourse—particularly in the networked, AI eras—has changed drastically. Yet in both cases, we cling to the old, inaccurate map.

Ultimately, the space for discourse, an integral part of democratic society, faces three problems that the world-map controversy does not. First, the space for discourse is imagined. It cannot be measured or observed in the same way as a physical space. It remains an imagined space that resides in individual minds, not shared observations. Second, the longitude and latitude lines of an Enlightenment map—that truth is generally universal and discoverable and that individuals are similarly rational—are fundamentally flawed. Just as with Mercator's projection, we've known this for decades. Legal scholar Jerome Barron came to this conclusion when he introduced access theory in 1967, reasoning the marketplace approach was a "romantic conception of free expression," and "if ever there were a self-operating marketplace of ideas, it has long ceased to exist."[8] Of course, thinkers throughout this book have come to similar conclusions. Oliver W. Holmes, who is often mistakenly credited with mapping the Enlightenment-based marketplace of ideas, rejected absolute truth and questioned one-size-fits-all human rationality. He explained to Judge Learned Hand, in a 1918 letter the year before his groundbreaking free-expression opinions *Schenck* and *Abrams* decisions:

> When I say a thing is true, I mean that I can't help believing it – and nothing more. But as I observe that the cosmos is not always limited by my Cant Helps I don't bother about absolute truths or even inquire whether there is such a thing, but define the Truth as the system of my limitations.[9]

He put it more concisely in a letter several years later: "Absolute truth is a mirage."[10] Holmes bristled against those who boasted ownership of absolutely true knowledge.[11] Constitutional scholar Edwin Baker couldn't have agreed more, concluding decades later that "The marketplace of ideas theory is unworkable, dangerous, and inconsistent with a reasonable interpretation of the purpose of the First Amendment."[12] These thinkers are not identifying cosmetic problems with a long-loved rationale for freedom of expression. These are fundamental problems

# Conclusion

found at the very roots of the map upon which US legal thinkers have based expansive safeguards for free expression. Mercator's assumptions about the world were incorrect and they led to a skewed map. The marketplace's foundational rationales include the same problems. They were wrong from the beginning, and they have led to an incorrect imagining of the space for discourse.

These are just the old problems. The map has always been flawed. Despite its cartographic problems, the concept of an Enlightenment-founded marketplace of ideas has persisted as a centerpiece rationale for free expression. The third problem, or a host of new problems, which were primarily addressed in chapter 6, have made the long-standing imperfections in the map for the space for discourse as untenable as Mercator's representation of Europe as larger than South America when the former is half the size of the latter. In the marketplace's case, powerful algorithms influence the ideas and individuals with whom people engage. Once corporations' algorithms have finished sorting people into generally like-minded communities based on the personal information they have gathered about them, individuals—placed in the unenviable position of selecting the information and ideas they wish to encounter in a choice-rich environment—winnow down their information worlds even further. AI entities, such as bots, as well as misinformation and disinformation, flow freely in these spaces, feeding individuals with information they are primed to accept—even if it is fabricated or misleading.

Some of these challenges to the space for discourse, though they remain unresolved, hardly seem new, as fresh challenges have already grabbed headlines away from them. Increasingly believable deepfakes, which use advanced machine-learning technologies, and other manipulated content are already undermining truth and reality in virtual spaces. The metaverse, the next frontier of online discourse, promises to supercharge the power and influence of AI communicators as they gain human-like forms and can be tailored to reach individual users in a space in which people live, rather than visit.

Ultimately, this list of challenges adds up to a crisis for the map of the space for discourse in democratic society. These changes have fundamentally altered the features and landmarks of the space for discourse. It's time to stop holding, stubbornly, to an inaccurate and fundamentally

240

*Revising the Space*

flawed map of the space for discourse. This final chapter outlines the steps and building blocks needed to redraw the space, beginning with the most crucial move—admitting the marketplace model has never been a static, unchanging map.

## REVISION ONE: A NEW FRAME

The space for discourse is an imagined place. When jurists or others describe it, as was discussed in chapter 1, they are doing so without having been there. It is an idea, something that cannot reside as an exact copy in more than one mind at a time. Ideas have different fundamental properties than physical spaces. Since no one has physically been to the space for discourse, when we read and think about it, we can only imagine how others have pictured it. Such a dynamic makes it nearly impossible for a single, static conceptualization of the space for discourse to exist. At best, we can agree on principles and assumptions regarding the space, which is what this book has sought to do and focus on in its conclusions. Thus, the most important principle of an imagined space for discourse is that, as an idea, it is dynamic and fluid, rather than static and unmoving. Such a conclusion must be at the heart of any reconceptualization of the space. It is a mistake to understand the space for discourse as being static and unchanging. The dynamism of the space can be understood in three ways.

First, on a conceptual level, ideas are incredibly malleable. The marketplace of ideas is an idea, rather than a place. Changing the map of a physical space, such as the Grand Canyon, requires facts and evidence that the current map is incorrect for one reason or another. Those who disagree with changes to the map could go to the canyon themselves and see what the space looks like. The canyon exists in a physical world, which allows it to be experienced and shared. We can disagree on all manner of issues regarding a phenomenon in a physical space, but throughout that discussion the actual thing always exists to guide how it is perceived and understood. A discussion of an idea lacks the potential for a shared, physical phenomenon. Thus, the building blocks for a space for discourse are not the same as they are for a physical phenomenon. We must stop assuming a space for ideas can be defined using the

## Conclusion

characteristics used to understand physical spaces. For ideas, their bases are in foundational assumptions rather than observable phenomena. They act as the idea's DNA. The internally created nature of the building blocks requires the imagined space to be conceptualized as a liquid rather than a solid.

Second, the history of the marketplace of ideas reinforces the logic that an idea should not be treated like a physical phenomenon. Ideas are dynamic. The marketplace of ideas' story and development, as drawn by justices and thinkers, is characterized by changes, which, in chapter 2, were framed as fits and starts because the space has gone through periods of change and stability from its inception. To effectively revise the space for discourse in the networked, AI eras, we must rid ourselves of the fable that the Enlightenment-founded marketplace of ideas was, from the beginning, the map for the space for discourse. It was not the map the Framers created in 1791 or the Court established in its first First Amendment decisions in 1919. History tells a far different, more nuanced, story, which was primarily examined in chapters 4 and 5.

Holmes made only a passing reference to a "the market" in 1919 in the first opinion in which a justice argued a law should be struck down because it conflicted with the First Amendment.[13] While Holmes referred to his market-based argument as "the theory of our Constitution," he never mentioned it again, despite several opportunities in similar First Amendment cases and countless free-expression related discussions in his letters in the years that followed.[14] His potential reference to Enlightenment-founded marketplace thinking lacks any substantial support that he intended to create a hard-and-fast, positivist approach to free-expression rationales. Crucially, Holmes rejected dogmatic thinking and disagreed with Enlightenment assumptions about truth and human rationality, repeatedly rejecting assumptions that truth had any inherent universality to it or that people share a similar understanding of the world around them.[15] Thus, nearly 130 years after the First Amendment was ratified, no precedent for an Enlightenment-based marketplace of ideas existed.

The Court struggled to construct the space in the 1920s and '30s, with Justice Louis Brandeis averring to some Enlightenment ideas to rationalize protecting unpopular ideas in his concurring opinion in

242

## Revising the Space

*Whitney v. California*, and Chief Justice Charles Evans Hughes—grasping to find any precedent in the first case in which the Court struck down a law because it violated the First Amendment—drawing from British precedent and the Constitution's authors' ideas to rationalize the Court's decision.[16] Nearly a decade later, in *Thornhill v. Alabama*, the "market" concept reappeared for the first time in more than two decades, triggering a thirty-year period of gradual construction as justices installed Enlightenment ideas into the space for discourse's foundations.[17] Holmes's mentee, Justice Felix Frankfurter, referred to the "free trade in ideas" in his dissent a year later in 1941 in *Bridges v. California*.[18] In 1953, nearing thirty-five years after Holmes's only reference to the market concept and more than 160 years into the First Amendment's existence, the Court used the "marketplace of ideas" as a complete phrase for the first time, reasoning "This publisher bids for the minds of men in the marketplace of ideas."[19] Just more than a decade later, the Court created the modern First Amendment in *New York Times v. Sullivan*, drawing Enlightenment assumptions and Holmes's "market" reference into the landmark decision's arguments.[20]

The Enlightenment-based marketplace of ideas was taking shape, but it was doing so here and there, as slowly and imperceptibly as highway construction. Such a history of change, in a few decisions each decade or so, tells a far different tale than the monolith-like fable that the marketplace concept was created as a complete idea during the Constitution's framing or in Holmes's dissent in *Abrams* in 1919. Five years after *Sullivan*, justices completed the decades-long installation project, rationalizing in *Red Lion Broadcasting v. FCC* that "It is the purpose of the First Amendment to preserve an uninhibited marketplace of ideas in which truth will ultimately prevail."[21] Still, justices continued to erase and redraw the shapes and contours of the Enlightenment-funded map of the space for discourse in the years that followed. Beginning with *Red Lion,* the Court debated whether the government could limit expression to protect the space for discourse—the path EU lawmakers and courts have selected.[22] The US Supreme Court, over the course of many years, rejected the idea that government could protect the space, instead putting even more weight on the truth-and-human-rationality assumptions they had installed into the marketplace's foundations.

243

## Conclusion

Crucially, there is no one landmark moment when the Enlightenment-based marketplace of ideas was created. That's the point. The space has evolved over the course of a century and it continues to do so. The EU, as discussed in the preceding chapter, has drawn a substantially different map of the space. EU promises of free expression are *protected* by the government, which is placed in a curatorial role that seeks to safeguard the space from distortion or harm. The bloc's space also includes a careful tension between freedom and responsibility, as lawmakers and jurists balance promises of freedom of expression with the expectation that such rights will be used for the good, rather than detriment, of society. The existence of the EU's substantially different map of the space further reinforces the crucial understanding that the marketplace approach is not an objective, unmoving thing, like the Grand Canyon. The space is imagined, and the most accurate constructions will account for its fluid, idea-based nature. Such a conclusion does not require the map of the space be redrawn daily. Instead, it emphasizes the value of a map that is flexible to changes in the landscape, rather than rigidly holding to a set of ideas that fails to properly describe the space.

Third, rigid versus dynamic approaches were also on trial in the decades-long disagreement within the Supreme Court between friends and nemeses Hugo Black and Felix Frankfurter. As examined in chapter 7, Black contributed mightily to the Enlightenment-based marketplace of ideas. His simple, dogmatic approach reasoned: "Congress shall make no law" means "Congress shall make no law."[23] In other words, Black constructed a map of the space for discourse using permanent marker. He set it in stone. Nearly any limitation on expression was rejected, from the start, by Black's hard-and-fast test. When the Court incorporated Enlightenment-based arguments into the birth of the modern First Amendment in *Sullivan*, Black concurred, writing separately to emphasize the Court didn't go far enough in protecting free expression. He explained, "An unconditional right to say what one pleases about public affairs is what I consider to be the minimum guarantee of the First Amendment."[24] Black, by his rigid approach and spare, direct writing contributed to the dominant, Enlightenment-based marketplace. Frankfurter dismissed Black's simple approach. The law, to Frankfurter, required balance and nuance. In the

244

## Revising the Space

crucial *Dennis v. United States* political speech case in 1951, Frankfurter wrote a 12,500-word, argument for why the boundaries for free expression should be balanced with other concerns and identified by the public, rather than the law. Frankfurter explained:

> The demands of free speech in a democratic society as well as the interest in national security are better served by candid and informed weighing of the competing interests, within the confines of the judicial process, than by announcing dogmas too inflexible for the non-Euclidian problems to be solved.[25]

Black wrote a 725-word dissent that rejected Frankfurter's proposed balanced approach. He emphasized, "I cannot agree that the First Amendment permits us to sustain laws suppressing freedom of speech and press on the basis of Congress's or our own notions of mere 'reasonableness.'"[26] The disagreement placed their differing positions in stark contrast.

While we need not accept Frankfurter's often convoluted free-expression legacy, his arguments against "mechanical jurisprudence" and "oversimplified formulas" remain instructive.[27] Frankfurter's disagreement with Black regarding the meaning of free expression and how the space for discourse operated shouldn't distract us from his most important contribution to our question regarding the future of the space for discourse. Frankfurter emphasized our approaches to ideas should not be rigid—they should be dynamic. In one opinion, Frankfurter quoted his mentor, Holmes, who wrote "To rest upon a formula is a slumber that, prolonged, means death."[28] Both feared the dangers of strict judicial formulas. Conditions change. The map of the space for discourse should be capable of changing with them. Accepting the dynamic nature of the space does not require a diminished set of free-expression rights. Rather, it allows us to continuously update the map of the space. Thus, the first, crucial revision to the space for discourse must be in how we understand its nature. Whether we examine the space through the inherently dynamic building blocks of ideas, the lens of history, or Frankfurter's warning that unchanging, mechanical tests can endanger discourse, the outcome remains that the space is best conceptualized a liquid—something that shifts and changes—than a solid.

*Conclusion*

## REVISION 2: ANOTHER TRUTH

Truth assumptions make up the heart of marketplace theory. A new map of the space, therefore, requires a change of heart. The theory's Enlightenment-based truth assumptions, which were added over time to the foundations of the approach, construct truth as generally objective and universal to all.[29] Alongside this monolithic approach to truth is the assumption that individuals are rational and capable of discerning truth from falsity. Together, these truth-and-rationality building blocks have led those who understand the space for discourse through the marketplace lens to assume truth has an innate, discernible quality that allows rational individuals to discern it from falsity. Truth, in this approach, awaits discovery like a diamond awaits a miner. The theory assumes truth will shimmer and show its worth when it is discovered, and individuals will yield to its inherent value. The Supreme Court, based on these assumptions, has generally rejected limitations on expression, reasoning when ideas move freely, truth will succeed, and falsity will fail. These assumptions make up the core of marketplace theory.

These are also at the source of the approach's problems. The Enlightenment-based truth and human rationality assumptions create an incongruent association between the natures of truth and ideas. They are mismatched. If ideas are constructed in each person's mind, rather than observed via physical phenomena, then a map of the space for the exchange of ideas must account for the inability of individuals to share exact versions of the appearances and features of the space. Truth, in this line of thinking, isn't a diamond that has always awaited discovery; it is an individual concluding something *is a* diamond based on the lens of ideas and past experiences they bring to the mine. Such an approach requires a different set of assumptions about truth and how people come to understand the world around them. When a person, bringing with them the full weight of their personal influences and biases, concludes something is true, their process relies on an emergent, rather than static, construction of truth. In this regard, human rationality is conceptualized on an individual level, rather than as a one-size-fits-all reality. These revised truth understandings construct a different map for discourse, one that more accurately accounts for the dynamic nature of ideas, than the

246

*Revising the Space*

Enlightenment approach. Revising the space for discourse's truth-and-rationality understandings helps create a match between the dynamic nature of the space and the nature of its foundational assumptions. Historically, the mismatch between a changing, imagined space—as examined above—and the Enlightenment's unmoving, concrete understanding of truth, has undermined marketplace theory's assumptions.

This conflict is not new. Baker, for example, noted "truth is not objective" when he concluded marketplace theory is "unworkable."[30] Legal scholar Stanley Ingber similarly emphasized the need to "pierce the myth of the neutral marketplace of ideas and expose the flawed market model assumptions of objective truth and the power of rationality."[31] Legal scholar Frederick Schauer also highlighted the flaws in the theory's truth assumptions, contending "Our increasing knowledge about the process of idea transmission, reception, and acceptance makes it more and more difficult to accept the notion that truth has some inherent power to prevail in the marketplace of ideas."[32] While these scholars did not frame truth assumptions as a problematic mismatch between a dynamic space and a static conceptualization of truth, as is being done here, they identified the marketplace approach's construction of truth as the theory's most fundamental structural flaw. German thinker Hannah Arendt, whose ideas were examined in chapter 9, went several steps further in deconstructing the problems with Enlightenment truth-and-rationality assumptions.

Arendt imagined conclusions about phenomena as falling into two categories: appearances and truth. Absent thought, she reasoned, many accept what appears to be as truth rather than engaging with ideas and coming to conclusions about them. Her concerns overlap with Holmes's skepticism about absolute truth, but Arendt constructed her ideas differently. She highlighted that some truths, particularly those that people do not wish to comprehend, struggle to find acceptance. When people criticized her construction of Nazi logistics mastermind Adolf Eichmann as a fool, rather than an evil, hate-filled monster, she noted "The clamor centered on the 'image' of a book which was never written, and touched upon subjects that often had not only not been mentioned by me but had never occurred to me before."[33] Truth, she observed, took on a life of its own. People were constructing it based on how the phenomena appeared.

## Conclusion

What factors caused the fictions to arise in the place of the truths she sought to convey? Emotion. Experience. Societal influences. Ultimately, the *truth* of Eichmann's guilt could not be boiled down to a good or bad product that succeeded or faltered in the free exchange of ideas. The story was far more complex. What people concluded from her work was fraught with countless immeasurable factors that were projected upon the ideas Arendt offered. Many chose to cling to appearances, which were fueled by individual biases, rather than to examine her ideas in a search for truth. She reflected on this in her final work, *The Life of the Mind*. Arendt reasoned, "The simple-minded positivism that believes it found a firm ground of certainty if it only excludes all mental phenomena from consideration and holds fast to observable facts, the everyday reality given to our senses" fails to grasp truth.[34] Arendt separated "truth" and "appearances," emphasizing Enlightenment ideas often confuse the appearance of a phenomena with the truth of its existence.[35] She contended something more is needed—a different standard—than Enlightenment-based truth. Her solution—thought. People must do more than accept simple appearances, she reasoned.

The problems with the appearances and personal biases Arendt identified have only become more concerning as non-human actors, such as algorithms and AI communicators, alongside the choice-rich information environment, have fundamentally changed the shape and contour of the space and introduced new types of distortions that undermine the already problematic objective-truth foundations. The chances of the faulty Enlightenment-based truth and human-rationality assumptions working, despite their flaws, have become increasingly unlikely as the static marketplace that was envisioned becomes increasingly deserted as algorithms and personal choices draw people into a multiverse of smaller, more idea-focused side streets and alleys. A dynamic construction of the space creates more flexibility in how we map the space. Such flexibility requires, however, an equally pliable conceptualization of truth.

A more flexible construction of truth does not suggest a truthless world. Crucially, Arendt and others have emphasized the Enlightenment's approach to truth doesn't necessarily yield truth. That's why removing the faulty construction of truth that has driven the space for discourse's foundational assumptions and replacing it with a more functional truth

*Revising the Space*

regime is crucial to revising how we understand the map of the space. Put differently, the Enlightenment-based approach posits truth is generally universal and the same for all, but that has never been an accurate understanding. In replacing it, we can consider the truth conceptualizations put forth by thinkers in the preceding chapters. William James and John Dewey, in chapter 8, for example, constructed American pragmatism based on assumptions that truth is made within each person, rather than found. These conclusions align with Arendt's thinking regarding the power of individual tendencies to lead people to accept appearances that align with their preconceptions. James, who shared in his old friend Holmes's influences when they were growing up, reasoned, "The truth of an idea is not a stagnant property inherent in it. Truth happens to an idea. It becomes true."[36]

Truth, in James's thinking, was conditioned upon experience. Though Holmes preferred to disagree with James, their conclusions overlapped in this regard. Holmes was more cynical, however. He wrote as much to James when his friend sent him a copy of *Pragmatism* in 1907. He told James, "I heartily agree with much—but I am more skeptical than you are."[37] Holmes framed experience as a bias-creating influence on individually constructed truths, while James simply believed people revised their truths as they learned and experienced more.[38] Skeptical or not, Holmes's and James's constructions of truth required accounting for the personal experiences and biases that color each person's interaction with the world around them.

Dewey, whose ideas Holmes lauded, applied James's pragmatic conception of truth to a social, rather than psychological level, contending truth *emerges* via discourse with others.[39] In this regard, Dewey introduced the need for community, emphasizing truth as the emergent result of discourse. He explained, "To learn to be human is to develop through the give-and-take of communication an effective sense of being an individually distinctive member of a community."[40] He also emphasized democracy is a "way of life," rather than a stagnant institution.[41] Thus, when Enlightenment truth is removed from the construction of the space for discourse and pragmatic truth is inserted in its place, the dynamic space gains a matching, pliable conceptualization of truth. The space and the construction of truth align in that they are both dynamic. At

## Conclusion

that point, a space that exists only in the minds of individuals is paired with an understanding of truth that assumes the same—truth is made internally and communicated externally. This shift in the nature of truth has consequences for how we map the space for discourse. The rationales become oriented toward safeguarding the ability of individuals to engage with others and for truth to emerge from that discourse. Thus, protecting the emergence of that truth, rather than the discovery of a persistent, universal truth, requires different rationales. Distortive influences on the space, such as purposeful information and AI-related babble that pushes human speakers from engaging with each other, become problems that must be addressed, rather than requiring that they be accepted as other competitors in a marketplace where truth is assumed to defeat falsity.

### REVISION 3: A PRINCIPAL-BASED APPROACH

As with the first two revisions—how we understand the *nature of ideas* and *assumptions regarding truth*—our last, shifting from a physical space- to a principle-based model, represents conceptual, rather than cosmetic, concerns regarding how we should understand the space for discourse. The space we seek to map and protect is conceptual—an imagined space—so constructing it as if it existed as a physical space automatically creates functionality problems. We must divest ourselves from imagining an idealized physical space as a representation of an imagined one. Those who constructed the Enlightenment-based marketplace of ideas, for example, conjured visions of pastoral, cobblestoned streets of seventeenth and eighteenth-century Europe when they structured the space. Justices have referred to "town criers" communicating ideas on public squares and lonely pamphleteers distributing messages when they use marketplace-based assumptions.[42] These types of imaginings of speakers acting in a physical space creates three problems that continue to undermine the viability of the marketplace model. First, an idea-based space for discourse cannot be accurately replicated in a physical one.

Ideas and physical spaces for discourse do not share the same properties. Imagined spaces can be described. They cannot, however, be accurately replicated to represent an imagined space. Features are always

*Revising the Space*

lost in the translation from an imagined space to a metaphorical physical realm. The physical cannot replicate the imagined because they are fundamentally different in nature. Second, the rigidity of a physical space's mold makes it difficult for the space for discourse to change and adapt to shifts in technology and society. The marketplace model, for example, struggles to adequately represent the fragmented nature of community and communication in the networked, AI eras. Finally, the idealized European marketplaces jurists and thinkers have conjured when they have structured the space were never truly spaces for the free exchanges of ideas. Many factors, such as race, gender, and socioeconomic position, limited who could participate in the space. Imagining the traditional conceptualization of the marketplace as a historic space of equality and the free exchange of ideas seeks to turn fiction into reality.

In this regard, the final crucial revision is to eschew constructing the space for discourse as if it resembled a physical space. An imagined space, in other words, should be constructed using conceptual, rather than physical, building blocks. Only then can that space adequately safeguard the flow of ideas. The building materials, in other words, should be apples to apples, not apples to oranges. Physical spaces and imagined spaces have different properties. They are governed by different rules. It is a mistake to ignore these differences. Revising our construction of the space from a metaphorical or comparative model, such as the marketplace approach, to a principle-based space creates an alignment between the imagined nature of the space and the properties used to describe it. This revision is particularly crucial in the networked, AI eras, as any vestige of the already problematic construction of the physical European town square marketplace fails to capture the contours and shapes of the space for discourse. Algorithms limit the ideas and communicators with which people engage. AI communicators create and boost certain messages, manipulating algorithms, flooding the spaces with ideas, and, at times, pushing human communicators' ideas from the space.

Humans have their part to play in this process as well. A choice-rich information environment generally leads to more homogenic communities.[43] These communities generally limit the spectrum of acceptable ideas, leading people to become wary and unused to encountering perspectives that diverge from their own. Finally, the metaverse threatens

## Conclusion

to make all these matters, which were examined in more detail in chapter 6, worse, ushering them into virtual reality. In the metaverse, the chatbot we encountered on a traditional social media app is represented by a human-like AI entity whose appearance and language has been selected based on algorithms that signal the AI entity regarding which approaches will be most effective on each individual audience member. The AI entity shows human-like qualities, such as disappointment or sadness. Changes such as these to the space for discourse seem overwhelming. Can any model account for all of them? A crucial step to addressing this concern is to stop thinking of the space as if it's a physical one. A physical world or metaphorical representation cannot do the job. A principle-based approach is required.

The first two revisions have already started our move toward a conceptual rendering of the space by drawing us into different ways to understand and build it. Thinkers in the preceding chapters also provided lenses through which a conceptual space for discourse can be constructed. Arendt and Dewey, in their own ways, emphasized that a space for discourse requires individuals to live active, meaningful lives in the public realm. Arendt added an admonition against an unthinking life, or a space dominated by base or frivolous matters, to her building blocks.[44] These thinkers indicated the space must protect human community and discourse, particularly when it involves matters of public concern. While the space for discourse should not include mandates that individuals lead active, meaningful lives, and avoid frivolity, it can be constructed upon principles that safeguard these types of discourse-supporting building blocks.

The EU's construction of the space aligns with this approach. The EU system, while imperfect, is constructed on a series of principles, rather than an imagining of a physical space. Lawmakers and jurists in the bloc generally do not subscribe to the marketplace approach. Instead, the principle-based approach has created a malleable system, allowing lawmakers to experiment with solutions to challenges posed by big tech firms, AI, and deepfakes.[45] The EU space for discourse is characterized by principles, such as human dignity, tolerance for others, duty to community, morality, public order, and the well-being of democratic society.[46] These principles, while they are imperfectly executed, guide the

252

*Revising the Space*

construction of the space for discourse. They create a map filled with landmarks that guide the way. They also create a tension between freedom of expression and the expectation that people use their rights responsibly. Many of these principles have no place in the United States' free-expression story. They don't have to. The crucial step is to recognize the need for a principle-based approach, one that replaces problematic dependencies on metaphorical imaginings of physical spaces.

## THE DISCURSIVE MARKETPLACE

Mercator's world map is plagued by surface-level problems. The sizes of entire continents are terribly misrepresented. These surface-level problems demand simple solutions. Redraw the map. Cartographers have a myriad of tools at their disposal to revise the map's features, so it accurately represents the space it claims to describe. All that is needed is the will to depart from the traditional map and fix the flawed, but long-accepted, representation of the space. Fixing the space for democratic discourse is more difficult. The dominant, Enlightenment-based marketplace approach's problems are not on the surface. They are deep within its core. Attempts to correct the existing map for the space for discourse will not be successful as long as flaws remain in the space's foundational assumptions. That's why this book has focused on conceptual, rather than cosmetic, revisions. We must change *how we understand* the space for discourse, shifting conceptualizations from incorrect assumptions that the space is static and unchanging to accepting it as dynamic. Within this changing space, we must correct the *flawed truth assumptions*, replacing positivist Enlightenment thinking with understandings of truth that accept that truth is formed from within, rather than from without. Finally, the space for discourse's building blocks must be *principles* rather than comparisons to the features of metaphorical physical spaces. We cannot think of the space in terms of bricks and mortar and buyers and sellers. We must alter the foundational materials, substituting guiding principles in the places of metaphors that compare the space to physical realms.

These three revisions do far more than fix cosmetic problems within the rationales we use to protect the free exchange of ideas. We're not

253

## Conclusion

redrawing misrepresented continents. We're digging into the earth's very mantle. These revisions change the space's nature from its core. When we conceptualize the space as dynamic, we not only make its frame more accurate, we normalize adjusting the space to account for changes in society and technology. The ability to adjust the space does not mean historical amnesia. That's where visualizing the space as composed of principles rather than imagining an idealized physical space helps. A dynamic, changing space can be adjusted, but the revisions are at all times guided by the stated principles of the space. Primarily among the principles of the space for discourse are the flow of ideas and emergences of truth. When we revise truth rationales so expression is no longer protected so truth can vanquish falsity in an open exchange of ideas, the focus shifts to protecting the ability of individuals to engage with others so truth can emerge via discourse. The adjustment is subtle, but crucial. Traditional marketplace reasoning emphasizes that static, same-for-all-truth has a special quality that allows rational people to separate it from falsity. The revised model constructs truth so it is attained on a personal level. The shift adjusts the space's assumptions, so the emphasis is protecting the formation of truth, rather than its discovery. In this approach, the model safeguards the flow of ideas and engagements among individuals in which truth emerges. Such a set of rationales leaves room for limitations on that which distorts the flow of ideas and emergence of truth. AI actors that push human speakers out of the space or distort which ideas people encounter could be limited, for example, because the goal is to protect truth-creating discourse, not the discovery of static truths.

These are careful, nuanced adjustments. Do they conflict with the nation's free-speech tradition? Only if we pretend the Enlightenment-based marketplace was a monolith that fell from the sky in 1791, 1919, or some other year. That was not the case. Our free-speech tradition is defined by change. These revisions do not turn their back on what is known about free expression. They work alongside it. They create a malleable system that more accurately reflects the formation of truth and is guided by foundational free-expression principles.

# NOTES

*Introduction*

1. Abrams v. United States, 250 U.S. 616 (1919).

2. Heywood Broun, "Act Three—The Courtroom," *New York Tribune*, Oct. 27, 1918, 21.

3. Hold Four, Charged with Advocating Overthrow of American Government," *Buffalo Enquirer*, March 12, 1919, 3.

4. "Russian Girl Held for Showering Pamphlets from Rooftop," *New York Daily News*, Sept. 19, 1919, 2.

5. "Girl Creates Stir at Anarchist Trial," *New York Times*, Oct. 11, 1919, Page 24.

6. "Girl Creates Stir."

7. Ibid.

8. "Molly Steimer, Red Agitator, Is Arrested," *New York Tribune*, Oct. 19, 1919, 1.

9. See Jacob Riis, *How the Other Half Lives* (Cambridge, MA: Harvard University Press, 2010); Andrew Cornell, *Unruly Equality* (Berkeley, CA: University of California Press), 21–26, regarding immigration, poverty, labor strife, and anarchism during this period.

10. "Haymarket Affair," *Britannica*, last updated June 9, 2023, https://www.britannica.com/money/topic/Haymarket-Affair.

11. "Arrest 41 Pickets for Suffrage at the White House," *New York Times*, November 11, 1917, 1.

12. See David M. Rabbin, *Free Speech in its Forgotten Years* (Cambridge, UK: Cambridge University Press, 1997), 2–8, for discussion regarding the catalyzing nature of the Espionage Act in inducing the Supreme Court to make its first decisions about the First Amendment's meaning.

# Notes to Introduction and Chapter One

13. One of the original six conspirators was acquitted. Another died in jail while awaiting trial.

14. "'Cheer Up!' Girl Red Tells Weeping Mother at Parting in the Tombs," *New York Tribune*, May 2, 1920, 1.

15. Steimer and Abrams weren't the first critics the government deported. Emma Goldman, who was influential to Abrams and Steimer, was deported, along with 248 other dissidents, in December 1919. See "Burford Reaches Hango and Deported Radicals Go on to Russia by Train," *New York Times*, Jan. 18, 1920, 1.

16. See "Girl 'Red' Leader 'Totally Indifferent' At Her Arraignment," *New York Tribune*, Sept. 19, 1919, 20; "Goldman's Power Gone," *St. Joseph News-Press*, Dec. 17, 1919, 2, for examples.

17. See *Abrams,* 250 U.S. at 617–619 regarding Abrams' presence in the case. Abrams is the only one of the four who were convicted who is mentioned in the Supreme Court case. See also Robert Post, "Reconciling Theory and Doctrine in First Amendment Jurisprudence," *California Law Review* 88 (200): 2358–2360; Edward S. Corwin, "Freedom of Speech and Press Under the First Amendment Resume," *Yale Law Journal* 30, no. 1 (1920): 50–55, for examples of the impact Holmes' dissent in the *Abrams* decision had on free expression.

18. *Abrams,* 250 U.S.at 616 and 630 (Holmes, J., dissenting).

19. See chapter 3 for a full discussion of how Holmes understood truth.

20. Ibid.

21. Ibid.

22. *Abrams,* 250 U.S. at 630 (Holmes, J., dissenting).

23. Ibid.

24. Oliver Wendell Holmes, Sr., "My Hunt After the Captain," *The Atlantic*, December 1862.

25. See Letter from Felix Frankfurter to Oliver W. Holmes (Nov. 26, 1919) (on file with Harvard Law School Digital Suite), for an example. See also chapter 3.

### Chapter One

1. Arches National Park. 2021. "Traffic & Travel Tips." National Park Service. Accessed June 25, 2021, https://www.nps.gov/arch/planyourvisit/traffic .htm.

2. Abrams v. United States, 250 U.S. 616, 630 (1919) (Holmes, J., dissenting).

3. Grand Canyon National Park was established February 26, 1919. The Supreme Court announced its decision in Schenck v. U.S., 249 U.S. 47 (1919), the first case in which justices addressed the First Amendment less than a week later. Abrams was announced November 10, 1919 and Zion National Park was added nine days later. See Grand Canyon Information. 2021. "A Sight Beyond Words: Grand Canyon National Park." National Parks Foundation. Accessed June 25, 2021, https://www.nationalparks.org/connect/ explore-parks/grand-canyon-national-park; History of Zion National Park.

## Notes to Chapter One

2021. "A History Lesson on Zion National Park." Greater Zion. Accessed, June 25, 2021, https://greaterzion.com/articles/history-zion-national-park/.

4. Benedict Anderson, *Imagined Communities: Reflections on the Origin and Spread of Nationalism* (London: Verso, 2016), 6. Anderson emphasizes citizens must believe they share things in common for a nation to function. While a citizen might not know every other citizen, they must imagine they share habits or attributes in common with them.

5. Holmes was shot on three different occasions during the Civil War. In two instances, his wounds appeared fatal. Holmes often made references to war in his legal and personal writings. In his Memorial Day speech in 1884, he said "the generation that carried on the war has been set apart by its experience. Through our great good fortune, in our youth our hearts were touched with fire." See Oliver Wendell Holmes, *Speeches* (Boston: Little, Brown, and Company, 1934), 11; Louis Menand, *The Metaphysical Club* (New York: Farrar, Straus and Giroux, 2001), 38; Mark DeWolfe Howe, "The Positivism of Mr. Justice Holmes," *Harvard Law Review* 64 (1951), 535; Jared Schroeder, "The Holmes Truth: Toward a Pragmatic, Holmes-Influenced Conceptualization of the Nature of Truth," *British Journal of American Legal Studies* 7, no. 1 (2018): 177–178.

6. *Abrams*, 250 U.S. at 630 (Holmes, J., dissenting).

7. See Richard A. Posner, *The Essential Holmes* (Chicago: University of Chicago Press, 1992), xii; Vincent Blasi, "Holmes and the Marketplace of Ideas," *Supreme Court Review* 2004: 2; Robert Post, "Reconciling Theory and Doctrine in First Amendment Jurisprudence," *California Law Review* 88 (2018): 2361; Frederick Schauer, "Oliver Wendell Holmes, the Abrams Case, and the Origins of the Harmless Speech Tradition," *Seton Hall Law Review* 51 (2020):205–206, for discussion regarding the impact of the opinion on United States law.

8. *Abrams*, 250 U.S. at 624–631 (Holmes, J., dissenting).

9. Justice Brandeis, who joined Justice Holmes's dissent in *Abrams*, took the lead in most free-expression related cases after 1919. This was intentional. Brandeis regretted joining Holmes's opinions, rather than writing his own, in the 1919 case, see letter from Louis Brandeis to Felix Frankfurter (Aug. 8, 1923), in Melvin I. Urofsky, "The Brandeis-Frankfurter Conversations," *Supreme Court Law Review* (1985): 323–324. The primary exception was Holmes's dissent in Gitlow v. New York, 268 U.S. 652, 672–673 (1925) (Holmes, J., dissenting). In the dissent, Holmes famously contended "Every idea is an incitement."

10. See letter from Felix Frankfurter to Oliver W. Holmes (Nov. 26, 1919) (on file with Harvard Law School Digital Suite), https://iiif.lib.harvard.edu/manifests/view/drs:42879149$17i; and Zechariah Chafee, *Freedom of Speech* (New York: Harcourt, Brace, and Howe, 1920), 375–377.

11. See letter from Oliver W. Holmes to Harold Laski (January 11, 1929) in Posner, *The Essential Holmes*, 107; Felix S. Cohen, "The Holmes-Cohen

*Notes to Chapter One*

Correspondence," *The History of Ideas* 9 (1948): 3 (emphasis included); Oliver Wendell Holmes, Jr., *The Common Law* (New York: Dover Publishers, 1991), 1, for examples.

12. See Thornhill v. Alabama, 310 U.S. 88, 105 (1940); United States v. Rumely, 345 U.S. 41, 42–43 (1953); New York Times v. Sullivan, 376 U.S. 254, 269 (1964); Red Lion v. Federal Communications Commission, 395 U.S. 367, 390 (1969), for examples.

13. *Red Lion*, 395 U.S. at 390.

14. See Virginia State Board of Pharmacy v. Virginia Citizens Consumer Council, 425 U.S. 748 (1976); First National Bank v. Bellotti, 435 U.S. 765 (1978); Reno v. ACLU, 521 U.S. 844 (1997); Brown v. Entertainment Merchants, 564 U.S. 786 (2011); for examples of instances when the Court extended preexisting free-expression safeguards to include new categories.

15. Clay Shirky, *Here Comes Everybody* (New York: Penguin Books, 2008), 59–60.

16. See Jared Schroeder, "Saving the Marketplace from Market Failure: Reorienting Marketplace in the Era of AI Communicators," *William & Mary Bill of Rights Journal* 28 (2020): 699–700. The idea of a multiverse of marketplaces was influenced by Brian McNair, *Cultural Chaos: Journalism, News, and Power in a Globalized World* (New York: Routledge, 2006), 137.

17. See Cass Sunstein, *#Republic* (Princeton, NJ: Princeton University Press, 2017), 1–30, where he discusses the concept of the "daily me." *Also*, Jared Schroeder, "Information, Community, and Change: A Call for a Renewed Conversation About First Amendment Rationales," *First Amendment Law Review* 18 (2020): 123.

18. See Rik Peeter and Marc Schuilenburg, *The Algorithmic Society: Technology Power and Knowledge* (New York, Routledge, 2021), 1–2; Jack M. Balkin, "Free Speech in the Algorithmic Society: Big Data, Private Governance, and New School Speech Regulation," *University of California Davis Law Review* 51 (2018): 1157–1159.

19. See e.g., Molly K. McKew, "How Twitter Bots and Trump Fans Made #ReleaseTheMemo Go Viral," *Politico*, Feb. 4, 2018, https://www.politico.com/magazine/story/2018/02/04/trump-twitter-russians-release-the-memo-216935; Tess Owen, "Nearly 50% of Twitter Accounts Talking About Coronavirus Might Be Bots," *Vice*, April 23, 2020, https://www.vice.com/en_us/article/dygnwz/if-youre-talking-about-coronavirus-on-twitter-youre-probably-a-bot; Kate Starbird, "Disinformation's Spread: Bots, Trolls and All of Us," *Nature*, July 24, 2019, https://www.nature.com/articles/d41586-019-02235-x..

20. Bobby Chesney and Danielle Citron, "Deep Fakes: A Looming Challenge for Privacy, Democracy, and National Security," *California Law Review* 107, no. 6 (December 2019): 1780–1781; Nina I. Brown, "Deepfakes and the Weaponization of Disinformation," *Virginia Journal of Law & Technology* 23, no. 1 (Spring 2020): 10–12.

*Notes to Chapter One*

21. H. C. Andersen, *The Emperor's New Clothes*, H. C. Andersen Center, https://andersen.sdu.dk/vaerk/hersholt/TheEmperorsNewClothes_e.html. The emperor and his trusted minister trusted the clothes the swindlers were making existed, even though they could not see them.

22. Jerome A. Barron, "Access to the Press: A New First Amendment Press," *Harvard Law Review* 80, no. 8 (June 1967): 1641.

23. Ibid.

24. 447 U.S. 557, 592 (1980) (Rehnquist, C. J., dissenting).

25. Ibid.

26. Jurgen Habermas, *The Structural Transformation of the Public Sphere*, trans. Thomas Burger and Frederick Lawrence (Cambridge, MA: MIT Press, 1999), 31–32.

27. 521 U.S. 844, 870 (1997).

28. 573 U.S. 464, 496 (2014).

29. David A. Hollinger, "The Enlightenment and the Genealogy of Cultural Conflict in the United States," in *What's Left of the Enlightenment*, eds. Keith Michael Baker and Peter Hanns Reill (Stanford, CA: Stanford University Press, 2001).

30. John Milton, *Areopagitica and of Education with Autobiographical Passages and Other Prose Works*, ed. George H. Sabine (Arlington Heights, IL: Harland Davidson, 1951), 50.

31. 310 U.S. 88, 105 (1940).

32. 376 U.S. 254, 269 (1964).

33. United States v. Alvarez, 567 U.S. 709 (2012).

34. Ibid., 728.

35. 538 U.S. 343, 358 (2003) (citing *Abrams*, 250 U.S. 616, 630 (Holmes, J., dissenting)).

36. 435 U.S. 765, 789 (1978).

37. Ibid., 784.

38. Ibid., 810 (White, J., dissenting).

39. 558 U.S. 310, 349–350 (2010).

40. Ibid., 349.

41. Ibid.

42. Younghee Noh, "Imagining Library 4.0: Creating a Model for Future Libraries," *The Journal of Academic Librarianship* 41, no. 6 (2015): 789–790. Web 1.0 was characterized by massive information availability. Web 2.0 added citizen publishers and social media. Web 3.0 included more intrinsic connections between knowledge and data. Web 4.0 includes increasingly integrated interactions between human and AI communicators.

43. See Gerald F. Gaus, *Contemporary Theories of Liberalism* (London: Sage, 2003), 2–3; Fred S. Siebert, "The Libertarian Theory of the Press," in *Four Theories of the Press: The Authoritarian, Libertarian, Social Responsibility, and Soviet Communist Concepts of What the Press Should Be and Do*,

## Notes to Chapter One

eds. Fred S. Siebert et al. (Urbana, IL: University of Illinois Press, 1956), 40; Peter J. Gade, "Postmodernism, Uncertainty, and Journalism," in *Changing the News: The Forces Shaping Journalism in Uncertain Times*, eds. Wilson Lowrey and Peter J. Gade (New York: Routledge, 2011), 64.

44. C. Edwin Baker, *Human Liberty and Freedom of Speech* (New York: Oxford University Press, 1989), 12.

45. William James, *Pragmatism and the Meaning of Truth* (Cambridge, MA: Harvard University Press, 1978), 97.

46. Hans-Georg Gadamer, *Truth and Method* (London: Continuum, 1989), 269. Gadamer, along with Hannah Arendt, was one of Martin Heidegger's students.

47. Letter from Oliver W. Holmes to Harold Laski (January 11, 1929) in Posner, *The Essential Holmes*, 107.

48. Oliver Wendell Holmes, "Natural Law," *Harvard Law Review* 32 (1918): 43.

49. Letter from Oliver W. Holmes to Frederick Pollock (August 30, 1929) in Posner, *The Essential Holmes*, 107.

50. *Abrams*, 250 U.S. 616, 630 (1919) (Holmes, J., dissenting) (emphasis added).

51. Letter from Felix Frankfurter to Oliver W. Holmes (Nov. 26, 1919) (on file with Harvard Law School Digital Suite), https://iiif.lib.harvard.edu/manifests/view/drs:42879149$17i.

52. Ibid.

53. Zechariah Chaffee, *Freedom of Speech* (New York: Harcourt, Brace and Howe, 1920), 1. Chaffee's 1919 law review article, "Freedom of Speech in War Time," had critiqued the Court's initial First Amendment decisions, all of which were written by Holmes and announced in Spring 1919. See Zechariah Chafee, "Freedom of Speech in War Time," *Harvard Law Review* 32, no. 8 (1919).

54. Chaffee, *Freedom of Speech*, 1. Milton, *Areopagitica*, 50.

55. Justice Holmes said Frankfurter "walked deep into my heart." Justice Brandeis called him "half brother, half son." See *Half Brother, Half Son: The Letters of Louis D. Brandeis and Felix Frankfurter*, eds Melvin Urofsky and Daid W. Levy (Norman, OK: University of Oklahoma Press, 1991), 5; Joseph P. Lash, *From the Diaries of Felix Frankfurter* (New York: W. W. Norton & Company, 1975), 7–8, 16–18.

56. See R. Hooykaas, "The Rise of Modern Science: When and Why?" *British Journal for the History of Science* 20 (1987): 455–456; Emilio Prospero, Diego Illuminati, Anna Marigliano, Paolo Pelaia, Christopher Munch, Pamela Barbadoro, and Marcello M. D'Errico, "Learning from Galileo: Ventilator-Associated Pneumonia Surveillance," *American Journal of Critical Care Medicine* 186 (2012): 1309.

57. See Hannah Arendt, *The Human Condition* (Chicago: University of Chicago Press, 1998), 259–263.

## Notes to Chapter One

58. Ibid., 262.

59. H. B. Acton, "Comte's Positivism and the Science of Society," *Philosophy* 26, no. 99 (1951): 291.

60. See Milton, *Areopagitica*, 45; John Locke, *The Second Treatise of Government and a Letter Concerning Toleration* (Mineola, NY: Dover Publications, 2002), 35; Jean-Jacques Rousseau, *Discourse on Political Economy and the Social Contract*, trans. Christopher Betts (Oxford: Oxford University Press, 1994), 32–34, for examples.

61. Locke, *Second Treatise*, 38.

62. See "Declaration of Independence: A Transcription," *National Archives*, accessed July 26, 2021, https://www.archives.gov/founding-docs/declaration -transcript. John Dickinson, *Letters from a Farmer in Pennsylvania to the Inhabitants of the British Colonies* (New York: The Outlook Company, 1903), 76–78. Dickinson cites Locke multiple times. Also, Benjamin Franklin, *The Writings of Benjamin Franklin*, ed. Albert Henry Smith, vol. 3 (London: Ardent Media, 1970), 174.

63. Franklin, *The Writings of Benjamin Franklin*, 174.

64. Compare Locke, *Second Treatise*, 38, and "Declaration of Independence: A Transcription," *National Archives*, accessed July 26, 2021, https:// www.archives.gov/founding-docs/declaration-transcript.

65. Baker, *Human Liberty*, 6.

66. Ibid., 13.

67. Frederick Schauer, "The Role of the People in First Amendment Theory," *California Law Review* 74 (1986): 777.

68. Derek E. Bambauer, "Shopping Badly: Cognitive Biases, Communications, and the Fallacy of the Marketplace of Ideas," *University of Colorado Law Review* (2006): 653.

69. Holmes, *Natural Law*, 40–41.

70. Ibid., 40.

71. Ibid., 41.

72. Hollinger, "The Enlightenment and the Genealogy of Cultural Conflict," 8–9.

73. Ibid., 8.

74. Bambauer, "Shopping Badly," 653.

75. "Voter's Reflections on the 2020 Election," *Pew Research Center*, January 15, 2021, https://www.pewresearch.org/politics/2021/01/15/ voters-reflections-on-the-2020-election/.

76. Kaleigh Rogers, "The Birther Myth Stuck Around for Years. The Election Fraud Myth Might Too," *FiveThirtyEight*, https://fivethirtyeight .com/features/the-birther-myth-stuck-around-for-years-the-election-fraud -myth-might-too/.

77. Ibid.

78. Mark Jurkowitz, "Republicans Who Relied on Trump for News More Concerned Than Other Republicans About Election Fraud," *Pew*

## Notes to Chapter One

*Research Center*, January 11, 2021, https://www.pewresearch.org/fact
-tank/2021/01/11/republicans-who-relied-on-trump-for-news-more-concerned
-than-other-republicans-about-election-fraud/.

79. Sheera Frenkel, Ben Decker, and Davey Alba, "How the 'Plandemic' Movie and its Falsehoods Spread Widely Online," *New York Times*, May 20, 2020, https://www.nytimes.com/2020/05/20/technology/plandemic-movie -youtube-facebook-coronavirus.html.

80. Angelo Fichera, Saranac Hale Spencer, D'Angelo Gore, Lori Robertson and Eugene Kiely, "The Falsehoods of the 'Plandemic Video," *Factcheck. org*, May 8, 2020, https://www.factcheck.org/2020/05/the-falsehoods-of-the -plandemic-video/; "False Claim: 'Plandemic' Video on COVID-19," *Reuters*, May 15, 2020, https://www.reuters.com/article/uk-factcheck-plandemic -video/false-claim-plandemic-video-on-covid-19-idUSKBN22R2ZC; Martin Enserink and Jon Cohen, "Fact-Checking Judy Mikovits, the Controversial Virologist Attacking Anthony Fauci in a Viral Conspiracy Video," *Scientific American*, May 8, 2020, https://www.sciencemag.org/news/2020/05/ fact-checking-judy-mikovits-controversial-virologist-attacking-anthony-fauci -viral.

81. Kate Kelland, "'Crazy and Evil': Bill Gates Surprised by Pandemic Conspiracies," *Reuters*, January 27, 2021, https://www.reuters.com/article/ us-health-coronavirus-gates-conspiracies/crazy-and-evil-bill-gates-surprised -by-pandemic-conspiracies-idUSKBN29W0Q3.

82. "Poll: 44% of Republicans Think Bill Gates to Use COVID-19 Vaccine to Implant Tracking Chip," CBS Austin, May 26, 2020 https://cbsaustin.com/ news/local/poll-44-of-republicans-think-bill-gates-to-use-covid-19-vaccine -to-implant-tracking-chip.

83. Alice Miranda Ollstein, "Politico-Harvard Poll: Most Americans Believe Covid Leaked from Lab," *Politico*, July 9, 2021, https://www.politico .com/news/2021/07/09/poll-covid-wuhan-lab-leak-498847.

84. Shanto Iyengar and Kyu S. Hahn, "Red Media, Blue Media: Evidence of Ideological Selectivity in Media Use," *Journal of Communication* 59 (2009): 34; Jared Schroeder, "Marketplace Theory in the Age of AI Communicators," *First Amendment Law Review* 17 (2018): 41–44; Sunstein, *#Republic*, 41–44.

85. Itai Himelboim, Stephen McCreery and Marc Smith, "Birds of a Feather Tweet Together: Integrating Network and Content Analyses to Examine Cross-Ideology Exposure on Twitter," *Computer-Mediated Communication* 18 (2013): 166–171; W. Lance Bennett and Shanto Iyengar, "A New Era of Minimal Effects? The Changing Foundations of Political Communication," *Journal of Communication* 58 (2008): 720–722; Manuel Castells, *The Rise of the Network Society* (Oxford: Blackwell Publishers, 2000).

86. Sunstein, *#Republic*, 57.

87. Castells, *Rise of the Network Society*, 3.

88. Ibid.

*Notes to Chapter One*

89. Arielle Pardes, "Need Some Fashion Advice? Just Ask the Algorithm," *Wired*, September 12, 2019, https://www.wired.com/story/stitch-fix-shop-your -looks/.

90. Dipayan Ghosh, *Terms of Disservice* (Washington, DC: Brookings Institution Press, 2020), 23–34; Jose Van Dijck, *The Culture of* Connectivity (Oxford: Oxford University Press, 2013), 29–41.

91. Hunt Allcott and Matthew Gentzkow, "Social Media and Fake News in the 2016 Election," *Journal of Economic Perspectives* 31, no. 2 (2017): 212–213.

92. Frenkel, Decker, and Alba, "How the 'Plandemic' Movie and its Falsehoods Spready Widely Online," *New York Times*, May 21, 2020, https:// www.nytimes.com/2020/05/20/technology/plandemic-movie-youtube -facebook-coronavirus.html.

93. Soroush Vosoughi, Deb Roy and Sinan Aral, "The Spread of True and False News Online," *Science* 359 (2018): 1148.

94. Jeff Horwitz and Deepa Seetharaman, "Facebook Executives Shut Down Efforts to Make the Site Less Divisive," *Wall Street Journal*, May 2, 2020, https://www.wsj.com/articles/facebook-knows-it-encourages-division -top-executives-nixed-solutions-11590507499.

95. Ibid.

96. Ibid.

97. Karen Ho, "YouTube is Experimenting with Ways to Make its Algorithm Even More Addictive," *MIT Technology Review*, Sept. 27, 2019, https://www.technologyreview.com/2019/09/27/132829/youtube-algorithm -gets-more-addictive/; Zeynap Tufekci, "YouTube, the Great Radicalizer," *New York Times*, March 10, 2018, https://www.nytimes.com/2018/03/10/ opinion/sunday/youtube-politics-radical.html.

98. See McKew, "How Twitter Bots and Trump Fans Made #ReleaseTheMemo Go Viral," regarding how bots can infiltrate and overpower a national debate. For a more detailed discussion about the power of bots to influence discourse, see Schroeder, "Marketplace Theory," 30–32.

99. "How Much to Fake a Trend on Twitter? In One Country, About £150," *BBC*, March 2, 2018, https://www.bbc.com/news/blogs-trending-43218939.

100. Chesney and Citron, "Deep Fakes: A Looming Challenge for Privacy, Democracy, and National Security," 1753.

101. Lex Haris, "CBS News Asks Facebook to Remove 'Deepfake' Video of Mark Zuckerberg with Unauthorized CBSN Trademark," *CBS News*, June 12, 2019, https://www.cbsnews.com/news/cbs-news-asks-facebook-to-remove -deep-fake-video-of-mark-zuckerberg-with-unauthorized-cbsn-trademark/.

102. The "cheap fake" manipulated clip of Pelosi appeared in May 2019 and again in August 2020. See Hannah Denham, "Another Fake Video of Pelosi Goes Viral on Facebook," *Washington Post*, August 3, 2020, https:// www.washingtonpost.com/technology/2020/08/03/nancy-pelosi-fake-video -facebook/.

*Notes to Chapter Two*

**Chapter Two**

1. Legal scholars have acknowledged, qualified, and questioned the narrative. See Rodney A. Smolla, "The Meaning of the 'Marketplace of Ideas' in First Amendment Law," *Communication Law & Policy* 24, no. 4 (2019): 437; Vincent Blasi, "Holmes and the Marketplace of Ideas," *The Supreme Court Review* (2004): 1–2; Derek E. Bambauer, "Shopping Badly: Cognitive Biases, Communications, and the Fallacy of the Marketplace of Ideas," *University of Colorado Law Review* 77, no. 3 (2006): 667, for examples.

2. Abrams v. United States, 250 U.S. 616, 624–631 (Holmes, J., dissenting).

3. See Robert Schmuhl and Robert G. Picard, "The Marketplace of Ideas," in *The Press*, eds. Geneva Overholser and Kathleen Hall Jamieson (Oxford: Oxford University Press, 2005), 141–142; Hannah Arendt, *The Human Condition* (Chicago: University of Chicago Press, 1998), 159–161.

4. See United States v. Alvarez, 567 U.S. 709, 718 (2012); Central Hudson Gas & Electric v. Public Service Commission, 447 U.S. 557, 592–598 (Rehnquist, C. J., dissenting); C. Edwin Baker, *Human Liberty and Freedom of Speech* (Oxford: Oxford University Press), 6–15; First National Bank v. Bellotti, 435 U.S. 765, 777 and 788–789 (1978).

5. See United States v. Alvarez, 567 U.S. 709 (2012) and Citizens United v. Federal Election Commission, 558 U.S. 310 (2010).

6. Zygmunt Bauman, *Liquid Modernity* (Cambridge: Polity, 2000), 2.

7. Ibid., 2–9.

8. Learned Hand, "Mr. Justice Holmes," *Harvard Law Review* 43, no. 6, 857 (1930); Louis Menand, *The Metaphysical Club* (New York: Farrar, Straus and Giroux, 2001), 424–427.

9. See letter from Oliver W. Holmes to Learned Hand (April 19, 1918) (on file with Harvard Law School Digital Suite), https://iiif.lib.harvard.edu/manifests/view/drs:43005319$4i; Letter from Oliver W. Holmes to Learned Hand (March 9, 1920) (on file with Harvard Law School Digital Suite), https://iiif.lib.harvard.edu/manifests/view/drs:43005319$18i; Letter from Oliver W. Holmes to Learned Hand (March 9, 1921) (on file with Harvard Law School Digital Suite), https://iiif.lib.harvard.edu/manifests/view/drs:43005319$20i.

10. Letter from Oliver W. Holmes to Learned Hand (June 24, 1918) (on file with Harvard Law School Digital Suite), https://iiif.lib.harvard.edu/manifests/view/drs:43005319$8i.

11. Letter from Oliver W. Holmes to Learned Hand (April 3, 1919) (on file with Harvard Law School Digital Suite), https://iiif.lib.harvard.edu/manifests/view/drs:43005319$14i; Menand, *Metaphysical Club*, 427.

12. The three cases were Debs v. United States 249 U.S. 211 (1919), Frohwerk v. United States, 249 U.S. 204; and Schenck v. United States, 249 U.S. 47 (1919). In regard to the Espionage Act of 1917, see David Rabban, *Free Speech in the Forgotten Years* (Cambridge: Cambridge University Press, 1997), 249–255.

13. *Schenck*, 294 U.S. at 52.

## Notes to Chapter Two

14. U.S. Constitution, amendment 1.

15. *Schenck*, 294 U.S. at 50–51. For context, see Jeffrey Rosen, *The Supreme Court: The Personalities and Rivalries that Defined America* (New York: Times Books/Henry Holt and Company), 119–120.

16. See Rabban, *Free Speech in the Forgotten Years*, 1–8.

17. See Menand, *Metaphysical Club*, 30–33; Lochner v. New York, 198 U.S. 45, 75–76 (1905) (Holmes, J., dissenting).

18. Justice Holmes was generally indifferent to civil liberty concerns. See Yosul Rogat, "The Judge as Spectator," *University of Chicago Law Review* 31, no. 2, 254 (1964). In personal correspondence, he generally dismissed civil liberty concerns. He dismissed *Abrams's* expression as a question of the right of a "donkey to drool," see letter from Oliver W. Holmes to Lewis Einstein (June 4, 1925) (on file with Harvard Law School Digital Suite), http://library .law.harvard.edu/suites/owh/index.php/item/42876801/53.

19. Menand, *Metaphysical Club*, 421.

20. The most pointed criticism was in the *New Republic*. See Harry Kalven, "Ernst Freund and the First Amendment Tradition," *University of Chicago Law Review* 40, no. 2 (1973): 239–242, which reprints the entirety of the article.

21. Letter from Oliver W. Holmes to Harold Laski (April 4, 1939) (on file with Harvard Law School Digital Suite), https://iiif.lib.harvard.edu/manifests/ view/drs:43012649$26i.

22. See Masses v. Patten, 244 F. 535 (S.D.N.Y. 1917).

23. Ibid., 540. Judge Hand's reasoning was not supported by the appeals court, which overturned his ruling, 246 F. 24 (2d Cir. 1917).

24. Letter from Learned Hand to Oliver W. Holmes (April 1, 1919) (on file with Harvard Law School Digital Suite), https://iiif.lib.harvard.edu/manifests/ view/drs:43005322$17i.

25. Ibid.

26. Letter from Oliver W. Holmes to Learned Hand (April 3, 1919) (on file with Harvard Law School Digital Suite), https://iiif.lib.harvard.edu/manifests/ view/drs:43005319$14i.

27. Menand, *Metaphysical Club*, 427.

28. Zechariah Chafee, "Freedom of Speech in War Time," *Harvard Law Review* 32, no. 8 (1919): 943–944.

29. Ibid., 944.

30. See chapter 3, which connects Holmes's legal and scholarly contributions to his life experiences and personal philosophy, as outlined in his letters and other texts.

31. Letter from Oliver W. Holmes to Frederick Pollock (June 17, 1919) (on file with Harvard Law School Digital Suite), https://iiif.lib.harvard.edu/ manifests/view/drs:43019755$82i.

32. Letter from Oliver W. Holmes to John Wigmore (June 7, 1919) (on file with Harvard Law School Digital Suite), http://library.law.harvard.edu/suites/ owh/index.php/item/43024949/13.

## Notes to Chapter Two

33. Letter from Oliver W. Holmes to Harold Laski (March 16, 1919) (on file with Harvard Law School Digital Suite), https://iiif.lib.harvard.edu/manifests/view/drs:42882402$15i.

34. Ibid.

35. Letter from Harold Laski to Oliver W. Holmes (March 18, 1919) (on file with Harvard Law School Digital Suite), https://iiif.lib.harvard.edu/manifests/view/drs:42882402$17i.

36. See Kalven, "Ernst Freund and the First Amendment Tradition, 239–242. The article reprints the entirety of Freund's argument.

37. Ibid., 242.

38. *Abrams*, 250 U.S. 616 (1919).

39. Ibid., 630 (Holmes, J., dissenting).

40. Ibid.

41. Historians and legal scholars offer a range of conclusions about the differences between Justice Holmes's reasoning in *Schenck* and *Abrams*. See Rabban, *Free Speech in the Forgotten Years*, 342–345; Menand, *Metaphysical Club*, 429–431; Sam Lebovic, *Free Speech and Unfree News* (Cambridge: Harvard University Press, 2016); Lee C. Bollinger and Geoffrey R. Stone, *The Free Speech Century* (Oxford: Oxford University Pres, 2019), 1, for examples.

42. See letter from Morris Cohen to Oliver W. Holmes (Dec. 4, 1919) (on file with Harvard Law School Digital Suite), http://library.law.harvard.edu/suites/owh/index.php/item/42978028/5; Letter from Learned Hand to Oliver W. Holmes (Nov. 25, 1919) (on file with Harvard Law School Digital Suite), http://library.law.harvard.edu/suites/owh/index.php/item/43399522/45; Letter from Felix Frankfurter to Oliver W. Holmes (Nov. 12, 1919) (on file with Harvard Law School Digital Suite), https://iiif.lib.harvard.edu/manifests/view/drs:42879149$13i; Letter from Oliver W. Holmes to Felix Frankfurter (Nov. 30, 1919) (on file with Harvard Law School Digital Suite), https://iiif.lib.harvard.edu/manifests/view/drs:42879149$21i, for examples.

43. Letter from Learned Hand to Oliver W. Holmes (Nov. 25, 1919) (on file with Harvard Law School Digital Suite), http://library.law.harvard.edu/suites/owh/index.php/item/43399522/45.

44. Letter from Oliver W. Holmes to Learned Hand (Nov. 26, 1919) (on file with Harvard Law School Digital Suite), https://iiif.lib.harvard.edu/manifests/view/drs:43399522$53i.

45. Letter from Felix Frankfurter to Oliver W. Holmes (Nov. 26, 1919) (on file with Harvard Law School Digital Suite), https://iiif.lib.harvard.edu/manifests/view/drs:42879149$17i. Written by John Milton in 1644, *Areopagitica* is a seminal Enlightenment work. In particular, it emphasizes the victory of absolute, discoverable truth over falsity in a free exchange of ideas among rational individuals. See John Milton, *Areopagitica and of Education with Autobiographical Passages and Other Prose Works*, ed. George H. Sabine (Arlington Heights, IL: Harland Davidson, 1951), 50.

46. *Abrams*, 250 U.S. 616, 630 (1919) (Holmes, J. dissenting).

266

## Notes to Chapter Two

47. Justice Brandeis wrote to Felix Frankfurter, who he mentored, in 1925 that he regretted joining Justice Holmes's opinions in *Schenck* and *Debs*. See letter from Louis Brandeis to Felix Frankfurter (Aug. 8, 1923), in Melvin I. Urofsky, "The Brandeis-Frankfurter Conversations," *Supreme Court Law Review* 1985 (1985): 323–324.

48. United States v. Rumely, 345 U.S. 41, 56 (1953) (Douglas, J., concurring).

49. See letter from Oliver Wendell Holmes, Jr. to Harold Laski (Jan. 27, 1929) in *The Essential Holmes*, ed. Richard Posner (Chicago: University of Chicago Press, 1992), 107; Letter from Oliver Wendell Holmes, Jr. to Frederick Pollock (Aug. 30, 1929), in Posner, *The Essential Holmes*, 108; Oliver Wendell Holmes, Jr., *The Common Law* (Cambridge: Harvard University Press, 1881), 1; Oliver Wendell Holmes, "Natural Law," *Harvard Law Review* 32 (1918): 43, for examples when Justice Holmes questioned objective truth and human rationality.

50. The laws included New York's criminal anarchy law, New York Penal Law §§ 160, 161 (1902); the California Criminal Syndicalism Act, Gen. Laws, Act 8428 (1919); the Michigan criminal syndicalism law, No. 255, Public Acts (1919); and Minnesota's "public nuisance" law, Chapter 285 of the Session Laws of Minnesota (1925).

51. Gitlow v. New York, 268 U.S. 652, 631–32 (1925) (Holmes, J., dissenting).

52. Ibid., 673.

53. Ibid.

54. Posner, *The Essential Holmes*, xii.

55. Letter from Oliver W. Holmes to Lewis Einstein (July 11, 1925) ((on file with Harvard Law School Digital Suite), http://library.law.harvard.edu/suites/owh/index.php/item/42876801/53.

56. Ibid.

57. Rabban, *Free Speech in the Forgotten Years*, 77–83.

58. Ruthernberg v. Michigan, 273 U.S. 782 (1927). See also, People v. Ruthenberg, 229 Michi. 315 (Mich. 1925), and Ronald K. L. Collins and David M. Skover, "Curious Concurrence: Justice Brandeis's Vote in Whitney v. California," *Supreme Court Law Review* 2002, no. 1 (2005): 372.

59. Vincent Blasi, "The First Amendment and the Ideal of Civic Courage: The Brandeis Opinion in *Whitney v. California*," *William & Mary Law Review* 29, no. 4 (1988): 668.

60. Whitney v. California, 274 U.S. 357, 375–377 (1927) (Brandies, J., concurring).

61. Schenck v. United States, 249 U.S. 47, 52 (1919).

62. *Whitney*, 274 U.S. 357, 374 (Brandeis, J., concurring).

63. Ibid., 376.

64. Ibid., 377.

65. Ibid., 375.

*Notes to Chapter Two*

66. Ibid., 377–378.

67. See Near v. Minnesota, 283 U.S. 697, 707 (1931); Bridges v. California, 314 U.S. 252, 261–262 (1941); New York Times v. Sullivan, 376 U.S. 254, 270 (1964); Brandenburg v. Ohio, 395 U.S. 444, 447 (1969), in which the Court rejected the Whitney decision, favoring Justice Brandeis's approach; Alvarez v. United States, 567 U.S. 709, 727 (2012), for examples.

68. Fred W. Friendly, *Minnesota Rag* (New York: Random House, 1981), 37.

69. See John R. Vile, "Continental Congress: Letter to the Inhabitants of the Province of Quebec," *The First Amendment Encyclopedia* (2009), https:// www.mtsu.edu/first-amendment/article/862/continental-congress-letter -to-the-inhabitants-of-the-province-of-quebec (discussing the history of the Letter to the Inhabitants of the Province of Quebec).

70. *Near*, 283 U.S. at 717 (quoting John Dickinson, *Letter to the Inhabitants of the Province of Quebec* (October 1774)).

71. Roy Branson, "James Madison and the Scottish Enlightenment," *Journal of the History of Ideas* 40, no. 2 (1979): 236. Branson concluded that Princeton president John Witherspoon, who came from Scotland, exposed Madison to these thinkers. Madison placed Hume's and Smith's works on the first list of books for the Library of Congress.

72. *Near*, 283 U.S. at 718 (quoting James Madison, "Report to the Virginia House of Delegates" (1800)).

73. Ibid., 713–714 (quoting William Blackstone, *Commentaries: Book the Fourth* (1765), 151).

74. Andrew Cohen, "Today is the 50th Anniversary of the (Re-)Birth of the First Amendment," *The Atlantic*, March 9, 2014, https://www.theatlantic .com/national/archive/2014/03/today-is-the-50th-anniversary-of-the-re-birth -of-the-first-amendment/284311/; Roy Gutterman, "The Landmark Libel Case *Times v. Sullivan*, Still Resonates 50 Years Later," *Forbes*, March 4, 2014, https://www.forbes.com/sites/realspin/2014/03/05/the-landmark-libel -case-times-v-sullivan-still-resonates-50-years-later/?sh=4eaa8ae4585a.

75. *Sullivan*, 376 U.S. 254, 270 (1964).

76. Ibid., 271–272 (quoting N.A.A.C.P. v. Button, 371 U.S. 415, 435 (1963)).

77. Ibid., 269 (quoting Roth v. United States, 354 U.S. 476, 484 (1957). Brennan wrote the Court's opinion in *Roth*, which marked the Court's first clear ruling about limitations on obscene speech.

78. 381 U.S. 301, 306–307 (1965) (Brennan, J., concurring). Justice William Douglas used the phrase "marketplace of ideas" for the first time in the Court's history in U.S. v. Rumely, 345 U.S. 31, 56 (1953) (Douglas, J., concurring).

79. *Sullivan*, 376 U.S. at 270 (quoting *Whitney*, 274 U.S. 357, 375–376 (1927) (Brandeis, J., concurring)).

80. Ibid., 279. See Milton, *Areopagitica*, 50–51; John Stuart Mill, *On Liberty* (New York: Dover, 2002), 27, for examples of central Enlightenment ideas Justice Brennan cited. See Christoph Bezemek, "The Epistemic Neutrality of the Marketplace of Ideas: Milton, Mill, Brandeis, and Holmes on

*Notes to Chapters Two and Three*

Falsehood and Freedom of Speech," *First Amendment Law Review* 14 (2015): 165–167.

**Chapter Three**

1. Louis Menand, *The Metaphysical Club* (New York: Farrar, Straus and Giroux, 2001), 6. Emerson, in particular, left an impact on him. In 1930, nearly fifty years after Emerson's death, Holmes wrote, "The only firebrand of my youth that burns to me as bright as ever is Emerson." See letter from Oliver Wendell Holmes, Jr. to John Pollack (May 20, 1930) in *The Essential Holmes*, ed. Richard Posner (Chicago: University of Chicago Press, 1992), 16.

2. Oliver W. Holmes, "The Class of 1861: A Poem," in *The Mind and Faith of Justice Holmes*, ed. Max Lerner (Boston: Little, Brown ad Company, 1943), 8.

3. See Lewis Einstein, "Introduction," in *The Holmes-Einstein Letters*, ed. James Bishop Peabody (New York: St. Martin's Press, 1964), xvi-xvii; Menand, *Metaphysical Club*, 55; letter from Oliver Wendell Holmes, Jr. to his parents (May 16, 1864) in *Touched with Fire*, ed. Mark de Wolfe Howe (London: Oxford University Press, 1946), 121–123.

4. Einstein, *The Holmes-Einstein Letters*, xvi.

5. Ibid., xviii-xix; Menand, *Metaphysical Club*, 67–68.

6. Letter from Oliver W. Holmes to Harold Laski (December 28, 1924) (on file with Harvard Law School Digital Suite), https://iiif.lib.harvard.edu/manifests/view/drs:42885078$14i.

7. Letter from Oliver Wendell Holmes to Harold Laski (Feb. 19, 1920) in Posner, *The Essential Holmes*, 38.

8. Letter from Oliver W. Holmes to Harold Laski (March 4, 1920) (on file with Harvard Law School Digital Suite), http://library.law.harvard.edu/suites/owh/index.php/item/42885056/1.

9. Letter from Oliver W. Holmes to Felix Frankfurter (June 14, 1925) (on file with Harvard Law School Digital Suite), http://library.law.harvard.edu/suites/owh/index.php/item/42879156/11.

10. Letter from Oliver W. Holmes to Frederick Pollock (April 27, 1919) (on file with Harvard Law School Digital Suite), http://library.law.harvard.edu/suites/owh/index.php/item/43019755/70.

11. Ibid.

12. See Jared Schroeder, "Fixing False Truths: Rethinking Truth Assumptions and Free-Expression Rationales in the Networked Era," *William & Mary Bill of Rights Journal* 29, no. 4 (2022): 1104–1116 for an examination of how truth became inseparable from how free expression is understood in the United States.

13. Jeffrey Rosen, *The Supreme Court* (New York: Henry Holt and Company, 2007), 77; Menand, *Metaphysical Club*, 66–67. Brandeis, who, with Holmes, developed the initial free-expression rationales, was a progressive. Holmes never became involved in any political movement and rejected almost

## Notes to Chapter Three

any group's belief in ideas. See Pnina Lahav, "Holmes and Brandeis: Libertarian and Republican Justifications for Free Speech," *Journal of Law & Politics* 4 (1988): 465–466.

14. Alexander Meiklejohn, *Free Speech and its Relation to Self-Government* (New York: Harper Collins, 1948), 70. Meiklejohn constructed his own theory of the First Amendment. His work is cited in more than thirty Supreme Court decisions.

15. Ibid. See also letter from Oliver W. Holmes to Felix Frankfurter (March 1, 1924) (on file with Harvard Law School Digital Suite), http://library.law .harvard.edu/suites/owh/index.php/item/42885074/1.

16. 249 U.S. 47 (1919); 250 U.S. 616, 624–631 (1919) (Holmes, J., dissenting); 268 U.S. 652, 672–673 (1925) (Holmes, J., dissenting).

17. Holmes diary, *Touched with Fire*, 23.

18. Ibid., 23–24.

19. Rosen, *The Supreme Court*, 86.

20. Ibid.

21. Menand, *Metaphysical Club*, 3; letter from Oliver W. Holmes to Canon Sheehan (Sept. 21, 1908) (on file with Harvard Law School Digital Suite), http://library.law.harvard.edu/suites/owh/index.php/item/43291261/7. In the letter, he refers to drinking the glass of wine alone to "the living and the dead, it being the anniversary of Antietam."

22. Oliver W. Holmes, "Memorial Day," in Lerner, *Mind and Faith*, 12.

23. Holmes's diary, *Touched with Fire*, 117.

24. Oliver W. Holmes, "Memorial Day," in Lerner, *Mind and Faith*, 16.

25. Ibid.

26. Menand, *Metaphysical Club*, 6.

27. Ibid., 7–9.

28. Letter from Oliver Wendell Holmes, Jr. to George Kain (March 22, 1930) (on file with Harvard Law School Digital Suite), http://library.law.harvard.edu/ suites/owh/index.php/item/43006891/5.

29. Letter from Oliver Wendell Holmes, Jr. to Ralph Waldo Emerson (April 16, 1876) (on file with Harvard Law School Digital Suite), http://library.law .harvard.edu/suites/owh/index.php/item/42978047/2.

30. Menand, *Metaphysical Club*, 23.

31. Letter from Oliver W. Holmes to Amelia Holmes (his mother) (May 1, 1861), in *Touched with Fire*, 3. See also Lerner, *Mind and Faith*, xxiii.

32. Menand, *Metaphysical Club*, 35.

33. Lerner, *Mind and Faith*, xxii; Menand, *The Metaphysical Club*, 21.

34. Holmes diary, *Touched with Fire*, 26.

35. Ibid., 25.

36. Ibid., 27.

37. Ibid.

38. Ibid., 32.

39. Lerner, *Mind and* Faith, xxiv.

*Notes to Chapter Three*

40. See letter from Oliver Wendell Holmes, Jr. to John Palfrey (Oct. 21, 1911) (on file with Harvard Law School Digital Suite), http://library.law.harvard.edu/suites/owh/index.php/item/43026619/9;, letter from Oliver Wendell Holmes, Jr. to Nina Gray (May 3, 1903) (on file with Harvard Law School Digital Suite), http://library.law.harvard.edu/suites/owh/index.php/item/43095316/45; letter from Oliver Wendell Holmes, Jr. to Harold Laski (May 8, 1918) (on file with Harvard Law School Digital Suite), https://iiif.lib.harvard.edu/manifests/view/drs:42882399$17i, for examples.

41. Letter from Oliver Wendell Holmes, Jr. to Harold Laski (May 8, 1918) (on file with Harvard Law School Digital Suite), https://iiif.lib.harvard.edu/manifests/view/drs:42882399$17i.

42. Ibid.

43. Menand, *Metaphysical Club*, 41.

44. Letter from Oliver W. Holmes to Oliver W. Holmes Sr. and Amelia Holmes (his parents) (April 23, 1862), in *Touched with Fire*, 45.

45. Letter from Oliver W. Holmes to Oliver W. Holmes Sr. and Amelia Holmes (his parents) (June 2, 1862), in *Touched with Fire*, 50–51.

46. Ibid.

47. Letter from Oliver W. Holmes to Oliver W. Holmes Sr. and Amelia Holmes (his parents) (Sept. 22, 1862), in *Touched with Fire*, 68. The letter included two sketches Holmes drew for his parents.

48. Ibid.

49. The Union, under General Burnside's new leadership, lost 12,600 soldiers in a stinging defeat in the Battle of Fredericksburg. The Confederacy lost 5,300 soldiers. See Letter from Oliver Wendell Holmes, Jr. to Lewis Einstein (Aug. 27, 1917) (on file with Harvard Law School Digital Suite), http://library.law.harvard.edu/suites/owh/index.php/item/42876796/52.

50. Letter from Oliver W. Holmes to Amelia Holmes (his mother) (Dec. 12, 1862), in *Touched with Fire*, 74.

51. Letter from Oliver W. Holmes Jr. to Oliver W. Holmes Sr. (Dec. 20, 1862), in *Touched with Fire*, 80.

52. Ibid.

53. Letter from Oliver W. Holmes to Amelia Holmes (his sister) (Nov. 16, 1862), in *Touched with Fire*, 73. Amelia was two years younger.

54. Ibid.

55. Oliver W. Holmes, "Memorial Day," in Lerner, *Mind and Faith*, 9.

56. Rosen, *The Supreme Court*, 86.

57. Oliver W. Holmes, "The Soldier's Faith," in Lerner, *Mind and Faith*, 20.

58. Menand, *Metaphysical Club*, 54–55. The Bloody Angle of Spotsylvania, in particular, included some of the most gruesome fighting of the war. See Gary W. Gallagher, *The Spotsylvania Campaign* (Chapel Hill, NC: University of North Carolina Press, 1998), x-xi.

59. Letter from Oliver W. Holmes to Amelia Holmes (his mother) (May 11, 1864), in *Touched with Fire*, 114.

271

## Notes to Chapter Three

60. Menand, *The Metaphysical Club*, 55. See Robert Krick, "Spotsylvania's Bloody Angle," in *The Spotsylvania Campaign*, ed. Gary W. Gallagher, 80–126.

61. Holmes diary (May 12, 1864), *Touched with Fire*, 116.

62. Letter from Oliver W. Holmes to Amelia Holmes (his mother) (June 7, 1864), in *Touched with Fire*, 143.

63. Ibid.

64. Holmes had thirteen of Spencer's works in his personal library when he died, see Estate of Justice Holmes: The Library (on file with Harvard Law School Digital Suite), http://library.law.harvard.edu/suites/owh/index.php/item/42864701/55. See also, however, Lochner v. New York, 198 U.S. 45, 75 (1905) (Holmes, J., dissenting) and letter from Oliver W. Holmes to Harold Laski (Dec. 31, 1916), in *Essential Holmes*, 30.

65. *Lochner*, 198 U.S. at 75–76 (Holmes, J., dissenting).

66. Letter from Oliver W. Holmes to Harold Laski (Dec. 31, 1916), in *Essential Holmes*, 30.

67. Letter from Oliver W. Holmes to Clara Sherwood Stevens (Dec. 27, 1915) (on file with Harvard Law School Digital Suite), http://library.law.harvard.edu/suites/owh/index.php/item/43026648/17.

68. Letter from Oliver W. Holmes to William James (March 24, 1907) (on file with Harvard Law School Digital Suite), https://iiif.lib.harvard.edu/manifests/view/drs:43006888$37i; Letter from Oliver W. Holmes to William James (April 1, 1907) (on file with Harvard Law School Digital Suite), https://iiif.lib.harvard.edu/manifests/view/drs:43006888$42i; Letter from Oliver W. Holmes to William James (Oct. 13, 1907) (on file with Harvard Law School Digital Suite), https://iiif.lib.harvard.edu/manifests/view/drs:43006888$40i.

69. Holmes met Mill in 1866 during a tour of Europe, see Lerner, *Mind and Faith*, xxvi.

70. 250 U.S. 616, 624–631 (1919) (Holmes, J., dissenting).

71. 268 U.S. 652, 672–673 (1925) (Holmes, J., dissenting).

72. Letter from Oliver W. Holmes to Harold Laski (May 7, 1917) (on file with Harvard Law School Digital Suite), http://library.law.harvard.edu/suites/owh/index.php/item/42882395/17.

73. Estate of Justice Holmes: The Library: Beverly Farms (on file with Harvard Law School Digital Suite), https://iiif.lib.harvard.edu/manifests/view/drs:43258460$1i and https://iiif.lib.harvard.edu/manifests/view/drs:42864695$89i.

74. Letter from Oliver W. Holmes to John T. Morse (Aug. 21, 1905) (on file with Harvard Law School Digital Suite), http://library.law.harvard.edu/suites/owh/index.php/item/43095319/19.

75. Letter from Oliver W. Holmes to Harold Laski (Dec. 4, 1926) (on file with Harvard Law School Digital Suite), http://library.law.harvard.edu/suites/owh/index.php/item/42889873/23.

## Notes to Chapter Three

76. Letter from Oliver W. Holmes to Nina Gray (Aug. 15, 1929) (on file with Harvard Law School Digital Suite), http://library.law.harvard.edu/suites/owh/index.php/item/42882384/11.

77. Holmes downplayed his involvement in the group in a letter to a Charles Peirce biographer in 1927. See letter from Oliver W. Holmes to Charles Hartshorne (Aug. 25, 1927) (on file with Harvard Law School Digital Suite), https://iiif.lib.harvard.edu/manifests/view/drs:43024973$6i. See also Menand, *Metaphysical Club*, 201–232, for a history of the club.

78. Letter from Oliver W. Holmes to Harold Laski (Nov. 29, 1923) (on file with Harvard Law School Digital Suite), http://library.law.harvard.edu/suites/owh/index.php/item/42885072/7.

79. See William James, *Pragmatism* (Cambridge, MA: Harvard University Press, 1978).

80. Menand, *Metaphysical Club*, 206–07.

81. letter from Oliver W. Holmes to Charles Hartshorne (Aug. 25, 1927) (on file with Harvard Law School Digital Suite), https://iiif.lib.harvard.edu/manifests/view/drs:43024973$6i.

82. Letter from Oliver W. Holmes to Frederick Pollock (Aug 30, 1929), in *Essential Holmes*, 108.

83. Menand, *Metaphysical Club*, 206.

84. Letter from Chauncey Wright to Simon Newcomb (May 18, 1865), in *The Letters of Chauncey Wright: With Some Account of His Life* (James Bradley Thayer ed., 1878), 74.

85. Letter from Oliver W. Holmes to Harold Laski (Nov. 29, 1923) (on file with Harvard Law School Digital Suite),
http://library.law.harvard.edu/suites/owh/index.php/item/42885072/7.

86. Letter from Oliver W. Holmes to Frederick Pollock (Aug 30, 1929), in *Essential Holmes*, 108.

87. Ibid.

88. 250 U.S. 616, 630 (1919) (Holmes, J., dissenting) (emphasis added).

89. Ibid.

90. "Pragmatism," *Stanford Encyclopedia of Philosophy*, April 6, 2021, https://plato.stanford.edu/entries/pragmatism/.

91. Ralph Barton Perry, *The Thought and Character of William James* (Nashville, TN: Vanderbilt University Press, 1948), 12. The passage is from an undated excerpt from Henry James's diaries.

92. Ibid., 11, regarding William James Sr.'s temper. See letter from Oliver W. Holmes to Harold Laski (March 15, 1917), in *Essential Holmes*, 37 and letter from Oliver W. Holmes to Lewis Einstein (June 17, 1908), in *The Holmes-Einstein Letters*, 35, regarding William James Jr.'s temperament.

93. Letter from Oliver W. Holmes to William James (Dec. 15, 1867), in *Thought and Character*, 89.

94. Menand, *Metaphysical Club*, 205.

*Notes to Chapter Three*

95. Letter from William James to Henry James (July 5, 1876), in *Thought and Character*, 99.

96. James retired from Harvard in 1907. His book was published the same year.

97. James, *Pragmatism*, 35–36.

98. Ibid., 83.

99. Ibid., 97.

100. William James, "A Defence of Pragmatism," *Popular Science Monthly*, March 1907, 193–206.

101. Letter from Oliver W. Holmes to William James (March 24, 1907) (on file with Harvard Law School Digital Suite), https://iiif.lib.harvard.edu/manifests/view/drs:43006888$37i.

102. Ibid.

103. Ibid.

104. Letter from Oliver W. Holmes to William James (Oct. 13, 1907) (on file with Harvard Law School Digital Suite), https://iiif.lib.harvard.edu/manifests/view/drs:43006888$40i.

105. Letter from Oliver W. Holmes to Charlotte Moncheur (Aug. 31, 1910) (on file with Harvard Law School Digital Suite), https://iiif.lib.harvard.edu/manifests/view/drs:43095328$30i.

106. Oliver W. Holmes, "Natural Law," *Harvard Law Review* 32 (1918): 42.

107. Oliver W. Holmes, "Law and the Court," in *The Holmes Reader* (New York: Oceana Publications, 1955), 98. The speech was originally given in 1913 at a dinner for the Harvard Law School Association in New York.

108. Lerner, *Mind and Faith*, xxvi.

109. See letter from Oliver W. Holmes to Ralph Waldo Emerson (April 16, 1876) (on file with Harvard Law School Digital Suite), http://library.law.harvard.edu/suites/owh/index.php/item/42978047/3, as well as Menand, *Metaphysical Club*, 57–59.

110. Oliver W. Holmes, *The Common Law* (Boston: Little, Brown and Company, 1881), iii.

111. See "Apotheosis of the Reasonable Man," *New York Times Literary Supplement*, June 27, 1968 (on file with Harvard Law School Digital Suite), http://library.law.harvard.edu/suites/owh/index.php/item/43199388/49; Peabody, *Homes-Einstein Letters*, v; Rosen, *The Supreme Court*, 89–90.

112. "Apotheosis of the Reasonable Man," *New York Times Literary Supplement*, June 27, 1968 (on file with Harvard Law School Digital Suite), http://library.law.harvard.edu/suites/owh/index.php/item/43199388/49.

113. Holmes, *Common Law*, 1.

114. Ibid., 2

115. Holmes, "Natural Law," 40.

116. Ibid., 41.

274

*Notes to Chapters Three and Four*

117. Letter from Oliver W. Holmes Jr. to Oliver W. Holmes Sr. (Dec. 20, 1862), in *Touched with Fire*, 80; Letter from Oliver W. Holmes to Amelia Holmes (his sister) (Nov. 16, 1862), in *Touched with Fire*, 73.

118. Holmes, "Natural Law," 41.

119. Ibid., 43.

120. Holmes, "Law and the Court," in *The Holmes Reader*, 97.

121. Holmes, "Ideals and Doubts," *Illinois Law Review* 10, no. 1 (1915): 2–3.

122. Ibid., 2.

123. See Kovacs v. Cooper, 336 U.S. 77 (1949) (Frankfurter, J., concurring); Callanan v. U.S., 364 U.S. 587 (1961), for examples.

124. See Schroeder, "Fixing False Truths," 1107–1122.

125. Ibid.

**Chapter Four**

1. Abrams v. United States, 250 U.S. 616, 630 (1919) (Holmes, J., dissenting).

2. 395 U.S. 367, 390 (1969).

3. See Hannah Arendt, *The Human Condition* (Chicago: University of Chicago Press 1998), 274–275; Thomas Kuhn, *The Copernican Revolution* (Cambridge, MA.: Harvard University Press, 1957), 192–194.

4. John Donne, *An Anatomy of the World* (London: Samuel Macham 1611), 13. Kuhn concluded the poem was influenced by the Copernican Revolution (see Kuhn, *Copernican Revolution*, 192–194).

5. Arendt, *Human Condition*, 274.

6. Ibid., 275.

7. C. D. Broad, "Francis Bacon and Scientific Method," *Nature*, October 2, 1926, 487–488.

8. Francis Bacon, *Novum Organum*, ed. Joseph Devey (New York: P. F. Collier & Son,1902), 44. The book was published in 1620 and outlines a system of logic that is based on empiricism and inductive thinking.

9. Ibid., 7.

10. Anton M. Matytsin, *The Specter of Skepticism in the Age of Enlightenment* (Baltimore: Johns Hopkins Press, 2016), 206–207.

11. See *The Ideas That Made the Modern World: The People, Philosophy, and History of the Enlightenment* (London: Encyclopedia Britannica, 2008), 171–73; D. W. Hamlyn, *Western Philosophy* (London: Penguin Books, 1987), 206–216. See also John Locke, *The Second Treatise of Government* (Mineola, NY: Dover Publications), 2–7; John Milton, *Areopagitica and of Education with Autobiographical Passages and Other Prose Works*, ed. George H. Sabine (Arlington Heights, IL: Harland Davidson, 1951), 17–18; Jean-Jacques Rousseau, *The Social Contract and the First and Second Discourses*, ed. Susan Dunn (New Haven, CT.: Yale University Press, 2002), 83–84, for specific examples.

12. Marshall Grossman, *The Seventeenth Century Literature Handbook* (Malden, MA: Blackwell Publishing, 2011), 204.

275

*Notes to Chapter Four*

13. Ibid.

14. Ibid., 203–206.

15. Ibid. See also Milton, *Areopagitica*, 45–50, for examples.

16. Milton, *Areopagitica*, 50.

17. Ibid., 45.

18. Letter from Felix Frankfurter to Oliver W. Holmes (Nov. 26, 1919) (on file with Harvard Law School Digital Suite), https://iiif.lib.harvard.edu/manifests/view/drs:42879149$17i.

19. 376 U.S. 254, 279, Note 19 (1964).

20. Hamlyn, *Western Philosophy*, 134.

21. See Locke, *Second Treatise*, 6–7, for example.

22. Ibid., 2.

23. Ibid, 3. Also, Thomas Jefferson, et al., *Declaration of Independence* (1776); U.S. Constitution amendment V.

24. Hamlyn, *Western Philosophy*, 188–190.

25. David Hume, *A Treatise of Human Nature*, ed. L. A. Selby-Bigge (London: Oxford, 1896), 529.

26. John S. Tanner and Justin Collings, "How Adams and Jefferson Read Milton and Milton Read Them," *Milton Quarterly* 40, No. 3 (2006): 210.

27. Benjamin Franklin, *The Writings of Benjamin Franklin*, ed. Albert H. Smyth (New York: MacMillan Company, 1907), 174.

28. Milton, *Areopagitica*, 50.

29. Tanner and Collings, "How Adams and Jefferson Read Milton," 207.

30. John Dickinson, "Olive Branch Petition," *Avalon Project*, accessed April 1, 2022, https://avalon.law.yale.edu/18th_century/contcong_07-08-75.asp, which was published July 5, 1775; John Dickinson, "Letter to the Inhabitants of the Province of Quebec," *Wikisource*, accessed April 1, 2022, https://en.wikisource.org/wiki/Letter_to_the_Inhabitants_of_the_Province_of_Quebec, originally published October 26, 1774. See generally Jane E. Calvert, "Liberty Without Tumult: Understanding the Politics of John Dickinson," *The Pennsylvania Magazine of History and Biography*, 131, No. 3 (2007), for background on Dickinson's contributions and support of Locke's work.

31. Jefferson, *Declaration of Independence*.

32. See Alexander Tsesis, *For Liberty and Equality* (Oxford: Oxford University Press, 2012), 37.

33. Roy Branson, "James Madison and the Scottish Enlightenment," *Journal of the History of Ideas* 40, No. 2 (1979): 236–237; "Report on Books for Congress, January 23, 1783," National Archives, accessed April 1, 2022, https://founders.archives.gov/documents/Madison/01-06-02-0031.

34. Mark G. Spencer, "Hume and Madison on Faction," *William & Mary Quarterly* 59, No. 4 (2002): 873; Douglass Greybill Adair, "The Intellectual Origins of Jeffersonian Democracy," *Yale University ProQuest Dissertations* (1943): 252.

## Notes to Chapter Four

35. "Signing of the Constitution," *Explore the Capitol Campus/Art,* last accessed April 1, 2022, https://www.aoc.gov/explore-capitol-campus/art/signing-constitution.

36. David E. Hollinger, "The Enlightenment and the Genealogy of Cultural Conflict in the United States," in *What's Left of the Enlightenment,* ed. Keith Mitchell Baker and Peter Hans Reill (Stanford, CA.: Stanford University Press), 9.

37. C. Edwin Baker, *Human Liberty and Freedom of Speech* (Oxford: Oxford University Press, 1989), 3.

38. Central Hudson Gas & Electric v. Public Service Commission of New York, 447 U.S. 557, 592 (1980) (Rehnquist, C. J., dissenting).

39. Ibid.

40. Jerome Barron, "Access to the Press: A New First Amendment Right," *Harvard Law Review* 80, No. 8 (1967): 1641.

41. Stanley Ingber, "The Marketplace of Ideas: A Legitimizing Myth," *Duke Law Journal* 1984, No. 1 (1984): 90.

42. Baker, *Human Liberty,* 13.

43. Frederic Schauer, "The Role of the People in First Amendment Theory," *California Law Review* 74, No. 3 (1986): 777.

44. Derek E. Bambauer, "Shopping Badly: Cognitive Biases, Communications, and the Fallacy of the Marketplace of Ideas," *University of Colorado Law Review* 77 (2006): 651; Leonard M. Niehoff and Deeva Shah, "The Resilience of Noxious Doctrine: The 2016 Election, the Marketplace of Ideas, and the Obstinacy of Bias," *Michigan Journal of Race & Law* (2017): 269; Vincent Blasi, "Holmes and the Marketplace of Ideas," *Supreme Court Review* 2004 (2004): 2.

45. See 323 U.S. 214, 233–242 (1944) (Murphy, J., dissenting).

46. See Roger K. Newman, *Hugo Black: A Biography* (New York: Pantheon Books, 1994), 306.

47. See Felix Frankfurter diary entry January 30, 1943, in *From the Diaries of Felix Frankfurter,* Joseph P. Lash ed. (New York: W. W. Norton & Company, 1975), 174–175

48. Near v. Minnesota, 283 U.S. 697 (1931) and Grosjean v. American Press Co., 297 U.S. 233 (1936) were likely the most relevant First Amendment decisions.

49. See 283 U.S. 697 (1931), as well as chapter 2, for context regarding the first instance in which the Supreme Court struck down a law because it conflicted with the First Amendment.

50. See 283 U.S. at 714–718 regarding Chief Justice Hughes's references to Madison's and Dickinson's work.

51. 310 U.S. 88, 97 (1940) (citing *Near,* 283 U.S. at 713).

52. Ibid., citing Milton, *Areopagitica.*

*Notes to Chapter Four*

53. See 249 U.S. 47, 52 (1919); 250 U.S. 616, 630 (1919) (Holmes, J., dissenting).

54. *Thornhill*, 283 U.S. at 105.

55. See Newman, *Hugo Black*, 296–297; Frankfurter, January 30, 1943 diary entry, *Diaries of Felix Frankfurter*, 174–175. See also Melvin I. Urofsky's collection of Douglas's letters, which includes a chapter simply titled "Felix," which highlights Douglas's struggle, often alongside Black, with Frankfurter. See Melvin I. Urofsky, *The Douglas Letters* (Bethesda, MD: Alder & Alder, 1987).

56. Newman, *Hugo Black*, 235–237.

57. Bridges v. California, 314 U.S. 252, 258–259 (1941). See also Newman, *Hugo Black*, 289.

58. Frankfurter, January 30, 1943 diary entry, *Diaries of Felix Frankfurter*, 176.

59. *Bridges*, 314 U.S. at 263.

60. Ibid., 283 (Frankfurter, J., dissenting).

61. 341 U.S. 494, 495–497 (1951).

62. Ibid., 581 (Black, J., dissenting).

63. Jay Walz, "High Court Upholds Guilt of 11 Top U.S. Communists; Other Prosecutions are Set," *New York Times*, June 5, 1951.

64. Dennis v. United States, 341 U.S. at 580 (Black, J., dissenting) (citing Bridges v. California, 314 U.S. 252, 263 (1941).

65. Ibid.

66. Ibid., 584–585 (Douglas, J., dissenting).

67. Ibid., 584.

68. Ibid. (emphasis added).

69. Ibid.

70. Ibid., 519 (Frankfurter, J., concurring).

71. See Richard Polenberg, "The National Committee to Uphold Constitutional Government, 1937–1991," *Journal of American History* 52, No. 3 (1965): 592.

72. United States v. Rumely, 345 U.S. 41, 56 (1953) (Douglas, J., dissenting).

73. Ibid., 56 (quoting *Grosjean*, 297 U.S. 233, 247 (1936)).

74. Ibid., 57.

75. Newman, *Hugo Black*, 483.

76. William J. Brennan IV, "Remembering Justice Brennan: A Biographical Sketch," *Washburn Law Review* 37 (1998): xii.

77. See Anthony Lewis, *Make No Law* (New York: Vintage Books, 1992), 164–165.

78. New York Times v. Sullivan, 376 U.S. 254, 272 (1964).

79. Ibid., 270; See also Newman, *Hugo Black*, 533. Newman called Brennan's opinion for the Court in *Sullivan* "one of the enduring landmarks of Constitutional law."

## Notes to Chapters Four and Five

80. Ibid., 269 (quoting Roth v. United States, 354 U.S. 476, 484 (1957). Brennan wrote the Court's landmark obscenity decision in *Roth* seven years before *Sullivan*.

81. Ibid., 279, Note 19.

82. Milton, *Areopagitica*, 50.

83. *Sullivan*, 376 U.S. at 274–76.

84. Ibid., 271 (quoting United States v. Associated Press, 52 F.Supp. 362, 372 (D.C.S.D.N.Y.1943)).

85. *Sullivan*, 376 U.S. at 269.

86. Lamont v. Postmaster General, 381 U.S. 301, 305 (1965).

87. Ibid., 307 (quoting *Sullivan*, 376 U.S. 265, 270 (1964).

88. Ibid., 308 (Brennan, J., concurring).

89. Ibid.

90. Red Lion Broadcasting v. FCC, 395 U.S. 367, 390 (1969).

### Chapter Five

1. See Red Lion Broadcasting v. FCC, 381 F.2d 908, 910–911 (D.C. Cir., 1967).

2. See Fred J. Cook, *Barry Goldwater: Extremist of the Right* (New York: Grove Press, 1964). See Louis A. Powe, "Or of the Broadcast Press," *Texas Law Review* 55 (1976): 39–40, for context.

3. Fred Cook, "Radio Right: Hate Clubs of the Air," *The Nation*, May 25 (1964): 526.

4. See Red Lion Broadcasting v. FCC, 395 U.S. 367, 369–370 (1969).

5. Letter from John Norris to unnamed FCC official (Dec. 9, 1965), quoted in *Red Lion Broadcasting*, 381 F.2d at 914.

6. Ibid.

7. *Red Lion Broadcasting*, 395 U.S. at 390 (emphasis added).

8. See Dipayan Ghosh, *Terms of Disservice* (Washington, DC: Brookings Institution Press, 2020); Itai Himelboim, Stephen McCreery, and Marc Smith, "Birds of a Feather Tweet Together: Integrating Network and Content Analyses to Examine Cross-Ideology Exposure on Twitter," *Journal of Computer-Mediated Communication* 18 (2013): 166–171.

9. See Cass R. Sunstein, *#Republic* (Princeton, NJ: Princeton University Press, 2017), 138–142; Jared Schroeder, "Fixing False Truths," *William & Mary Bill of Rights Journal* 29, no. 4 (2021): 1099–1100; Manuel Castells, *The Rise of the Network Society* (Oxford: Blackwell Publishing, 2nd ed., 2000), 3–4, for deeper discussion about the effects these changes are having on human discourse.

10. See Castells, *Rise of the Network Society*, 3–4; Sunstein, *#Republic*, 57; Jared Schroeder, "Information, Community, and Change: A Call for a Renewed Conversation About First Amendment Rationales," *First Amendment Law Review* 18 (2020): 133–135.

## Notes to Chapter Five

11. See Sherry Turkle, *Reclaiming Conversation* (New York: Penguin Books, 2015), 3–17, for more about how networked technologies lead to declining levels of empathy in users.

12. Castells, *Rise of the Network Society*, 3.

13. See Nils Köbis and Luca D. Mossink, "Artificial Intelligence Versus Maya Angelou: Experimental Evidence that People Cannot Differentiate AI-Generated from Human-Written Poetry," *Computers in Human Behavior* 114 (2021): 5–6.

14. Cook, "Hate Clubs of the Air," 523.

15. Ibid., 526.

16. *Red Lion Broadcasting*, 395 U.S. 367, 390 (1969).

17. Ibid.

18. 403 U.S. 713, 729 (1971) (Stewart, J., concurring).

19. 408 U.S. 169, 180–181 (1972).

20. 412 U.S. 94, 123 (1973).

21. Ibid., 95.

22. Ibid., 184 (Brennan, J., dissenting).

23. Ibid., 194.

24. 287 So.2d 78, 84 (Fla., 1973).

25. Ibid.

26. 418 U.S. 241, 256 (1974).

27. See Clay Calvert, "First Amendment Battles Over Anti-Deplatforming Statutes: Examining *Miami Herald Publishing Co. v. Tornillo*'s Relevance for Today's Online Social Media Platform Cases," *New York University Law Review* 97, no. 1 (2022), regarding *Tornillo* and recent laws.

28. See Keith Wittington, *Political Foundations of Judicial Supremacy* (Princeton, NJ: Princeton University Press, 2007), 222–226, for a brief history of Nixon's intentional effort to make the Court more conservative.

29. *Bigelow*, 421 U.S. 809, 826 (1975).

30. *Virginia State Board*, 425 U.S. 748, 765 (1976).

31. *Bigelow*, 421 U.S. at 832 (Rehnquist, J., dissenting).

32. Ibid., 833.

33. *Virginia State Board*, 425 U.S. at 781 (Rehnquist, J., dissenting).

34. Ibid.

35. 424 U.S. 1 (1976). See Trever Potter, "Buckley v. Valeo, Political Disclosure and the First Amendment," *Akron Law Review* 33, no. 1 (1999): 103–106; Kenneth J. Levit, "Campaign Finance Reform and the Return of Buckley v. Valeo," *Yale Law Journal* 103 (1993): 488–489, for discussion about the impact and legacy of *Buckley*.

36. First National Bank of Boston v. Bellotti, 435 U.S. 765, 789–790 (1978).

37. Ibid., 777

38. Ibid.

39. Ibid., 803 (White, J., dissenting).

280

*Notes to Chapters Five and Six*

40. Ibid., 804–05.

41. Ibid., 823 (Rehnquist, J., dissenting) (quoting Dartmouth College v. Woodward, 4 Wheat. 518, 636 (1819)).

42. Ibid., 824.

43. Central Hudson Gas & Electric Corp. v. Public Service Commission of New York, 447 U.S. 557 (1980).

44. Ibid., 562.

45. Ibid., 563.

46. Ibid., 527 (Brennan, J., concurring).

47. Ibid., 592 (Rehnquist, C. J., dissenting).

48. See Reuters Pitchbot (Satire). "@ReutersPitchbot." Twitter. Accessed May 6, 2022, https://twitter.com/ReutersPitchbot?ref_src=twsrc%5Egoogle %7Ctwcamp%5Eserp%7Ctwgr%5Eauthor

49. "Reuters Pitchbot (Satire), Twitter, April 25, 2022, https://twitter.com/ ReutersPitchbot/status/1518670928732897280.

50. See Ahmed Al-Rawi, Jacob Groshek, and Li Zhang, "What the Fake? Assessing the Extent of Networked Political Spamming and Bots in the Propagation of #fakenews on Twitter," *Online Information Review* 43 (2019): 65; Kate Starbird, "Disinformation's Spread: Bots, Trolls, and All of Us," *Nature* 571 (2019): 449; Emilio Ferrara, Onur Varol, Clayton Davis, Filippo Menczer, and Alessandro Flammini, "The Rise of Social Bots," *Communications of the ACM* 59, no. 7 (2016): 96–104, for more about bots and misinformation and disinformation.

51. Austin v. Michigan Chamber of Commerce, 494 U.S. 652, 660 (1990).

52. See 376 U.S. 254, 256–279 (1964) regarding Brennan's crucial role in incorporating Enlightenment assumptions into the space for human discourse. Also, see chapter 4.

53. 491 U.S. 397, 414 (1989).

54. *Austin*, 494 U.S. at 670 (Brennan, J., concurring).

55. Ibid., 677.

56. Ibid., 679 (Scalia, J., dissenting).

57. Ibid.

58. 558 U.S. 310, 349 (2010).

59. Ibid., 354.

60. Ibid., 376 (Roberts, C. J., concurring).

61. 562 U.S. 443 (2011).

62. Ibid., 461.

63. Brown v. Entertainment Merchants, 564 U.S. 786, 790 (2011).

64. Ibid., 790 (quoting Burstyn v. Wilson, 343 U.S. 495, 503 (1952)).

65. 567 U.S. 709, 726 (2012).

### Chapter Six

1. Ben Dooley and Hisako Ueno, "This Man Married a Fictional Character. He'd Like You to Hear Him Out," *New York Times*, April 24, 2022,

## Notes to Chapter Six

https://www.nytimes.com/2022/04/24/business/akihiko-kondo-fictional -character-relationships.html; Emiko Jozuka, "Beyond Dimensions: The Man Who Married a Hologram, *CNN*, Dec. 29, 2018, https://www.cnn .com/2018/12/28/health/rise-of-digisexuals-intl/index.html.

2. See "Gatebox – Promotion Movie 'Okaeri,'" *Gatebox*, Dec. 13, 2016, https://www.youtube.com/watch?v=nkcKaNqfykg.

3. See "The AI Companion Who Cares," *Replika*, https://replika.com/.

4. See Keith Collins, "This New Twitter Account Hunts for Bots that Push Political Opinions," *Quartz*, Oct. 25, 2017, https://qz.com/1110481/this-new -twitter-account-hunts-for-bots-that-push-political-opinions/.

5. See Manuel Castells, *The Rise of the Network Society* (Oxford, UK: Blackwell Publishing, 2001), 3; Cass Sunstein, #Republic (Princeton, NJ: Princeton University Press, 2017), 57–62.

6. Bobby Chesney and Danielle Citron, "Deep Fakes: A Looming Challenge for Privacy, Democracy, and National Security," *California Law Review* 107, no. 6 (2019): 1758–1762; John Villasenor, "Artificial Intelligence, Deepfakes, and the Uncertain Future of Truth," *Brookings Institution*, Feb. 14, 2019, https://www.brookings.edu/blog/techtank/2019/02/14/artificial-intelligence -deepfakes-and-the-uncertain-future-of-truth/

7. See Eric Ravenscraft, "What is the Metaverse, Exactly?" *Wired*, April 25, 2022, https://www.wired.com/story/what-is-the-metaverse/; Brian X. Chen, "What's All the Hype About the Metaverse?" *New York Times*, Jan. 18, 2022, https://www.nytimes.com/2022/01/18/technology/personaltech/ metaverse-gaming-definition.html.

8. See Itai Himelboim, Stephen McCreery, and Marc Smith, "Birds of a Feather Tweet Together: Integrating Network and Content Analyses to Examine Cross-Ideology Exposure on Twitter," *Journal of Computer-Mediated Communication* 18, no. 2 (2013): 156–171; W. Lance Bennett and Shanto Iyengar, "A New Era of Minimal Effects? The Changing Foundations of Political Communication," *Journal of Communication* 58 (2008): 720; Castells, *Rise of Network Society*, 3–4.

9. Richard Weissbourd, Milena Batanova, Virginia Lovison, and Eric Torres, *Loneliness in America: How the Pandemic has Deepened an Epidemic of Loneliness and What We Can Do About It*, Harvard Making Caring Common Project, February 2021, https://mcc.gse.harvard.edu/ reports/loneliness-in-america; Emily B. O'Day and Richard Heimberg, "Social Media Use, Social Anxiety, and Loneliness: A Systemic Review," *Computers in Human Behaviors Reports* 3 (2021): 8–9.

10. Sherry Turkle, *Alone Together* (New York: Basic Books, 2011), 11–12.

11. Zizi Papacharissi, *A Networked Self: Identity, Community, and Culture on Social Network Sites* (New York: Routledge, 2011), 307.

12. José Van Dijck, *The Culture of Connectivity* (Oxford: Oxford University Press, 2013), 30–39; Dipayan Ghosh, *Terms of Disservice* (Washington, DC: Brookings Institution, 2020), 28–44.

*Notes to Chapter Six*

13. See Sherry Turkle, *Reclaiming Conversation* (New York: Penguin Books, 2016), 3–4; Manuel Castells, *The Power of Identity* (Oxford: Wiley-Blackwell, 2010), xxiii-xxviii; Francine Edwards, "An Investigation of Attention-Seeking Behavior Through Social Media Post Framing," *Athens Journal of Mass Media and Communications* 3, no. 1 (2017): 41–43.

14. See Himelboim, et al., "Birds of a Feather Tweet Together," 167–171; Itai Himelboim, Marc A. Smith, Lee Rainie, Ben Shneiderman, and Camila Espina, "Classifying Twitter Topic-Networks Using Social Network Analysis," *Social Media+Society* 3, no. 1 (2017): 10–12.

15. Sunstein, *#Republic*, 9.

16. Castells, *Rise of the Networked Society*, 3.

17. Ibid.

18. A. M. Turing, "Computer Machinery and Intelligence," *Mind* 49, no. 236 (1950): 433–434.

19. Turkle, *Alone Together*, 23–24.

20. Ibid., 23.

21. Michael Cavna, "'Nobody Knows You're a Dog': As Iconic Cartoon Turns 20, Creator Peter Steiner Knows the Joke Rings as Relevant as Ever," *Washington Post*, January 1, 2013.

22. See Rui Fan, Oleksandr Talvera, and Vu Tran, "Social Media Bots and Stock Markets," *European Financial Management* 26, no. 3 (2020): 774–775; Emilio Ferrara, Onur Varol, Clayton Davis, Filippo Menczer, and Alessandro Flammini, "The Rise of Social Bots," *Communication of the ACM* 59, no. 7 (2016): 99; Ran Tao, Chi-Wei Su, Yidong Xiao, Ke Dai, and Fahad Khalid, "Robo Advisors, Algorithmic Trading and Investment Management: Wonders of Fourth Industrial Revolution in Financial Markets," *Technological Forecasting and Social Change* 163 (2021): 167.

23. See Helen A. S. Popkin, "AP Latest Victim in String of Twitter Break-Ins by Syrian Electronic Army," *NBC News*, April 23, 2013, https://www.nbcnews.com/tech/tech-news/ap-latest-victim-string-twitter-break-ins-syrian-electronic-army-flna6c9567459.

24. See Steven Goldberg, "Could Computerized Trading Cause Another Market Crash?" *Kiplinger*, April 3, 2018, https://www.kiplinger.com/article/investing/to41-coo7-soo1-could-computerized-trading-cause-another-market-cr.html; Ferrara et al., "The Rise of Social Bots."

25. Ran Tao et al., "Robo Advisors," 167.

26. See Alessandro Bessi and Emilio Ferrara, "Social Bots Distort the 2016 U.S. Presidential Election Online Discussion," *First Monday*, 21, no. 11 (2016), https://firstmonday.org/ojs/index.php/fm/article/download/7090/5653.

27. See Emilio Ferrara, "Bots, Elections, and Social Media: A Brief Overview," in *Disinformation, Misinformation, and Fake News in Social Media*, ed. Kai Shu, Suhang Wang, Dongwon Lee, Huan Liu (Cham, Switzerland: Springer, 2020), 100–112.

## Notes to Chapter Six

28. Molly K. McKew, "How Twitter Bots and Trump Fans Made #ReleaseTheMemo Go Viral," *Politico*, February 4, 2018, https://www.politico.com/magazine/story/2018/02/04/trump-twitter-russians-release-the-memo-216935/.

29. Ibid.

30. A. J. Vicens, "Researchers Say They've Uncovered a Massive Facebook Bot Farm from the 2020 Election," *Mother Jones*, May 10, 2021, https://www.motherjones.com/politics/2021/05/facebook-bot-farm/.

31. McKenzie Himelein-Wachowiak, Salvatore Giorgi, Amanda Devoto, Muhammad Rahman, Lyle Ungar, et al., "Bots and Misinformation Spread on Social Media: Implications for COVID-19," *Journal of Medical Internet Research* 23, no. 5 (2021): 5.

32. See Jürgen Habermas, *The Structural Transformation of the Public Sphere*, trans. Thomas Burger (Cambridge, MA: MIT Press, 1999), 14–15.

33. Ibid., 16–23.

34. See Soroush Vosoughi, Deb Roy, and Sinan Aral, "The Spread of True and False News Online," *Science*, March 9, 2018, https://www.science.org/doi/epdf/10.1126/science.aap9559.

35. Sarah Mervosh, "Distorted Videos of Nancy Pelosi Spread on Facebook and Twitter, Helped by Trump," *New York Times*, March 24, 2019, https://www.nytimes.com/2019/05/24/us/politics/pelosi-doctored-video.html.

36. Ibid.

37. Reuters Staff, "Fact Check: Video Showing Joe Biden Falling Asleep During Live Interview is Manipulated," *Reuters*, Sept. 1, 2020, https://www.reuters.com/article/uk-factcheck-biden-asleep-altered/fact-check-video-showing-joe-biden-falling-asleep-during-live-interview-is-manipulated-idUSKBN25S63S.

38. See Nils C. Köbis, Barbora Doležalová, and Ivan Soraperra, "Fooled Twice: People Cannot Detect Deepfakes but They Think They Can," *iScience* 24, no. 11 (2021), https://www.sciencedirect.com/science/article/pii/S2589004221013353.

39. Bobby Chesney and Daniel Citron, "Deep Fakes: A Looming Challenge for Privacy, Democracy, and National Security," *California Law Review* 107, no. 6 (2019): 1785–86.

40. Ibid., 1785.

41. Brenda Wiederhold, "Ready (or Not) Player One: Initial Musings on the Metaverse," *Cyberpsychology, Behavior, and Social Networking* 25, no. 1 (2022): 1–2.

42. See "Fortnite Presents . . . The Rift Tour Featuring Ariana Grande," *Epic Games*, Aug. 9, 2021, https://www.epicgames.com/fortnite/en-US/news/fortnite-presents-the-rift-tour-featuring-ariana-grande, to watch the performance.

43. See Suchi Rudra, "The Metaverse is Already Here and K-12 Schools are Using it for Education," *EdTech*, June 1, 2022, https://edtechmagazine.com/k12/article/2022/06/metaverse-already-here-and-k-12-schools-are-using-it-education;

## Notes to Chapter Six

Kathy Hirsch-Pasek, Jennifer M. Zosh, Helen Shwe Hadani, Roberta Michnick Golinkoff, Kevin Clark, Chip Donohue, and Ellen Wartella, "A Whole New World: Education Meets the Metaverse," *Brookings*, Feb. 14, 2022, https://www.brookings.edu/research/a-whole-new-world-education-meets-the-metaverse/.

44. Rani Molla, "10 Ways Office Work Will Never be the Same," *Vox*, March 23, 2021, https://www.vox.com/recode/22331447/10-ways-office-work-pandemic-future-remote-work; Danielle Abril, "Workers are Putting on Pants to Return to the Office Only to be on Zoom All Day," *Washington Post*, Sept. 27, 2021, https://www.washingtonpost.com/technology/2021/09/27/return-to-work-in-person-hybrid/.

45. See Roberto Di Pietro and Stefano Cresci, "Metaverse: Security and Privacy Issues," *Third IEEE International Conference on Trust* (2021): 281.

46. Sunstein, *#Republic*, 18–20.

47. Castells, *The Power of Identity*, xxiii.

48. Ibid.

49. Ibid., xxvi.

50. Andrei Boutyline and Robb Willer, "The Social Structure of Political Echo Chambers: Variation in Ideological Homophily in Online Networks," *Political Psychology* 38, no. 3 (2017): 565–566; Elanor Colleoni, Alessandro Rozza, and Adam Arvidsson, "Echo Chamber or Public Sphere? Predicting Political Orientation and Measuring Political Homophily in Twitter Using Big Data," *Journal of communication* 64, no. 2 (2014): 328–329.

51. Turkle, *Reclaiming Conversation*, 83.

52. See Stefania Milan, "When Algorithms Shape Collective Action: Social Media and the Dynamics of Cloud Protesting," *Social Media+Society* 1, no. 2 (2015): 8; Ronald J. Deibert, "The Road to Digital Unfreedom: Three Painful Truths About Social Media," *Journal of Democracy* 30, no. 1 (2019): 32–33.

53. See generally, *The Facebook Papers*, https://apnews.com/hub/the-facebook-papers, a collection of reporting by the Associated Press about the internal documents leaked by former product manager Frances Haugen in October 2021.

54. Dan Milmo and David Pegg, "Facebook Admits Site Appears Hardwired for Misinformation, Memo Reveals," *The Guardian*, Oct. 25, 2021, https://www.theguardian.com/technology/2021/oct/25/facebook-admits-site-appears-hardwired-misinformation-memo-reveals.

55. See Zeynap Tufekci, "YouTube, the Great Radicalizer," *New York Times*, March 10, 2018, https://www.nytimes.com/2018/03/10/opinion/sunday/youtube-politics-radical.html; Brendan Nyhan, "YouTube Still Hosts Extremist Videos. Here's Who Watches Them," *Washington Post*, March 10, 2021, https://www.washingtonpost.com/outlook/2021/03/10/youtube-extremist-supremacy-radicalize-adl-study/; Kevin Roose, "The Making of a Radical," *New York* Times, June 8, 2019, https://www.nytimes.com/interactive/2019/06/08/technology/youtube-radical.html; Ryan Mac and Cecilia Kang,

*Notes to Chapters Six and Seven*

"Whistle-Blower Says Facebook 'Chooses Profits Over Safety,'" *New York Times*, Oct. 27, 2019, https://www.nytimes.com/2021/10/03/technology/whistle-blower-facebook-frances-haugen.html?searchResultPosition=2.

56. See Sheera Frenkel, "The Storming of Capitol Hill was Organized on Social Media," *New York Times*, Jan 6., 2021, https://www.nytimes.com/2021/01/06/us/politics/protesters-storm-capitol-hill-building.html; Rebecca Heilweil and Shirin Ghaffary, "How Trump's Internet Built and Broadcast the Capitol Insurrection," *Vox*, Jan. 8, 2021, https://www.vox.com/recode/22221285/trump-online-capitol-riot-far-right-parler-twitter-facebook.

57. Sophie Bushwick, "What the Capitol Riot Data Download Shows About Social Media Vulnerabilities," *Scientific American*, Jan. 27, 2021, https://www.scientificamerican.com/article/what-the-capitol-riot-data-download-shows-about-social-media-vulnerabilities/; Travis M. Andrews, "The Capitol Rioters Kept Posting Incriminating Things on Social Media. Unsurprisingly, They Were Mocked—and Arrested," *Washington Post*, Jan. 19, 2021, https://www.washingtonpost.com/technology/2021/01/19/capitol-riot-social-media/.

58. See Itai Himelboim, Marc A. Smith, Lee Rainie, Ben Shneiderman, and Camila Espina, "Classifying Twitter Topic-Networks Using Social Network Analysis," *Social Media+Society* 3, no. 1 (2017): 2.

59. Ronald S. Burt, *Structural Holes: The Social Structure of Competition* (Cambridge, MA: Harvard University Press, 1995), 18.

60. Himelboim et al., "Classifying Twitter Topic Networks," 10–11.

### Chapter Seven

1. Melvin I. Urofsky, "The Failure of Felix Frankfurter," *University of Richmond Law Review* 26, no. 1 (1991): 175.

2. R. L. Duffus, "Felix Frankfurter: The Man Behind the Legend," *New York Times Magazine*, Jan. 15, 1939, 3.

3. See, for example, Felix Frankfurter, "The Case of Sacco and Vanzetti," *The Atlantic*, March 1927, 409, www.theatlantic.com/magazine/archive/1927/03/the-case-of-sacco-and-vanzetti/306625/

4. Joseph P. Lash, *From the Diaries of Felix Frankfurter* (New York: W. W. Norton & Company, 1975), 64–65.

5. Ibid., 54.

6. Ibid., 64.

7. Jefferey Rosen, *The Supreme Court* (New York: Holt Paperbacks, 2007), 148.

8. Ibid.

9. Lash, *The Diaries*, xi.

10. Roger K. Newman, *Hugo Black* (New York: Pantheon Books, 1994), 287.

11. Letter from Oliver Wendell Holmes to Harold Laski (March 4, 1920) (on file with Harvard Law School Digital Suite), http://library.law.harvard.edu/suites/owh/index.php/item/42885056/1http://library.law.harvard.edu/suites/owh/index.php/item/42885056/1.

## Notes to Chapter Seven

12. Louis Menand, *The Metaphysical Club* (New York: Farrar, Straus and Giroux, 2001), 68.

13. Melvin I. Urofsky and David W. Levy, *Half Brother, Half Son: The Letters of Louis D. Brandeis and Felix Frankfurter* (Norman: University of Oklahoma Press, 1991), 5.

14. Letter from Oliver W. Holmes to Lewis Einstein (April 26, 1918) in *The Holmes-Einstein Letters*, ed. J. B. Peabody (New York: St. Martin's Press, 1964), 164.

15. Urofsky and Levy, *Half Brother, Half Son*, 5.

16. Ibid., 6.

17. Letter from Felix Frankfurter to Oliver W. Holmes (May 15, 1919) (on file with Harvard Law School Digital Suite), https://iiif.lib.harvard.edu/manifests/view/drs:42879149$7i.

18. Letter from Oliver W. Holmes to Harold Laski (June 1, 1919) in *The Essential Holmes*, ed. Richard Posner (Chicago: University of Chicago Press, 1992), 109–110.

19. Letter from Oliver W. Holmes to Felix Frankfurter (Sept. 25, 1919) (on file with Harvard Law School Digital Suite), https://iiif.lib.harvard.edu/manifests/view/drs:42880786$32i.

20. Lash, *The Diaries*, 52–53.

21. Robert G. McCloskey, *The American Supreme Court* (Chicago: University of Chicago Press, 2010), 110.

22. See Oliver W. Holmes, *The Common Law* (Boston: Little, Brown and Company, 1881), 1.

23. Urofsky and Levy, *Half Brother, Half Son*, 6–7.

24. See Justice Harlan Stone's famous Footnote 4 in United States v. Carolene Products, 304 U.S. 144, 152 (1938).

25. Newman, *Hugo Black*, 234.

26. Ibid., 280.

27. Letter from William O. Douglas to Felix Frankfurter (Dec. 8, 1933) in *The Douglas Letters*, ed. Melvin Urofsky (Bethesda, MD: Adler & Adler, 1987).

28. Letter from William O. Douglas to Felix Frankfurter (April 1, 1937) in *The Douglas Letters*, 81.

29. Letter from William O. Douglas to Felix Frankfurter (May 29, 1954) in *The Douglas Letters*, 85.

30. William Domnarski, *The Great Justices, 1941–53* (Ann Arbor: University of Michigan Press, 2006), 90.

31. Newman, *Hugo Black*, 284.

32. Ibid.

33. Minersville School District v. Gobitis, 310 U.S. 586, 591 (1940).

34. Ibid., 593.

35. Lash, *The Diaries*, 70.

36. Felix Frankfurter, journal entry June 14, 1943, in Lash, *The Diaries*, 254.

37. Ibid.

*Notes to Chapter Seven*

38. Newman, *Hugo Black*, 284.

39. Ibid.

40. Conversation between William O. Douglas and Walter F. Murphy, taped 1961–1963, available online via the Seeley G. Mudd Manuscript Library, Princeton University, at https://findingaids.princeton.edu/catalog/MC015_c03.

41. West Virginia State Board v. Barnette, 319 U.S. 624, 644 (1943) (Black, J., concurring).

42. Felix Frankfurter, journal entry June 14, 1943, in Lash, *The Diaries*, 253–254.

43. *West Virginia State Board*, 319 U.S. at 646 (Frankfurter, J., dissenting).

44. See multiple journal entries between June 1 and June 14, 1943, in Lash, *The Diaries*, 252–255.

45. *West Virginia State Board*, 319 U.S. at 649 (Frankfurter, J., dissenting), citing Missouri, Kansas & Texas R. Co. v. May, 194 U.S. 267, 270 (1904).

46. Lash, *The Diaries*, 70–72.

47. Conversation between William O. Douglas and Walter F. Murphy, taped 1961–1963, available online via the Seeley G. Mudd Manuscript Library, Princeton University, at https://findingaids.princeton.edu/catalog/MC015_c03.

48. 314 U.S. 252, 258–260 (1941).

49. Ibid., 279 (Frankfurter, J., dissenting).

50. Ibid., 283 (Frankfurter, J., dissenting) (quoting Abrams v. United States, 250 U.S. 616, 630 (1919) (Holmes, J., dissenting).

51. See Schenck v. United States, 249 U.S. 47 (1919), *Abrams*, 250 U.S. at 624 (Holmes, J., dissenting), and Whitney v. California, 274 U.S. 357, 372 (1925) (Brandeis, J., concurring). See also chapter 4.

52. *Bridges*, 314 U.S. at 264.

53. Ibid.

54. U.S. Const. amend. I.

55. 312 U.S. 287, 291–292 (1941).

56. Ibid., 294.

57. Ibid., 293.

58. Ibid., 294.

59. Ibid., 301–302 (Black, J., dissenting).

60. Ibid., 302.

61. Ibid.

62. Lash, *The Diaries*, 15.

63. Ibid., 57.

64. Ibid., 72; Noah Feldman, *Scorpions: The Battles and Triumphs of FDR's Great Supreme Court Justices* (New York: Twelve, 2010), 232; Russell W. Galloway Jr., "The Roosevelt Court: The Liberals Conquer (1937–1947) and Divide (1941–1946)," *Santa Clara Law Review* 23 (1983): 510–516.

65. Galloway, "The Roosevelt Court," 516.

66. Lash, *The Diaries*, 74.

## Notes to Chapter Seven

67. Kovac v. Cooper, 336 U.S. 77, 89 (1949) (Frankfurter, J., concurring).

68. Ibid., 88.

69. See 304 U.S. 144 (1938), Footnote 4.

70. See Smith v. California, 361 U.S. 147, 157 (1959), for example.

71. Don Pember and Clay Calvert, *Mass Media Law* (New York: McGraw-Hill, 2011), 43 (emphasis added).

72. *Kovac*, 336 U.S. at 96 (Frankfurter, J., concurring).

73. Ibid., 96–97.

74. Ibid., 101 (Black, J., dissenting).

75. Chicago v. Terminiello, 332 Ill. App. 17, 21 (Ill. App. Ct., 1947).

76. Terminiello v. Chicago, 337 U.S. 1, 4 (1949).

77. Ibid.

78. Ibid.

79. Ibid., 11 (Frankfurter, J., dissenting).

80. Letter from William O. Douglas to Hugo Black (June 22, 1941) in *The Douglas Letters*, 107.

81. Ibid.

82. Ibid.

83. See Urofsky, *The Failure of Felix Frankfurter*, 175; Alpheus Thomas Mason, "The Chief Justice of the United States: Primus Inter Pares," *Journal of Public Law* 17 (1968): 21. Regarding the "Switch in time," see generally, Felix Gilman, "The Famous Footnote Four: A History of the *Carolene Products* Footnote," *South Texas Law Review* 46 (2004–2005).

84. Felix Frankfurter, journal entry Oct. 19, 1946, in Lash, *The Diaries*, 274.

85. *Dennis*, 341 U.S. 494, 555 (1951) (Frankfurter, J., concurring).

86. Ibid., 549 (Frankfurter, J., concurring).

87. Ibid., 580 (Black, J., dissenting).

88. Ibid., 584 (Douglas, J., dissenting).

89. Ibid.

90. See Erika J. Pribanic-Smith and Jared Schroeder, "Breaking the White Circle: How the Press and Courts Quieted a Chicago Hate Group, 1949–1952," 38, no. 4 (2021): 418–421.

91. People v. Beauharnais, 408 Ill. 512, 513–514 (Ill., 1951).

92. Beauharnais v. Illinois, 343 U.S. 250, 263 (1952).

93. Ibid., 275 (Black, J., dissenting).

94. Ibid.

95. Ibid., 285 (Douglas, J., dissenting).

96. Ibid.

97. Newman, *Hugo Black*, 518–20.

98. Hugo L. Black, "*Mr. Justice Frankfurter*," *Harvard Law Review* 78 (1965): 1522.

99. For more about Frankfurter's understandings of the marketplace, see Jared Schroeder, "Justice Frankfurter's Contextual Marketplace," *Rutgers Law Review* 74 (2022): 576–581.

## Notes to Chapter Eight

**Chapter Eight**

1. Letter from William James to Thomas W. Ward, March 27, 1866, in *The letters of William James*, ed. by Henry James (son) (Boston: Little, Brown, and Company, 1926), 19.

2. Ibid.

3. See Oliver W. Holmes personal journal entry, May 3, 1864, in *Touched with Fire*, ed. Mark de Wolfe Howe (London: Oxford University Press, 1946), 101; Holmes personal journal entry, May 28, 1864, in *Touched with Fire*, 128, for examples.

4. See Louis Menand, *The Metaphysical Club* (New York: Farrar, Straus and Giroux, 2001), 6.

5. See letter from Oliver W. Holmes to Amelia Holmes (May 26, 1866) (on file with Harvard Law School Digital Suite), https://iiif.lib.harvard.edu/manifests/view/drs:43005328$2i; letter from Amelia Holmes to Oliver W. Holmes (July 3, 1866) (on file with Harvard Law School Digital Suite), https://iiif.lib.harvard.edu/manifests/view/drs:43005329$2i.

6. Letter from Amelia Holmes to Oliver W. Holmes (July 3, 1866) (on file with Harvard Law School Digital Suite), https://iiif.lib.harvard.edu/manifests/view/drs:43005329$2i.

7. Ibid.

8. Gay Wilson Allen, *William James* (Minneapolis: University of Minnesota Press, 1970), 5.

9. Ibid., 6–10.

10. Menand, *Metaphysical Club*, 75.

11. See letter from Oliver W. Holmes to Harold Laski (Nov. 29, 1923) (on file with Harvard Law School Digital Suite), https://iiif.lib.harvard.edu/manifests/view/drs:42885072$7i; Menand, *Metaphysical Club*, 216–217, regarding Wright's influence on Holmes. See Robert D. Richardson, *William James* (Boston: Houghton Mifflin Company, 2006), 130–131, regarding James's relationship with Wright.

12. Richardson, *William James*, 128–129.

13. Schenck v. United States, 249 U.S. 47 (1919).

14. Abrams v. United States, 250 U.S. 616, 624–631 (1919) (Holmes, J., dissenting).

15. Richardson, *William James*, 130; Menand, *Metaphysical Club*, 200–204.

16. Charles Sanders Peirce, "How to Make Our Ideas Clear" in *The Pragmatism Reader*, eds. Robert B. Talisse and Scott F. Aikin (Princeton, NJ: Princeton University Press, 2011), 57.

17. See William James, *Pragmatism: A New Name for Some Old Ways of Thinking* (Cambridge: Harvard University Press, 1907), 28–29, for example. See also William James, "A Defence of Pragmatism," *Popular Science Monthly* 70 (1907): 351–364; Menand, *Metaphysical Club*, 349–351.

18. James, *Pragmatism*, 10.

19. Ibid., 31.

290

## Notes to Chapter Eight

20. Ibid.

21. See Richardson, *William James*, 304; John Dewey, "The Development of American Pragmatism," in *The Essential Dewey, Vol. 1*, eds. Larry A. Hickman and Thomas M. Alexander (Bloomington, IN: University of Indiana Press, 1998), 5–7, regarding the impact James's *Principles of Psychology* had on Dewey's thinking.

22. Dewey, "From Absolutism to Experimentalism," in *The Essential Dewey*, 19.

23. John Dewey, "Creative Democracy—The Task Before Us," in *The Essential Dewey*, 342.

24. Estate of Justice Holmes: The Library, in Oliver Wendell Holmes Jr., Harvard Law School Library Digital Suite, http://library.law.harvard.edu/suites/owh/index.php/item/42,864,692/49.

25. Letter from Oliver Wendell Holmes to Nina Gray (Jan. 2, 1927) (on file with Harvard Law School Digital Suite), https://iiif.lib.harvard.edu/manifests/view/drs:42882378$12i.

26. Richardson, *William James*, 41.

27. Menand, *Metaphysical Club*, 74; Gerald E. Myers, "Introduction," in *The Correspondence of William James, Vol. 1 William and Henry 1861– 1884*, eds. Ignas K. Skrupskelis and Elizabeth M. Berkeley (Charlottesville, VA: University Press of Virginia, 1992), xxv.

28. Letter from William James to Henry James (July 5, 1876), in *The Thought and Character of William James*, ed. Ralph Barton Perry (Nashville, TN: Vanderbilt University Press, 1996), 99.

29. Henry James (William James's son), *The Letters of William James, Vol. 1* (Boston: The Atlantic Monthly Press, 1920), 63.

30. See Richardson, *William James*, 51; Myers, "Introduction," xxiii; for further discussion of James's mental health challenges during the period.

31. See Richardson, *William James*, 65–69; Menand, *Metaphysical Club*, 119–123, regarding Agassiz's expedition and disagreements regarding Darwin's conclusions.

32. Letter from William James to Henry James (May 3, 1865), in *The Correspondence of William James*, 6.

33. Richardson, *William James*, 111.

34. Ibid., 112.

35. Ibid., 111–113; Henry James, *Notes of a Son and Brother* (London: MacMillan and Co., 1913), 479.

36. Henry James, *Notes of a Son and Brother*, 479.

37. See Robert C. LeClair, "Henry James and Minny Temple," *American Literature* 21, no. 1 (1949): 36–37; Myers, "Introduction," xlvii, regarding parallels between Minny Temple and the leading women in Henry James's novels.

38. Letter from Henry James to William James (March 29, 1870), in *The Correspondence of William James*, 153.

## Notes to Chapter Eight

39. William James, "The Will to Believe," *Will to Believe and Other Essays in Popular Philosophy* (New York: Longmans, Green, and Co., 1897), 19.

40. Ibid., 14.

41. Menand, *Metaphysical Club*, 350.

42. Ibid.

43. Letter from William James to Theodore Flournoy (March 26, 1907), in *The Letters of William James, Vol. 2,* ed. Henry James (William James's son) (Boston: The Atlantic Monthly Press, 1920), 380.

44. Ibid.

45. James, *Pragmatism*, 30.

46. Ibid., 10–15.

47. Ibid., 22.

48. Ibid., 97.

49. Ibid., 83.

50. Ibid., 32

51. William James, *The Meaning of Truth* (Cambridge: Harvard University Press, 1975), 68.

52. Ibid.

53. James, *Pragmatism*, 38.

54. Ibid., 86.

55. Ibid., 98.

56. Menand, *Metaphysical Club*, 286–287; George Dykhuizen, "John Dewey: The Chicago Years," *Journal of the History of Philosophy,* 2, no. 2 (1964): 228.

57. Richardson, *William James*, 345.

58. Menand, *Metaphysical Club*, 273–274.

59. George Dykhuizen, *The Life and Mind of John Dewey* (Carbondale, IL: Southern Illinois University Press, 1973), 77.

60. Menand, *Metaphysical Club*, 288.

61. Dykhuizen, *Life and Mind of John Dewey*, 30–31; Steve Rockefeller, *John Dewey: Religious Faith and Democratic Humanism* (New York: Columbia University Press, 1991), 76–77.

62. Dewey, "From Absolutism to Experimentalism," in *The Essential Dewey*, 17.

63. Ibid., 19.

64. Charlene Haddock Seigfried, *Feminist Interpretations of John Dewey* (University Park, PA: The Pennsylvania State University Press, 2022), 7–8; Jay Martin, *The Education of John Dewey* (New York: Columbia University Press, 2002), 164–165; Dykhuizen, *Life and Mind of John Dewey*, 104–106.

65. Rockefeller, *John Dewey: Religious Faith and Democratic Humanism*, 208.

66. Maurice Hamington, "Jane Addams," *The Stanford Encyclopedia of Philosophy*, July 7, 2022, https://plato.stanford.edu/entries/addams-jane/.

292

## Notes to Chapter Eight

67. Jane Addams, "Eulogy for Gordon Dewey" (on file with the Jane Addams Digital Collection), https://digital.janeaddams.ramapo.edu/items/show/3621.

68. William Neumann, "Prefatory Note on Jane Addams' Life," in *Jane Addams: A Centennial Reader*, ed. Emily Cooper Johnson (New York: The MacMillan Company, 1960), x; Rockefeller, *John Dewey: Religious Faith and Democratic Humanism*, 206–207.

69. See "Hull House," in *Encyclopedia Britannica*, https://www.britannica.com/topic/Hull-House, for an overview of the settlement house's programs. See also, Jane Addams, "Hull House and its Neighbors," *Charities* (May 7, 1904) (on file with the Jane Addams Digital Collection), https://digital.janeaddams.ramapo.edu/items/show/3619, for an example of how Addams described the settlement house's programs.

70. Dykhuizen, *Life and Mind of John Dewey*, 105.

71. Jane Addams, "The Subjective Necessity for Social Settlements," *Protest and Reform Gallery*, http://www.sscnet.ucla.edu/history/waughj/classes/gildedage/private/protest_and_reform/documents/protest_and_reform_document_002.html.

72. See Hamington, "Jane Addams," https://plato.stanford.edu/entries/addams-jane/; Charlene Haddock Seigfried, "Shared Communities of Interest: Feminism and Pragmatism," *Hypatia* 8, no. 2 (1993); 4.

73. See James, *Pragmatism*, 34–37, for example.

74. Dewey, "From Absolutism to Experimentalism," in *The Essential Dewey*, 19.

75. See Dewey, "From Absolutism to Experimentalism," in *The Essential Dewey*, 17, regarding his admission he struggled to match his academic and personal interests early in his career. In many ways, he matched the two at Hull House.

76. Letter from Oliver W. Holmes to John T. Morse (Dec. 11, 1931) (on file with Harvard Law School Digital Suite), https://iiif.lib.harvard.edu/manifests/view/drs:43006908$29i. Morse was a historian, who published a biography of Oliver W. Holmes Sr. in 1896.

77. John Dewey, *The Public and its Problems* (Athens, OH: Swallow Press, 1927), 35.

78. Ibid., 31.

79. See Itai Himelboim, Stephen McCreery, and Marc Smith, "Birds of a Feather Tweet Together: Integrating Network and Content Analyses to Examine Cross-Ideology Exposure on Twitter," *Journal of Computer-Mediated Communication* 18, no. 2 (2013): 156–171; Henry Jenkins, *Convergence Culture* (New York: New York University Press, 2006), 51–58; Manuel Castells, *Communication Power* (Oxford: Oxford University Press, 2009), 20–26, regarding community formation in the networked era. See also chapter 6.

80. Dykhuizen, *Life and Mind of John Dewey*, 104.

81. Dewey, *The Public and its Problems*, 150.

*Notes to Chapters Eight and Nine*

82. Ibid., 154.

83. See Dewey, "Creative Democracy—The Task Before Us," in *The Essential Dewey*, 342, for a concise, focused version of his understanding of an active democratic life.

84. See John Locke, *The Second Treatise of Government* (Mineola, NY: Dover Publications), 6–7, for an example of individual-based Enlightenment thought. See also, Fred S. Siebert, "The Libertarian Theory of the Press," in *The Four Theories of the Press*, eds. Fred S. Siebert, Theodore Peterson, and Wilbur Schramm (Urbana, IL: University of Illinois Press, 1956), 40–41, regarding the overall construction of Enlightenment thought.

85. Dewey, *The Public and its Problems*, 168.

86. Dewey, "Creative Democracy—The Task Before Us," in *The Essential Dewey*, 343.

87. Dewey, *The Public and its Problems*, 155.

88. Ibid., 167.

89. Dewey, "Creative Democracy—The Task Before Us," in *The Essential Dewey*, 342.

90. Ibid.

91. Dewey, "Logic Method and Law," in *The Essential Dewey*, 357 (quoting Oliver W. Holmes, *The Common Law* (New York: Dover Publications, 1991), 1).

92. Letter from Oliver W. Holmes to Elizabeth Shepley Sergeant (Jan. 28, 1927) (on file with Harvard Law School Digital Suite), https://iiif.lib.harvard .edu/manifests/view/drs:38003485$11i.

93. Letter from Oliver W. Holmes to Lewis Einstein (April 1, 1928) (on file with Harvard Law School Digital Suite), https://iiif.lib.harvard.edu/manifests/ view/drs:43393924$96i.

94. See letter from Oliver W. Holmes to Felix Frankfurter (May 21, 1926) (on file with Harvard Law School Digital Suite), https://iiif.lib.harvard.edu/ manifests/view/drs:42879157$7i; letter from Oliver W. Holmes to Morris Cohen (Sept. 14, 1923), https://iiif.lib.harvard.edu/manifests/view/drs:43097 589$29i; letter from Oliver W. Holmes to Harold Laski (Feb. 26, 1918) (on file with Harvard Law School Digital Suite), https://iiif.lib.harvard.edu/manifests/ view/drs:42882398$24i, for examples of Holmes's willingness to critique and cast aside thinkers' ideas.

### Chapter Nine

1. Michael Berenbaum, "Adolf Eichmann." In *Britannica Academic*, Encyclopedia Britannica, April 6, 2020, https://academic.eb.com/levels/collegiate/ article/Adolf-Eichmann/32112.

2. Ibid.

3. "Killer of 6,000,000: Adolf Eichmann," *New York Times,* May 26, 1960, https://timesmachine.nytimes.com/timesmachine/1960/05/26/105436870.html ?pageNumber=18.

*Notes to Chapter Nine*

4. Moshe Pearlman, *The Capture and Trial of Adolf Eichmann* (New York: Simon & Schuster, 1963), 52–56.

5. Elisabeth Young-Bruehl, *Hannah Arendt: For Love of the World* (New Haven, CT: Yale University Press, 2004), 328.

6. "Killer of 6,000,000: Adolf Eichmann," *New York Times,* May 26, 1960, https://timesmachine.nytimes.com/timesmachine/1960/05/26/105436870 .html?pageNumber=18.

7. Young-Bruehl, *Hannah Arendt,* 329.

8. Letter from Hannah Arendt to Elizabeth Washburne (January 2, 1961) (on file with the Library of Congress), https://www.loc.gov/resource/mss11056dig .025900/?st=pdf&pdfPage=23.

9. Ibid.

10. Hannah Arendt, *Eichmann in Jerusalem: A Report on the Banality of Evil* (New York: Penguin Books, 1964), 5.

11. Ibid.

12. Ibid., 33.

13. Ibid., 252. See Young-Bruehl, *Hannah Arendt,* 347–355, regarding the criticism Arendt's coverage of the Eichmann trial created.

14. Arendt, *Eichmann in Jerusalem,* 28.

15. Ibid., 33.

16. Ibid.

17. Ibid., 32.

18. Ibid., 252.

19. Hannah Arendt, *The Origins of Totalitarianism* (New York: Meridian Books, 1958), vii.

20. Young-Bruehl, *Hannah Arendt,* 11–12.

21. Ibid.

22. See Derwent May, *Hannah Arendt* (New York: Penguin Books, 1986), 15, regarding Arendt's experience. See also Arendt, *The Origins of Totalitarianism,* 56–68, to see how she framed the experiences in her own words.

23. Arendt, *The Origins of Totalitarianism,* 56.

24. Young-Bruehl, *Hannah Arendt,* 19.

25. Ibid., 30.

26. Ibid., 33–34.

27. Ibid., 36.

28. Young-Bruehl, *Hannah Arendt,* 48. See Taylor Carman, "Foreword," in *Being and Time,* Martin Heidegger, trans. John Macquarrie and Edward Robinson (New York: Harper Perennial, 2008), xiii, for a brief description of Heidegger's project.

29. Young-Bruehl, *Hannah Arendt,* 49.

30. Ibid.

31. Ibid., 465. Young-Bruehl quoted from a letter from Arendt to Mary McCarthy (August 22, 1975).

295

## Notes to Chapter Nine

32. Theodore Kisiel, "Heidegger's Apology: Biography as Philosophy and Ideology," in *The Heidegger Case: On Philosophy and Politics*, eds. Tom Rockmore and Joseph Margolis (Philadelphia: Temple University Press, 1992), 31.

33. Young-Bruehl, *Hannah Arendt*, 166.

34. Arendt, *The Origins of Totalitarianism*, 293.

35. Ibid., 295–296.

36. Ibid., 296.

37. Hannah Arendt, *The Human* Condition (Chicago: University of Chicago Press, 1958), 7.

38. Ibid., 30.

39. Ibid., 7.

40. Ibid., 58.

41. Ibid., 41.

42. Arendt, *The Origins of Totalitarianism*, 296–300.

43. Ibid., 299.

44. Ibid., 299.

45. Arendt, *The Human* Condition, 199.

46. Ibid., 160.

47. Ibid., 324.

48. Ibid., 160.

49. Ibid.

50. Arendt, *Eichmann in Jerusalem*, 92.

51. Arendt, *The Human* Condition, 203.

52. Ibid., 50.

53. See Martin Heidegger, *Being and Time*, trans. John Macquarrie and Edward Robinson (New York: Harper Perennial, 2008), 26–28, for a brief explanation of the thinker's conceptualization of *Dasein*. See also Hannah Arendt, *The Life of the Mind* (San Diego: A Harvest Book, 1978), 120–122, for an example of how Arendt discussed Heidegger's conceptualizations of being and truth.

54. Arendt, *The Origins of Totalitarianism*, 301.

55. See chapter 8, which examines the pragmatism-based assumptions for the space for human discourse.

56. Young-Bruehl, *Hannah Arendt*, 349.

57. See "Letters to the Editor: 'Eichmann in Jerusalem,'" *New York Times*, June 23, 1963, https://timesmachine.nytimes.com/timesmachine/1963/06/23/89935369.html?pageNumber=212, and "Letters to the Editor: 'Eichmann in Jerusalem,'" *New York Times*, July 14, 1963, https://timesmachine.nytimes.com/timesmachine/1963/07/14/356860072.html?pageNumber=178, regarding the responses to Arendt's book.

58. Michael A. Musmanno, "Man with An Unspotted Conscience," *New York Times*, May 19, 1963, https://timesmachine.nytimes.com/timesmachine/1963/05/19/86709120.html?pageNumber=160.

## Notes to Chapters Nine and Ten

59. "Letters to the Editor: 'Eichmann in Jerusalem,'" *New York Times*, June 23, 1963, https://timesmachine.nytimes.com/timesmachine/1963/06/23/89935369.html?pageNumber=212.

60. Young-Bruehl, *Hannah Arendt*, 348–349.

61. Letter from Hannah Arendt to Siegfried Moses (July 17, 1963) (on file with the Library of Congress), https://www.loc.gov/resource/mss11056dig.020960/?sp=29.

62. Arendt, *Eichmann in Jerusalem*, 283.

63. Hannah Arendt, "Truth and Politics," in *The Portable Hannah Arendt*, ed. Peter Baehr (New York: Penguin Books, 2000), 545.

64. Ibid.

65. Arendt, *The Human Condition*, 259–262.

66. Ibid., 262.

67. Arendt, *The Life of the Mind*, 39.

68. Ibid., 5–7.

69. See Heidegger, *Being and Times*, 51–54, regarding the thinker's understandings about truth and appearances. See Arendt, *The Life of the Mind*, 156–158, for an example of how she referenced his ideas about this topic.

70. See chapter 8, regarding Dewey's pragmatic construction of an experience-influenced form of truth.

71. Arendt, *The Human Condition*, 9.

72. Arendt, *The Life of the Mind*, 49 (emphasis in original).

73. Heidegger, *Being and Times*, 26–27.

74. Hans-Georg Gadamer, *Truth and Method*, trans. Joel Weinsheimer and Donald G. Marshall (London: Continuum, 2006), 271.

75. Arendt, *The Human Condition*, 9.

76. Ibid., 152.

77. Ibid., 121.

78. Ibid., 147.

79. Ibid.

80. Ibid., 151.

81. Ibid.

82. Arendt, *The Life of the Mind*, 6.

83. Ibid., 4.

84. Arendt, *The Human Condition*, 172.

85. Ibid., 146.

86. Ibid., 158.

87. Ibid., 19.

### Chapter Ten

1. Susan Palmer and Bryan Sentes, "The International Raëlian Movement," in *The Cambridge Companion to New Religious Movements*, eds.

*Notes to Chapter Ten*

Olav Hammer and Mikael Rothstein (Cambridge: Cambridge University Press, 2012), 167–169.

2. Gina Kolata and Kenneth Change, "For Clonaid, a Trail of Unproven Claims," *New York Times*, Jan. 1, 2003, https://www.nytimes.com/2003/01/01/us/for-clonaid-a-trail-of-unproven-claims.html.

3. Palmer, "Raëlian Movement," 172–183.

4. Mouvement Raëlien Suisse v. Switzerland, no. 16354/06, §16, 13 July 2012, https://hudoc.echr.coe.int/fre?i=001-112165.

5. Ibid., §76.

6. Ibid., §61.

7. Ibid., §71.

8. Ibid., §72.

9. See Jared Schroeder, "Meet the EU Law that Could Reshape Online Speech in the U.S.," *Slate*, Oct. 27, 2022, https://slate.com/technology/2022/10/digital-services-act-european-union-content-moderation.html.

10. See Silvia Amaro, "How Europe Became the World's Top Tech Regulator," *CNBC*, March 25, 2021, https://www.cnbc.com/2021/03/25/big-tech-how-europe-became-the-worlds-top-regulator.html; "The Brussels Effect: The EU Wants to Become the World's Super-Regulator in AI," *The Economist*, April 24, 2021, https://www.economist.com/europe/2021/04/24/the-eu-wants-to-become-the-worlds-super-regulator-in-ai; Matina Stevis-Gridneff, "EU's New Digital Czar: 'Most Powerful Regulator of Big Tech on the Planet,'" *New York Times*, Sept. 10, 2019, https://www.nytimes.com/2019/09/10/world/europe/margrethe-vestager-european-union-tech-regulation.html, for examples.

11. European Convention on Human Rights, Article 10, §1.

12. Ibid., §2.

13. Mouvement Raëlien Suisse v. Switzerland, no. 16354/06, §52, 13 July 2012, https://hudoc.echr.coe.int/fre?i=001-112165.

14. Rantsev v. Cyprus and Russia, no. 25965/04, §277, January 7, 2010, https://hudoc.echr.coe.int/eng?i=001-96549.

15. See Lawrence B. Solum, "Originalism and Constitutional Construction," *Fordham Law Review* 82 (2013), 456–457; Robert Post and Reva Siegel, "Originalism as a Political Practice: The Right's Living Constitution," *Fordham Law Review* 75 (2006): 545–548; Thomas B. Colby and Peter J. Smith, "Living Originalism," *Duke Law Journal* 59, no. 2 (2009): 241–244, for analyses of jurists' obsessions with Constitutional originalism since the 1970s.

16. See chapter 4 for more about the influential role Enlightenment thinkers had over those who framed early American thought. See also Darren Staloff, *Hamilton, Adams, Jefferson: The Politics of Enlightenment and the American Founding* (New York: Hill and Wang, 2005), 3–4.

17. See Roy Branson, "James Madison and the Scottish Enlightenment," *Journal of the History of Ideas* 40, No. 2 (1979): 236–237; Jane E. Calvert, "Liberty Without Tumult: Understanding the Politics of John Dickinson," *The*

## Notes to Chapter Ten

*Pennsylvania Magazine of History and Biography*; Alexander Tsesis, *For Liberty and Equality* (Oxford: Oxford University Press, 2012), 37, for examples.

18. See Lyrissa Barnett Lidsky, "Nobody's Fools: Rational Audience as First Amendment Ideal," University of Illinois Law Review, 2010, no. 3 (2010): 801–802; Fred S. Siebert, "The Libertarian Theory," in *Four Theories of the Press*, eds. Fred S. Siebert, Theodore Peterson and Wilbur Schramm (Urbana, IL.: University of Illinois Press,1956), 40–41; R. Randall Kelso, "The Natural Law Tradition on the Modern Supreme Court: Not Burke, but the Enlightenment Tradition Represented by Locke, Madison, and Marshall," *St. Mary's Law Review* 26 (1995): 1074–1076, for perspectives on the truth and rationality assumptions at the foundations of US free expression.

19. See Nikolas Bowie, "The Constitutional Right of Self-Government," *Yale Law Review*, 130 (2021): 1658–1659; William Sutton Fields, "The Third Amendment: Constitutional Protection from the Involuntary Quartering of Soldiers," *Military Law Review* 195 (1989): 199–202; Stephen P. Halbrook, "Encroachments of the Crown on the Liberty of the Subject: Pre-Revolutionary Origins of the Second Amendment," *University of Dayton Law Review* 91 (1989): 119–123, for examples.

20. "Universal Declaration of Human Rights: History of the Declaration," United Nations, accessed December 6, 2022, https://www.un.org/en/about-us/udhr/history-of-the-declaration.

21. Ibid.

22. Universal Declaration of Human Rights, Article 1.

23. "Universal Declaration of Human Rights," United Nations.

24. Universal Declaration of Human Rights, Article 29.

25. See generally, "Universal Declaration of Human Rights," United Nations, accessed December 6, 2022, https://www.un.org/en/udhrbook/pdf/udhr_booklet_en_web.pdf.

26. European Convention on Human Rights, Article 10.

27. Mouvement Raëlien Suisse v. Switzerland, no. 16354/06, §76, 13 July 2012, https://hudoc.echr.coe.int/fre?i=001-112165.

28. Handyside v. United Kingdom, no. 5493/72, §49, 7 December 1976, https://hudoc.echr.coe.int/eng?i=001-57499.

29. Ibid.

30. Ibid.

31. Mouvement Raëlien Suisse v. Switzerland, no. 16354/06, §35, 13 July 2012, https://hudoc.echr.coe.int/fre?i=001-112165.

32. Ibid., Judge De Albuquerque dissenting.

33. Animal Defenders v. United Kingdom, no. 48876/08, §116, 22 April 2013, https://hudoc.echr.coe.int/eng?i=001-119244.

34. Ibid.

35. Ibid., §125.

36. Hertel v. Switzerland, no. 25181/94, 25 August 1998, https://hudoc.echr.coe.int/eng?i=001-59366.

## Notes to Chapter Ten

37. Ibid., §51.

38. Delfi v. Estonia, no. 64569/09, §110, 16 June 2015, https://hudoc.echr.coe.int/eng?i=001-155105.

39. Magyar Helsinki Bizottság v. Hungary, no. 18030/11, §180, 8 November 2016, https://hudoc.echr.coe.int/eng?i=001-167828.

40. Ibid.

41. Ibid., §176.

42. European Convention on Human Rights, Article 10.

43. See "Tackling Online Disinformation," *European Commission*, last accessed December 7, 2022, https://digital-strategy.ec.europa.eu/en/policies/online-disinformation, for example.

44. Mouvement Raëlien Suisse v. Switzerland, no. 16354/06, §74–76, 13 July 2012, https://hudoc.echr.coe.int/fre?i=001-112165.

45. Delfi v. Estonia, no. 64569/09, §56, 16 June 2015, https://hudoc.echr.coe.int/eng?i=001-155105.

46. Animal Defenders v. United Kingdom, no. 48876/08, §18, 22 April 2013, https://hudoc.echr.coe.int/eng?i=001-119244.

47. Ibid., §99.

48. Aquilina v. Malta, no. 25642/94, §43, 29 April 1999, https://hudoc.echr.coe.int/eng?i=001-58239.

49. Steel and Morris, no. 68416/01, §11-12, 15 February 2005, https://hudoc.echr.coe.int/eng?i=001-68224.

50. Ibid., §85-87.

51. Ibid., §88.

52. Ibid., §89.

53. See Zana v. Turkey, no. 69/1996/688/880, §51, 25 November 1997, https://hudoc.echr.coe.int/eng?i=001-58115, regarding the centrality of the public-good expectation. See also, Hertel v. Switzerland, no. 25181/94, §46, 25 August 1998, https://hudoc.echr.coe.int/eng?i=001-59366, in regard to how the thinking has persisted.

54. Zana v. Turkey, no. 69/1996/688/880, §46, 25 November 1997, https://hudoc.echr.coe.int/eng?i=001-58115.

55. "The Digital Services Act; Ensuring Fair and Open Digital Markets," European Commission, accessed December 6, 2022, https://ec.europa.eu/info/strategy/priorities-2019-2024/europe-fit-digital-age/digital-markets-act-ensuring-fair-and-open-digital-markets_en.

56. Khari Johnson, "Europe Prepares to Rewrite the Rules of the Internet," *Wired*, Oct. 28, 2022, https://www.wired.com/story/europe-dma-prepares-to-rewrite-the-rules-of-the-internet/.

57. See Clothilde Goujard, "WTF is DSA? What Europe's New Content Moderation Law Means for the Internet," *Politico*, Oct. 27, 2022, https://www.politico.eu/article/5-things-to-know-about-the-eu-content-moderation-law-digital-services-act/; "EU Law Targets Big Tech Speech, Disinformation,"

# Notes to Chapter Ten

*Associated Press*, April 23, 2022, https://www.npr.org/2022/04/23/1094485542/
eu-law-big-tech-hate-speech-disinformation, regarding the DSA's requirements.

58. "The Digital Services Act; Ensuring Fair and Open Digital Markets,"
European Commission, accessed December 6, 2022, https://ec.europa.eu/
info/strategy/priorities-2019-2024/europe-fit-digital-age/digital-markets-act
-ensuring-fair-and-open-digital-markets_en.

59. Schroeder, "Meet the EU Law." See also, "Complete Guide to GDPR
Compliance," European Union, accessed December 6, 2022, https://gdpr.eu/,
for more about a law that can help us understand the global impact the DSA
might have.

60. Arkansas State Parks, accessed December 6, 2022, https://www
.arkansasstateparks.com/. See bottom of the main page for GDPR compliance information; Mount Rushmore National Memorial, accessed December 6, 2022, https://www.mtrushmorenationalmemorial.com/privacy
-policy/. See "Your EU/Other Privacy Rights" section.

61. "Laying Down Harmonised Rules on Artificial Intelligence (Artificial Intelligence Act) and Amending Certain Union Legislative Acts," European Council, May 21, 2021, last accessed December 6, 2022, https://
artificialintelligenceact.eu/the-act/.

62. Ibid.

63. See Kate Starbird, "Disinformation's Spread: Bots, Trolls and All of
Us," *Nature*, July 24, 2019, *https://www.nature.com/articles/d41586-019
-02235-x*; Jeanna Smialek, "Twitter Bots Helped Trump and Brexit Win,
Economic Study Says," *Blooomberg*, May 21, 2018, last accessed December
6, 2022, https://www.bloomberg.com/news/articles/2018-05-21/twitter-bots
-helped-trump-and-brexit-win-economic-study-says?leadSource=uverify
%20wall, for examples of AI entities' influences on elections. See also Danielle Citron, "How Deepfakes Undermine Truth and Threaten Democracy,"
*TED Talk*, September 2019, last accessed December 6, 2022, https://www
.ted.com/speakers/danielle_citron; Bobby Chesney and Danielle Citron,
"Deep Fakes: A Looming Challenge for Privacy, Democracy, and National
Security," *California Law Review* 107 (2019): 1785–1786, regarding deepfakes and democracy.

64. "Blueprint for an AI Bill of Rights," *The White House*, last accessed
December 6, 2022, https://www.whitehouse.gov/ostp/ai-bill-of-rights/.

65. "Establishing a Common Framework for Media Services in the Internal Market (European Media Freedom Act) and Amending Directive 2010/13/
EU," European Commission, Sept. 16, 2022, last accessed December 6, 2022,
https://eur-lex.europa.eu/legal-content/EN/TXT/?uri=CELEX:52022PC0457;
Foo Yun Chee, "EU Wants to Ensure Independent Media, Tougher Media
Merger Rules," *Reuters*, Sept. 16, 2022, https://www.reuters.com/world/
europe/eu-wants-tougher-rules-media-pluralism-mergers-against-spying
-journalists-2022-09-16/.

## Notes to Chapter Ten

66. "The 2022 Code of Practice on Disinformation," European Commission, June 2022, last accessed December 6, 2022, https://digital-strategy.ec.europa.eu/en/policies/code-practice-disinformation.

67. Ibid.

68. Ibid. See also Jared Schroeder, "SLAPP Fight: How Journalists are Pushing Back on Nuisance Lawsuits," *Global Investigative Journalism Network*, September 14, 2021, https://gijn.org/2021/09/14/slapp-fight/, for more information about SLAPPs.

69. "Recommendation on the Protection, Safety and Empowerment of Journalists," European Commission, September 16, 2021, last accessed December 6, 2022, https://digital-strategy.ec.europa.eu/en/library/recommendation-protection-safety-and-empowerment-journalists.

70. Ibid.

71. "European Media Freedom Act: Commission Launches Public Consultation," European Commission, January 10, 2022, last accessed December 6, 2022, https://ec.europa.eu/commission/presscorner/detail/en/ip_22_85, quoting Vice President for Values and Transparency Věra Jourová.

72. "Directive of the European Parliament and of the Council on Protecting Persons Who Engage in Public Participation from Manifestly Unfounded or Abusive Court Proceedings," European Council, April 27, 2022, last accessed December 6, 2022, https://eur-lex.europa.eu/legal-content/EN/TXT/?uri=CELEX%3A52022PC0177.

73. "Tackling Online Disinformation," European Commission, last accessed December 6, 2022, https://digital-strategy.ec.europa.eu/en/policies/online-disinformation.

74. See "European Democracy Action Plan," European Commission, December 3, 2020, last accessed December 6, 2022, https://ec.europa.eu/info/sites/default/files/edap_factsheet8.pdf, regarding the EU's broad, proactive approach to safeguarding the space for discourse.

75. Chaplinsky v. New Hampshire, 315 U.S. 568, 572 (1941).

76. See *Chaplinksy*, 315 U.S. at 527, for example, in which the Court reasoned,

> It has been well observed that such utterances are no essential part of any exposition of ideas, and are of such slight social value as a step to truth that any benefit that may be derived from them is clearly outweighed by the social interest in order and morality.

See also Roth v. United States, 354 U.S. 476, 484 (1957).

77. See Albert B. Gerber, "Suggested Solution to the Riddle of Obscenity," *University of Pennsylvania Law Review* 112 (1964): 855–856, regarding the narrow interpretation of the Miller Test; Mark A. Rabionwitz, "Nazis in Skokie: Fighting Words or Heckler's Veto," *DePaul Law Review* 28 (1979): 259–260, regarding the disappearing role of "fighting words" limitations.

*Notes to Chapter Ten and Conclusion*

78. European Convention on Human Rights, Article 10 §2.

79. Mouvement Raëlien Suisse v. Switzerland, no. 16354/06, §76, 13 July 2012, https://hudoc.echr.coe.int/fre?i=001-112165.

80. Hertel v. Switzerland, no. 25181/94, §51, 25 August 1998, https://hudoc.echr.coe.int/eng?i=001-59366.

*Conclusion*

1. See Michele Albee, "The Spread of the Mercator Projection in Western European and United States Cartography," *The International Journal for Geographic Information*, 56, no. 2 (2021): 151–152, regarding long-standing flaws in Mercator's map. See also, Carolyn Eisele, "Charles S. Peirce and the Problem of Map-Projection," *The Proceedings of the American Philosophical Society*, 107, no. 4 (1963): 300–301, regarding American pragmatist Charles Sanders Peirces's observations regarding Mercator's map.

2. See Donald Houston, "Five Maps that Will Change How You See the World," *The Conversation*, March 22, 2017, https://theconversation.com/five-maps-that-will-change-how-you-see-the-world-74967; Joanna Walters, "Boston Public Schools Map Switch Aims to Amend 500 Years of Distortion," *The Guardian*, March 23, 2017, https://www.theguardian.com/education/2017/mar/19/boston-public-schools-world-map-mercator-peters-projection, regarding the reaction to Boston schools' map change.

3. Leo Doran, "Boston Public Schools Adopt New World Map," *Chicago Tribune*, June 15, 2017.

4. Alex Tolkin, "Why You Should Be Upset Boston Public Schools Adopted a New Map," *Medium*, March 21, 2017, https://alextolkin.medium.com/why-you-should-be-upset-boston-public-schools-has-adopted-a-new-map-c694e6f8cd7.

5. *The West Wing*, season 2, episode 16, "Somebody's Going to Emergency, Somebody's Going to Jail," directed by Jessica Yu, written by Aaron Sorkin and Paul Redford, aired Feb. 28, 2001, https://www.youtube.com/watch?v=vVX-PrBRtTY.

6. See Colin Dwyer, "Boston Students Get a Glimpse of a Whole New World, With Different Maps," *NPR The Two Way*, March 21, 2017, https://www.npr.org/sections/thetwo-way/2017/03/21/520938221/boston-students-get-a-glimpse-of-a-whole-new-world-with-different-maps; M. A. Zuber, "The Armchair Discovery of the Unknown Southern Continent: Gerardus Mercator, Philosophical Pretensions and a Competitive Trade," *Early Science and Medicine*, 16, no. 6 (2011): 521–523, regarding Mercator's motivations when creating his maps.

7. See chapter 4 for a more complete discussion of the roots and influences upon Enlightenment thought.

8. Jerome Barron, "Access to the Press. A New First Amendment Right," *Harvard Law Review* 80, no. 8 (1967): 1641.

*Notes to Conclusion*

9. Letter from Oliver W. Holmes to Learned Hand (June 24, 1918) (on file with Harvard Law School Digital Suite), https://iiif.lib.harvard.edu/manifests/view/drs:43005319$8i.

10. *The Essential Holmes: Selections from the Letters, Speeches, Judicial Opinions and Other Writings of Oliver Wendell Holmes, Jr.*, ed. Richard A. Posner (Chicago: University of Chicago Press, 1992), 107.

11. See for examples Oliver W. Holmes, "Natural Law," *Harvard Law Review* 32 (1918): 42; Oliver W. Holmes, "Law and the Court," in *The Holmes Reader* (New York: Oceana Publications, 1955), 98. The speech was originally given in 1913 at a dinner for the Harvard Law School Association in New York. See also chapter 3, which focuses on Holmes's thinking.

12. C. Edwin Baker, *Human Liberty and Freedom of Speech* (Oxford: Oxford University Press, 1989), 3.

13. Abrams v. United States, 250 U.S. 616, 630 (1919) (Holmes, J., dissenting).

14. See Pierce v. United States, 252 U.S. 239 (1920); Schaefer v. United States, 251 U.S. 466 (1920); Gilbert v. Minnesota, 254 U.S. 325 (1920), Milwaukee Social Democratic Publishing v. Burleson, 255 U.S. 407 (1921); Whitney v. California, 274 U.S. 357 (1927) for examples of free-expression cases that followed *Abrams*. Holmes did not return to the "market" metaphor or expand on his "theory of our Constitution" reasoning from *Abrams*.

15. See Holmes, *Natural Law*, 40–41; Oliver W. Holmes, "Ideals and Doubts," *Illinois Law Review* 10, no. 1 (1915): 2–3, for examples of his rejection of generally shared human rationality and universal truths. See also chapter 3 for a more complete discussion about Holmes and truth.

16. See Near v. Minnesota, 283 U.S. 697, 713–720 (1931).

17. 310 U.S. 88, 105 (1940).

18. 314 U.S. 252, 283 (1941) (Frankfurter, J., dissenting).

19. United States v. Rumely, 345 U.S. 41, 56 (1953) (Douglas, J., dissenting).

20. See 376 U.S. 254, 279, Note 19 (1964).

21. Red Lion Broadcasting v. FCC, 395 U.S. 367, 390 (1969).

22. See chapter 10 for more about the EU's system.

23. This approach was expressed most explicitly in Smith v. California, 361 U.S. 147 (1959) (Black, J., concurring). See also Dennis v. United States, 341 U.S. 494, 580 (1941) (Black, J., dissenting) citing Bridges v. California, 314 U.S. 252, 263 (1941), for more regarding Black's approach.

24. New York Times v. Sullivan, 376 U.S. at 297 (Black, J., concurring).

25. *Dennis*, 341 U.S. at 525 (Frankfurter, J., concurring).

26. Ibid., 580 (Black, J., dissenting).

27. Kovac v. Cooper, 336 U.S. 77, 96 (1949) (Frankfurter, J., concurring).

28. Ibid. Frankfurter quotes Holmes, "Ideals and Doubts," 3.

29. See chapter 4 for a more complete explanation of how Enlightenment understandings of truth and human rationality were installed into marketplace theory's foundations.

304

*Notes to Conclusion*

30. Baker, *Human Liberty*, 12.

31. Stanley Ingber, "The Marketplace of Ideas: A Legitimizing Myth," *Duke Law Journal* 1984, no. 1 (1984): 90.

32. Frederic Schauer, "The Role of the People in First Amendment Theory," *California Law Review* 74, no. 3 (1986): 777.

33. Hannah Arendt, *Eichmann in Jerusalem: A Report on the Banality of Evil* (New York: Penguin Books, 1964), 283.

34. Hannah Arendt, *The Life of the Mind* (San Diego: A Harvest Book, 1978), 39.

35. See Arendt, *Eichmann in Jerusalem*, 283; Hannah Arendt, "Truth and Politics," in *The Portable Hannah Arendt*, ed. Peter Baehr (New York: Penguin Books, 2000), 545, for examples of Arendt's separation between truth and appearances.

36. William James, *Pragmatism: A New Name for Some Old Ways of Thinking* (Cambridge: Harvard University Press, 1907), 97.

37. Letter from Oliver W. Holmes to William James (Oct. 13, 1907) (on file with Harvard Law School Digital Suite), https://iiif.lib.harvard.edu/manifests/view/drs:43006888$40i.

38. See Holmes, "Natural Law," 40–41; James, *Pragmatism*, 35, for examples.

39. See John Dewey, *The Public and its Problems* (Athens, OH: Swallow Press, 1927), 154 and 168; John Dewey, "Creative Democracy—The Task Before Use," in *The Essential Dewey, Vol. 1*, eds. Larry A. Hickman and Thomas M. Alexander (Bloomington, IN: University of Indiana Press, 1998), 343, for examples. See also chapter 8 for a full discussion of Dewey's understandings regarding truth and community.

40. Dewey, *The Public and its Problem*, 154.

41. See Dewey, "Creative Democracy—The Task Before Us," in *The Essential Dewey*, 342, for a concise, focused version of his understanding of an active democratic life.

42. See 44 Liquormart v. Rhode Island 517 U.S. 484, 495 (1996); Texas v. Johnson, 491 U.S. 397, 438 (1989) (Rehnquist, C. J., dissenting); Reno v. ACLU, 521 U.S. 844, 870 (1997); Branzburg v. Hayes, 408 U.S. 665, 704 (1972), for examples.

43. See Itai Himelboim, Stephen McCreery, and Marc Smith, "Birds of a Feather Tweet Together: Integrating Network and Content Analyses to Examine Cross-Ideology Exposure on Twitter," *Journal of Computer-Mediated Communication* 18, no. 2 (2013): 156–171; W. Lance Bennett and Shanto Iyengar, "A New Era of Minimal Effects? The Changing Foundations of Political Communication," *Journal of Communication* 58 (2008): 720; Manuel Castells, *The Rise of the Network Society* (Oxford, UK: Blackwell Publishing, 2001), 3–4, for discussions of the like-minded tendencies of virtual communities.

44. See Hannah Arendt, *The Human Condition* (Chicago: University of Chicago Press, 1958), 203, 324; Arendt, *Eichmann in Jerusalem*, 92, for

## Notes to Conclusion

examples of Arendt's concerns about an unthinking society. See also chapter 9 for a fuller examination of Arendt's reasoning on this matter.

45. See chapter 10 for a more complete examination of laws such as the Digital Services Act, Digital Markets Act, Artificial Intelligence Act, and the European Media Freedom Act.

46. See European Convention on Human Rights, Article 10; §1; Universal Declaration of Human Rights, Article 1 and 29, for examples.

# INDEX

Abrams, Jacob, 4, 6, 11

Abrams v. United States: facts of, 4; and Holmes' dissent, 7, 12–22, 53, 61–70; and the marketplace of ideas, 36–42, 71–75, 82–84, 91, 151, 239

Acton, H. B., 21

Adams, John, 76–77

Addams, Jane, 170, 178–84

Aguilina v. Malta, 225

AIA (Artificial Intelligence Act), 229–32

Alien and Sedition Acts, 5

Alvarez, Xavier, 111

Anderson, Benedict, 12

Animal Defenders v. United Kingdom, 221

Arendt, Hannah: experience of, 191–211; influence of, 247–49, 252; quotes from, 21, 73

Areopagitica: and Frankfurter, 37; and Holmes, 13, 21; as Milton's work, 20, 47, 74–79, 82, 90

Austin v. Michigan Chamber of Commerce, 108–10

Bacon, Francis, 20, 73–74

Baker, C. Edwin, 19, 22, 79–80, 239, 247

Bambauer, Derek, 22

Barron, Jerome, 15, 79, 239

Bauman, Zygmunt, 32

Beauharnais v. Illinois, 160–64

Bigelow v. Virginia, 101–6

Bill of Rights, 31, 77–78, 151–52, 217–18, 231

Bipartisan Campaign Reform Act, 109

Black, Hugo, 81–88, 98, 138–65, 244–45

Blackstone, William, 44–45

Brandeis, Louis, 38–47, 83, 139–54, 242

Brennan, William J., Jr., 47, 75, 87–91, 98–109, 164–65

Bridges v. California, 83–87, 150–53, 228, 243

307

## Index

*Buckley v. Valeo*, 103
Burger, Warren, 101

California Criminal Syndicalism
Act, 41
Castells, Manuel, 25, 118, 129
*Central Hudson v. Public Service
Commission*, 15, 106–7
Chafee, Zechariah, 20, 35
ChatGPT, 18
*Citizens United v. Federal Election
Commission*, 17, 109–12
Cohen, Morris, 53, 67, 154–55
*Columbia Broadcasting v. Demo-
cratic National Committee*, 99
Cook, Fred, 93–98
Copernican Revolution, 73–75

*Declaration of Independence*, 21,
76–77, 217
Deepfake: European Union's regula-
tion on, 216–17, 231, 236, 252;
example of, 28; harm of, 14, 29,
116–17, 126–36, 240
*Delfi v. Estonia*, 222–36
*Dennis v. United States*, 84–87,
160–62, 245
Dewey, John, 61–62, 170–89,
200–211, 249–52
Dickinson, John, 21, 44–45, 77, 217
DMA (Digital Markets Act), 229–32
Douglas, William O., 83–91,
138–65, 172
DSA (Digital Services Act), 229–35

ECHR (European Court of Human
Rights), 216–34
Eichmann, Adolf, 190–211, 247–48
ELIZA, 119–20
Emerson, Ralph Waldo, 49, 55, 65,
68, 166
Enlightenment: assumptions of, 7,
14–28, 31, 48, 64, 70, 94–97,

119, 126, 134, 177, 205, 215;
description of, 15, 188, 201; development of, 73–74; influence of,
70–88, 90–92, 111–12, 124–28,
136, 140–43, 162–71, 184–85,
217–18, 228–29, 234–44, 246–
54; and justices, 102–8, 132, 152;
thinkers of, 13, 45, 61
Espionage Act, 1–3, 5, 7, 33–36, 39,
41

fairness doctrine, 13, 94
*First National Bank v. Bellotti*, 17,
103
Frankfurter, Felix: experience and in-
fluence of, 138–65, 182, 243; and
Harvard Law School, 20, 35–37;
and Holmes, 51–53, 67–69, 75;
and other justices, 82–88
Franklin, Benjamin, 21, 76, 217
Freund, Ernst, 36

Galileo, 20–21, 205
Gannett, Frank, 86
Gitlow, Benjamin, 39, 51
*Gitlow v. New York*, 40–43, 53, 61
Guilford, Howard, 43–44

Hamlyn, D. W., 75
Hand, Learned, 32–37, 53, 141–46,
239
*Handyside v. United Kingdom*,
220–27, 236
Hargis, Billy James, 93, 97–98
Haymarket Riot, 3
*Healy v. James*, 99
*Hertel v. Switzerland*, 222–27, 236
Hollinger, David, 23
Holmes, Oliver Wendell, Jr.: Civil
War experience of, 49–70; and
Dewey, 182–88; as Frankfurter's
mentor, 140–45, 148–49, 151–56,
161, 245–49; and James, 166–68,

308

# Index

171–72; and marketplace of ideas, 4–7, 11–23, 30–48, 79–75, 81–84, 239, 242–43

Holmes, Oliver Wendell, Sr., 55, 65

Hughes, Charles Evans, 82–84, 139, 147–51, 159, 243

Hughes, John, 44–45

Hume, David, 44–45, 74–78, 217

Ingber, Stanley, 79, 247

James, William, and Holmes, 61–68; experience of, 154, 166–89; and pragmatism, 19, 53, 200, 206, 211, 217, 249

Jefferson, Thomas, 21, 76–77, 85, 217

Kant, Immanuel, 65, 170, 188, 194–95

*Korematsu v. United States*, 81

*Kovac v. Cooper*, 155–59

*Lamont v. Postmaster General*, 47, 90–91

Laski, Harold, 20, 35–36, 51–56, 61–67, 142–46, 154

*Lochner v. New York*, 61

Locke, John, 21, 44–45, 74–78, 217

Longfellow, Henry Wordsworth, 55, 65, 166

Madison, James, 44–45, 77–78, 82, 90, 217

*Magyar Helsinki Bizottság v. Hungary*, 224

*McCullen v. Coakley*, 15

Meiklejohn, Alexander, 52

Metaphysical Club, The, 62–67, 168

MFA (European Media Freedom Act), 232–33

*Miami Herald v. Tornillo*, 100

Mill, John Stewart, 11, 47, 61, 68, 90, 166

Milton, John: as author of Areopagitica, 47, 82, 90; as Enlightenment thinker, 7, 13, 21, 44, 217; influence of, 76; thoughts from, 21, 37, 74

*Minersville School District v. Gobitis*, 147

*Mouvement Raëlien Suisse v. Switzerland*, 215–16, 221–24, 236

Murphy, Frank, 81–87, 148–51

National Woman's Party, 3

Near, Jay, 43

*Near v. Minnesota*, 43–46, 82

Newton, Isaac, 20, 73–75

*New York Times v. Sullivan*: and Brennan, 87, 100; facts of, 46–47; influence of, 16, 75, 88, 90, 91, 103, 108, 243–44

Nineteenth Amendment, 3

Paul, Alice, 3

Peirce, Benjamin, 65–68, 166

Peirce, Charles Sanders, 62–63, 167–68, 174–78, 188

*Pennsylvania Gazette*, 21, 76; Pitchbot, 107

Plandemic, 24, 26–27

Pollock, Frederick, 19, 35, 60–63

Posner, Richard, 40

Pound, Roscoe, 20, 35

Powell, Louis, 74, 104–6

preferred position, 70, 156, 163

*Red Lion v. Federal Communications Commission*, 13, 71, 91–110, 243

Rehnquist, William, 15, 79, 102–8, 103–5

*Reno v. American Civil Liberties Union*, 15

Roberts, John, 31, 110, 150

Roosevelt, Franklin, 20, 81–86, 139–59

309

## Index

*Roth v. United States*, 47
Rumely, Edward, 84, 86–87
*Ruthenberg v. Michigan*, 41

*Saturday Press*, 43
Scalia, Antonin, 109
Schauer, Frederick, 22, 80, 247
*Schenck v. United States*, 33–47, 53, 68, 82, 151, 239
*SLAPP* (strategic lawsuits against public participation), 232, 233
Smith Act, 74, 160
Smith, Adam, 45, 74, 77
*Snyder v. Phelps*, 110
Spencer, Herbert, 61, 173
*Steel and Morris v. United Kingdom, 225–27*
Steimer, Mollie, 1–6, 11, 36
Sunstein, Cass, 25, 118, 129

*Terminiello v. Chicago*, 157–59
*Texas v. Johnson*, 108
Thornhill, Byron, 80–81
*Thornhill v. Alabama*, 16, 81–83, 152, 243

UDHR (Universal Declaration of Human Rights), 218–24, 234
*United States v. Alvarez*, 111
*United States v. Carolene Products*, 156
*United States v. Rumely*, 84

*Virginia State Pharmacy Board v. Virginia Citizens Consumer Council*, 101
*Virginia v. Black*, 17
Voltaire, 21, 74–77

Warren, Earl, 89, 101, 165
Weeks, Bartow, 1–4
*West Virginia State Board v. Barnette, 149*
White, Byron, 17, 104–5
Whitney, Anita, 41
*Whitney v. California*, 41–47, 151, 243
Wigmore, John, 35
Wright, Chauncey, 62–68, 167–73

*Zana v. Turkey*, 227

Printed and bound by CPI Group (UK) Ltd, Croydon, CR0 4YY

11/06/2025

14688089-0002